The Vatican, Islam, and the Middle East

Contemporary Issues in the Middle East

The Vatican, Islam, and the Middle East

Edited by Kail C. Ellis, O.S.A.

SYRACUSE UNIVERSITY PRESS

Library of Congress Cataloging-in-Publication Data

The Vatican, Islam, and the Middle East.

(Contemporary issues in the Middle East)
Papers of a conference held Oct. 25–26, 1985 at
Villanova University and sponsored by the Institute for
Contemporary Arab and Islamic Studies of Villanova
University.
Includes bibliographies and index.
1. Islam—Relations—Christianity—Congresses.
2. Catholic Church—Relations—Islam—Congresses.
3. Christians—Middle East—Congresses.   4. Catholic
Church—Relations (diplomatic)—Arab countries—
Congresses.   5. Catholic Church—Relations (diplomatic)
—Israel—Congresses.   6. Arab countries—Foreign
relations—Catholic Church—Congresses.   7. Israel—
Foreign relations—Catholic Church—Congresses.
8. Jewish-Arab relations—1949–   —Congresses.
I. Ellis, Kail C.   II. Villanova University.   Institute
for Contemporary Arab and Islamic Studies.   III. Series.
BP172.V38   1987   261.2'7   87-10153
ISBN 0–8156–2415–8 (alk. paper)

Contents

Preface

On 25–26 October 1985, a conference was held at Villanova University, Villanova, Pennsylvania, on the subject of the Vatican, Islam, and the Middle East. Sponsored by the Institute for Contemporary Arab and Islamic Studies of Villanova University, the meeting sought to shed light on the often nebulous and little understood role of the Holy See in the volatile Middle East region, and on the new interfaith relationships that the Catholic Church has sought to develop with Islam in the aftermath of the Second Vatican Council of 1962.

Some of the conclusions of that church conclave, convened by His Holiness, Pope John XXIII, were codified the following year in the papal encyclical *Pacem in Terris*. This gave seminal Catholic Church recognition to the concept that the followers of Islam share a common God with Christians, and hence should be accorded the same measure of respect extended to adherents of the other great monotheistic religions. It was a significant step in interfaith ecumenicalism.

In the ensuing two decades, this new Catholic posture toward Islam and its followers, implemented perforce in diverse sociopolitical environments, has slowly and sometimes painfully evolved. Generally speaking, its progress has escaped the attention of the majority of Middle East observers, most of whom are more intent on analyzing political and economic than spiritual phenomena. Apart from a number of European journals dealing with religious matters, few of which are widely read in this country outside of specialist circles, and an occasional article or newspaper account in the United States, little has appeared in print on the subject. (One notable exception is George Irani's recent book, *The Papacy and the Middle East*, published by the University of Notre Dame Press in 1986.) Thus, the Villanova conference constituted a pioneering effort in exploring achievement to date and examining ancillary problems associated with that effort.

Among the conference attendees were two Catholic prelates, Catholic clergymen from various countries and religious orders, lay scholars, former diplomats, and a number of Muslim dignitaries from the *Rabita,* or Muslim League, organization of Mecca, Kingdom of Saudi Arabia. The latter group was headed by Dr. Maʿaruf Dawalibi, former prime minister of Syria and for many years a distinguished royal counsellor at the Saudi Arabian court.

Various papers were presented on different aspects of the conference theme, followed by questions from the floor. Although the relatively brief duration of the conference precluded the full analysis of all aspects of the theme, the panels and papers highlighted many salient elements thereof. It is the fifteen separate essays presented at that conference, together with a masterly introduction by Father Kail Ellis, O.S.A., who conceived of and spearheaded the organization of the meeting, that constitute the subject matter of this volume. (Father Ellis's introduction categorizes and provides a conceptual framework for the conference essays.)

The foreign policy-making processes of the Holy See have always been something of a mystery, and they continue to remain so. Debate within the Roman *curia* on policy issues concerning the Middle East is a closely guarded secret, although rumors of divergent views among its senior members sometimes leak out to the media. The Vatican, while not a nation state, has its own interests in the Middle East, as elsewhere. These it seeks to protect and promote, utilizing the limited diplomatic instruments at its disposal. Chief among the latter is the internationally recognized moral force that it represents. Skeptics may scoff at the value of any such intangible instrument of diplomacy, but its residual effectiveness in certain situations should not be dismissed. The Holy Father, standing symbolically for the great Apostle of Peace of the Christian religion, has consistently added his voice to the cause of resolving the bitter, multiple conflicts that have for so long convulsed the Middle East region, and of establishing some measure of true peace and harmony among the peoples and states of the area.

On a practical level, the Vatican must be concerned with trying to safeguard the rights of indigenous Catholic communities in the Middle East—many of them marginal in terms of the demographics of the polities in which they live—that they may pursue their Christian faith without hindrance; the rise in the past seven years of what has come to be known is Islamism, sometimes in a form that is both militant and restrictive of other faiths, lends a special urgency to this objective. The Vatican also seeks to protect those monasteries, convents, educational institutions, and the like in that strife-torn region that belong to it or to individual Catholic orders. It is equally anxious that its missionary activities abroad not be constrained—a recurrent subject of controversy with Muslim communities, who abhor what they see as the encouragement of apostasy.

The issue of satisfactorily resolving the difficult and emotionally laden question of Jerusalem, the city of peace that is sacred to the three great monotheistic religions of the world, must also be high on the list of Vatican priorities in the Middle East. Like the United States, it is caught between the competing claims of Muslims and Jews for sovereignty over that immemorial city. It doubtless has its own ideas on how that issue might optimally be resolved, perhaps by some form of internationalization, but has little capability to translate these concepts into reality. Rather, it must accept the situation as it is.

In political science terms, as Father J. Bryan Hehir points out in his perceptive essay, the Catholic Church can be considered a "transnational actor." As such, its operating dynamics require analyses at separate center-periphery, periphery-center, and periphery-periphery levels. The Vatican, as the center, provides guidance to both Catholic communities and orders abroad on matters pertaining to church doctrine and interfaith relations. For their part, the discrete Catholic peripheral communities in the Middle East (as elsewhere) seek to influence the Roman center on matters of particular concern to them, and to solicit its support. These same peripheral Catholic communities, some of them Uniate and each with special interests of its own, must work with similar peripheral communities in order to resolve outstanding issues between and among them. In the latter context, the Roman center must sometimes mediate conflicting claims—often a thankless albeit essential task.

Geographically and functionally, the topics explored by the various conferees ranged widely and illustrated all three aspects of the aforementioned "transnational actor" role of the Catholic Church. Geographically, Christian-Muslim relations, as they have developed in the past quarter of a century, were explored from Egypt and Lebanon eastward as far as the Philippines, with points in between. The status of the small, marginal Christian communities in Pakistan and in India—the first immersed in an overwhelmingly Islamic society, the second in a Hindu-dominated but also religiously pluralistic state—

were assayed. So was the reverse of these situations: the status of the quasi-insurgent minority Muslim community in the predominantly Catholic Republic of the Philippines.

Functionally, various essays dealt with comparative Christian-Muslim theosophy, the historical development of Eastern Catholic communities, structural similarities between the Christian church and Sunni and Shiʿi Islam, and the evolving position of the Holy See on the matter of Jerusalem, and included a critical assessment by a Sudanese Muslim scholar and lawyer of the statutory disabilities to which *dhimmis,* or non-Muslim but protected People of the Book, are subjected in those Islamic states where the legal system is based entirely or primarily on the *shariʿa.* (The latter presentation, incidentally, evoked the ire of Muslim participants from the *Rabita,* who vehemently denied that any such legal disabilities exist.)

In short, the compendium of essays represents a wide spectrum of both intellectual and practical insights into the new Catholic-Islamic dialogue and changing attitudinal approaches of the Catholic church to various Middle East affairs. All of the participants, clergy and laity alike, were extraordinarily knowledgeable of the Middle East countries in which they have worked. Rarely have I participated in a conference in which so many of the participants possessed not only theoretical, but extensive practical, experience. In my view, the distillation of this theoretical knowledge and practical experience into the various essays give them particular relevance. For those concerned with the complex problems of the Middle East, including the current compelling topic of whether the West can work with militant Islamic communities, they fill some critical interstices in our comprehension of that critical part of the world.

I would conclude by making a personal point pertinent to the role of representatives of the Catholic Church in the Middle East. As a former American diplomat who has spent well over three decades working in the Middle East, I have had frequent opportunity to meet with papal *nuncios,* their staffs, and Catholic educators serving in countries of that region, and to exchange views with them on current developments. They may not always have been in the vortex of the swirl of diplomatic activities that characterizes the Middle East capitals, but their observations on local conditions and sociopolitical problems were invariably perceptive and comprehensive. The educators among them were truly selfless men, who have left indelible ethical and "value" impressions upon the generations of Middle East students that have been privileged to know them. The papal representatives were uniformly men of deep compassion, who also understood human frailties, emotions, and practical issues. Collectively, they represented, in the tradition of the Holy See, morality and decency in the highest sense of those terms—commodities so often lacking in international conduct and, as the protracted agony of Lebanon bears sad witness, in intercommunal relationships as well. I have benefited immeasurably from their wisdom, knowledge, experience, and impartiality and, as a non-Catholic Christian, I am honored to have the opportunity to acknowledge my debt to them.

Boston University   Hermann Frederick Eilts
November 1986

Contributors

GEORGES C. ANAWATI, O.P., entered the Dominican order in 1933. After completing doctoral work in philosophy and theology, he began advanced studies in such subjects as Islamic philosophy and theology, as well as the history of the sciences in the Arab world. Father Anawati has been deeply involved in the Christian-Islamic dialogue since 1944, when he established contacts with prominent intellectuals at the University of Cairo and Al-Azhar University.

Father Anawati has been a visiting lecturer at the universities of Montreal, Louvain, the Angelicum, and Southern California. He was a special consultant on Islam for the Vatican secretariat for non-Christians and was recently appointed by Pope John Paul II as a member of the newly created pontifical council of culture.

ABDULLAHI AHMED AN-NA'IM is professor of law at the University of California at Los Angeles. He studied at the University of Khartoum and at Cambridge University, and in 1976 received his doctoral degree from the University of Edinburgh. Dr. An-Na'im has lectured widely on such subjects as "Islamization and Human Rights in the Sudan," "A Modern Approach to Human Rights in Islam," and "Constitutional Issues and Islamic Reform in the Sudan." He has also published, in English and Arabic, a number of works on criminal procedure, and is currently working on a textbook to be called *General Principles of Criminal Responsibility in the Sudan*. Dr. An-Na'im's English translation of Mahmoud Mohamed Taha's *Second Message of Islam* was published in 1987.

TAHSEEN BASHEER, one of Egypt's most distinguished diplomats, was his country's ambassador to Canada until his retirement from the foreign service in 1985. He had also served as Egypt's ambassador to Norway, the Arab League, and as Egyptian delegate to the United

Nations. Ambassador Basheer was supervisor of press affairs for President Anwar al-Sadat, as well as spokesman for the Egyptian delegation at the peace talks that began in 1973 and culminated two years later with the signing of the second Sinai accord.

Ambassador Basheer spent a year at the Center for International Affairs at Harvard University, and was a visiting fellow at the American Enterprise Institute. He continues to lecture widely in the United States and Europe on the subjects of the Middle East and Arab politics, and is the author of many articles, in both Arabic and English, on subjects of international interest.

JAMES A. BILL is professor of government and Middle Eastern studies at the University of Texas at Austin. A graduate of Assumption College, Worcester, Massachusetts, he earned his master's and doctoral degrees at Princeton University. Dr. Bill has focused his research on the comparative aspects of classes and groups in the process of political development, with special emphasis on the countries of the Middle East. His most recent research concerns the issues of stability and revolution in that troubled part of the world, as well as the resurgence of Islam in the third world and United States foreign policy toward Middle Eastern countries. Dr. Bill's published works include *The Politics of Iran* (1972), *The Middle East: Politics and Power* (1974), and *Politics in the Middle East* (1979), as well as numerous articles in political science journals.

JOSEPH CARDINAL CORDEIRO is archbishop of Karachi, Pakistan. Educated in Karachi, where he attended St. Patrick's High School and D. J. College, he pursued theological studies at the papal seminary in Kandy, Ceylon (now Sri Lanka). From 1948 to 1950 he was engaged in educational work in Karachi and in Quetta, Pakistan.

Named archbishop of Karachi by Pope Pius XII in 1958, Cordeiro was elevated to the cardinalate in 1973 by Paul VI. He continues to serve on papal commissions, having most recently been named by Pope John Paul II as papal legate to the international eucharistic congress in Nairobi, Kenya, in 1985. Cardinal Cordeiro's accomplishments in the fields of education and social service were acknowledged by President Zia-ul-Haq of Pakistan in 1984 with the award of the prestigious *Sitara-i-Imtiaz* [Star of Honor].

ROBERT M. HADDAD is Sophia Smith professor of history at Smith College, where he also teaches religion. He received his doctorate in history and Middle Eastern studies from Harvard University in 1965, and has done extensive research in both the Middle East and Europe as a Fulbright scholar, Ford Foundation fellow, and recipient of a grant from the Social Science Research Council. Professor Haddad is the author of *Syrian Christians in Muslim Society: an Interpretation* (1981), as well as of a number of articles concerned primarily with the interaction between Islam and Eastern Christianity.

FATHER J. BRYAN HEHIR is currently secretary of the department of social development and world peace at the U.S. Catholic Conference in Washington, D.C. He is also senior research scholar at the Kennedy Institute of Ethics at Georgetown University, and research professor of ethics and international politics at Georgetown's School of Foreign Service. Father Hehir, who holds a Th.D. from the Harvard Divinity School, was a member of the Vatican delegation to the United Nations special session on disarmament in 1973, as well as to the General Assembly. An advisor to the U.S. bishops at the fourth international synod of bishops in Rome in 1974, Father Hehir also played an important role in the National Conference of Catholic Bishops' Ad Hoc Committee on War and Peace (Bernardin Committee) between 1981 and 1983. He is the author of numerous articles in such publications as *Worldview, Foreign Policy,* and *Commonweal.*

GEORGE EMILE IRANI, who was born in Ghana of Lebanese parents, received his B.A. degree in political science from the Catholic University of Milan in 1974. He earned his master's degree in international relations (1980), and a doctorate from the University of Southern California (1984). Dr. Irani is director of international student advisement at USC's college of letters, arts, and sciences. He has contributed papers to numerous conferences, and his pivotal study, *The Papacy and the Middle East: The Role of the Holy See in the Arab-Israeli Conflict,* was published in 1986.

WILLIAM SOLIMAN KILADA studied at the University of Cairo, where he received his licentiate (1944) and his doctorate (1954) in law. He is the former vice president of the Egyptian state council, and counsellor for the supreme administrative court.

Dr. Kilada's published works include *Teachings of the Prophet, Dialogue among Religions,* and *On the Principles of an Egyptian Formula for National Unity with One People and One Homeland* (all in Arabic). In addition, several of his articles have been published by the Center for

Strategic and Political Studies of the Cairo newspaper, *Al-Ahram*, and he has addressed a number of international conferences.

FRED J. KHOURI is professior emeritus of political science at Villanova University, having joined the faculty in 1951. He earned his university degrees, including his doctorate in 1953, at Columbia University. From 1961 to 1964, Dr. Khouri was visiting professor at the American University of Beirut. He has lectured widely on Middle Eastern affairs, especially on the Arab-Israeli conflict, and was a member of the Brookings Institution Middle East study group, where he helped to produce that group's influential report, "Towards Peace in the Middle East."

Dr. Khouri was senior fellow at the University of Pennsylvania's Middle East center for two years, and is currently a fellow of the Middle East Studies Association. He is the author of numerous essays and articles addressing Middle Eastern affairs, as well as of the seminal *Arab-Israeli Dilemma* (1985).

CESAR ADIB MAJUL received his doctorate from Cornell University in 1957, after which he began a long association with the University of the Philippines, serving variously as dean of the university college; dean of the college of arts and sciences; professor of political and Islamic philosophy; and finally as dean of the institute of Islamic studies. When he retired from the university in 1979, he was given the title of University Professor in recognition of his many years of distinguished service.

Dr. Majul's published works include *The Political and Constitutional Ideas of the Philippine Revolution* (1957); *Mabini and the Philippine Revolution* (1960); *Apolinario Mabini: Revolutionary* (1964); *The Muslims in the Philippines* (1973); and *Islam and Development: A Collection of Essays* (1980), in addition to numerous monographs and scholarly articles on the role of Islam in the Philippines.

FATHER YOAKIM MOUBARAC studied at St. Joseph's University in Beirut, and earned his doctorate in theology at the Institut Catholique in Paris. He also holds doctorates in letters and Islamic studies from the Sorbonne. Father Moubarac is currently professor at the Institut Catholique, and at Louvain-la-Neuve in Brussels. He has participated in a number of Christian-Muslim colloquia and was spokesman for the Maronite Church at the Second Vatican Council. Father Moubarac is the author of several scholarly books on Islam and Christianity, most recently the multi-volume *Pentologie Maronite* (1985). He counts the French Orientalist, Louis Massignon, as a major influence on his work.

JOSEPH L. RYAN, S. J., is director of the Pontifical Mission for Palestine in Amman, Jordan, a position he assumed in 1984. From 1945 to 1948 Father Ryan taught at Baghdad College secondary school, leaving Iraq to visit Palestine during the summers of 1946 and 1947. He returned to Iraq to serve as dean (1956–66) and academic vice president (1966–68) of Al-Hikma University in Baghdad. From 1969 to 1971, Father Ryan was visiting fellow at the Cambridge (Mass.) Center for Social Studies. In 1971 he became a member of CEMAN (the Center for the Study of the Modern Arab World) at St. Joseph's University, Beirut. He remained at the Center, which is involved in the research of social and cultural change in the Arab Middle East, until 1975.

MICHAEL J. SCANLON, O.S.A., is professor of systematic theology at the Washington (D.C.) Theological Union, and president of the Catholic Theological Society of America. Father Scanlon entered the Augustinian order in 1956. Upon graduation from Villanova University in 1960, he pursued graduate studies at the Catholic University of America, where he received the doctorate in sacred theology in 1969.

Father Scanlon taught systematic theology at Augustinian College in Washington, D.C., from 1965 to 1968, at which time he joined the faculty at Washington Theological Union. In addition, he regularly teaches at Villanova's summer sessions. Father Scanlon was a co-founder and second president of the Washington Theological Consortium, an ecumenical institute seeking cooperation among the area's Catholic and Protestant schools of theology.

CHRISTIAN W. TROLL, S.J., pursued philosophical and theological studies at the universities of Bonn and Tübingen, West Germany, and studied Arabic and Islamics at St. Joseph's University in Beirut. He entered the Society of Jesus in 1963, and from 1964 to 1976 studied philosophy, Urdu, Persian, and South Asian history, in addition to further studies of Arabic and Islamics. Father Troll did research at the department of history of South Asia of the school of Oriental and African studies at the University of London, where he was awarded his doctorate in 1976. He is currently professor of Islamic studies at Vidyajyoti Institute of Religious Studies in New Delhi, as well as a research fellow at Woodstock Theological Center, Georgetown University, Washington, D.C.

JOHN ALDEN WILLIAMS is professor of art and Middle Eastern studies at the University of Texas at Austin. He received a Woodrow Wilson fellowship in Oriental studies from Princeton, was a Fulbright Scholar in Egypt, and was holder of the Near East fellowship at Princeton in 1957. He received his doctorate from that university the following year. From 1966 to 1969, Dr. Williams was director of the Center for Arabic and Islamic Studies at the American University in Cairo, followed by a term as senior research fellow at the Center for Middle East Studies at the Harvard Center for Study of World Religions from 1971 to 1972.

Dr. Williams is the author of *Islam* (1961), *Themes of Islamic Civilization* (1971), *Annals of the Early Caliphate, 744–54* (1985), and *The Abbasid Revolution* (1985). He is also a frequent contributor to scholarly publications.

The Vatican, Islam, and the Middle East

Introduction

KAIL C. ELLIS

In 1965, the Second Vatican Council issued a statement that signaled a remarkable change in the Catholic Church's approach to Islam. The declaration, *Nostra Aetate*, by stressing the common beliefs of Muslims and Christians attempted to discredit the commonplace, crusading ideology which viewed Islam as a fanatical religion of power and ignorance. The declaration stated that "the Church looks with esteem" upon Muslims, and that "although in the course of the centuries many quarrels and hostilities have arisen between Christians and Muslims [it urged] all to forget the past and to strive sincerely for mutual understanding."[1]

The Catholic Church's emphasis on Muslim-Christian cooperation was, in large part, inspired by Pope Paul VI. It was during his pontificate that the Vatican Secretariat for Non-Christians was established in 1964, the Pontifical Institute for Arab and Islamic Studies reorganized in the same year, and the Commission for Religious Relations with Islam founded in 1974.

Pope John Paul II expanded upon these initiatives in several meetings with Muslims in such diverse places as Kenya, Ghana, France, Germany, Pakistan, the Philippines, Portugal, Belgium, Turkey, Morocco, and Bangladesh. In Morocco in August 1985, for example, he stated that "dialogue between Christians and Muslims is today more necessary than ever," and that Muslims and Christians must give witness to God "in a world which is becoming more secularized and at times even atheistic." In Bangladesh in November 1986, he stressed that Muslims and Christians have "many spiritual resources in common which we must share with one another as we work for a more human world." He also reaffirmed that the Catholic Church is committed "to a path of dialogue and collaboration with men and women of good will of every religious tradition."[2]

It is then, as a religio-political institution that the Catholic Church enters into dialogue with other religions as a "witness of faith in the world," while at the same time using its status as a transnational actor to exercise influence in the world of international politics. Its administrative structures, especially its diplomatic corps, as well as the person of the pope, are employed to promote international understanding, peaceful development among nations, and the welfare of its adherents.

The Vatican maintains formal diplomatic relations with over a hundred states.[3] Although its diplomacy is concerned generally with the critical issues of world peace, its special concern in the Middle East is the welfare of the Christian minorities in the Islamic states. To promote the goals of peace, human rights, social justice, and religious freedom in the region, the Vatican sends ambassadors (nuncios) to several Arab and Islamic states, including Algeria, Bangladesh, Egypt, Indonesia, Iran, Iraq, Kuwait, Lebanon, Morocco, Pakistan, Syria, Sudan, Tunisia, and Turkey. In addition, there is an apostolic delegate for Jerusalem and Palestine who represents the Vatican to the Church hierarchies of Jordan and Israel. There are no formal diplomatic relations with either government, however. An apostolic delegate also represents the Vatican in Libya.

The purpose of this volume, therefore, is to explore the complex relationship between Catholicism and Islam as a contribution toward the mutual understanding called for by the Council and the many recent papal statements. Four aspects of this relationship will be examined: (1) Islam and Western Christianity; (2) Vatican diplomacy and the Middle East; (3) The Vatican and Muslim-Christian relations in the Middle East; and (4) resurgent Islam and Christian-Muslim relations.

Islam and Western Christianity

Muslim-Christian relations are analyzed from a theological and structural perspective by three authors in this section. "Fidelity to Monotheism: Christianity and Islam" by Michael J. Scanlon, O.S.A., examines the notion of monotheism in terms of its religious, anthropological, and cultural consequences. Muslims have interpreted the Christian doctrine of the Trinity as explicit tritheism, while for Christians the undifferentiated monotheism of Muslims evokes images of a strongly transcendent and even deist notion of God. Scanlon attempts to reconcile the Christian concept of God's "immanence" as personal presence or fidelity to his creation, through Jesus and the Holy Spirit, with the Quran's reference to God's *ruh* and *amr* (God's spirit and command). The *ruh min amr-Allah* (which can be translated as "All that is given, is given from God, including one's own soul"), according to Scanlon, seems to mean the spirit of prophecy authenticating the revelation given to the Prophet Muhammad. *Ruh* expresses the "how" of divine revelation, while *amr* expresses the "what" of revelation.

For Scanlon, a certain complement exists between the Islamic and Christian notions of monotheism. On the one hand, Islam provides all religious traditions with a powerful reminder of the dangers inherent in one-sided emphasis on divine immanence, which can lead to polytheism and pantheism. On the other hand, Christianity's emphasis on God's immanence guards against a transcendent notion of God that can lead to voluntarism (the doctrine that will is the dominant factor in experience or in the world) and nominalism (which holds that only individuals, not abstract entities, exist). These are extreme doctrines which can lead to deism and atheism.

Scanlon also touches upon the Christ question. While for Christians, Jesus as the Christ is the presence of God in the world of humanity, for Muslims the Quran is God's living word, not in human form but as spoken revelation. Islamic orthodoxy disclaims any mediation between God and humanity; however, lived Islamic faith, especially in Sufism, has always been inspired and guided by the *sunna* of the Prophet, who was called the "Proof" of God's Word. "Christians," according to Scanlon, "will note the similarity with their own faith in Christ as a paradigmatic human being."

The three main attitudes of Catholics toward Islam are discussed by Georges Anawati, O.P., in his chapter, "An Assessment of the Christian-Islamic Dialogue." The "minimalists" reflect basically the attitude of pre-Vatican II Catholicism and are unsympathetic to Islam. The "maximalists" are totally sympathetic to Islam in their acceptance of the prophethood of Muhammad and the revealed character of the Quran, but gloss over the Quran's explicit denial of basic Christian beliefs. The third attitude is of those who maintain a sympathetic and broad-minded approach to Islam but who also take into account the unique character of Islam and Islam's rejection of the fundamental Christian mysteries of the Trinity, Incarnation, and Redemption through Christ. Authentic dialogue, Anawati cautions, does not ignore obvious differences. In order to avoid the "dead end" of exaggerated conciliatory trends, therefore, it is important to maintain a proper sense of and regard for truth. Thus, theological understanding is deepened only out of respect for one's interlocutors.

Anawati calls for mutual respect between the two faiths. He calls upon Muslims to accept that the faith of Christians is without absurdity and, like theirs, is based on true sources. He suggests that dialogue between Muslims and Christians might also provide other benefits as, for example, through the use of exegesis, which helps explain and critically interpret texts. Anawati belives that exegesis, which uses the new acquisitions of modern philology, critical history, and the history of dogma, could give Muslim theologians a precious tool which would enable them "to extract from their classical commentaries that which is abiding while rejecting that which is mere folklore and superstition."

The third chapter in this section, "Shi'i Islam and Roman Catholicism: An Ecclesial and Political Analysis," by James Bill and John Alden Williams, suggests that although the Shi'ite and Catholic religious systems have basic differences, each also has some enduring and essential doctrinal, structural, and sociopolitical characteristics which are strikingly similar. Listed among the similarities are: meditation upon the significance of the passion of an innocent victim who took upon himself the sins of the community and atoned for them; belief that God's grace is mediated through earthly and heavenly hierarchies; faith in intercessors; the intercession and the accessibility of the friends of God, the saints; emphasis on a great mother-figure as a leading intercessor, a pattern for woman, and a refuge for those in trouble; the great value of martyrdom and redemptive suffering— that individual suffering can become part of a "treasury of grace" to benefit co-religionists; and the belief by each community that it is led by a charismatic leader who is guided by God, preserved from error, and accepting of a religious hierarchy which shares his authority and disseminates his teaching.

Perhaps as intriguing as the above list is the authors' comparison of the Catholic and Shi'i models of politics and the state. Although neither system has simple, universally accepted models of politics and the state, the authors contend that both have certain accepted principles that are identifiable in their teachings. These include the emphasis upon the normative foundations of political systems; the preeminence of divine and natural law over human law; the ideal state as furthering the moral and spiritual fulfillment of the individual and the human community; the stress on the common good and on the community taking precedence over the individual (it is only in the community that human beings can attain their moral good); and in the increasing contemporary concern for the downtrodden and oppressed.

Bill and Williams see certain similarities between "populist Islam" as evidenced among the Shi'i communities, and "liberation theology" as practiced by certain Roman Catholic clerics in some other third world countries, especially in Latin America. Inasmuch as liberation theology questions the separation of church and state, the authors conclude, it comes closer to populist Islamic ideology.

Vatican Diplomacy and the Middle East

The belief that left unchecked, the conflicts in the Middle East could trigger a superpower confrontation and threaten the entire world underlies the diplomacy of most nations in the region and that of the United States. This section focuses on the Vatican's diplomacy as it affects the crucial issues of peace in the Middle East in four papers: "The Catholic Church and the Middle East: Policy and Diplomacy," by Father J. Bryan Hehir; "The Holy See and the Israeli-Palestinian Conflict," by George Irani; "The Jerusalem Question and the Vatican," by Fred J. Khouri; and "The Holy See and Jordan," by Joseph L. Ryan, S.J.

Hehir's paper offers a useful introduction to this section by analyzing the Vatican's role as a transnational actor. Although sovereign states remain the central actors in the contemporary state system, transnational actors, Hehir states, occupy an unrivaled status: "they are based in one place, present in several states, and in possession of a trained corps of personnel, a single guiding philosophy, and a sophisticated communications system."

This point is reiterated in Ryan's study on Jordan. Most of the world is desirous of having good relations with the Vatican, Ryan states, because it is such an effective transnational actor. The Vatican exerts world-wide moral authority, and it has a long history of far-sighted diplomacy; but because it is in constant communication with bishops, priests, and other Catholics throughout the world, the Vatican has access to grassroots information which makes diplomatic relations with it valuable to various states. These advantages have been recognized by a number of Arab countries which, like Lebanon and Egypt, established diplomatic relations with the Holy See as early as the late 1940s, seeking thereby the Vatican's support and influence to have particular United Nations resolutions regarding Jerusalem and Palestine implemented.

Hehir is careful to point out the mistake in focusing only on the diplomacy of the Holy See in the classical model of church-state relations. Since the Second Vatican Council, he states, primary emphasis has been placed on the Church's role in society as an advocate of social change, human rights, and human dignity.

In an attempt to understand the potential as well as the complexity of the Church's role, Hehir distinguishes three levels of activity involving the "Center," Rome as embodied in the Pope and the Vatican Secretariat of State, and the "Periphery," the local church, principally the local bishops conferences. He outlines how each interacts and coexists in the transnational community of the Church. This analysis enables us to see how the Vatican formulates and projects an international policy on major Middle East questions such as Jerusalem, Palestinian rights, the Arab-Israeli conflict, and the Lebanese civil war. It also explains why only the Center has the capacity to attract attention for its positions.

Conversely, the relationship of the Periphery to the Center involves the activities of the Arab Christian communities in the Middle East, both as a source of pastoral concern and of information and perspective which influence the specific positions the Vatican takes on the Middle East. When the issues at stake directly affect the local church, as in the case of the Lebanese civil war, tensions can occur. The Vatican's advocacy of Lebanon's territorial integrity, a more equitable distribution of the country's political and economic resources, its support of Palestinian nationalism, as well as its overall concern with the position of the Christian minorities in the Middle East put it at odds with the predominantly Maronite Lebanese Front and its supporters among the Order of Maronite monks.

The Vatican's conciliatory and equidistant attitude in the Lebanese conflict points out that without legitimation from the Center, the local church has difficulty breaking new ground on policy issues. It also indicates, however, that stalemate can occur when no meaningful substitute can be found for lack of support from the Center.

In his paper, "The Holy See and the Israeli-Palestinian Conflict," George Irani contends that the Vatican has adopted a pragmatic stance toward that conflict since 1967. The Holy See, he states, has the advantage of being in permanent contact with all the parties involved in the conflict, and its prestige and influence in international institutions such as the United Nations clearly motivates the parties to the conflict to pay close attention to the Vatican's positions. Irani informs us, for example, that the apostolic delegate for Jerusalem and Palestine has frequent contacts with the Israeli Foreign Ministry and the Ministry of Religious Affairs and communicates frequently with Jordanian officials. In addition, the governments of both Jordan and Israel have access to the Vatican through their embassies in Italy.

The Holy See, according to Irani, adopted a stand sympathetic to the plight of the Palestinians from the beginning of the Israeli-Palestinian dispute. This stance was motivated primarily by the Vatican's concern for the fate of Catholics in Palestine and the humanitarian needs of the Palestinian refugees. Irani concludes that there are three major goals of Vatican policy in the Middle East: (1) the preservation and maintenance of a Catholic presence in the Holy Land; (2) the promotion of the right of self-determination for the Palestinians; and (3) recognition of the *de facto* existence of the Jewish state and its right to secure and defined borders. In addition, Pope John Paul II has asserted without ambiguity his opposition to acts of terrorism and the use of reprisals.

Fred Khouri states that the history of the Vatican's concern for Jerusalem began with the British Mandate period. After World War II, however, the Holy See believed that its interests and the cause of peace in the region would best be served if Great Britain were either to continue the Mandate, or if the Mandate were given to some other Christian nation. Failing that, Khouri states, the Vatican wished Palestine to be internationalized under United Nations control.

This policy explains the Holy See support for the 1947 proposal of the United Nations Special Committee on Palestine which provided for full territorial internationalization of Jerusalem and its environs *(corpus separatum)*. The Vatican wished to protect both the Holy Places and the Catholic community in Palestine, and it felt that internationalization would ensure the universal character of Jerusalem and prevent it from becoming part of either a Jewish or an Arab state. The Vatican solicited support for the partition plan for Palestine from many Catholic member states of the United Nations, especially those from Latin America. This support, however, was clearly contingent on the provision for the internationalization of Jerusalem.

Khouri states that the Vatican continued to press for the internationalization of the city after Israel seized control of the western or

New City portion of Jerusalem in the 1948 Palestine war and Transjordan (later Jordan) occupied East Jerusalem, which contains most of the Holy Places. It also opposed Israel's annexation of East Jerusalem after the June 1967 war.

By late 1967, however, the internationalization of Jerusalem was no longer considered a viable proposition by many of its former supporters in the United Nations. The Vatican continued to call for an internationally guaranteed statute for the city and its Holy Places, but did not reiterate its usual references to a *corpus separatum* for the Holy City. At this point, according to Khouri, the focus of Vatican policy shifted from internationalization to that of guarantees for freedom of worship, respect for the Holy Places, and preservation of the Christian presence in the Holy Land. In 1979, Pope John Paul II referred to the Vatican's "hope for a special statute that, under international guarantees would respect the particular nature of Jerusalem" in his address to the United Nations. The specific nature of those guarantees was left unspecified, however.

The status of Jerusalem remains a source of concern for the Vatican and a dangerous bone of contention between Israel, the Arabs, and over 800 million Muslims. In the context of an overall settlement in the Middle East, it is probably the most intractable of the issues to be settled. Yet, Khouri cautions, it would be unwise to ignore it, as no solution to the Middle East conflict can be finalized until an acceptable agreement is reached on East Jerusalem.

Jordan does not have diplomatic relations with the Holy See. Yet its intimate involvement with the question of Jerusalem and the Israeli-Palestinian conflict gives it a special reason for cultivating good relations with the Vatican. Joseph L. Ryan, S.J., traces the history of these relations in his paper, "The Holy See and Jordan."

Contacts at the highest level between the Holy See and Jordan began in 1953, the year King Hussein was crowned. In that same year, Hussein went to the Vatican and was received in audience by Pope Pius XII. This was the first of many contacts between the King and a pope, and Ryan believes that it is this continuity, due in large part to Hussein's personal leadership, that accounts for the favorable relations between Jordan and the Vatican.

Few non-Arab countries have given as consistent and conspicuous support to the Palestinian cause and Jerusalem as has the Holy See, according to Ryan. Indeed, Jordan has actively sought that support, just as it seeks support from Christians from every quarter—for example, from the Orthodox Patriarch of Constantinople and the Archbishop of Canterbury. It should not be forgotten, Ryan states, that it is also in the Vatican's interest to cultivate good relations with Jordan. Not only is Jordan's special role regarding Jerusalem and the West Bank of interest to the Vatican, but the presence of Christians, and particularly of Catholics who live on both sides of the Jordan River, is also a matter of concern.

Ryan believes that the personalities of the Popes Paul VI and John Paul II have been important factors in developing relations between the Vatican and the predominantly Arab Muslim countries of the Middle East such as Jordan. Pope Paul VI's interest in Islam, he states, is evident in the Second Vatican Council's declaration *Nostra Aetate*, his contacts with scholars sympathetic to Islam such as Louis Massignon, and in his founding in 1974 of the Secretariat for Non-Christians with its special section devoted to Muslims. The establishment of diplomatic relations with a number of Muslim countries during the pontificate of Pope Paul VI also has contributed to the favorable attitudes of the Islamic countries to the Vatican.

Pope John Paul II's interest in Islam was highlighted by Cardinal Francis Arinze, the president of the Secretariat for Non-Christians, during this address to the participants in Villanova University's conference, "The Vatican, Islam and the Middle East." Pope John Paul II, Cardinal Arinze said, has "met in private audience with the heads of the important international Islamic organizations, such as the Organization of the Islamic Conference and the World Muslim League, and has discussed matters of common concern with Islamic religious leaders, heads of state, and members of the diplomatic corps."

Formal diplomatic relations between the Holy See and Jordan, however, seem to be only a remote possibility. The question is inextricably linked with the question of possible diplomatic status between the Holy See and Israel and that, as Ryan points out, depends upon a settlement of the Israeli-Palestinian-problem—an event that, unhappily, seems to be far into the future.

Actual state-to-state relations between the Vatican and an Islamic country are examined in Tahseen Basheer's paper, "Egypt's Diplomatic Relations with the Holy See." Egypt and the Holy See established full embassies in the 1960s. Basheer, however, a former ambassador of Egypt to Canada and Norway, speculates that because "there is little written or published in any language on the historical relationship between Vatican and Egypt," the *modus operandi* between the two must be quiet and patient diplomacy.

Egyptian-Vatican relations, Basheer states, "float on the ever changing currents of history." The perceptions of past events, such as the Crusades with their attempt to control Jerusalem and conquer

Egypt, and more recently, the unease felt by Coptic Christians over the Vatican's missionary activities, have had some negative effects on this relationship. Despite past perceptions, however, Egypt has welcomed the educational, medical, health, and social services provided by the missionary orders of the Church and relations between the two have matured. Interreligious dialogue has also progressed with the visits in 1965 of Vienna's Cardinal Franz Koenig to the Azhar and in 1974 of Cardinal Pignedoli to Cairo. President's Sadat's visit to Pope Paul VI in 1978 was an attempt to enlist the Vatican's support for Egypt's peace initiative with Israel.

As is the case with other Arab countries, according to Basheer, Egypt appreciates the Vatican's endorsement of the right of the Palestinian people to establish a homeland, its insistence on a peaceful settlement of the Palestinian problem, the status of Jerusalem and, more recently, its efforts to mediate the Lebanese conflict. Basheer, however, expressed a common concern among Arabs that dialogue between Catholics and Jewish leaders might exacerbate theological relations between Catholics and Eastern Churches and, most importantly from the Arab viewpoint, eventually undermine the Vatican's Middle Eastern stand.

The Vatican and Muslim-Christian Relations in the Middle East

This section examines the Vatican's role and interest in the Christian communities in the Middle East. Special attention is given to Muslim-Christian relations in Lebanon and Egypt, and to the Sudanese situation, which is often referred to as a religious conflict.

"Eastern Christians in Contemporary Arab Society" by Robert Haddad sets the framework for understanding the role of the Christian communities of Greater Syria. Haddad describes these communities as "marginal," a status, he says, which resulted from the Islamic invasions of the seventh century. He divides the history of the Christian communities into four phases: "The Twilight Age of Creative Christianity in Islamic Lands," corresponding to the development of the Caliphate; "The First Age of Transmission" (750–950), in which Christian translators transmitted to their Muslim conquerors Hellenistic philosophy and science; "The Age of Intellectual Irrelevance" (950–1850), a period of creative decline; and "The Second Age of Transmission" (1850–1950), when Arabic-speaking Christians, notably in Greater Syria, again became conduits between the culture of Western European Christianity and Islam.

The relationship among the Syrian Christian communities was an important determinant of their status in the predominantly Muslim society. Haddad shows that the Arabic-speaking Orthodox Melkites, in contrast to the ethnic Greeks, had been shielded from the bitter conflicts which led to the Great Schism with the Latin West by Islamic hegemony. By the same token, the Papacy's preoccupation with the Protestant Reformation afforded certain Uniate groups, such as the Maronites, *de facto* independence. Left to their own devices, the Maronite and Orthodox Melkite churches concluded a union around the year 1540 which was dictated by purely local circumstances and arranged without consultation with Rome and Constantinople. Although this union was aborted by Constantinople with Ottoman support, and Rome remained unaware of it, Haddad speculates on what its effects might have been. The vast majority of Syrian Christians, free of Rome and Constantinople, might have been able to confront a fragmented Syrian Islam, and the union might have precluded the emergence of the modern Lebanese state.

The fractionization of Syrian Christianity, Haddad states, was aggravated by Latin proselytism and abetted by the lure of European commercial opportunities. Although the divisions within Syrian Christianity gravely impaired its position vis-à-vis the Muslim majority, they eventually led the Christians to develop a non-Islamic principle of authority acceptable to Christians and Muslims alike. This set the stage for the "Second Age of Transmission" and the development of secular nationalist ideologies. According to Haddad, these sometimes unconscious attempts by members of marginal communities to provide a post-Islamic basis of political authority in Syria and in Arab society were generally led by members of the Orthodox Melkite community, notably Antun Saʿadah, the founder of the Syrian National Party, Michel ʿAflaq, chief ideologue and cofounder of the pan-Arab Baʿath Party, and George Habash, the Marxist creator of the Popular Front for the Liberation of Palestine.

Haddad asserts that the Second Age of Transmission has run its course. Eastern Christians no longer hold an educational edge over Muslims, and it is doubtful that Arabic-speaking Christians will be anything but politically and culturally marginal in Arab society. Although the heterogeneity of both the Muslim and Christian communities in the Middle East might preclude the establishment of fundamentalist regimes, Haddad concludes that this will not affect the position of the Christians. Current Arab regimes, he believes, will most likely adopt "a pattern of political behavior which is more supportive of Muslims than of non-Muslims."

The role of the Christian community in Lebanon is treated from a somewhat different perspective by Yoakim Moubarac. His paper, "The Lebanese Experience and Muslim-Christian Relations," is a philosophical and conceptual tract whose thesis is that the image of Lebanon as a beautiful mosaic does not adequately describe the communities which created Lebanon. Moubarac identifies three prototype communities in Lebanon, each of which has a universalist plan:

The Shi'ite Plan is evidenced by the resurgence of Iranian Shi'ism. The emergence in Lebanon of Imam Musa al-Sadr indicates a Shi'ite plan not only for Lebanon, but also for the entire Arab, Muslim, and non-Muslim world.[4]

The Druze plan is evidenced by the emergence of Druzism from the universalism of Shi'i Fatimism, by the fact that modern Lebanon was formed in the sixteenth century in the Druze environment, and in Kamal Jumblatt's philosophical understanding of Druzism out of which developed, according to Moubarac, "the most generous, if not the most coherent plan of Arab Socialism."

It is the "Maronite Plan," however, which forms the basis of Moubarac's thesis. According to Moubarac, the Maronite role converged with the Vatican's Islamic-Christian plan, which, since the founding of the Maronite College in Rome in 1584, sought to promulgate an ecumenical, cultural, and political undertaking for the Levant through Lebanon.

The ecumenical goal of the Maronite Plan was the unity of the Eastern Christians, but that quickly ended with the rise of "Uniatism," or the establishment of Eastern Churches united with Rome in separate Churches. Moubarac calls this development an "error" that has set back the cause of Antiochean Church unity by at least two centuries. The cultural aspect was most evident in the educational missions, but this, too, has led to the accusation that the Maronites collaborated in a colonialist undertaking ("Orientalism") in which knowledge was placed in the service of power.

The political design of the Maronite Plan involved the introduction of European technology to the Levant, the fostering of pluralism, particularly among the Maronites and Druzes during the Emirate of Fakhr al-Din II, and the movement toward emancipation and autonomy in the same period. The first was instrumental in the modernization process, while the mixing of the populations proved to be a benefit not fully appreciated in the atmosphere of communal conflict prevailing in today's Lebanon. The movement toward political emancipation was a harbinger of Arab nationalism for, as Moubarac points out, it occurred in the heart of the Ottoman Empire two centuries before its development in the Egypt of Muhammad Ali.

Moubarac's thesis is that the Maronites' political plan, under the Vatican's aegis and with the help of France, sought to create an egalitarian and modern Islamic-Christian society—Lebanon—which was to serve as a prototype for the nation-states of the Arab East. Palestine, too, was to be a model derived from this prototype—a place where Christians, Muslims, and Jews could realize more completely the benefits derived from the European Renaissance and the Arab Awakening. For these reasons, Moubarac states, the Vatican supported the movement for a modern Lebanon from the beginning and today continues to insist upon Lebanon's unity.

The United States, Moubarac contends, has no appreciation for these models. Despite the best efforts of American intellectuals and their colleagues, the United States has sacrificed both the Palestinian model and its Lebanese prototype to its policies in the Arab-Israeli conflict. Furthermore, Moubarac states, the United States' support of conservative Islamic regimes, such as Wahhabite Saudi Arabia, for strategic and economic interests, also works against the Lebanese and Palestinian models. When the "United States favors religious fundamentalism in one country," he warns, "it should not be surprised to see it arise forcefully in another, threatening not only conservative governments, but also the most liberal regimes in the region."

A third perspective on Muslim-Christian relations is provided in William Soliman Kilada's paper, "Christian-Muslim Relations in Egypt." Kilada's overall approach is irenic and emphasizes the importance of Egypt's historical experience of the last millennium in understanding the great possibilities for Muslim-Christian relations when mutual good will predominates in society.

Kilada outlines four bases for Muslim-Christian relations in Egypt: (1) the concept of humanity in Christianity and Islam which emphasizes dignity and freedom; (2) the sense of belonging to the land of Egypt which constitutes a unifying bond between Muslims and Christians; (3) the endeavors of the Egyptian people to regain their national, political, economic, social, and cultural independence; and (4) the previous phases of the Christian-Muslim relationship as providing a guide for future cooperation.

Kilada gives special attention to the Quranic concept that humanity is God's Khalif, or representative on earth, with responsibility for the world's welfare and prosperity. This concept was lost when, under the Umayyads, the notion of the Khalif-as-ruler took precedence and emphasis was placed on man-as-governed. Legal scholars, as a consequence, were required to exhaust their talents in safeguarding the head of state, regardless of whether the ruler fulfilled the prerequisites of the Khalifate.

The struggle of the Egyptian people to regain their independence, however, is the historical basis for congenial relations between the Muslim and Christian communities. Kilada gives special note to al-Tahtawi's acceptance that modern constitutional principles do not contradict traditional Islamic concepts, al-Tahtawi's advocacy of freedom of religion, and his support for the principle that citizenship is based on one's relationship to a country, nation, or homeland *(watan)*. The Islamic concept of *ijma* or consensus as the source of rules, Kilada concludes, preceded the living experiences of the Egyptian communities. He is convinced that the Quaranic concept of humanity, the Medinan constitution, the Biblical and Patristic legacies, and the actual living experience of the Egyptians form the foundations for the future of Muslim-Christian relations in Egypt.

The final paper in this section identifies some of the religious aspects of the north-south conflict in the Sudan. Abdullahi Ahmed An-Na'im's "Christian-Muslim Relations in the Sudan: Peaceful Coexistence at Risk" stresses that religious issues are only one dimension of the Sudanese conflict. He recounts that Christianity was established in the Sudan when the Arab-Muslim invasion of Egypt took place in 642. Islam, however, came to northern and central Sudan through gradual migration and conversion rather than military conquest. The transfer of political power to the Muslims of these regions was, therefore, a consequence rather than the cause of the conversion of the population to Islam. Christianity was introduced in the southern part of the country through missionary activity only in the mid-nineteenth century. Although Christians today constitute only an estimated 7 to 9 percent of the Sudan's population of 20 million, they nevertheless represent the educated leaders of tribes and communities in the south.

According to An-Na'im, when the Sudan achieved independence in 1956, the question immediately arose whether its proposed constitution should be Islamic or secular. When the Transitional Constitution of 1956 was introduced, its provisions for a multi-party parliamentary system based on British constitutional practices were challenged by some Muslims. Proponents of an "Islamic" constitution were either imprisoned or driven into exile.

In 1977, President Nimeiri sought and achieved "national reconciliation" by giving proponents of the Islamic constitution prominent roles in various political and executive organizations. By 1983, he decided to play the "fundamentalist card" and, according to An-Naᶜim, claim credit for implementing *shariᶜa* law. Nimeiri's violation of the Addis Ababa Agreement of 1972, which provided for regional self-government in the south, however, led the southern Sudanese into open armed revolt. The hasty and repressive manner in which the *shariᶜa* law was applied eventually generated wide dissatisfaction and led to Nimeiri's overthrow in April 1985.

The debate over Islamization in the Sudan continues, An-Naᶜim points out, because the laws which purported to transform the nature of the constitutional and legal system of the Sudan to a *shariᶜa* Islamic state remain in force. An-Naᶜim argues that the final resolution of this debate will have a profound effect on Egypt, Sudan's northern neighbor. Egypt, he believes, will regard Islamization in the Sudan as a dangerous precedent likely to have a profound effect on Muslim-Christian relations in the Middle East generally.

Resurgent Islam and Christian-Muslim Relations

The effect of resurgent Islam on Christian-Muslim relations in three non-Arab countries, Pakistan, India, and the Philippines, is the final topic of this discussion on the Vatican and Islam. "The Christian Minority in an Islamic State: The Case of Pakistan," by Joseph Cardinal Cordeiro, the Catholic Archbishop of Karachi, describes the attempts of the Christian minority (a little over 1 percent out of population of 90 million) to coexist in a country that is both officially Islamic and overwhelmingly Muslim.

The Christian community in Pakistan, Cordeiro relates, originated in the last quarter of the nineteenth century, when Protestant and Catholic missionaries began to evangelize the depressed classes in the Punjab. The descendants of the Punjabi converts, educated in Christian schools and using English in their conversation and liturgy, soon spread to other provinces in Pakistan. After independence, the

English schools conducted by the Church enjoyed prestige and prosperity and expanded to various parts of the country. As Muslims strove to find their Islamic identity, Cordeiro recounts, adverse feelings toward the Christian schools and missionaries began to surface. The schools were perceived as catering to the elite, and the Church's identification with the English language caused it to be regarded as a holdover of imperialism. As a result, English-speaking Christians began to migrate to the United Kingdom, Canada, and Australia. The Christians who remained, however, identified with Punjabi culture, and Urdu came into their consciousness and usage.

Cardinal Cordeiro makes an interesting comparison between the process of Islamization and the experience of Church renewal after the Second Vatican Council. He reminds us that neither the Catholic Church nor the community of Islam has been monolithic in the process of renewal. Just as the Second Vatican Council struggled with a wide spectrum of opinion, tensions, compromise, and post-Conciliar dissension and deadlock, even at the parish level, so too has the process of Islamization been slow to get off the ground in Pakistan. To give some idea of the spectrum of Muslim thinking regarding Christians in Islamic Pakistan, Cordeiro cites the theories of four Muslim writers: (1) Mawlana Maudoodi, who states that Christians are to be classed as *dhimmis,* that is, protected citizens who may convert non-Muslims to their faith, but not Muslims; (2) Dr. Parveen Shaukat Ali, who assures Christians of the continued "tolerance" of Islam; (3) Professor Rafi Ullah, who asserts that the same rights and obligations apply to Christians and Muslims; and (4) Rias Ahmed, who states that in Pakistani society there is no need to maintain a Muslim or for that matter a Christian identity. The Muslim identity, he says, has already been achieved in the world and in Pakistan, and there is no need to prove it through legislation.

The Christian community, for its part, feels threatened from three quarters: (1) their small numbers and related to this the prohibition against proselytizing, which assures their continued minority status; (2) the demands of a government-prescribed syllabus on Christian education; and (3) the dangers inherent in mixed marriages, mainly because Christian women are better educated than Christian men and, Cordeiro points out, "a woman of superior attainments often must settle for someone second-rate in order to remain in the Christian faith and in the community."

Cardinal Cordeiro concludes that the future of Muslim-Christian relations in Pakistan will depend on whether the Christians make every effort to be integrated into the country under its present form and way of life (Islamization). "If they live aloof and in a ghetto mentality," he warns, "they will not survive."

"Christian-Muslim Relations in India" by Christian Troll, S.J., describes a situation in which the adherents of both Islam and Christianity are minorities (11 percent and 3 percent of the population respectively). As a consequence, the adherents of both religions have, in a sense, come together to achieve mutual understanding in a pluralistic society.

The Muslims of India, in particular, face the challenge of religio-cultural pluralism, modernity, and the sharing of political power in a democracy as legally equal citizens. Their numbers and influence were drastically reduced by the partition of 1947. When prominent members of their community switched their allegiance to Pakistan, especially in the 1950s, the Muslims who remained became suspect in the eyes of the majority Hindu community. The Muslim remnant, some 80 million, according to Troll, are being asked how they intend to contribute to the common good of the nation and how they view their relationship with non-Muslim Indians.

Minority status for India's Christians was less problematic, since they did not find the new secular constitution alien to Christian thought and experience. Christianity, at least in its formative and normative stage, did not have the support of a "Christian" political structure or state. This was in contrast to the experience of Islam, where, Troll points out, the decision for the Medinan state and its development date from the earliest period of Islamic history. Troll's detailed descriptions of the various efforts on behalf of Muslim-Christian dialogue indicate that the relations between the two communities are generally good because both labor under minority status.

The last case study deals with Muslims living in a state which has a Christian majority (Muslims are 5 percent of the population of over 90 million). Cesar Adib Majul's "Muslims and Christians in the Philippines: A Study in Conflict and Efforts at Reconciliation" is a detailed account of the communal conflict of the past two decades, which has resulted in a hundred thousand dead, the displacement of hundreds of thousands of Muslims from their ancestral lands, and a Muslim secessionist movement.

The history of the conflict covers three centuries of Spanish rule, three decades of American rule, and forty years of independence. Muslims, Majul states, neither individually nor collectively participated in the Philippine revolutions of 1896 and 1898 against Spain.

Nor have they ever cultivated a sympathy or an understanding for a "Filipino" identity. Historically, the Spanish had called the Christian Filipinos "indios," and the Muslims "moros," and for many years after independence in 1946, the terms "Filipino" and "Christian" were interchangeable in the minds of the majority of Muslims.

Majul's account of the conflict in Mindanao is comprehensive. He cites a number of appeals regarding the conflict which Muslim leaders have addressed to the Catholic hierarchy on the assumption that it exercises strong moral influence on the faithful. He acknowledges that past meetings between Muslim leaders and the Church hierarchy have been difficult because of the fragmented nature of Muslim leadership. Nevertheless, he relates, the Archbishop of Manila, Jaime Cardinal Sin, has expressed his sympathy for the sufferings of the Muslim refugees and promised to bring their problems to the attention of the political and military leaders of the country.

The visit of Pope John Paul II to Davao City in February 1981 was also a sign of hope. The Pope addressed the Muslims as "brothers" and reminded them that it is only within the "framework of religion and its shared promises of faith that one can really speak of mutual respect, openness and collaboration between Christians and Muslims." Yet, Majul points out, there are still several areas of serious concern for Muslims, many of them stemming from the conflict in Mindanao. In a situation where thousands of uprooted Muslim families and orphans live in poverty and are subjected to disease and other deprivations, Muslims fear that Christian missionaries who have resources and outside support, as well as the protection of the authorities, will take advantage of the situation to proselytize. The future of Muslim-Christian relations in the Philippines, Majul concludes, depends on the willingness of Christians to grant to Muslims what Islam has always granted to Christianity, namely that revelation is found in both Islam and Christianity.

Conclusion

Christian-Muslim relations, especially as they relate to theological, political, and socioeconomic issues, have taken on critical importance in the last decade. The papers in this volume have tried to analyze the phenomena of these relations on three levels: the theological dialogue between Islam and Christianity, the diplomacy of the Vatican as it relates to the Middle East, and the course of Muslim-Christian relations.

Events since the Islamic revolution in Iran in 1979 and the emergence of the Shi'ite movement in Lebanon, especially after the Israeli invasion of 1982, have contributed both to a new stereotyping of Islam and to a new emphasis on its impact and influence.[5] The old tendency of Western Orientalists to deny Islam its originality and divine inspiration by attributing the major components of Islamic belief and practices to borrowings from Judaism and Christianity has given way to a new tendency, signaled by references to such terms as "Islamic revolutionaries," "Mullah regimes," "Islamic fundamentalists," and "Islamic Jihad," to describe those seeking an Islamic identity as at best obscurantist, and at worst as evil, backward, anti-Western fanatics.

Such stereotyping, insulting to a religion which regards itself as Abrahamic and whose very name signifies both the individual's and the community's response and submission to the will of God, is also a tragic constraint on a major world religion which extols piety, patience, charity, and human concern as the highest virtues and which claims over 800 million adherents. The papers in this volume, therefore, have tried to continue both in the tradition of the Second Vatican Council's 1965 declaration on the Muslims and in the spirit of Pope John Paul II's numerous statements on the need for dialogue between Muslims and Christians and his stress on working on common concerns.[6]

With regard to Vatican diplomacy, it should be noted that perhaps no other area of the world has been the focus of such sustained Vatican interest and concern as the Middle East. The papers of this volume have sought to analyze the reasons for the Vatican's activity in the region. These include the region's status as the birthplace of Christianity; the Vatican's continuous concern for the city of Jerusalem, "the city of God, which he made the object of his satisfaction and where he revealed the great mysteries of his love for man"; and desire for peace between Israelis and Palestinians, and for an end to the tragic conflict in Lebanon.[7]

Two caveats must be kept in mind when considering Vatican diplomacy, however. The first is that one should not focus only on the diplomacy of the Holy See in the classical sovereign-state model. There is the danger of confusing the Holy See's role as a transnational actor—in constant communication with bishops, priests, and Catholics throughout the world, and thus with access to valuable grassroots information—with that of an intelligence-gathering agency. The second caveat is not to expect new insights into the Vatican's decision-making process.

Since the Second Vatican Council, the Holy See's primary emphasis has been on the Church's role in society and the influence it can bring to bear on behalf of social change and human rights. Thus, although papal nuncios and apostolic delegates may not be at the center of Middle East politics (and intrigues), the Holy See continues to play a central role in the region through its religious ministry and its stress on shaping the conditions which determine how power will be used. This role has been played out on two levels: (1) from Rome through papal statements and the activities of the Vatican Secretariat of State concerning Middle East peace, Palestinian rights, the maintaining of the presence of Arab Christians in Jerusalem and the Holy Land, as well as in the general concern for the Christian minorities in the Arab and Islamic world; and (2) through the local episcopal conferences which influence their countries' policy debates on the Middle East. Father Bryan Hehir, a key figure in the formulation of the U.S. bishops' positions in policy debates on many issues, including the Middle East, highlights the importance of episcopal conferences for U.S. policy in his study. "Precisely because no other outside power has such influence in the region," he states, "the role of the local bishops conference in the United States is a unique one."

Perhaps one of the most tantalizing questions in considering Vatican policy in the Middle East is that of its decision-making process. Unfortunately, other than the convenient center-periphery taxonomy outlined in Father Hehir's paper and the coherent statement of general principles and interests in papal encyclicals, official statements, and contacts with heads of state, analyzed in this volume's other studies, the reader should not expect to find new insights into the Vatican's decision-making process. The administrative structure of the Holy See is not easily susceptible to outside scrutiny. Nor is it generally subject to pressures or "lobbying" to embark upon particular policies, such as the diplomatic recognition of Israel or Jordan.[8] Such decisions, it is clear from the papers which follow, must await a peace settlement that determines the borders of both countries and the future of Jerusalem, and reaches a just settlement of the Palestinian issue in all its aspects. The reasons the Vatican's administrative structure cannot be penetrated are admittedly the subject of speculation. Some observers, however, have pointed to the long history of papal diplomacy, the transnational character of the Holy See's activities, and the selection process of its diplomats. What this volume does offer the reader, however, is a multi-faceted, coherent approach to the issues of Christian-Muslim relations and the Vatican's approach to the Middle East.

Finally, a word on the course of Muslim-Christian relations in the case studies presented in this volume. It is generally conceded that the dynamics of Muslim-Christian relations affect the prospects for peace in three of the countries studied: Lebanon, Egypt, and the Sudan. The Christian population of these countries is of such size and the history of intercommunal conflicts of such significance that an in-depth analysis of the relationships between the two communities is required. Such analysis, it is hoped, can contribute to mutual understanding and thus to the beginnings of a possible resolution of the problems facing them.

The other case studies deal with Pakistan, the Philippines, and India—one society overwhelmingly Muslim, the second overwhelmingly Christian, and the last a society in which both the Muslim and the Christian communities form a minority. The conclusions offered us in these case studies vary in their emphasis. Some authors have tried to overlook the fears of the minority community, preferring instead to accentuate the bases for cooperation, while others have given a critical assessment of legal disabilities as interpreted through Islamic law. Still others have expressed forthrightly the fears which stem from minority status.

The topics of all of these case studies are deemed important because they deal with the basic issues of human dignity, civil and political rights, and equality of opportunity in diverse societies. Such questions, however, are not confined to the Middle East or to other less-developed countries. Yvonne Haddad reminds us that Islam is also an American religion, with an estimated three million adherents in the United States. If the current growth rate continues, she states, Islam will become the second largest religion (after Christianity) in the United States by the year 2015.[9] The importance of establishing a sound basis for Muslim-Christian relations, therefore, is not confined to distant lands.

The case studies in this volume drive home the lesson that bridges of understanding and mutual cooperation must be built up to sustain a fruitful Muslim-Christian encounter. They point out that one way to achieve this understanding is through an appreciation of the common theological heritage of the one God and the common Abrahamic tradition of Judaism, Christianity, and Islam. Such an appreciation can also form the basis for a greater understanding of human freedom and the fostering of human rights, and so offer the hope that cooperation between Islam and Christianity can further the cause of justice and peace in the world.

Notes

1. Walter M. Abbott, gen ed., *The Documents of Vatican II*, "Declaration on the Relationship of the Church to Non-Christians" *(Nostra Aetate)*, (New York: The America Press: 1966), p. 663.

2. "John Paul II in Morocco: Dialogue between Christians and Muslims," *Origins* 15, no. 11 (August 29, 1985): 174–76; and "Homily at Ordination Mass in Ershad Stadium in Dhaka," *L'Osservatore Romano*, Weekly Edition in English, November 24, 1986, p. 3.

3. This volume uses the designations "Vatican" and the "Holy See" interchangeably. The Vatican refers to the State of Vatican City, which was established by the Lateran Treaty with Italy on February 11, 1929. The Holy See designates Rome as the bishopric of the Pope and the Curia, the administrative structure of the Church. Diplomats are accredited to the Holy See. The sovereign state of Vatican City, occupying 108.7 acres of land and with an estimated population of 738, is located completely within the city of Rome.

4. For a detailed study of Musa al-Sadr and the evolution of the Shi'ite role in Lebanon, see Fouad Ajami, *The Vanished Imam: Musa al-Sadr and the Shia of Lebanon* (Ithaca, NY: Cornell University Press, 1986).

5. See: "After Israeli's Asia Visit, The Debate Continues," *New York Times*, December 7, 1986, p. A 6, concerning the reaction to the visit of President Chaim Herzog of Israel to Southeast Asia and the Pacific. President Herzog's visit to the Philippines was canceled at the last minute because of "political considerations." The cancelation, according to the report, has "brought into focus emergent policy makers who want to redirect traditional pro-Western alliances and move more into line with other third-world nations." A speech to diplomats in Manila by Mamintal Tamano, a Philippines deputy foreign minister, called for "a greater 'Islamic factor' in Manila diplomacy."

6. *Origins*, pp. 174–76. In his speech to thousands of Muslim youths in Casablanca, the Pope reiterated the necessity for dialogue between Christians and Muslims, stating that "it flows from our fidelity to God and supposes that we know how to recognize God through faith and to give witness to him through prayer and action in a world which is becoming more and more secularized and at times even atheistic."

7. See "The Crisis of the Middle East," *Origins* 12, no. 16 (September 30, 1982): 241, 243.

On Lebanon, Pope John Paul said: "Lebanon needs to recover its serenity and peace and sovereignty over all its territory with respect for legal authority. To this end the country needs the real and efficient collaboration of all its ethnic and religious components."

On the Palestinian-Israeli issue, the Pope said: "The Holy See is convinced that there will not be able to be true peace without justice; and that there will not be able to be justice if the rights of all the people involved are not recognized and accepted, in a stable mode, fair and equal." He went on to ask: "Is it unrealistic, after so many disappointments, to hope that one day these two peoples [Israelis and Palestinians], each accepting the existence and reality of the other, can find a way to a dialogue that makes them arrive at a just solution, in which both live in peace, in their own dignity and liberty, mutually giving each other a commitment of tolerance and reconciliation?" He went on to hope that "they abandon every recourse to war, to violence and to all forms of armed struggle, some of which in the past have been particularly ruthless and inhuman."

8. See: "Perez and Pope Meet at Vatican," *New York Times*, February 20, 1986, p. A. 3, where it was reported that "the Vatican has made it clear in the last week that it is not likely to recognize Israel in the near future"; Joseph Berger, "Jewish Leader Asks Cardinal to Seek Vatican-Israel Links," *New York Times*, November 7, 1985, p. A 1, which reported that Edgar Bronfman, the president of the World Jewish Congress, in remarks at a dinner honoring John Cardinal O'Connor of New York, appealed to O'Connor to press the Vatican for diplomatic recognition of Israel; and an op-ed article, "Rome Must Recognize Israel," by Arthur Hertzberg, the vice president of the World Jewish Congress, *New York Times*, December 4, 1985, p. A 31. For a reaction to Hertzberg's article, see letter by Msgr. John M. Oesterreicher, "Vatican Ties Would Solve None of Israel's Problems," *New York Times*, December 14, 1985, p. A 26.

9. Yvonne Yazbeck Haddad, "Islam in the U.S.: More Than Marginal," *National Catholic Reporter*, November 28, 1986, p. 16.

Part l

Islam and Western Christianity

·⁺◄❧ **1** ❧►⁺·

Fidelity to Monotheism
Christianity and Islam

MICHAEL J. SCANLON, O.S.A.

In the past twenty years, significant progress has been made in Islamic-Christian dialogue. For Catholicism, this movement away from a pattern of centuries of conflict was initiated by the Second Vatican Council in its official recognition of non-Christian religions *as religions*, with significant references of respect for Muslims.[1] Since the Council, popes Paul VI and John Paul II have often referred to the moral and spiritual values of Islam.[2] Further evidence in support of such an observation was made recently by the internationally known Catholic theologian, Hans Küng: "Islam has now grown closer to us than ever before, and that in a wider sense then purely one of geography and mobility."[3] This new spirit of open dialogue with the goal of mutual understanding must continue if religion is to make its contribution to a new world order more in accord with universal human longings for peace and justice.

Successful interreligious dialogue has proven the value of finding a basic area of agreement for a point of departure. By now, the claim that both Christianity and Islam are "monotheistic" religions, that both are heirs to the Biblical witness to the One and Only One God, is a commonplace of the wider ecumenical dialogue of our time. However, when one examines the apposite literature, one finds that even this seemingly basic agreement is in need of nuance. For some, the very notion of monotheism is ambiguous in terms of its religious, anthropological, and cultural consequences.[4] Among some Christians, for example, undifferentiated monotheism evokes images of a starkly transcendent—even deist—notion of God. Among Muslims, further, there is a general contention that the Christian doctrines of Incarnation and Trinity in fact deny monotheism. In response to this criticism I will attempt in the pages that follow to make a case for the thesis that these doctrines are not merely compatible with mono-

27

theism, but that they concretely explicate the monotheistic faith of
Christianity.

Trinity and Incarnation

Many Muslims have interpreted the Christian doctrine of the
Trinity as an example of explicit tritheism.[5] While the orthodox tradition of the Catholic Church has always rejected this interpretation, it
cannot be denied that some Christian theologians have presented
understandings of the Trinity that might fairly be said to confirm
critical suspicions of tritheism. In the course of the development of
this trinitarian understanding of the Christian God, some theologians—philosophic kin to Muslims in this regard—rejected immanent Trinitarianism (that is, the doctrine that God is eternally triune,
and not merely historically active in a triune way) in fidelity to the
divine "monarchy."[6] These theologians produced an understanding
of the Trinity which became known as *modalism:* the eternally One
God acting triunely in the history of salvation. Against these extreme
positions, the orthodox Christian tradition has always sought to formulate its trinitarian understanding of God in terms of a mean between the maximalism of tritheism on the right and the minimalism
of modalism on the left. (By way of comparison, the doctrine of
creation can be similarly understood as a mean between dualism on
the right and pantheism on the left.)[7] During the centuries subsequent to the Catholic church's definition of the doctrine of the Trinity
at its first and second ecumenical councils (Nicea in 325 and Constantinople in 381, respectively), basically orthodox trinitarian theologies can be seen as evincing tendencies toward one or the other of
these extreme positions. Thus, one might observe that Eastern
(Greek) Christian Trinitarianism tilts toward crypto-tritheism, while
Western (Latin) Christian Trinitarianism displays a crypto-modalist
tendency.
    It follows that, as a Western Christian, I am an heir of the latter
tendency—a position which makes me theologically akin to the Muslim witness to monotheism! With the Jew who avers that there is only
one God and Yahweh is his name, Christians explicitly concur. With
the Muslim who avers that there is only one God and Allah is his
name, Christians again explicitly (since Vatican II, in the case of

Roman Catholics) concur. But the Christian, as Christian, also avers that there is only one God and his name is the Father of Jesus Christ and He mediates through Christ in the Spirit of all humanity.

In the Western theological tradition, significant dissatisfaction with the tri-personal language of Trinitarianism has been registered since the time of Augustine. Before the Council of Nicea, Origen in the East had posited a neo-Platonic schema on the relationship between God and the *logos* that seemingly protected the divinity of the latter at the cost of rendering the *logos* a "second god" (albeit subordinated to the Father).[8] This Origenist vision can easily inspire a literal ditheism: it does not question the external pre-existence of the divine *logos* but what eternally pre-exists is a god somewhat less than God the Father. The Nicene *homoousios* overcame this subordinationist ditheism in basic fidelity to New Testament monotheism.

In the West, Tertullian developed the Latin trinitarian vocabulary, but his uncritically materialist cast of mind led him to envision the *logos* as a "portion" of the substance of the Father.[9] All later development of Trinitarianism in the West was inspired by Augustine. His remark on the "personal" trinitarian vocabulary he inherited is of course famous: Faced with the issue of "three in God," Augustine concluded that human speech had reached its limits, so that "if we say three Persons, it is not so much to affirm something as to avoid saying nothing."[10] For Augustine, God is not an object of human thought; rather, God is the principle of self-conscious life. With his "psychological" approach to the doctrine of the Trinity, the Triune God becomes the ground of, variously, human existence (the Father), human cognition (the Son), and human conation (the Holy Spirit). This Augustinian understanding of the trinitarian God as the ground of human subjectivity resonates with much contemporary Catholic "transcendental" theology.[11]

Recent trinitarian theology in the West illustrates the continuing influence of Augustine's "crypto-modalism."[12] But before turning to a consideration of some contemporary systematic theologians, a few observations on recent linguistic philosophy and biblical criticism are in order.

Among the key turns or shifts in contemporary theology, one of the most fruitful has been the "linguistic turn."[13] Theologians familiar with developments in the philosophy of language have become aware of the pervasive linguisticality of human life.[14] Paul Ricoeur, among others, has alerted theologians to the special kind of language that is spontaneously employed by people in expressing specifically religious experiences.[15] In brief, religious language is fundamentally symbolic, rather than conceptual, language. As multivalent mediations of meaning, symbols are peculiarly suited to express the finally ineffable referent of religious experience, the *mysterium tremendum et fascinans*.[16] The perennial symbols of the Christian tradition testify to the power of the "analogical imagination" of people who perceive a divine epiphany, in nature and/or history.[17] If God is the Creator of the world, and if *omne agens agit simile sibi*, then the world of space and time can reveal to the attuned hospitality of human openness intimations, adumbrations, traces—in a word, *signs* of its divine Author. As these signs become effective in structuring the religious imagination of a people, a symbol system revelatory of a symbolic whole becomes the self-identification of a lasting religious tradition. While these symbols are specific enough to identify a religion as "one and the same" diachronically, they are elastic enough *as symbols* to beget an ongoing, dynamically re-creative synchronicity in the history of their transmission, somehow transcending the inevitable losses and discontinuities that describe temporal passage. As long as a religious tradition lives— as long as its religious symbols are able to illuminate the ever-changing totality of a people's lived experience—these symbols not only give an ultimate meaning to life, but also evoke conversion in light of this meaning and enable fidelity in the *praxis* of daily life.[18]

Central to the Christian symbol system are the symbols of *logos* and *pneuma*. What follows will focus on the symbol of *logos* (and on its cognate, *sophia*), with tangential observations on the symbol *pneuma* where relevant. In point of fact, pneumatic symbolism developed in Christianity as a corollary to sapiential symbolism.) To interpret the *sophia* symbolism (Paul) and the *logos* symbolism (John) as applied to Jesus in the New Testament, most scholars today turn to the Wisdom Literature of late Judaism. Given the heightened perception of divine transcendence in late Judaism (especially those in apocalyptic circles that had some relationship with the Jewish sages),[19] an attempt to balance, if not to mollify, this experience of divine distance is evident in the development of such consolatory symbols of divine immanence as the Wisdom, the Word, the Spirit of God, the Angels, and so forth.

The symbols *sophia*, *logos*, and *pneuma* are similar in meaning and cosmic in scope, expressing as they do the universal presence and efficacy of God.[20] The cognate symbols *sophia* and *logos*, with their "noetic" connotations, evince a certain affinity with the Hellenistic cast of mind.[21] However, there is a significant difference between Greek cosmology and Jewish ctisiology. For the Greek, the world is *cosmos*—

an intelligible, harmonious whole, inviting and sustaining the human quest for knowledge; the world's order is immanent in its intelligible structure. In Hebraic thought, however, cosmocentrism yields to anthropocentrism, and—from the perspective of the human longing for meaning and value in life—the world often appears to be *chaos* rather than *cosmos*. In Genesis, the drama of creation is presented as the work of God overcoming primeval *chaos*.[22] Thus, for Hebrew anthropocentrism (the human being as image and likeness of God in Genesis), a world without the continuously creative presence of God is a world without order. To express their faith in the ordering of the world through the divine immanence (rather than through its own immanent structure), the Jewish sages speak symbolically of the personified *sophia* of God.[23] As a symbol of divine immanence, *sophia* expresses God's presence as implanting meaning in the world.[24] The world's meaning or order does not lie immanent in cosmic structures; its meaning or order results from the dynamic presence of God, realizing his plan for his creation. To the extent that it is dynamic, activating, energizing, and life-giving, God's presence is aptly symbolized as the divine *pneuma;* to the extent that it is effective of God's intentionality for order, form, and meaning, God's presence is appropriately symbolized as the divine *sophia* (or *logos*).

In translating this religious symbolism into the idiom of our contemporary, evolutionary, or processive worldview, we might say that the divine *pneuma* names God's power effecting genuine novelty in the creative advance of the universe, while the divine *sophia* (or *logos*) names God's effective plan or purpose realized naturally and historically in the world. Novelty without order would indeed be *chaos*, but order without novelty is a *cosmos* whose cost is the eternal repetition of the same.

When we turn to New Testament usage of these symbols of divine immanence, we find grounds for a contemporary presentation of the Christian doctrines of Trinity and Incarnation which not only do not betray monotheism but which in fact reinforce it by explicating its religious or salvific import. Recent scholarship has focused its investigation of the meaning of New Testament sapiential Christology in dialogue with the Old Testament sapiential literature. Thus, it is immediately apparent that the strictly monotheistic self-identiy of the Hebrew tradition could have incorporated symbols of divine immanence only in faithful accord with the demands of Yahwism: "Hear, O Israel, the Lord thy God is One."[25] Accordingly, *pneuma, sophia,* and *logos* signify the immanence of the One God; they do not name parallel or subordinate deities. Thus, when linguistic exuberance portrays *sophia* as personal, what is intended is poetic personification. Or, to state it another and perhaps better way, *sophia* is portrayed personally because she symbolizes the presence of the Personal God to his creation.

When Paul proclaims Jesus "the Wisdom of God," the meaning of this confession must be consonant with the Old Testament symbol of *sophia*. If, in Judaism, that symbol expressed the meaning that God implants in his creation, then Paul is claiming that Jesus is the apocalypse of Wisdom—that Jesus is the embodiment of the divine plan or purpose behind the creation of the world—that Jesus is indeed, the divine "secret hidden from the ages."[26]

For the Christian, Jesus is the chief clue in any attempt to answer the question of the ultimate meaning of reality. In Jesus God reveals "what it's all about," if you will; Jesus is God's answer to the human Why about the world. For Paul is not presenting the descent of a preexistent divine hypostasis: he is, rather, universalizing the significance of Jesus the Christ through whom he has found salvation. Thus, Paul's sapiential Christology is an illustration of that tendency to universalism inherent in all the great world religions. As a strict Jewish monotheist, Paul is convinced that God alone can be our salvation. He is also convinced that the only God there is has encountered him through Jesus. Thus, the universal significance of Jesus as God's Wisdom is a testimony to monotheism.

The Johannine Prologue is another illustration of the Christological use of protological symbolism to universalize the significance of Jesus. This prologue is, obviously, the *locus classicus* for the Christian doctrine of the Incarnation: the Word became flesh. Here we seem to have a clear (literal?) presentation of the descent of a preexistent divine *logos* (person?). I am convinced, however, that this interpretation is too simple. In my opinion, we should interpret the Johannine "incarnation of the *logos*" in rapport with the interpretation given above to Paul's Wisdom Christology. It seems to me that Paul and John, in their use, respectively, of Wisdom and Word symbolism, assert the cosmic significance of Jesus as divine meaning incarnate.

James Dunn (with whose interpretation of Paul's Wisdom Christology I happen to concur) holds that the doctrine of preexistence emerges with John: "The Fourth Evangelist was the first Christian writer to conceive clearly of the personal pre-existence of the *logos*-Son and to present it as a fundamental part of his message."[27] With Dunn's interpretation of the pre-existence of the *logos* in John, however, I respectfully disagree. John's Christology is quite "high," to be sure, but John is *not* a pre-existent Origen! On the other hand, I find J.A.T. Robinson's observations on the Christology of the Fourth Gospel both congenial and convincing.[28] Robinson insists that sonship in John's Gospel is fundamentally Hebraic in its meaning, designating "a functional relationship marked by character."[29] Citing as evidence John 8: 34–47, Robinson claims that to be a son is to reveal the style of action characteristic of the father. Jesus' "moral affinity" with God, his perfect imaging of the One he called Father, flowed from the fact that his entire life was lived "from God":

> It is this sense of belonging elsewhere, this sense that the source and ground of his being and acting and speaking is not "of himself", nor "of the world", but "from above", that John seeks to express, spatially and temporally, in the late-Jewish, Hellenistic myth of pre-existence.[30]

Thus interpreted, Johannine *logos* Christology is in basic continuity with Pauline *sophia* Christology. In both, we are presented with the evocative language of the symbol rather than with the literal language of the concept.

Contemporary Theology

In what follows I intend to illustrate the recent recovery in Christian theology of the humanity of Christ as the concrete point of departure for new understandings of what the Christian doctrines of Incarnation and Trinity mean. It seems to me that the theologians I have chosen as illustrations are all sensitive to the demands of monotheism as they attempt in similar ways to present Christ and Spirit as explications of that monotheism which is distinctive of Christianity.

The Catholic "Church Father" of the twentieth century is, of course, the German Jesuit Karl Rahner. Throughout his theological career Rahner was always the "mystagogue"—one who lived from his profound experience of the gracious nearness of the transcendent God, and who sought to lead others into that experience. While

Rahner is a Christocentric (never Christomonist) theologian, his Christ is always the mediator of the One Divine Mystery.

Vatican Council I charged Catholic theologians with the task of showing the interconnection of the doctrines of the tradition in reference to the final end of the human person. At Vatican Council II the Church accepted the principle of the hierarchy of dogma: "Catholic theologians. . . should remember that in Catholic teaching there exists an order of 'hierarchy' of truths, since they vary in their relationship to the foundation of the Christian faith."[31]

Some "foundational truths" define the reality of Christian faith for all Christians (beyond confessional disagreements). Throughout his theological investigations, Karl Rahner often refers to this hermeneutical norm for establishing the "essence" of Christianity. He frequently insists on the clear formulation of this "basic substance" of the faith to address the burning issue of "the possibility of belief today."[32]

Basic to Christianity as a monotheistic religion is its doctrine of God. To refer to the incomprehensible and ineffable reality of God, Rahner characteristically speaks of the Mystery (or the Holy Mystery). To underscore Christian monotheism, Rahner reminds us that the word *Theos* in the New Testament almost always signifies the One Jesus called Father.[33] This God is both the Yahweh of the Old Testament and the Allah of the Quran. Again, this God of the New Testament is the Personal One of the prophets of Israel.[34] Thus, when Christians speak of the Personal God or of God as a Person, they mean the God whom Jesus called *Abba* and whom the disciples of Jesus dared to call "our Father." In speaking of this God (the Father) as Person, Christians are not speaking anthropomorphically. Our modern notion of human personhood is derived ultimately from the prophetic revelation of God as Personal Will, calling humanity to responsible (personal) existence.[35]

When we turn to the classical Christian expression of the Divine Mystery in relation to the world and to humanity, we come with Rahner to the "basic substance" of the faith—and that basic substance is expressed in the doctrine of the Trinity. However, we must be careful here: To speak of the eternal "tri-personal" God as the definition of Christian Trinitarianism is misleading. The traditional language of "three Persons in One God" is misleading precisely in its relation to our modern notion of personhood, defined in terms of consciousness and freedom. To employ our modern notion of personhood to define the meaning of the "three persons" in God would result in three gods. We do not find this doctrine in the New Testament, however. What we do find there is what is called *economic* Trinitarianism, the story of God's self-revelation to the world through Jesus Christ and in the Spirit. For Christians, to encounter Christ in the power of the Spirit is to encounter the One and only One God. This experience of God in the "economy" of salvation is the basis for the later doctrine of the eternal Trinity, the doctrine known as immanent Trinitarianism. In this doctrine, Christians assert that the economic Trinity is the immanent Trinity. The logic of the faith here moves from actuality to possibility. If encountering Christ is encountering the definitive epiphany of God in history, then it follows that this actuality must always have been a possibility in God. If the experience of the Spirit is the experience of the divine presence in the world, graciously grounding both the possibility of the Christ and the Christian's recognition of the Christ, then this divine presence in creation must always have been a real possibility in God: "The unoriginated God (called 'Father') has from eternity the opportunity of an historical self-expression and likewise the opportunity of establishing himself as himself at the innermost center of the intellectual creature as the latter's dynamism and goal."[36] It is indeed misleading to call these "eternal real possibilities" in God "persons."

The *logos* and the *pneuma* name the two modes of the immanence of the transcendent God—two modes that mutually condition each other. One way to express this mutual conditioning would be an analogy taken from human self-understanding. Theologians have traditionally described the basic structure of the human being in a bidimensional manner. On the one hand, the human person is a being *in* the world, a bodily being in history; on the other hand, the human person is simultaneously *beyond* the world, a spiritual being in transcendence over the world. Thus, the human person is a being both of history and of transcendence.

Now, these two dimensions of being mutually condition one another. Transcendence names the ground of—or the presupposition behind—human self-enactment in history. Historical self-enactment is the concrete mediation of transcendence. If we apply this way of understanding the human being to God's modes of presence to the world, we can say that the *pneuma* grounds and conditions the historical incarnation of the *logos*, while the *logos* incarnate historically mediates the *pneuma*. The Spirit thus designates the dynamic presence of the One God in the world. Christology becomes "a moment in a universal Pneumatology."[37] Christ for the Christian focuses the Spirit as God's self-communication to the world.

As *logos* or *sophia* incarnate, Jesus Christ becomes for Christians the apocalypse of universal Grace (the *pneuma*). In the words of the New Testament: "In him dwelt all the fulness [*plerōma*] of the godhead bodily."[38] Behind this confession is the general Christian conviction expressed by Paul: "God was in Christ reconciling the world unto himself."[39] Thus for Christians does Jesus the Christ become the symbol, the effective visibility of the invisible God. As symbol, Jesus is the effective focus of God's universal presence in the spirit because he is grounded in what is symbolized: God for us.

As a summary statement of their faith, Christians confess that Jesus is God. (Never, by the way, that God is Jesus.) But the meaning of this summary statement must be clearly understood. It is a very special linguistic usage of the copula. The "is" here affirms a mysterious union—not an identity—between God and the man Jesus. Since the time of the Council of Chalcedon in A.D. 451 the Christian tradition has expressed this mystery as the *hypostatic union*. (Today we would speak of a "personal union.") In this union or coincidence of the human and the divine, Jesus is the Grace-grounded fulfillment of an anthropology that affirms that the human being is the *finitum capax infiniti*—an anthropology inspired by Genesis 1: 26–27, wherein humanity is described as the image and likeness of God.

A similar understanding of Trinity and Incarnation is proposed by the Dutch theologian Piet Schoonenberg.[40] According to Schoonenberg the central problem with classical Christology was the trinitarian concept of the eternal *logos* as a divine person. Just as before the Council of Chalcedon Apollinaris replaced the human soul of Jesus with the *logos,* so after Chalcedon the neo-Chalcedonian theologian Leontius of Byzantium replaced the human personhood of Jesus with the pre-existent divine person of the *logos.* Schoonenberg overcomes this last vestige of "replacement Christology" with a neat inversion of the position of Leontius: since the word *hypostasis* (trinitarian "person") does *not* include the notions of consciousness and freedom, the *logos* and the *pneuma* are "modes of God's presence, extensions of the Father's being."[41] Accordingly, the position of Leontius should be inverted so that the *logos* becomes a person in the man Jesus, rather than the human nature of Jesus becoming a person through the *logos.*

Jesus is a human person. In terms of our understanding of person, the Triune God would be One Person (the Father). Only through the human personhood of Jesus is there an "I-Thou" relation in God. Pre-existence is a temporal image of transcendence. Thus, the only God we know is the One who *becomes* triune through the process of history.

With Schoonenberg, we have come a long way from the immutable God of Greek metaphysics. History is not alien to God; indeed, history becomes the drama of divine freedom, the arena of God's self-determination to *become* our God. Here, as with so much contemporary Christology, we are reminded of the beautiful words of Irenaeus: "The glory of God is humanity fully alive."

In his recent book on Christology, theologian John Dwyer proposes "a new language for faith,"[42] adding that "the sixteen centuries during which Christology was dominated by Greek categories of thought . . . are over."[43] Dwyer envisions a thorough reconstruction of Christology in light of our contemporary understanding of the mindset of the New Testament. For Dwyer, Jesus is the manifestation of God—specifically, of God's freedom to be what He does not have to be. The eternally self-sufficient God wills not to be alone: God wills to be for us. Word and Spirit (a Rahnerian echo can be heard here) name the conditions in God that make possible the realization of the divine freedom to become our God: "Word is the real condition of possibility, within God, for the existence of anyone or anything outside him, and Spirit is the condition of possibility for his accepting and loving presence with things and persons outside him."[44] Word and Spirit are not persons in our sense of the term. They name the personal forms of relatedness of the One God who "is, in the modern sense, one person, not three."[45]

Dwyer's Christology is a clear example of a contemporary theological effort to situate traditional Christocentrism within a broader theocentrism. This project is an attempt to literally explicate the significance of the New Testament's use of the preposition *through* as applied to Jesus. Christian faith moves *through* Jesus *to* God. *Through* Jesus Christian faith learns the meaning of the word, God.

"When Christology is at its best it is about God, not about the mode of the incarnation or the make-up of the person of Christ."[46] In the long history of the interaction of Athens and Jerusalem in Christian thought, the inherited Greek concept of God was allowed to preside over theological development. Through this philosophical notion of God as eternal, necessary, one, and immutable, biblical monotheism was basically retained. However, this pre-Christian understanding of God did not "leave room for Jesus' understanding of God to influence the church's understanding of what God was like."[47] A major awakening is taking place among Christians today because of contemporary efforts to construct a "theological christology."[48] For Christians, Jesus remains the revelation of what humanity means, but he is so because he is first and foremost the revelation of what divinity means.

It seems to me that these new directions in Christological reflection are most significant for Muslim-Christian dialogue. Among others, Smail Balić has been severely critical of all presentations of Jesus that fail to point consistently away from him to "the God of revelation":

> If Jesus is so interpreted that we no longer refer to the concept of God as found in revelation, then Christianity and Islam have nothing at all in common. . . . The Western theologians who distance themselves from the God of revelation open up a gulf which could make Muslim-Christian dialogue impossible.[49]

I trust that Balić would approve of the theocentric thrust of much contemporary Christology.

Islamic Monotheism

In her recent book, *Contemporary Islam and the Challenge of History*, Yvonne Yazbeck Haddad speaks positively of a certain kind of non-Muslim interpretation of Islam:

> It may be the case that the non-Muslim willing to approach his material with sensitivity and appreciation is in a good position to balance attempts at sympathetic interpretation with the objectivity that sometimes only distance can afford.[50]

In what follows, "sympathetic interpretation" is intended and "objectivity" is hoped for.

Both Islam and Christianity continue to prove themselves to be living religious traditions in terms of the quality of human life they inspire, nourish, and promote. For both traditions, this humanism is the practical result of the divine initiative in revelation. For Christians, that revelation is found basically in the Scriptures, but "in the Scriptures as received and understood throughout the centuries by the whole Church's lived faith."[51] For Muslims, that revelation is found in the Quran. Now, many Muslims would stop with that last period, holding that the Quran's "maturity as revelation, if we may so speak, is immediate. It does not incorporate into its nature the public reception of its message, except in the very narrow sense that controversy within the preaching years is mirrored in its pages."[52] The absolute character of the Quran as Word of God is a traditional tenet of Islamic orthodoxy. Some contemporary Islamic theologians, however, find evidence in the Quran itself for the significance of the reception of revelation. According to Fazlur Rahman, for example:

> Orthodoxy (indeed all medieval thought) lacked the intellectual capacity to say both that the Quran is entirely the Word of God and, in an ordinary sense, also entirely the word of Muhammad. The Quran obviously holds both. . . . The Quran is . . . pure Divine Word, but, of course, it is equally intimately related to the inmost personality of the Prophet Muhammad . . . the Divine Word flowed through the Prophet's heart.[53]

This sensitivity to the reception of revelation on the part of the Prophet opens the door, it seems to me, to a critical appropriation of the Quran as the Word of God in vital rapport with subsequent Islamic self-understanding up to—and with urgent focus on—present Islamic self-understanding inspired by the resources of the same Quran. Fazlur Rahman has continued to unfold the ramifications of his antifundamentalist position in a recent book on Islam in tension with modernity. With a concern similar to the efforts of Christian theologians to formulate a "hierarchy of dogma," Rahman calls for an understanding of the Quran as a unity, or as an interconnected whole that is then to be brought into correlation with the present situation of Muslims. The first movement, as he puts it, is "from the specifics of the Quran to the eliciting and systematizing of its general principles, values, and long-range objectives," while "the second is to be from this general view to the specific view that is to be formulated and realized *now*.[54] As an antifundamentalist Catholic who repudiates the pseudo-fidelity of nonhistorical "orthodoxy," I cannot help but register my own congenial reception of Rahman's renovating approach to his own religious tradition.

Nor is Rahman alone in his recognition of the need for a critical approach to both the Quran and Islamic tradition. Rudi Paret observes that "Islam is as much in need as Christianity of demythologization."[55] Paret extends this demand for demythologization to the whole of the Quran. He is convinced that as long as critical study of the Quran is not pursued for extraneous purposes, Muslims will more easily be able "to free themselves from the fear that an historical understanding of the Quran would mean the end of their religion."[56] With Rahman, Paret is confident that critical appropriation of the Quran would mean a new beginning, a new vitality for the Muslim community.

The Quran is the religious masterpiece of testimony to monotheism and to the ramifications of monotheistic faith for the quality of human life. In what follows I offer the reflections of a Christian on the vital testimony of Islam's fidelity to the One and only One God.

Monotheistic faith means faith in a transcendent God. In their fidelity to monotheism Judaism, Christianity, and Islam all witness to the divine transcendence, and, of course, this common witness displays both similarities and differences. For all of these traditions God, as Creator of the world, surpasses, transcends, "is beyond" everything finite. But this understanding of God as transcendent is not the result of philosophical reasoning. It is rather, rooted in the religious experience of the faithful, formed by the religious traditions normatively expressed in the Scriptures and in the Quran. As a *religious* understanding of God, the notion of divine transcendence becomes the vision of a *personal* God. And, since the very essence of personhood is freedom, the transcendent God is the eminently free God, determined or constrained by nothing outside of himself. As a testimony to this God (the only God there is), the Quran vigorously proclaims the freedom of God who reveals his freedom in his fidelity to his people. Indeed, it has been said "that the Muslim's radical commitment to the absolute, sovereign freedom of God is the decisive issue behind all other questions, including that of a 'unitarian' over against a 'trinitarian' confession."[57]

In the Quran, as in the Scriptures, God is protrayed in terms of will, and revelation is the disclosure of the divine will for humanity. As eternal Will and Freedom God is Person, and as Person transcendent over all creation. But this transcendent God of the Quran and of the

Scriptures is not the deistic God of the Enlightenment, the God who is not involved with his creation. The only God there is is the God of freedom who reveals his freedom in his fidelity to (his "involvement" with) his creation. Thus it seems to me that sustained reflection on the *religious* implications of the notion of divine transcendence leads us to an appropriate understanding of divine immanence. Immanence becomes, not a crypto-polytheistic reification of the divine, but rather the personal presence or fidelity of God to his creation. As immanent in this sense, the transcendent God can freely deign to come into association with his creatures. He can reveal his will; he can speak to the prophets; he can reveal the Quran to the Prophet Muhammad. Thus, the Quran affirms divine immancence in terms of the language of revelation and prophecy. Especially pointed is Sura 50.16: "I am nearer to you than your jugular vein"—an image far more graphic than Augustine's famous *intimior intimo meo.*

Regarding the issue of divine immanence, a Christian cannot help but be fascinated by those sections of the Quran that speak of God's *ruh* and *amr.*[58] Both Christian and Jewish theologians have attempted to explain these terms as influences of the Scriptures on the Quran. Implicit in these attempts, of course, is the reductionistic bias that denies any originality to the Prophet of Islam. I intend no such reductionism. Again, I register my fascination with what I would call these symbols of the immanence of the Divine Mystery in the Quran. In those texts that refer to the *ruh min amr-Allah, ruh* seems to mean the Spirit of prophecy, authenticating the revelations given to the Prophet:[59]

> The accent here can be either on the Spirit of Prophecy itself, by virtue of which the Prophet receives his revelations, or rather on the revelation the Spirit communicates.[60]

At any rate, it is through the Spirit that Muhammad both warns (Sura 16,2; 40,15) and guides (Sura 42, 52). Thus it seems to me that the *ruh* expresses the "how" of divine revelation, while the *amr* expresses the "what". "What the Spirit reveals is 'with regard to the *amr* (dispensation) of God'."[61] In the Quran, "the word [*amr*] indicates God's sovereign Command and Commandment, His design and dispensation in governing the universe, revealed to the Prophet."[62]

The affinity between what I would call the Quranic symbols of *ruh* and *amr* and the Scriptural symbols of *pneuma* and *logos (sophia)* seems clear to me. Here we can note what might be called the experiential logic of a religious tradition that envisions the divine as transcendent Person. God becomes the Supreme Subject of human history, the ultimate source and goal of cosmic order, meaning, and design *(amr)*, and the ultimate power *(ruh)* effecting all provisional realizations of cosmic order unto that final order of Resurrection and the Day of Accounting.[63]

Both Islam and Christianity have at times so emphasized the transcendence of God that the Divine Will has been portrayed as disconcertingly arbitrary. Such a tendency in medieval Catholicism was characteristic of the philosophies of Voluntarism and Nominalism. The neo-orthodox thought of the twentieth century Protestant theologian, Karl Barth, is a modern illustration of this Christian emphasis on divine transcendence. (The American "Death of God" theologies of the 1960s could fairly be seen as the consequence of Barthian theology.) Extreme emphasis on divine transcendence can and does lead to deism and atheism; however, a living religious tradition provides safeguards against potentially dangerous nondialectical emphases. Islam, for instance, provides all religious traditions with a powerful reminder of the dangers inherent in such one-sided emphases on divine immanence, which can lead to pantheism and polytheism. It was against the polytheism of Arabia in the sixth and seventh centuries that the Quran proclaimed the *shahada:* "There is no God but God"—a testimony to monotheism that is the glory of Islam. And, as a religious tradition that lives from the presence of God, Islam knows that transcendence does not mean distance.

The religious witness in Islam to the transcendence of God implies a distinctively Islamic anthropology. As in Judaism and Christianity, in Islam the human being is defined primarily in terms of his relation to God. Thus, an understanding of humanity in relation to a transcendent God portrays humanity as transcendent over the rest of creation. Through Islam—literally, *self-surrender to God*—Muslims find their basic identity as servants of God. And enhancing human dignity still further is the Quranic portrayal of God's creation of Adam as his "representative" on earth—a religious anthropology that should remind the Christian of the biblical summons to humanity to become the image of God.[64]

Paradigmatic for Islamic anthropology is, of course, the Prophet. Indeed, "the person of Muhammad, as the Islamic confession avows, became inseparable from the proclamation of the oneness of God."[65] The message of God becomes concrete in the messenger even to the extent that "the conduct of the Prophet's *Jihad* becomes part of the revelation."[66] While Islamic orthodoxy disclaims any mediation between God and humanity, lived Islamic faith (especially in Sufism) has always been inspired and guided by the *sunna* of the Prophet who was called the Proof of God's Word.[67] In tension with doctrine, Islamic devotion became for many Muslims the *imitatio Muhammadi*. Wherever this cult of the Prophet as the perfection of humanity is expressed, Christians must note the similarity with their own faith in Christ as the paradigmatic human being.[68] Rejecting that form of mediation identified with the incarnation of a divine hypostasis, Muslims in practice express what might be called humanity's need of and longing for mediation. While speech about divine immanence and incarnational mediation is obviously "more at home in Christianity,"[69] Islamic theologians might be willing to entertain a recently formulated position of some Christian theologians: mediated immediacy. According to this understanding of the divine-human relationship, God remains immediately present to his spiritual creatures, but that very immediacy must somehow be concretely mediated to bodily constituted and historically formed human beings.[70] This notion of mediation is not intended to limit the divine agency. It has taken Christians a long time to overcome that pervasive religious presumption that the more an activity is divine the less it is human; but divine hegemony over creation does not entail the replacement of the finite by the Infinite. God acts in and through his creatures, and his freedom is effective in grounding the freedom of his human representatives. In the Quran God offers guidance, and guidance implies human freedom and responsibility.

The basic orientation of the Quran is practical:

> Muhammad's monotheism was, from the very beginning, linked up with a *humanism* and a sense of social and economic justice whose intensity is no less than the intensity of the monotheistic idea, so that whoever carefully reads the early revelations of the Prophet cannot escape the conclusion that the two must be regarded as expressions of the same idea.[71]

According to the Quran, God's will is dynamically creative of order in the world: "The basic elan of the Quran is moral, *whence* flows its emphasis on monotheism as well as on social justice."[72] Through *Islam,* their basic self-surrender to God, Muslims are awakened to moral responsibility. The God revealed through the Prophet Muhammad is the same God as the One revealed through the prophets of the Bible. This ethical monotheism is the religious *whence* of that structure of human existence which we today call personhood.[73] Submission to the only God there is raises the believer to personal responsibility, realized in ethical *praxis* unto the creation of a moral universe.

But, of course and also, human beings are petty, proud, and prone to ignorance; moral evil is an obvious fact in everyone's experience. Unlike Christianity, however, Islam has no doctrine of original sin, and hence no doctrine of redemption (although it is deeply aware of human frailty and sinfulness and God's merciful condescension to the human condition). Christians today are rethinking the doctrines of original sin and redemption. The former is the Christian recognition of the moral impotency of "man on his own," while the latter celebrates God's gracious empowerment of the human person to do good. To Christian ears, Islamic personalism has a somewhat Pelagian ring, and this impression seems corroborated when Islam refers to the divine assistance as "guidance." But again, Christian self-understanding is changing in our day. Excessive emphasis on moral impotency or depravity—traditionally, more characteristic of Protestantism than of Catholicism—concommitant with an understanding of redemption as the work of God alone has led some Christians to moral passivity. Catholic Christianity has traditionally taken human effort quite seriously, however; its theology of redemptive grace has typically followed Augustine's teaching on *gratia cooperans* ("what God does in us *with* us"). Even Pelagius can be retrieved dialectically as a symbol of human responsibility.[74] For Islam, human *praxis* is moral action guided by the Quran and exemplified by the Prophet; for Christianity, human *praxis* is Grace-enabled action in discipleship to Christ. Differences there are, to be sure; but perhaps the similarities are sufficient to inspire cooperation among peoples whose moral responsibility is, after all, rooted in the same ethical monotheism. Perhaps the hour of our history is a *kairos*.

Conclusion

For both Christianity and Islam, fidelity to monotheism demands both orthodoxy and orthopraxy. The religious reason for concern with orthodoxy is "to let God be God"; idolatry or *shirk* must be avoided by means of a diachronic fidelity to tradition. But orthodoxy loses its religious purpose when concern for purity of doctrine becomes an end in itself, disengaged from life. The demand for orthopraxy is evident from the fact that monotheism begets an anthropology wherein conation supersedes cognition—wherein, indeed, conation sublates cognition. Islam is realized in moral effort toward social justice; Christianity is realized in provisional anticipations on earth of the Kingdom of God.

In recent years Christian theology has made something of a praxiological turn; the primacy of *praxis* over theory is recognized in all of the representative forms of contemporary theology. While authentic Christians have always known the criterion of God's final judgment was the quality of their agapeic *praxis* in relation to their neighbor, Christian theology tended to be more idealistic than materialistic.[75] To paraphrase a famous thesis of Karl Marx, theology merely interpreted the world, while the point was, of course, to change it. Muslim thinkers have often criticized the "ascetic, 'dualistic' world view of Christianity."[76] (And given the otherworldliness of traditional Christian spirituality, this Muslim criticism is accurate.)

The praxiological turn in Christian thinking is in the process of overcoming religious other-worldliness, however. Many Christian theologians have opened themselves to the ramifications of historical consciousness. They have come to perceive time as the material of human freedom and history as the issue of human decisions. This new awareness of time has been evident in Roman Catholicism since Vatican II. The general tone of the conciliar documents evinces a shift of focus from eternity to history, from the other world to this world, from the soul to the body—in fine, from the private interiority of the individual believer to the public responsibility of the community of believers for the world. Ecclesiocentrism yielded to a sacramental understanding of the Church as servant of the world. The Synod of Bishops meeting in Rome in 1971 declared that working for social justice is a *constitutive* part of the Gospel. Since the Council this new orientation has been elaborated quite extensively, as contemporary political and liberation theologies make plain.

In these last decades of the twentieth century the great world religions have much to offer our chaotic world. Interreligious dialogue between Christians and Muslims must continue to overcome the polemics of the past and to increase mutual understanding and respect. But the present world crisis, the crisis of the very survival of historical existence, summons all who are faithful to the Creator to go beyond dialogue to a new planetary consciousness, concretized in cooperation by all for all. Christians need to embrace the "healthy worldliness of Muhammad."[77] For all Muslims, Jesus is a major prophet. As a matter of fact, some Muslims such as "Mahoud Ayoub and Ali Merad draw attention, with different nuances, to the Quranic recognition of the 'special humanity' of Jesus and his uniqueness."[78] The Prophet and the Christ define for us, Muslims and Christians, that personalism which describes "the anthropological function of monotheism."[79] Muslims and Christians alike realize that their religious personalism thrives only in a nurturing social matrix, and so we have reason to anticipate cooperation toward the construction of a new world order. But in the midst of our present global *chaos* we find consolation in our faith that persons as persons enjoy a divinely engendered freedom over every social construct that might constrain their pilgrimage to the God of freedom.

> Contemporary experience shows clearly that the value of the human person transcends any political society, whatever its coercive powers. It shows even more clearly that only the definition and justification conferred on the limits of the person by a religious faith can give it greater eminence and dynamism.[80]

To serve a humanity hoping against hope Muslims and Christians must continue to be faithful to monotheism, to the Personal God of both Quran and Bible who calls us to freedom. As a Christian I can only hope that all have heard the beautiful words the Quran places on the lips of Jesus:

> I have but said to them what you have ordered me: Adore God, my Lord and your Lord.[81]

Notes

1. Walter Abbott, ed., *The Documents of Vatican II* (New York: Guild Press, 1966), *Nostra Aetate*, 3; *Lumen Gentium*, 16; *Ad Gentes*, 11.

2. Cf. T. Michel, "Christianity and Islam: Reflections on Recent Teachings of the Church," *Encounters: Documents for Muslim-Christian Understanding* 112 (1985).

3. Hans Küng, "The Dialogue with Islam as One Model," *Harvard Divinity Bulletin* (December 1984–January 1985): 1–7.

4. Cf. Claude Geffre and Jean-Pierre Jossua, eds., *Monotheism, Concilium* 117 (Edinburgh: T. & T. Clark LTD, 1985).

5. In the Quran the Trinity is identified as the "Holy Family" (God, Mary, and Jesus). For Muslims Trinity has traditionally meant "three gods."

6. Sabellius is the famous illustration. To make his point he preferred a "patripassian" understanding of the Cross.

7. Cf. Langdon Gilkey, *Maker of Heaven and Earth* (Garden City: Doubleday, 1959).

8. Cf. William Rusch, ed., *The Trinitarian Controversy* (Philadelphia: Fortress Press, 1980), pp. 13–17.

9. *Ibid.*, pp. 9–11.

10. *De Trinitate*, IX, 12, no. 17.

11. For a superb treatment of Augustinian Trinitarianism cf. Charles Cochrane, *Christianity and Classical Culture* (London: Oxford University Press, 1940), pp. 399–455.

12. William Hill, *The Three Personed God* (Washington: Catholic University of America Press, 1982), p. 62. Hill describes this "crypto-modalism" in Augustine as "latent" and "unintentional."

13. Cf. David Tracy, *A Blessed Rage for Order* (New York: The Seabury Press, 1975), p. 72 ff.

14. Cf. Susanne Langer, *Philosophy in a New Key* (New York: New American Library, 1942).

15. Cf. Paul Ricoeur, *Symbolism of Evil* (Boston: Beacon Press, 1967).

16. Rudolf Otto, *The Idea of the Holy* (New York: Oxford University Press, 1958).

17. Cf. David Tracy, *The Analogical Imagination* (New York: Crossroad, 1981).

18. Cf. Gregory Baum, *Religion and Alienation* (New York: Paulist Press, 1975), pp. 238–62.

19. Cf. Christopher Rowland, *The Open Heaven: A Study of Apocalyptic in Judaism and Christianity* (New York: Crossroad, 1982).

20. Cf. Genesis 2:7; Wisdom 1:7, 12:1; Psalm 139:7–10.

21. According to contemporary scholarship, the influence of Hellenism on late Judaism and on the New Testament is pervasive.

22. Cf. John McKenzie, "creation," *Dictionary of the Bible* (Milwaukee: Bruce Publishing Company, 1965), pp. 157–60.

23. Cf. Proverbs 8 and Sirach 24.

24. Gerhard Von Rad, *Wisdom in Israel* (Nashville: Abingdon Press, 1972), p. 148.

25. Deuteronomy 6:4.

26. Colossians 1:26.

27. James Dunn, *Christology in the Making* (Philadelphia: Westminster Press, 1980), p. 249.

28. J. A. T. Robinson, "The Use of the Fourth Gospel for Christology Today," in B. Lindars and S. S. Smalley, eds., *Christ and Spirit in the New Testament* (Cambridge: Cambridge University Press, 1973), pp. 61–78.

29. *Ibid.*, p. 72.

30. *Ibid.*, p. 75.

31. *Unitatis Redintegratio*, 11.

32. Cf. Karl Rahner, "Thoughts on the Possibility of Faith Today," *Theological Investigations* (Baltimore: Helicon Press, 1966), 5: 3–22.

33. Karl Rahner, "Theos in the New Testament," *Theological Investigations* (Baltimore: Helicon Press, 1961), 1:79–148.

34. Cf. Paul Tillich, *Biblical Religion and the Search for Ultimate Reality* (Chicago: University of Chicago Press, 1955).

35. Cf. John Cobb, *The Structure of Christian Existence* (Philadelphia: Westminster Press, 1967), pp. 94–106.

36. Karl Rahner, "Oneness and Threefoldness of God in Discussion with Islam," *Theological Investigations* (New York: Crossroad, 1983), 28: 118.

37. Karl Rahner, *Foundations of Christian Faith* (New York: Seabury Press, 1978), p. 317.

38. Colossians 2:9.

39. II Corinthians 5:19.

40. Cf. Piet Schoonenberg, *The Christ* (New York: Seabury Press, 1969).

41. Piet Schoonenberg, "Trinity—The Consummated Covenant: Theses on the Doctrine of the Trinitarian God," *Sciences Religieuses [Studies in Religion]* (Fall 1975–76): 114.

42. John Dwyer, *Son of Man and Son of God* (New York: Paulist Press, 1983).

43. *Ibid.*, p. 154.

44. *Ibid.*, p. 121.

45. *Ibid.*, p. 122.

46. David Calvert, *From Christ to God* (London: Epworth Press, 1983), p. 65.

47. *Ibid.*, p. 65.

48. *Ibid.*, p. 67.

49. Smail Balić, "The Image of Jesus in Contemporary Islamic Theology," in Annemarie Schimmel and Abdoldjavad Falaturi, eds., *We Believe in One God* (New York: Seabury Press, 1979), p. 1.

50. Yvonne Yazbeck Haddad, *Contemporary Islam and the Challenge of History* (Albany: SUNY Press, 1982), p. xv.

51. Edmund Dobbin, "The Catholic College and the Magisterium" (paper presented for a symposium on "The Catholic College in the 1980s" at Merrimack College, North Andover, Mass., October 10, 1981), p. 3.

52. Kenneth Cragg, *Muhammad and the Christian* (Maryknoll, N.Y.: Orbis Books, 1984), pp. 19–20.

53. Fazlur Rahman, *Islam* (New York: Doubleday, 1966), pp. 26, 29.

54. Fazlur Rahman, *Islam and Modernity* (Chicago: University of Chicago Press, 1982), p. 7.

55. Rudi Paret, "Revelation and Tradition in Islam," in Schimmel and Falaturi, eds., *We Believe in One God*, p. 32.

56. *Ibid.*, p. 34.

57. Willem Bijlefeld, "The Relation of the Gospels to Islamic Culture and Religion," in Donald Miller and Dikran Hadidian, eds., *Jesus and Man's Hope* (Pittsburgh: Pittsburgh Theological Seminary, 1971), p. 276.

58. The Quranic texts in question are: 16,2; 17,85; 32,4; 40,15; 42,52; 65,12; 45,17,18; 97,3,4.

59. Ary A. Roest Crollius, *The Word in the Experience of Revelation in the Qur'an and Hindu Scriptures* (Roma: Universitá Gregoriana Editrice, 1974), p. 78.

60. *Ibid.*, p. 78.

61. *Ibid.*, p. 79.

62. *Ibid.*

63. Cf. Fazlur Rahman, *Major Themes of the Qur'an* (Chicago: Bibliotheca Islamica, 1980), p. 117.

64. 2, 30–33.

65. Cragg, *Muhammad and the Christian*, p. 21.

66. *Ibid.*, p. 27.

67. *Ibid.*, p. 54.

68. Cf. *ibid.*, p. 58.

69. W. Montgomery Watt, *Islam and Christianity Today* (London: Routledge & Kegan Paul, 1983), p. 52.

70. Cf. Charles Davis, *Body as Spirit* (New York: The Seabury Press, 1976).

71. Rahman, *Islam*, p. 2.

72. *Ibid.*, p. 27.

73. Cf. Cobb, *Christian Existence*.

74. Cf. Roger Haight, *The Experience and Language of Grace* (New York: Paulist Press, 1979), p. 51.

75. For Nicholas Lash, Christianity is "idealistic" when it "waits to see what God will do next"; Christianity can be called "materialistic" when it recognizes human *praxis* as constitutive of history. Cf. his *A Matter of Hope* (Notre Dame: University of Notre Dame Press, 1982), pp. 135–52.

76. Annemarie Schimmel, "The Prophet Muhammed as a Center of Muslim Life and Thought," in Schimmel and Falaturi, eds., *We Believe in One God*, p. 36.

77. *Ibid.*

78. Willem Bijlefeld, "Other Faith Images of Jesus: Some Muslim Contributions to the Christological Discussion," in Robert Berkey and Sarah Edwards, eds., *Christological Perspectives* (New York: Pilgrim Press, 1982), p. 211.

79. Michel Meslin, "The Anthropological Function of Monotheism," in Claude Geffré and Jean-Pierre Jossua, eds., *Monotheism*, p. 36.

80. *Ibid.*

81. 5, 117.

··✧❧ **2** ❦✧··

An Assessment
of the Christian-Islamic Dialogue

GEORGES C. ANAWATI, O.P.

On 20 October 1965, the Second Vatican Council, after many long discussions and emendations of the original text, promulgated a declaration on the relations of the Church with non-Christian religions. A part of the declaration was dedicated to Islam, marking the first time in history that the Church Magisterium had formulated an official position toward Islam as a major religion.

The declaration begins with the assurance that the Catholic Church regards her Muslim brothers "with esteem." It proceeds to detail the essential elements of Islamic doctrine, stressing those features that are common to the two religions; for example, Muslims are conceded to "adore the one God, living and enduring, merciful and all-powerful, Maker of heaven and earth." Further, without actually accepting the revealed character of the Quran the declaration observes that Muslims recognize that God "has spoken to men," and affirms that Muslims are anxious to submit themselves with all their souls to God's decrees even though the decrees be hidden, just as Abraham ("with whom the Muslim faith is pleased to associate itself") submitted himself to them.

A radical divergence, however, is noted on the role of Jesus Christ: "Though they [Muslims] do not acknowledge Jesus as God, they do revere Him as a prophet." Reference is made, too, to the exalted place occupied by Mary in Muslim doctrine: "They also honor Mary, his virgin mother; at times they call on her, too, with devotion." Concerning the "last things": "Muslims await the day of judgment when God will give each man his due after raising him up." A brief allusion is made to Muslim morality: "They prize the moral life and give worship to God especially through prayer, almsgiving, and fasting." And in conclusion, the Council addressed itself to Christians and Muslims alike:

Although in the course of the centuries many quarrels and hostilities have arisen between Christians and Moslems, this most sacred Synod urges all to forget the past, and to strive sincerely for mutual understanding. On behalf of all mankind, let them make common cause of safeguarding and fostering social justice, moral values, peace and freedom.[1]

The radical novelty of the declaration is obvious, as demonstrated by a flood of recently published books and articles that clearly present the attitude toward Islam of Christianity—in particular, of the Catholic Church—in the previous half-century.[2] The historical relationship between Christians and Muslims before the modern era may be divided into three periods. First is an age of ignorance, extending from the appearance of Islam to the beginning of the twelfth century, a period during which the West simply ignored the pressing reality of Islam. Since only meager information about the religion of the Arabs could be gleaned from the Bible (and that little only with great difficulty), churchmen adopted a somewhat apocalyptic vision of Islam. Imagination fermented this doubtful data to produce an Islam that appeared to the people of the West as a remote and inaccessible realm where there could be but little hope of conversion to Christianity.

The second period developed in the twelfth century, and was twofold in nature. On the one hand, a degree of direct contact with the religious activities of the Arab regions provided a more accurate knowledge of Islam to the West. Under the influence of Peter the Venerable, for example, the Quran and other more or less authentic Muslim texts were translated into Latin, while on the intellectual level Muslim philosophical and scientific texts were introduced into the curricula of European universities, leading to admiration of Islamic scholarship. On the other hand, the Mongol conquest of Baghdad stirred some hope that the Muslim peoples might yet be converted to Christianity—either by military means (the Crusades) or through the rational arguments of philosophy.

But these "hope-filled decades" soon gave way to disillusionment. In 1291, St. John of Acre fell to the Muslims, and hopes for Muslim domination by Christian military forces were dashed. While some in the West still advocated military intervention, the hereditary enemy became more threatening: a flood of Turkish Muslim armies overwhelmed the environs of Constantinople, and, in 1453, the great capital of the Byzantine empire finally crumbled under the weight of repeated assaults.

The fall of Constantinople marked the third phase of the history of Muslim-Christian relations. With all hope of a Christian military victory gone, some Europeans espoused a more peaceful approach to the problem. This took the form of a proposal for a conference with the Muslim elite to determine a common meeting-ground and establish peaceful "coexistence" with the Muslims—a kind of medieval detente, if you will. In this connection, the undertaking of Nicolas of Cusa in his famous book, *Cribratio Alcorni*, must be cited.[3]

What were the Church's "declarations" concerning Islam during these periods? Generally, the Church's attitude is reflected in a vigorous condemnation of Islam as an upstart religion intent on supplanting Christianity while denying its essential dogmas, such as the Trinity, the Incarnation, and the Redemption. Moreover, since Revelation had closed with the death of the last Apostle, the Church could not even consider the possibility of additional Revelation being transmitted by a new prophet positing a wholly new religious Law.

Since the Renaissance—and particularly since the nineteenth century—the new science of "Orientalism" has grown steadily, with Islam as one of its primary subjects: the Quran was translated into several Western languages; the life of the founder of Islam was scrutinized; the immense literature of the Arabs, both religious and secular, became widely known; and some Western scholars tried to give an objective view of Islam. On the dogmatic level, however, traditional positions remained unchanged until the beginning of the twentieth century; Islam was categorically condemned; Mohammad was not a prophet in any meaningful sense of the word; the Quran was a tissue of errors, with those marginal truths it contained mere borrowings from the Christian Bible; and so forth. The concomitant decline of the Muslim powers also served to reinforce the Western conviction that the Muslim peoples were victims of the fatalism preached by their religion.

One scholar who contributed enormously to the modern Christian reappraisal of Islam was Professor Louis Massignon.[4] Ironically, Massignon rediscovered his Catholic faith through the study of the great Muslim mystic al-Hallaj, and devoted his long and fruitful life to celebrating the richness of Islamic civilization and to pointing out to the Western world all that was truly valuable in Islam. Massignon was convinced that Christians had to accomplish what amounted to a

Copernican recentering in order to understand Islam—that is to say, place themselves at the very axis of Muslim doctrine, "this virginal point of truth which is at its center and that makes it live." In one of his many exceptional brief sketches, Massignon characterized the three monotheistic religions by saying that, if Judaism was the religion of hope and Christianity the religion of love, then Islam was the religion of faith. Receptive to the Muslim notion that the three religions issued from the same source, Massignon accepted the connection of Muslims to Abraham via Ismael: they were the heirs of his blessing, and of his vocation of being specially chosen. Moreover, Islam's stress on the absolute rights of God over man gave it a certain vocation toward Christianity.

Some of Massignon's disciples tried, though not always without exaggeration, to draw inferences from his intuitions. Nevertheless, it is largely thanks to Massignon and his disciples that a more favorable atmosphere for dialogue with Islam was gradually established. And it is in this historical context that we must seek to understand the Second Vatican Council's declaration on Islam referred to above.

In order to show clearly that the council's declarations were valid, His Holiness Pope Paul VI requested that the Secretariat for Non Christian Religions (which he had founded some months previously) promote a Muslim-Christian dialogue.[5] Many Catholic studies appeared as a result. With the texts of the council as a starting point, and in the light of past experience, a tentative plan was made to articulate a "theology of missions"—that is, an attempt to analyze the concept of dialogue, and compare it to that of mission in order to find meaning in the existence of Christians among Muslims. This question in particular was discussed in the encyclical *Ecclesiam Suam*, which identified dialogue with the Announcement of the Word of God and affirmed it as the mode best adapted to the missions.

Meetings between men of these different faiths began to increase, sometimes under the patronage of the Ecumenical Council of Churches, at other times on the initiative of the Secretariat of Non-Christians or under the sponsorship of private groups. The first meeting was held at Geneva Cartigny in March 1969, a second at Ajeltoun, Lebanon, in 1970, and a third at Broummana, Lebanon, in 1972.[6] Moreover, for the first time in the history of the venerable al-Azhar University—the heart and mind of the traditional Islamic world—a Catholic cardinal delivered a lecture. The two thousand Azharites and their turbanned professors were somewhat astonished to see the Roman purple in the chair once occupied by the great

Egyptian reformer, Shaykh Mohammad 'Abduh. Cardinal Koenig, Archbishop of Vienna, had carefully chosen as the theme of his historic lecture, "Monotheism in the Contemporary World."[7] The lecture's success was such that it was translated into Arabic to facilitate its diffusion throughout the Islamic world. As a matter of fact, scholars of al-Azhar also proposed to translate into Arabic a treatise on religions that had been published earlier under the direction of the cardinal.

Other visits took place. In December 1970, for example, a delegation of the High Council for Islamic Affairs—the most important organization in the world for the diffusion of Islam—was invited to Rome by the Secretariat for Non-Christians. In turn, Cardinal Pignedoli, accompanied by Monsignor Rossano and Father Abu Mokh, journeyed to Cairo, where they were joined by a group of Egyptian Catholic scholars. Together, they held working sessions with an official delegation of Muslim experts. Cardinal Pignedoli was received by President Sadat, and television and the press quickly made the public aware of the essence of the meetings. Following the discussions, resolutions were passed to ensure furture convocations. Similarly, in April 1974 Cardinal Pignedoli visited Saudi Arabia, where he was received in audience by King Faisal. His visit was returned that same year by a group of specialists in Islamic law who, while traveling in Europe, visited the Vatican and were received by the pope.

More spectacular was the Islamic-Christian Congress in Cordova, on 9–15 September 1974,[8] organized by the Spanish Association for Islamic-Christian Unity (A.I.C.). Among the participants were official delegations from Saudi Arabia, Algeria, Egypt, Iraq, Jordan, the Arab League, the Palestine Liberation Organization (P.L.O.), Syria, Tunisia, the Episcopal Conference of Africa, the Ecumenical Council of Churches, and various Spanish ministries. (Although Cardinal Duval, Archbishop of Algiers, and Monsignor Teisser, Bishop of Oran, took part in the Congress, neither the Vatican nor the Spanish Episcopate sent delegations.) Among those who did attend, however, the atmosphere was very cordial. Cordova, a caliphal city, seemed a logical choice for this democratic exchange between the representatives of Islam and of Christianity, all of whom were eager, in the interest of peace, to pursue the goals of mutual knowledge and justice between peoples. This perhaps accounts for the positive attitude taken toward the Palestinian problem, considered the problem par excellence of the contemporary Arab world. The culminating point of the Congress took place on 13 September, when Muslims gathered to pray in the ancient mosque-cathedral, which was opened to Islamic worship for the first time since 1236. The next day, a solemn mass was celebrated in the same cathedral in the presence of the Muslim delegates.

Perhaps the most significant of this series of meetings was the colloquium organized by the Center of Economic and Social Studies of Tunis. Here, for the first time, Muslims took the initiative and invited Christians to join them. The chosen theme was apt: "Muslim Conscience and Christian Conscience Confronted by Problems of Development." Among the Catholics present were professors Louis Gardet and Roger Arnaldez, and the White Fathers Demeersman, Caspar, and Lelong. Other eminent Christians invited, but unable to attend, included Louis Ricoeur, Pastor Lucas Vischer, and bishops Dom Helder Camara and Tchibangu.[9]

(While these meetings are certainly encouraging, one can detect in some of the Muslim delegations a desire to instill into the discussions a political element that might weigh on international opinion concerning the Palestinian problem—an issue that seems to hover over all contacts between Arabs and Westerners.)

What remains, however, is a radical problem that cannot fail to preoccupy Christian thinkers who ponder the dialectic with Muslims. What goals do they want to reach? What, finally, is represented by 800 million Muslims who have within their hearts a living faith transmitted to them by the Messenger of God through a Sacred Book which they consider to be the word of God? These questions confound both Christian theologians confronted by Islam and Christian Islamists who want to go beyond mere technical research and grasp the role of Islam in God's Plan of Salvation. The attitude of Christian theologians and students of Islam toward these issues certainly depends on a solution to the general problem of the status of non-Christian religions in the Kingdom of God and Salvation.

Reduced to its essential elements, the attitude of Catholics toward Islam consists of several main trends of unequal value. The minimalist trend, prominent before the Second Vatican Council and still very much alive, is unsympathetic to Islam, which it views as antagonistic to Christian dogmas and sensitivities. Simply put, the minimalists are incapable of appreciating the truths and richness of Islam. Their haughty and contemptuous attitude may be explained, if not excused, by the nature of the political atmosphere just prior to and immediately after the First World War: the decline of the Turkish Empire, with its former provinces slipping, one after the other, under the more or less veiled domination of Western colonialist powers, and the consequent damage to the prestige of Islam. In a public lecture in Cairo, Samuel Marinus Zwemer chillingly proclaimed Islam's incapacity to renew itself. This influential critic of Muslim sources, in particular of the Traditions *(hadith),* inclined some Orientalists to make judgments which, after the Second Vatican Council, look obsolete and even shocking. Even in the wake of Vatican II, the minimalist attitude has not totally disappeared. A rabid, anti-Quranic rage continues to so blind some minimalists that they are ready even to distort the recommendations of the Council concerning an Islamic-Christian dialogue.

The maximalist trend goes to the opposite extreme. Its representatives recognize, in a way, the prophethood of Muhammad and the revealed character of the Quran, but this acknowledgment leads them to exclude from the Quran any explicit denial of the Christian mysteries. For the maximalists, the Quran, at most, omits these mysteries. Their view is based on four points:

1. A material, realist interpretation of the blessing and the promise to Ismael mentioned in Genesis (17: 1–11): "In favor of Ismael also, I have heard you: I bless him, I will make him fecund and I will make him grow extremely, he will generate twelve princes and I will make of him a great people." In the maximalist view, the Arabs descend from Ismael, while Muhammad is a prophet sent by God in order to affirm monotheism in a special way and to return to the excluded Hagarites the promise and the hitherto denied privilege;

2. the providential role of Islam, as the reason millions of people believe in God;

3. the distinction between chronological time and what one might call *paracletic time,* or the time of the Holy Spirit; and

4. a tendentiously Christian reading of the Quran.

These principles, found in a more or less explicit formulation in the works of Massignon, have been diversely utilized by authors claiming to be the great master's disciples. While these authors represent a laudable desire to offer an acceptable concept of religion to Muslims, thereby completely reconciling them with Christians in a marvelously fruitful dialogue, their interpretations are illusory and rest on a fragile historical, exegetical, and theological base.

To begin with, the promise made by God to Abraham concerning Isaac has in fact already been realized by the Church: Christ is the decendent of Abraham by Isaac. He is also the Savior, and therefore all grace is a Christian—or, more exactly, a "Christic"—grace. The Church, which is Christ extended, the Mystical body, has members as numerous as the sands of the desert.

The promise concerning Ismael has, as its sole concern, certain worldly goods given to him and his descendants. There is no promise here of a parallel revelation of spiritual blessing. One simply cannot speak of a special mission entrusted to the "Arab race" with the promise that from it would come a prophet who would play a role in the plan of salvation. To St. Paul, "there is neither Jew nor Greek" (Gal. 3:28; Col. 3:1); we can confidently add: "nor Arab."

The second argument—namely, that Islam has been instrumental in bringing millions of people to believe in God—is somewhat ambiguous, and is easily refuted in any case. Some Christians might take the view that Islam, far from being providential, has been a great ordeal for Christianity. Islam has, through the centuries, swept Christianity from Asia Minor and North Africa; and is even now, trying to outpace Christianity in the conversion of the African peoples. At any rate, the argument is a ticklish one in the philosophy of history and cannot be supported by any serious theological hypothesis.

The distinction between chronological time and "paracletical" time might be acceptable from a poetic or mystical vision of the world, but not from any realistic one. The overlapping of two times, and of a Muhammad anterior "paracletically" to Christ, is a play on the imagination rather than a statement emanating from a firm grasp on reality. The reality of the Incarnation postulates that the Word of God took human nature "when the times were accomplished" (Eph. 1:15), or "when fullness of time came" (Gal. 4:4). It requires that one take seriously the successive appearance of the instants of time in history, rather than take refuge in some kind of gnostic "intemporality" in which there is neither before nor after. Christ, who is the meeting point between eternity and time, has decisively and irrevocably distinguished what was before his coming and what was to come.

Ultimately, too, the maximalist Christian reading of the Quran is methodologically defective. Even stopping short of considering the Quran a depository of revelation that the Muslim community has the mission to safeguard, normal scientific exegesis and the elementary laws of textual interpretation require a degree of consultation with those who have made it the core of their lives. It would be an aberration to take the Quran out of its historical context and the tradition that interprets it. To arrogantly dismiss the Quran's traditional interpretation in the belief that one has a better understanding of its text is to condemn oneself to constructing an absurdity—a new Islam devoid of any real Muslims who believe in it.

Finally, despite the brilliant and sometimes tumultuous dynamism of its defenders, the maximalist position rests on a very fragile base that is insufficient to support serious theology. Nourished by visions more poetic than historical, the maximalist position actually blocks all real dialogue and becomes entangled with non-issues.

The majority of Catholic Islamists, alert to the requirements of theology, prefer a middle road, a *via media*, to Christian-Muslim relations. While maintaining a sympathetic and broad-minded approach to Islam, they take into account the Muslim tradition of over a thousand years, a tradition that forms the basis of belief for the majority of Muslims. They also recognize the radical divergence of views that exists between the two religions, in particular Islam's rejection of the mysteries of the Trinity, the Incarnation, and of Redemption through Christ.

To simply point out these divergences, however, is not necessarily to say that one can immediately situate Islam in the plan of the Kingdom of Salvation. One of the foremost representatives of this position, my friend and collaborator Professor Louis Gardet, holds that it is premature to detail a theological argument regarding Islam. He writes:

> Is it really the first task of the Christian who asks himself about Islam to give, without delay, a theological note? Is it not our duty—and probably for yet a long time—to try to know Islam, really, then to take it as a fact, in its very complexity as a religion, a civilization and a community? Before being a subject for the theologian, has it not first to be examined by the historian and the philosopher?

A theology not based on scriptural text would be an "indiscreet theology"—and a lame one at that. One has to take into account the mystery of God, and, consequently, His Providence. But, one might object, what is the purpose of dialogue under these conditions? Will not our Muslim friends turn their backs on us, and accuse us of being intellectual imperialists, or even fanatics?

I do not think so. As a starting point, dialogue requires respect for the identity of the other. It does not ignore obvious differences, of course, for to do so would be of no use for either friendship or truth. What is important is the manner of the discourse, which must both be receptive to God's grace and engage all of one's heart and intelligence in order to safeguard the requirements of truth and charity.

In the minimalist and maximalist approaches noted above, insufficient attention is given to the unique character of Islam, which in an organic and undivided way is not only a religion, but a community and a civilization as well. In any relationship with Muslims, therefore, one must always be aware of the level of the discussion. Since Muslim interlocutors often do not distinguish among the three levels, but rather pass naturally from one to the other, they are apt to be astonished when Christians misunderstand them.[10] Taking this basic distinction into account, however, one may now ask how Christians can begin the dialogue or, once begun, pursue it.

On the religious level, several approaches seem possible. Dogmas, to be sure, are immutable, but new formulations are sometimes needed to make them understandable to contemporary interlocutors. The ferment of ideas that characterizes many in the Catholic milieu is a positive sign, reflecting as it does the desire to present classical truths in ways acceptable to the people of our times. Nevertheless, in order to avoid the dead end of exaggerated conciliatory trends, it is important to maintain a prudent sense of and regard for truth. Our Muslim friends will certainly not fail to appreciate this attitude. For instance, those writings about dialogue have been quoted with approval by Professor Talbi of the University of Tunis: "The more one is firm about the classical aspects of divergence, the better the contacts between us, in that they are marked by frankness and surprising efficacy, being based on a solid foundation."

I have said earlier that theological reflection on dogma may be presented in a new light. Our understanding of some notions and themes may be deepened out of respect for our interlocutors—for instance those pertaining to the Church, the Kingdom of God, and the supernatural faith of the non-Christians. Christians must also find ways to express to Muslims, in suitable theological and philosophical language, their main doctrines, and their implications and applications for the Christian life—for example, the love of God and the trinitarian life, the sacramental life, and the dignity of marriage.

A choice field for dialogue is Islamic mysticism, or Sufism, which intrigued Pope Pius XI and which the renewed interest in religious experiences is making increasingly important. Islam has always had generous souls who were thirsty for God, who tried to meet Him by a lived interiorization of the divine Mystery, and a study of these mystics would enrich some chapters of spiritual theology. By the same token, the great Christian mystics might also be examined and their riches made accessible to Muslim readers. Studies of the Bible and the Quran could also be undertaken. One must not mislead our Muslim friends into the exaggerations of a so-called rationalist exegesis, which adopts *a priori* the tendency to deny all supernatural phenomena. Nevertheless, a sane exegesis that is not only objective but which also respects religion does exist. This exegesis, which uses the new acquisitions of modern philology, critical history, and the history of dogmas, is cautious not to abandon the essential core of the religious message. It can give Muslim theologians a very precious tool, one that would enable them to extract from their classical commentaries what is abiding while rejecting what is mere folklore and superstition.

One can also work to clear the atmosphere by suppressing, particularly in schoolbooks, all that is mere fable and slanders both Islam and Christianity. This does not mean ignoring the differences and divergencies between Islam and Christianity. These must be expounded with objectivity, in order to avoid a false irenicism or syncretism.

On the second point, Islam as community—the modern concept of the state in some countries having a majority of Muslims—is a positive one. Christian minorities in these countries know that they are free citizens in a society that respects freedom of conscience and religion. As a result, they are eager to contribute actively to the welfare of their Muslim compatriots, as well as to the development and prosperity of the country as a whole. Moreover, the Church can put at the disposal of the state its social doctrines, which are the fruit of its long experience. It can also provide religious sisters for hospitals and dispensaries, and continue to put its schools and their devoted teachers at the service of the people and thus contribute to the spiritual dynamism of the state.

High-level dialogue between the Church hierarchy and the state could develop strong and constant mutual relationships, and facilitate a better understanding of the exceptional spiritual and social roles that the Church can play in the moral formation of all citizens. For one thing, politically Christianity and Islam agree completely. Both require that human rights be safeguarded, and that people work to help rather than to kill each other. Both also solemnly declare that God must not be excluded from the social community, and that human passions are and must be checked by acknowledging the glory and majesty of God.

Finally, dialogue between Christianity and Islam may have the best results in the areas of culture and civilization. All manner of arts and sciences in the two religions have celebrated the majesty of God, the riches of His Word, and the splendors of His Creation. Master-pieces in painting, sculpture, public monuments, mosques and cathe-drals, illuminations of scriptural texts and miniatures, music, philosophical and theological expositions, poetry, pious foundations, hospitals and scientific institutes, have all been animated by religious faith and put to the service of humankind in order to glorify God. Certainly, then, the study of common religious and cultural heritages is the surest way to safeguard the varied cultures existing in the world today. Cultural pluralism, a notion vigorously promoted by Jacques Maritain, guarantees this result in countries where diverse religions coexist and exercise their mutual influence.

Relationships between Christians and Muslims must be conceived in an atmosphere of respect for the person and his civil rights, of freedom of religious worship, of the guarantee of freedom of con-science, and of the right to freely propagate the Word of God. All that excites the passions, all that creates hatred and animosity, all that makes citizens of one country fight their neighbors on the other side of the border, must be systematically eradicated. In particular, Chris-tian and Muslim writers must show true magnanimity and, at the same time, strict scrupulous objectivity in working to promote fruitful and genuine brotherhood between fellow citizens.

The response to these advances by Christians toward Muslims remains to be seen. To be sure, the absence of an official magisterium in Islam does not allow for an official response. The previously mentioned meetings, however, indicate that certain groups are favor-able to dialogue. At the same time, it would be an illusion to believe that this represents a common opinion. The Old Guard, which pre-tends to defend steadfastly traditional positions and which refuses salvation to those who do not explicitly recognize the divine character of the Quaranic message, needs to be taken into account. True, attentive to Christian initiatives tilting toward dialogue, their voices become a bit more courteous; nevertheless, their positions remain firm, and any dialogue with them has small chance of success. One must address those with more open minds and hearts—those who, without renouncing the purity of their own faith, realize that the faith of their Christian friends is without absurdity and also flows from pure sources.

Several authors might be mentioned in this regard, but I will limit discussion to three. The first, Mahmud al-ʿAqqad, was a great writer who died some years ago. A varied and prolific essayist, he was for the most part circumspect, lucid, and moderate in his judgments. His great erudition—and his friendship with certain Christians—familiarized him with Christianity, though perhaps only in its Protestant or Coptic forms. His many books, however, also distinguish him as a strong apologist for Islam.

Paralleling his series of works on Muslim personalities considered to be "geniuses" (*'abaqira*), was his book *The Genius of Jesus ('Abqariyyat al-Masih)*. This life of Christ, addressed to a large Muslim audience, met with great success. The following characteristics of al-'Aqqad's approach should be noted:

1. He approaches the person of Jesus—that is, the Jesus of the Gospels—with an immense respect.

2. He vigorously defends the authenticity of the Gospels and the historicity of Jesus, declaring that they are the only sources for our knowledge of his life.

3. He rejects the rationalist prejudices against miracles, but—faithful to a method traced by him—does not utilize miracles in his exposition.

4. Finally, he correctly perceives certain aspects of Jesus' teaching: his stress on love, the complementary aspects of the Beatitudes, and the spiritual character of Christianity, which emphasizes conscience rather than religious law.

Among the inconsistencies found in his book is his arbitrary declaration regarding the Passion and death of Christ: "Here history ends and belief begins." Despite this, the rest of the book is based on a vigorous defense of the authenticity of the Gospels (although the dogmatic aspect of Christ's teaching is kept aside).

Dr. Kamel Hussein, former rector of the University of 'Ayn Shams at Cairo as well as a renowned physician and true humanist, also actively pursued the Christian-Muslim dialogue. The book which made him famous, *A City of Wrong [Qaryatun zalima]*, has been translated into English, French, and Spanish. Its title refers to Jerusalem, which condemned and grieved the Just One par excellence, Jesus the Messiah. The expression is Quranic, and the author expresses, with great tact and admirable reserve, his admiration for Jesus and his teaching.[11] Presented as an artistic work rather than a biography, the book is a personal meditation on the trial and condemnation of Jesus—a trial some consider to be the greatest crime in history. The story, in triptych form, begins on Good Friday, and describes, in a sober and elegant style, the attitude of the Jews, the Apostles, and the Romans toward the accused. Highlighting locales (such as Calvary, the meetings of the Apostles) as well as persons (Caiphas, Lazarus, Pilate,

Mary Magdelene), Hussein touches profound psychological features
to discuss such critical problems of metaphysics and morals as freedom, authority, God's existence, and the relationship between religion
and faith, conscience and politics. Without actually being described,
the visage of Christ is present everywhere. The essence of his mission
is to remind humankind that conscience (which is a participation in
the divine light) must be put above all else—even, if necessary, above
religion.

Very skillfully, in order to embarrass neither Christians nor Muslims, Hussein avoids discussing the Crucifixion. Although the book
converges on this central event—all the characters speak of it, and all
movement in the book leads to it—the author does not affirm that
Jesus was indeed crucified (although neither does he deny it). He only
mentions a Quranic verse—"God has elevated Jesus to him"—an
expression which, in this context, can be accepted by Christians.

In the last chapter, "Coming Back to the Sermon on the Mount,"
the author movingly develops the words of Christ and summarizes
them for our modern world in the following points:

1. To reject with force all false gods, whether they be money or
the state, or under guise of religion or the common good.

2. To truly live the precept of brotherly love.

3. To renounce all passions that threaten to veil the voice of
conscience.

The noble ideas of Dr. Kamel Hussein, and his pivotal role in the
opening of Muslim-Christian dialogue, have made him a leading
participant at certain international conferences. In an interview on
Canadian television in May 1965, he elaborated his comparison of
Christian and Muslim ideals, and was given the opportunity to refute
the notion of Islamic "fanaticism." Dr. Hussein answered with wisdom
and thoughtfulness questions relating to the unity of the Islamic
community, the love of God and of humans that characterizes both
religions, the relationship between science and faith, the place of the
Quran in Arabic civilization, and many other points. Later, in Rome,
Dr. Hussein was invited to expound the Muslim view of prayer in a
round table discussion on Italian television, and at the United Nations
in 1965 he delivered a lecture entitled, "International Cooperation
and World Peace."

Finally, in a more recent book called *The Sacred Valley* [*al-Wadi al-
Moqaddas*], Dr. Hussein reiterated his favorite theme: that in spite of
doctrinal conflicts, a meeting place exists on earth for all who believe—the Sacred Valley of his title. There, the voice of conscience is
clearly heard, asking that good be done without evasion, and un-

hesitatingly guiding believers toward the truth, as if God Himself were speaking.

Another contemporary Muslim thinker who shows a remarkable grasp of the essence of the Islamic-Christian dialogue is Mohammed Talbi, professor of history at the University of Tunis. In a lecture delivered at Rome under the auspices of the Pontifical Institute for Arabic Studies, Professor Talbi trenchantly analyzed both the conditions and the nature of the dialogue.[12] He demonstrated the necessity for Islam to engage in such dialogue, an invitation extended by Revelation itself. Stressing the handicaps of the past and the difficulties of the present, he expressed the need for the training of Muslim scholars in Christianity, as counterparts of the distinguished Christian Islamists. He dismissed two potentially disastrous attitudes—polemical confrontation and compromise (or superficial agreement)—and reiterated the dictum quoted above: "The more one is firm about the classical aspects of divergence, the better the contacts between us, in that they are marked by frankness and surprising efficacy, being based on a solid foundation." Professor Talbi assigned a precise function to dialogue: "Dialogue has as its aims to shake, to make move, and to hinder people from being caught in their convictions." One must go beyond "concordism," then, and renew an exegesis that "must integrate, without complex or fear, all that is integrable."

Finally, Professor Talbi reminds us, dialogue requires much patience. It should allow for the development of a progressive rapprochement, for the substitution of real friendship for indifference or hostile reserve, and for the diversity of beliefs and opinions. The function of dialogue is "to bring more clarity and openness to the debate, and also to allow the participants to go beyond their certitudes. The road toward the Kingdom of Light will be long, and God has willed that it be enveloped by mystery."

In conclusion, I repeat what I said some years ago at the Academy of Lincei, in Rome.[13] From the standpoint of the Catholic Church, the cause of the Muslim-Christian dialogue is definitely won, at least in principle. Catholic interest in Islam is constantly growing, and we have seen that some people (the maximalists) have even gone too far. Nevertheless, many prejudices have been eliminated, and it is likely that we are at last following the path paved by Louis Massignon and Father ʿAbd El-Jalil in discovering the true values of Islam.

On the Muslim side, we can at least say that the aforementioned authors are not the only ones interested in the Christian-Muslim dialogue. We recall, for example, the efforts of Professor ʿAli Merad of the University of Lyon who, in the Islamic-Christian Colloquium of Broummana, Lebanon, ably and rigorously analyzed the nature of the dialogue; of Professor Hassan Saab of the Lebanese University, who courageously asked his Muslim correligionists to renew their approach to the problem of Christian-Muslim relations; of Ahmad Taleb, the Algerian minister of foreign affairs, who, in his "Letters from Prison," showed an attentive sympathy to those Christians promoting the spirit of dialogue (Mounier and Naguid Baladi, among others); of Professor ʿAziz Lahbabi of Rabat, the promoter of "Islamic personalism," and an ardent partisan for dialogue; of Mohammad Arkoun, a professor at the University of Paris, who addressed a public appeal to Christians and proposed common research on the religious phenomenon; and the moving reactions of Professor ʿAskari, a Shiʿite at the University of Hayderabad, who stated that Islam needs "the idea of a suffering God." Obviously, the Spirit is manifested here and there, and touches the hearts of men.

Despite the terrible events currently devastating the Middle East, pitting one religious group against another in armed warfare, one must hope that reason will someday prevail, and that the efforts expended by both sides in recent years to promote dialogue between Christians and Muslims will continue, and with ardor. In this way, the Face of the One God, whom both adore, may appear more manifestly to all His creatures.

Notes

1. For the commentary on the text concerning Islam, cf. R. Caspar, "Le Concile et l'Islam," *Etudes* 9 (January 1966): 114–26; Vatican II Series, Collection Unam Sanctam (Paris: Le Cerf, 1966), pp. 201–36; and G. C. Anawati, "La religione musulman," *La religione non cristiane nel Vaticano II* (Torino: Elle di C., 1966), 171–99. For an English translation and commentary, cf. *The Documents of Vatican II, with Notes and Comments by Catholic, Protestant and Orthodox Authorities*, Walter M. Abbot, S.J., gen. ed.; Very Rev. Msgr. Joseph Gallagher, tr. ed. (New York: Guild Press, 1966).

2. Cf. R W. Southern, *Western Views of Islam in the Middle Ages* (Cambridge, Mass.: Harvard University Press, 1962); G. Thery, *Tolde, grande ville de la Renaissance medievale*, ed. Heintz (Oran, n.d.); Monneret de Villard, *Lo studio del Islam in Europa nel XII e nel XIII secolo*, Citta del Vaticano, Studi e Testi 110, 1944; M. TH. d'Alverny, "Deux traductions latines du Coron au moyen age," *Arch. d'Hist. doct. et litt. du M.A.* 16 (1948),

69–131; Dario Cabanelas Rodriguez, O.F.M., *Juan de Segovia y el problema islamico* (Madrid: University of Madrid, 1952); and especially Norman Daniel, *Islam and the West: the Making of an Image* (Madrid: University Press, 1952), J. Kritzeck, *Peter the Venerable and Islam* (Princeton, N.J.: Princeton University Press, 1964); and, by a pioneer of the dialogue, the remarkable book of Father Yoakim Moubarac, *Recherches sur la pensee chretienne et l'Islam dans les temps modernes et a l'epoque contemporaine* (Beirut: Publications de l'Universite libanaise, 1977).

3. Cf. G. C. Anawati, "Nicolas de Cues et le probleme de le l'Islam," *Nicolo Cusano agli inizi del mondo moderno*, Facolta di Magistero del mondo moderno di Padova XII (Florence: G. C. Sansoni, 1970), pp. 141–73.

4. On Massignon, cf. Anawati, "Vers un dialogue islamo-chretien," t. 64 (1964), n. 1, p. 292. Cf. also Massignon, *The Passion of al-Hallaj, Mystic and Martyr of Islam*, 4 vols. (Princeton, N.J.: Princeton University Press, Bollingen Series XCVIII, 1982), a masterpiece that has recently been translated from the French into English by Herbert Mason, and which features a long introduction on the life of Massignon.

Y. Moubarac, *Pentalogie islamo-chretienne*, vol. 1 (Beirut: Cenacle Libanais, 1972–73), 210 pp., gives a presentation of the life and the works of Massignon; cf. also his *Opera omnia*, 4 vols. (Recherches et Documents, Dar El-Maaref-Liban, 1963). The centenary of Massignon's birth has recently been celebrated at the University of Cairo and in Paris at the College de France and Unesco. See also G. Harpigny, *Islam et christianisme selon Louis Massignon* (Louvain: La Neuve, 1981), 335 pp.

5. M. L. Fitzgerald, "The Secretariat for Non-Christians is Ten Years Old," *Islamochristiana* 1 (1975): 87–96.

6. John B. Taylor, "The Involvement of the World Council of Churches (W.C.C.) in International Regional Christian-Muslim Dialogue," *Islamochristiana* 1 (1975): 97–102.

7. The lecture was delivered in English. A French translation has been published in *MIDEO* 8 (1964–66): 407–22. Cf. Emilio Galindo Aguilar, "Cordoue, capitale califale du dialogue islamo-chretien," in *Islamochristiana* 1 (1975): 103–14; Borrmans, "Le Congres islamo-chretien de Cordoue," *Bulletin, Secretariatus pro non-christianis* 28–29 (1975): 199–205.

8. Cf. Abdelmajid Charfi, "Quelques reflexions sur la rencontre islamo-chretienne de Tunis (11–17 Nov. 1974)," *Bulletin, Secretariatus pro non-christianis* 28–29 (1975): 196–98. For the important and spectacular "Seminar on Islamic Christian Dialogue" organized by Khaddafi and held in Tripoli 1–6 February 1976, see the long and accurate report of M. Borrmans in *Islamochristiana* 12 (1976): 135–70.

9. We have given a lecture in Rome before the promulgation of the Declaration whose title was: "L'Islam a l'heure du Concile: prolegomen menes a un dialogue islamo-chretien," and which has been reproduced in *Angelicum* 41 (1964): 145–68.

10. For the bibliography concerning the Islamic Christian dialogue, cf. R. Caspar, "Le dialogue islamo-chretien. Bibliographie," in *Parole et Mission* 33 (April 1966): 312–22; and *Parole et Mission* 34 (July 1966): 475–81; and G. C. Anawati, in *MIDEO* 9 (1967): 200–2. The review *Bulletin*, issued by the Secretariat for Non-Christians, is devoted to the dialogue. In 1975, the Institute Pontifical d'Etudes Arabes at Rome founded a new review, especially dedicated to Islamic-Christian dialogue, entitled *Islamochristiana;* it is an indispensable instrument and an invaluable source of information for what is done in the dialogue. For a synthetic presentation of the dialogue, see M. Borrmans, *Orientations pour un dialogue entre chretiens et musulmans* (Paris: Le Cerf, 1981), 192 pp.

Some other articles and books may also be mentioned: G. C. Anawati, "Vers un dialogue islamo-chretien," in *Revue thomiste* (1964): 280–336, 585–630; idem, "Polemique, apologie et dialogue islamo-chretiens. Positions classiques medievales et positions contemporaines," in *Euntes docete* 22 (1969): 375–472; Louis Gardet, *L'Islam, religion et communaute* (Paris: Desclee de Brouwer, 1967); Y. Moubarac, *Pentalogie islamo-chretienne,* 5 vols. (Beirut: Cenacle libanais, 1972–73); Denise Masson, *Monotheisme coranique et monotheisme biblique (Doctrines comparees),* 2d ed. (Paris: Desclee de Brouwer, 1976); J. Jomier, *Les grands themes du Coran* (Paris: Le Centurion, 1978), Michel Lelong, *Deux fidelites, une esperance: chretiens et musulmans, aujourd'hui* (Paris: Le Cerf, 1979); Roger Arnaldez, *Deux messagers, un seul Dieu* (Paris: Albin Michel, 1983).

11. Cf. a detailed presentation of this book in G. C. Anawati, "Jesus et ses juges d'apres la Cite inique du Dr. Kamel Hussein," *MIDEO* 2 (1955): 71–134. The text of Radio Canada's interview has been published in *MIDEO* 8 (1964–66): 359–67. The book has been translated into English from the Arabic by Bishop Kenneth Cragg, *City of Wrong, a Friday in Jerusalem* (Amsterdam: Djambatan, 1973), and into French by R. Arnaldez, *La Cite inique* (Paris: Sindbad, Coll. La Bibliotheque Arabe, 1973).

12. Mohammad Talbi, "Islam and Dialogue: Reflections on an Actual Theme" (Tunis: Maison Tunisienne de l'edition, 1972).

13. Cf. *Tavola Rotonda sul tema: Christianesimo e islamismo,* Roma 17–18 aprile 1972 (published in 1974), pp. 193–207.

Shi'i Islam and Roman Catholicism
An Ecclesial and Political Analysis

JAMES A. BILL AND JOHN ALDEN WILLIAMS

Introduction

Christianity and Islam are both Abrahamic faiths: that is, both worship the God of Abraham. This assertion is explicit in the Quran of Islam, which states that the revelation given to Muhammad is a restoration of the faith of Abraham, who was neither a Jew nor a Christian but a man of pure faith.[1] The Christian Scriptures also stress the importance of Abraham: "What fulfills the promise depends on faith, so that it may be a free gift and be available to all of Abraham's descendants, not only those who belong to the Law, but also those who belong to the faith of Abraham who is the father of all of us."[2]

St. John of Damascus, the Church father who knew Islam most intimately, identified it as a Christian heresy. Muslims recognize Jesus as the promised Messiah born of a virgin, but not as Lord; as word of God, but not as Son of God; as prophet and teacher, but not as atoning sacrifice or as Savior. Typologically, from the standpoint of Christian faith, Islam indeed appears as a deviant form of recognized Christian doctrine. Nevertheless, the fact remains: Islam has constituted itself as a religious system in its own right. Few Christians or Muslims today would wish to argue that Muslims are a sect of Christians. It is thus possible to point to congruities between a Christian system and a Muslim system precisely *because* Muslims are not Christians.

Christianity is an intricately thelogical approach to faith. Islam is not. Its concerns are primarily ethical: what are the right and wrong things to *do*. For many Muslims, theology begins and ends with the assertion that there is no God but God, and that Muhammad is His Messenger (though Shi'is will add that Ali is the Friend [*wali*] of God).

Aside from the theological implications of these preliminary statements, Muslim faith is expressed in action—in things done and not
done.

This study does not intend to concern itself primarily with theological comparisons, however. For one thing, Christian theology is a
matter of such importance and complexity that it should be left to the
professionals. For another, theological expertise is not the best avenue
to understanding Islam, since, as indicated above, Islam focuses its
concern on the ethical/legal aspect of faith rather than the theological
or philosophical. (There have, of course, been Islamic theologians,
just as there have been Christian canon lawyers, but the question is
one of the relative importance placed on each activity in these traditions.) The authors are concerned here with highlighting the parallels
in two discrete systems, believing as they do that such comparisons
may lead to heightened sensitivity and understanding. Comparative
analysis indicates how similar themes appear in the religious ideas of
two different though related traditions; it leads us from what we in
some measure understand to knowledge of what we know less well,
and in the process enables us to refine our conceptual and theoretical
approaches to these issues. The implications are, in the final sense,
social and political rather than theological; yet we believe that the
endeavor is worth some effort, both by believers and by nonbelievers
of these strikingly different but nevertheless entwined traditions.

As did late Judaism, both Christianity and Islam have had to
wrestle with the question of how man can seek to have any valid
knowledge of a transcendent God, a God whose ways are not man's
ways—a God who is, in point of fact, beyond knowledge. The Greek-
speaking Jews of Alexandria concluded in effect that man may know
God only through an intermediate principle, His *logos*—the divine
knowledge or wisdom through which He created all things, and which
permeated all things and ultimately made knowledge possible. This
name the Christians promptly applied to Christ. In the beginning was
the *logos;* all things were made by the *logos;* without the *logos* nothing
was made that has been made. In its life was the light of men. The
logos became flesh and was made man, and the apostles and disciples
beheld his glory.[3]

If the Greek term *logos* is replaced by the Arabic *kalima,* or Word,
then the pious Muslim is able to follow this paraphrase of the fourth
Gospel's hymn to the *logos* up to the last sentence. At this point,
however, he would be likely to say: "The Word became writing and
was made Book, and through the Apostle Muhammad it was given to

us in all its glory." It cannot be stressed too strongly that, as the *logos*, the Living Word of God, the Quran is given an importance high above that given to Christian scripture by even the most fundamentalist Christian: its position is parallel to that of Christ in the Christian teaching. Indeed, it is the *hadiths*—the doings and sayings, the teaching and epistles of their unique apostle—that are the Muslim parallel to the Christian scripture, even though the canon of the *hadiths* has not been fixed, even by Sunnis. In fact, the root of the disagreement between Sunnis and Shiʿis today can be found in the often sharp differences between the versions of the *hadiths* that each holds as authoritative.[4] This may require a few sentences of explanation.

To be accepted as true, a *hadith* must have a valid chain of transmitters who attest to its truth. The chains of authority or transmission accepted by Sunnis and Shiʿis usually differ, even when the same *matn*, or text, is being transmitted. Muhammad is held to have been guided by the "holy spirit"—i.e., the Archangel Gabriel—and his *hadith* is therefore second in importance only to the Quran as a source of Muslim law and ethics. But a legal and ethical question has divided Muslims almost from the moment of the Prophet's death: What disposition had Muhammad made for the leadership of the Community after his death? Was it correct for his Companions to elect one of themselves as his political successor, since he had left the question open, as Sunnis claim; or, contrariwise, had he, as Shiʿis hold, made quite explicit statements that he intended for the leadership to be vested in the family of his son-in-law and cousin Ali and Muhammad's own daughter Fatima? It is characteristic of Islam that its sectarian divisions are based on such politico-legal questions (rather than on theological differences), and that the politico-legal is exalted to almost metaphysical status.

Catholics believe in the primacy of Peter among the apostles, and in the primacy of his successor among the bishops. Religious authority for them is thus centralized and articulated in every age. The same may be said for Shiʿi Muslims, and this matter of the nature of religious authority is the first of the parallels that we may observe between Shiʿism and Roman Catholicism. There are many others. The authors are, of course, quite aware that these religious systems have fundamental differences, and that each has existed in history. But they believe also that besides existing in time (i.e., being exposed to change), each has some enduring and essential characteristics, and that certain of these characteristics are strikingly similar. These similarities are the subject of our analysis.

Catholicism and Protestantism / Shiʿi Islam and Sunni Islam

The link between the revealed and faith must be an infallible one, or God "dies" to faith. Thus, for Catholics it is the Church, which both wrote the scriptures and attests to their validity, that is infallible. Its infallibility is exercised through the series of successors to the apostles. For classical Protestantism, by comparison, it was the scriptures themselves that were the infallible guide, while the Church that wrote and canonized them was not only fallible but often errant.

Sunni Islam is sometimes referred to as "Catholic Islam" because for it, too, infallibility reposes in a Community of the Faithful, the *Umma*. If there is a difference of opinion within the Community, then the majority of those endowed with the religious knowledge, the *ulama*, are infallibly right. The Shiʿi position, however, is that the Community can only be infallible when it is led by the legitimate descendant of the Prophet, as his successor in every function of leadership save that of Prophecy (i.e., of bringing new revelation). Various Shiʿi sects have differing views as to which descendant was the rightful leader, but the Twelver Shiʿis we are concerned with here hold that a succession of twelve impeccable descendants of Muhammad led the Community. The last of these was taken into occultation due to the harassment of the Sunnis, but even in his absence, he is the true leader of the Community. He will reappear at the end of time along with the Messiah Jesus, in order to slay the Antichrist and usher in the triumph of true religion in the messianic age.

The claim of *'isma*, of impeccability, made for the Imams of the Twelver and the Ismaʿili Shiʿis goes considerably beyond the infallibility claimed for the Roman pontiff as leader of the successor of the apostles, as we shall observe. Still, the infallible link with revelation is vested for the Twelve in the Imams, and like the Prophet they are held to have been guided by Gabriel, the "holy spirit."[5]

The name *Sunni*, or *traditionalist*, refers to the tradition of the majority of the Companions of Muhammad, who elected and followed leaders not of his family after his death. The name *Shiʿi*, or *partisan*, refers to the partisans of the Prophet's family. According to the latter position, the majority of Muslims entered into serious error after the Prophet's death by overlooking the legitimate claim of his family to leadership. This was considered to be an act of treachery, of ingratitude, not only to the Messenger of God, but by extension to the message itself. Shiʿis have demonstrated their devotion to the Prophet by a willingness to be persecuted and put to death for their loyalty to his family. And it has often been the Sunni majority that has persecuted them.

The legal term for the leader of the Muslim Community, the *imam*, is common to all Muslims, whether Sunnis, Shi'is, or the third division, the Kharijis. For the Sunnis, the imam could be any physically sound member of the tribe of Quraysh who could adequately interpret the Law and defend the Community interests, and could be placed in office by agreement of the necessary number of magnates. For the Kharijis, any upright Muslim male who was fit for the duties of the office might be chosen, but if he lost the quality of rectitude he could be deposed. For the Twelvers, however, the imam could not be chosen by anyone less than God. The incumbent imam was guided by the angel Gabriel to announce on which of his sons the choice had fallen.[6] Since the Twelvers also hold that their imams were the best of mankind then living and that they were impeccable, no question of the consequences of a fall from rectitude could suggest itself.[7] (The Isma'ilis hold the same doctrine, but their imam is not in occultation. It is therefore the doctrine and practices of the Twelvers, indeed the majority of Shi'is today, that will be compared with those of Roman Catholicism in the following pages.)

The *Ithna'ashariya* or Twelvers represent more than 90 percent of the population of Iran, and slightly more than 50 percent of the Muslim population of Iraq. There is also a large Twelver population in Lebanon, mostly in the Central Valley and the South, estimated to be as much as 30 percent of the total population, and there are significant Twelver minorities in Syria and in the Arab states of the Gulf, including almost 500,000 in the eastern province of Saudi Arabia. Large and historically powerful Twelver communities are found in the Indian subcontinent as well. In total, perhaps 12 to 15 percent of the modern Muslim world is Twelver.

As minorities leveling trenchant criticism of the Establishment, all Shi'i sects may in that sense at least be labeled *protestant*. Despite this observation, our argument is that there are deeper, structural similarities between Catholicism and Shi'ism than between the latter and Christian Protestantism. Moreover, the Twelvers were signally unlike the Protestants of Europe in being slow to find princes to champion their cause. Although the Zaydis and the Isma'ilis were able to establish states during the third century A.H. (ninth century A.D.), the Twelvers were hampered by the fact that their imams were kept under strict surveillance and control by the Sunni Abbasid imam-caliphs, and the twelfth imam disappeared from view in Samarra about A.H. 260/A.D. 874. Leaders of the sect tried to make alliances with princes who might offer it protection from persecutors (for one, the pagan Mongols that destroyed Abbasid Baghdad), but it was not until the beginning of the tenth/sixteenth century that a Twelver state was established, by the Safavi shahs of Iran—although somewhat earlier, the Twelvers had found protectors in the shahs of three Muslim states of the Deccan in south central India.

For centuries, then, the Twelvers were a persecuted minority. What enabled them to survive in those difficult times was the practice of *taqiya,* or prudent dissimulation, enjoined on them by their imams. For example, it was not obligatory to proclaim one's faith; one might conceal it without dishonor if one's life or property would be endangered by open profession. "Mix with the enemies outwardly, but opppose them inwardly so long as the leadership is a matter of opinion," the sixth imam ordered.[8] These long intervals of fear, concealment, and frequent martyrdom are unlike anything faced by European Christians in the long period between the conversion of the Roman Empire and the Reformation. Unquestionably, they have burned deep in the Twelver experience, and—added to the trauma of the disappearance of the twelfth imam—they produced on the one hand a seeming willingness to compromise with almost any protector, and on the other a profound suspicion of any government in power. Fear of persecution has also produced in some Twelver communities—notably, Lebanon—an inward-looking quietism that has only very recently yielded to the desire to become actively involved in political affairs.

Matters were different for the Shi'is of Iran following 1500. Here at least they had a state, ruled over by shahs eager to implement Shi'i law and to advance the cause of Twelverism. Although the state was often invaded by the Ottoman Empire (as official defender of Sunnism) as well as by Sunni the Uzbeks of Central Asia, it was able to successfully repulse its attackers until 1722—in large part because of the devotion of the Persians to the Twelver cause. In the Deccan of India, and later in North India, where the princes of Awadh favored them (c. 1740–1856), the Twelvers also knew some political success. At the same time, because the imam was the true ruler yet could not rule, Twelvers had to recognize a *de facto* separation between church and state—a distinction foreign to the Muslim view of the proper nature of authority. Shi'i shahs might claim to be the *wakil,* or deputy of the absent imam, but this also exposed them to the watchful surveillance of the *mujtahids*, or interpreters of the Shiʿi law. Never at any time could a monarch validly claim to be the head of the religious community in the sense that a Protestant prince in Europe might claim to be the head of the Church in his realm. The most he could hope for was to manage it, as a king of Spain or of France might seek to manage the Church authorities. At the same time, due to the absence of the imam, religious authority among the Shiʿis inevitably devolved upon the *mujtahids*, who thus came to occupy a place of spiritual power and authority unique in Islam, and comparable to that of the high-ranking Catholic clergy.

Shiʿism and Catholicism:
A Comparative Analysis of Beliefs and Practices

Among the several parallels that we may observe between Twelver Shiʿism and Roman Catholicism, three are perhaps most telling: meditation upon the significance of the passion of an innocent victim who took upon himself the sins of the Community and atoned for them; belief that God's grace is mediated through earthly and heavenly hierarchies; and faith in intercessors. In Sunnism as in Protestantism, by comparison, the dominant view is that only Muhammad (or Jesus) is the intercessor—or even that the intercessory function has now been performed, and that therefore each believer must now "carry his own weight."[9] Shiʿism, in common with the *sufis* (the mystics of Islam), places great value on the model, the intercession, and the accessibility of the "friends of God," the saints.

In particular, both Catholicism and Twelverism emphasize an overarching mother-figure as a leading intercessor, a pattern for women, a refuge for those in trouble, a radiant "mother of sorrows" and hope for the sorrowing. Both emphasize the great value of martyrdom and of redemptive suffering, even to the extent that individual suffering can become part of a "treasury of grace" upon which coreligionists can draw. And finally, each community believes and proclaims that it is led by a charismatic leader who is guided by God and hence preserved from error, and believes further that there is a religious hierarchy that shares his authority and upholds and diffuses his teaching. This enables that hierarchy to speak with great confidence and authority, upheld as it is by the accompanying belief that God would never leave the faithful without such an infallible guide through the complexities of its religion.

These correspondences[10] are at times so striking that when one tradition observes them in the other, it produces something like a feeling of distrust and suspicion: Has the other sought to array itself in the garments of truth, to which of course it is not party? Is it a parody of the truth, drawing whatever strength it has from the reality that is the particular blessing of one's own community? Others would perhaps prefer to argue that each tradition possesses images, more or less perfectly understood, of archetypes which in a final sense are with God, and must be rendered back to Him. The authors will confine themselves here to discussing these parallels in the spirit of the declaration of the Church to non-Christians in the documents of the Second Vatican Council: "Although in the course of the centuries many quarrels and hostilities have arisen between Christians and Muslims, this most sacred Synod urges all to forget the past and to strive sincerely for mutual understanding."[11]

The Concept of Intercession and the Role of Sainthood

"The imams are also the intermediaries between man and God. To ask for their succour is to appeal to the channel God placed before man so as to enable man to return to Him."[12] Thus succinctly a modern Shi'i scholar states the role of the imams as intercessors. Great merit is attached to visiting the tombs of the eleven imams (and the place of disappearance of the twelfth) among the Twelvers, virtually as much as the Great Pilgrimage to Mecca. Some of the imams are buried at Medina, the city of the Prophet, in Arabia; others are buried in Baghdad or Samarra, the Iraqi capitals of the Abbasid caliphs who kept them under close surveillance. The eighth, Ali ibn Musa al-Rida, is buried in a village outside the city of Tus, in eastern Iran, that has become the important holy city of Mashhad ("Martyr-site").

Every year, hundreds of thousands of Twelvers visit these sacred sites and ask for the intercession of the imams. In many parts of the Shi'i world, icons of Ali, his sons, or other imams are displayed in homes and shops. Called timthal (likenesses), these icons usually display a noble and compassionate face surrounded by a halo, and are a significant exception to the general rule against religious pictures in Islam. Prayer books for the visitation of the tombs of the imams are sold, and the prayers are devoutly read and recited during the visits.

Imam Husayn was martyred by the troops of the Umayyad Caliph on the tenth day of Muharram in the year 61/680 at Karbala, in Iraq, while travelling from Mecca, where he had taken sanctuary, to Kufa, where his supporters had called him. This day, Ashura—the tenth of the holy month of Muharram—had originally been designated as the Muslim day of fast and atonement by the Prophet, directly patterned on Yom Kippur, the tenth day of the Jewish month of Tishri, with which it was originally simultaneous (the two calendars have since diverged). Subsequently Ashura was replaced as an obligatory fast by the mont of Ramadan; it remained as a voluntary fast, however, and is kept by devout Muslims everywhere.[13] For Shiʿis, the day, and the nine days preceding it, are made far more poignant by the recollection of the death of Husayn; according to the Shiʿis, Husayn knew perfectly that he would be martyred on this day and offered his life as an atonement for the sins of his grandfather's Community.[14]

It is an article of faith, placed in Twelver creedal statements by great *mujtahids* of the past, that all eleven imams were martyred, usually by poison, by their enemies: "He who says they were not has given them the lie and imputed falsehood to God."[15] Their sorrowful lives and deaths have cosmic significance, since the imams were given to the Muslims to guide them to the truth of God, both as rulers—as explainers of the Law of God—and as mystical guides.[16] "It is the Imam who directs man's spiritual life and orients the inner aspect of human action toward God. Clearly, his physical presence or absence has no effect on this matter. The Imam watches over men inwardly and is in communion with the soul and spirit of men even if he be hidden from their physical eyes."[17]

This is possible because Ali is the *wali* of God, and the imams are emanations from him. The word *wali* means friend, but it also has the connotation of *one who acts on behalf of.* It is usually translated in Western languages as *saint* when it is used to refer to the "Friends of God." Islam has an elaborate doctrine of saints, *awliya.* The earliest detailed hagiology to be set down (apparently for Sunnis), written in the third Islamic century (about A.D. 890) states that the friends of God have the following charisms: they remember God at all times (i.e., are united with Him in prayer); they overcome others by the power of truth alone; they are given clairvoyance and inspiration; whoever injures them soon receives retribution in the form of an evil death; all unite in praising them except those afflicted by envy; their prayers are answered; and signs occur such as disappearing into the earth, walking on water, and speaking with al-Khidr.[18] The latter is a mysterious

figure sometimes identified with the Prophet Elias—the instructor of
the saints, for the *sufis,* although usually replaced by the twelfth imam
among Twelvers. "The traditional and intellectual proofs of [Islam]
are to be found among the *ulama.* . . . Its visible proof is to be found
among the saints and the elect of God," writes a prominent theorist
around A.D. 1057.[19]

All friendship with God is referred to friendship with the imams,
who are among the greatest friends of God in the view of the Shi'is.
Sainthood is the very function of explaining the true meaning of
revelation. Hence, the saints are seen as the mystical family of the
imams, and consequently their intercession, like that of the imams, is
to be sought.[20] Shi'is share many saints with the Sunnis; some Sunnis
regard many of the twelve imams as great saints whose intercession is
to be greatly valued.[21] One of the few irenic areas of Shi'i-Sunni
relations is the doctrine of sainthood and intercession, though Sunnis
of course would not add the characteristic Shi'i explanation that it is
by virtue of their mystical relation with the imams that the saints are
saints (rather than by virtue of their direct relationship with God).

Similarly in Christendom, the first saints whose intercession seems
to have been sought were the martyrs—those who had literally laid
down their lives for Christ. Catholics would certainly agree that the
saints in their lives show forth the true meaning of faith, and that
during life or after death are accessible to those who seek the assistance of their prayers and intercession. (The Catholic church calendar is enlivened with the days of the saints.) There is, of course, no
process of canonization in Islam by which the saint is publicly and
officially commended to the faithful as an intercessor. People are
popularly recognized in a rather democratic way as models of faith,
particularly if there are stories of miracles connected with their lives
or their tombs. However, Catholics and Twelvers would agree that,
strictly speaking, God is always directly accessible to prayer, both
adding that there is yet great virtue and profit to the faithful in
seeking the friendship of these great friends of God.

The Blessed Virgin Mary and Sayyida Fatima

Mary, the mother of Christ, is a central figure and symbol for
Catholic Christianity. Especially blessed and immaculately conceived,
she was privileged to be the virginal mother of the *logos,* through
whom the world was created—hence, truly *"Theotokos"*: Mother of

God. As the mother of the prophet and promised Messiah, Mary is recognized as well in the Quran as "purified" and "chosen above all women" by God, who Himself ordained the virginal birth. The Virgin Mary is thus a sacred historical and theological link binding Christians and Muslims. Catholics and Orthodox Christians view her as mother of Christ the divine *logos*, and therefore the mother of God; Muslims consider her mother of the Messiah selected by God for this very special role.

An elaborate Catholic theology has developed about and involves the immaculate conception, the drama of the annunciation, the virginal birth, and the assumption of Mary into heaven. Roman Catholic teachings have sometimes even presented Mary as the Coredemptrix. Although she remains subordinated to Christ in the work of redemption, she is considered to be an integral part of the universal cause of human redemption. In this sense, she is viewed as a second redeemer and a second Eve.

Protestantism generally has tended to criticize what it considers to be the unseemly Catholic preoccupation with and glorification of Mary. The Catholic emphasis upon Mary's holiness and special grace and her "motherhood of God" is sometimes compared to pagan goddess worship. The Catholic stress upon the assumption of Mary, body and soul, into heaven is also seriously questioned, since this doctrine does not have an explicit scriptural foundation. The fact that Catholics seem to direct many of their prayers to Mary is considered to detract from the worship of God Himself, with many Protestants criticizing this intermediary and intercessionary role that Catholics have assigned to Mary.

With the (qualified) exception of the doctrine of the assumption, the differences in Catholic and Protestant views of Mary are reflected in actual religious practices. In Catholicism, the everyday cultural and devotional importance of Mary cannot be overemphasized. Although the emphasis has changed over the years in a kind of cyclical fashion, Catholics stress Mary in numerous feast days, litanies, prayers, songs, formal and informal devotions, and pilgrimages, as well as in such highly structured repetitive prayer practices as the rosary. The short but powerful Ave Maria is, with the Lord's Prayer, easily the most popular prayer recited by Catholic Christians. For them, the Virgin Mary, by virtue of her holiness and divine maternity, is a special intermediary and direct channel to God. Further, because Mary gave birth to Christ and is contained herself in God, she is often viewed as an emanation of the will and being of God. It is through Mary, who is herself immaculate, that many Catholics connect themselves totally to the Divine. Although this would seem to be particularly true of female Catholics, it is also true of many male practitioners of Catholicism.

The linking of the Catholic believer with God through Mary is strikingly similar to the relationship that Shiʿi Muslims hold with respect to the imams. The emanating chain of the imams links the divine and the human. Practicing Shiʿis bind themselves directly and totally into this chain. The Catholic-Shiʿi parallel here, however, is more than one between the Virgin Mary and the imams. Rather, it is one between Mary and Fatima, the daughter of the Prophet Muhammad, the wife of Imam Ali, and the mother of imams Husayn and Hasan. Fatima's entire being is linked to and inseparable from that of the Prophet Muhammad. According to Shiʿi sources, this special relationship is summarized in the following words attributed to the Prophet:

> The contentment of Fatima is my contentment, her anger is my anger. Whosoever loves my daughter Fatima loves me. Whosoever makes Fatima content makes me content. Whosoever makes Fatima unhappy makes me unhappy. Fatima is a part of my body. Whosoever hurts her, has hurt me, and whosoever hurts me has hurt God.[22]

Both Fatima and the Virgin Mary stand as female members of a central holy family; both are considered to be immaculate and impeccable; and both are emanating extensions of their fathers and sons. While Mary's personality is completely contained in that of her son Jesus, the figure of Fatima emanates forth from both her father Muhammad and her son Husayn. Mary and Fatima pass along the special grace derived directly from Christ and Muhammad, respectively, to practicing Catholics and Shiʿi Muslims.

The important symbolism of a linking and emanating source is seen in the images of radiant light that dominate the stories of both the Virgin Mary and of Fatima. Fatima is usually referred to as al-Zahra ("The Shining One"); at the moment of her birth, light is said to have spread over the sky and the earth, to the west and to the east. According to Shiʿi believers, Fatima, like Muhammad and Ali, received a special light from God and passed it along to all mankind. Mary is also believed to have emanated a special holy radiance, and is referred to in Catholic prayers as, variously, "Morning Star," "Our Light in Uncertainty," and "Radiant Mother."

Since emanation involves both a total acceptance of and a linking with another source (which is itself part of a chain of beings and consciousness), it also involves mediation and intercession. Shi'i Muslims ask Fatima's intercession and assistance through her special relationships with her father, her husband, and her sons—that is, the other members of the *Ahl al-Bayt*. Mary's analogous role is seen in the following powerful Catholic prayer of emanation-intercession:

> All that I am, all that I might be, my Lady and Queen, all that I have and hold in the order of nature as well as of grace, I have received from God through thy loving intercession; into thy sovereign hands I commit it all, that it may be returned to its noble original; wherefore we confess that thou art the channel whereby the graces of heaven descend upon us; thou art likewise the aqueduct which carries them back to their source; thou art, as it were, an electric wire, whereby we are put in direct communication with our heavenly Father; thou art the immaculate way which leads us safe to the Heart of God. Take, then, and accept all that I am, O Mary, Queen of every heart, and bind me to thee with the bonds of love, that I may be thine forever, and may be able to say in truth: "I belong to Jesus through Mary."[23]

Fatima, along with the Prophet Muhammad himself and the twelve imams, is considered by Shi'i Muslims to be of the "Fourteen Pure Ones," or "Fourteen Impeccables." Her significance is magnified, however, not only because of her close relation to the Prophet and Imam Ali, but also because, as the mother of Hasan and Husayn, she is considered to be the "Mother of the Imams." As the last daughter of the Prophet (who had no sons that survived infancy), Fatima is the one who inherits and passes on through history the honors and grace of the Muslim community: "The final link in this chain of Divine Justice, the rightful chain of truth is Fatima, the last daughter of a family who had anticipated a son."[24]

Both Roman Catholicism and Shi'i Islam emphasize the idea of a Holy Family, at the core of which resided a blessed, charismatic, and powerful woman. While Mary was the mother of Christ, Fatima was the mother of Imam Husayn. Both Christ and Husayn were later to undergo suffering and, ultimately, redemptive death. In Shi'i legend, the figures of Mary and Fatima, of Christ and Husayn, become curiously intertwined. Fatima is sometimes referred to by Shi'is as *al-Maryam al-Kubra* ("the Great Mary"), while Jesus is "in some sense, the brother of Husayn."[25] Although the concepts of virginal birth and assumption into paradise are alien to the story of Fatima, she is often titled *al-Muhaddatha* (the One Spoken to by Angels), "because angels spoke to her as to Mary, and she to them; they told her "God has chosen you and purified you; He has chosen you from among the women of the world."[26]

Both Fatima and Mary led lives in which they witnessed great suffering. As receptacles for and emanations of their sons, they shared in all experiences of these sons. While Mary suffered at the foot of the cross upon which her son was crucified, Fatima's image is bracketed by the traumatic death of her father, the Prophet Muhammad, and the martyrdom of her son Husayn. In Catholicism, many prayers begin with the phrase "O Mary Most Sorrowful," and the quintessential verse of sorrow is the *Stabat Mater:* "At the Cross her station keeping, / Stood the mournful mother weeping." In Shi'ism, Fatima is viewed as the mistress of the House of Sorrows, and a predominant Shi'i image of her is of a holy woman incessantly weeping. She was "one of the most tragic characters in all of human history . . . who dwelt all her short life in the House of Sorrows, becoming its mistress for all time until the Day of Resurrection, the day of her final vindication."[27] And like Mary's, Fatima's sorrow carries universal meaning: "All things weep in emulation of her tears, and the tears of the faithful here on earth are but a way of sharing in her sorrows and a means of bringing consolation to her broken heart."[28]

In the cases of both Mary and Fatima, the holy source of intercession is a sorrowful, weeping figure who—while reflecting the difficult lives of the faithful—yet holds out the hope of everlasting happiness. This drama of intercession is especially keen in the figure of Fatima: Shi'is believe that she will have a powerful voice in determining who will enter into and who will be barred from Paradise on the day of resurrection.

As supreme intercessors who have themselves witnessed great pain and sorrow, then, Mary and Fatima reflect compassion and mercy—especially toward the poor and the deprived. Fatima lived a life of considerable poverty and privation, particularly during the early years of her marriage to Ali, when she and her husband suffered frequent hunger and physical discomfort. Shi'i legend teaches that despite this poverty, however, Fatima gave away what little she had to those even poorer. On such occasions, she is reported to have tasted only water during the day and to have slept hungry at night. Similarly, in the *Magnificat,* in which Mary begins "My soul magnifies the Lord," the mother of Christ deprecates the proud, the mighty, and the rich while exalting the lowly, the hungry, and the poor (Luke I, 46–55).

In both cases, elaborate stories and interpretations have grown up around these two holy women, who have inspired entire systems of popular devotion. The major characteristics that they share, according to the beliefs of their followers (whether Roman Catholic or Shi'i Muslim), are the following:

1. Both Mary and Fatima are central female members of their respective Holy Families.
2. Both are considered to be immaculate and impeccable.
3. Both are critical links in a divine chain that connects the divine and the human.
4. While Mary is an emanation of her son, Jesus Christ, Fatima is an extension of the personalities of her father, the Prophet Muhammad, and of her son, Imam Husayn.
5. Both women are major intercessionary forces, to whom the faithful direct their prayers and their requests.
6. Both Mary and Fatima lived lives of extraordinary suffering, a suffering closely bound up with the martyrdom of their sons.
7. Both exhibited great compassion and have become symbols of mercy, providing succor and promising continual aid to the faithful.
8. Both Fatima and Mary have empathized particularly with the poor and the deprived, since they themselves experienced the greatest form of deprivation in their own lives.

The Place of Redemptive Suffering and Martyrdom

Suffering and martyrdom are central themes in both Islam and Christianity. These themes are most clearly stressed and fundamentally emphasized in Shi'ism and Roman Catholicism, where they dominate both belief and practice. In both cases, there is a critically important redemptive aspect to this suffering. In Catholicism, the doctrine of redemption is sharply and formally defined as part of Church teaching; it stresses the great offense of sin to God, and the need to satisfy his justice—something man unaided by Christ could not accomplish. Although Shi'ism has no such formally defined doctrine of redemption, suffering clearly helps to cut a path through to salvation. This occurs not only through the suffering of the individual Muslim, but also through the assistance and intercession of the martyred imams. "This intercession is the direct reward of the sufferings of the entire family of the Prophet, and of Husayn especially, as his status could be attained only through martyrdom. Redemption in Shiʻi piety must be understood within the context of intercession."[29] This is summarized well in lines taken from the Shiʻi passion play *(taʻziya),* where Gabriel delivers to the Prophet this message from God:

> None has suffered the pain and afflictions which Husayn has undergone. None has, like him, been obedient in My service. As he has taken no steps save in sincerity in all that he has done, thou must put the key of Paradise in his hand. The privilege of making intercession is exclusively his. Husayn is, by My peculiar grace, the mediator for all.[30]

Although both Catholicism and Shiʻism view suffering in the context of intercession and salvation, Catholics place more emphasis upon the cleansing of sin as part of the scenario.

Both Jesus Christ and Imam Husayn stand as central suffering figures, whose violent deaths at the hands of powerful temporal adversaries are revealed as preeminent, purifying, universal redemptive acts. Both deaths represented the climax of a terrible period of passion and suffering that helped cleanse the world of injustice, tyranny, and corruption, and opened the way to salvation. In their physical destruction and temporal defeat, both Christ and Husayn achieved major spiritual triumph and everlasting victory. In addition, their acts of ultimate sacrifice spawned a long history of similar acts of martyrdom by Christians and Muslims alike. In Roman Catholicism and Shiʻi Islam, these acts of martyrdom have been historically viewed as a form of blessed heroism that stands as continuing proof of the power of faith.

The concept and everyday force of martyrdom continues to this day in Shiʻi Islam, where the coincidence of religion, society, and politics results in situations in which martyrdom presents a viable choice. In Roman Catholic history, on the other hand, the division of church and state and the passing of periods of persecution have generally rendered the need for martyrdom considerably less urgent. In both cases, however, the drama of suffering and the legend of martyrdom have been institutionalized and remain living, integral parts of the system of faith. In Shi'ism and Catholicism alike, the passion and deaths of Christ and Imam Husayn are commemorated every day of every year. In Catholicism, this daily commemoration is of course the mass. In addition, yearly during the Lenten season (and especially during Holy Week, and, paramountly, Good Friday), Christ's crucifixion and death are a profound spiritual event in the life of the practicing Roman Catholic. Likewise in Shi'i Islam, the death of Imam Husayn at Karbala is vividly recalled throughout the year, in Shi'i mosques, prayer sessions, and devotional readings, while the commemorative mourning is dramatized each year in the first ten days of the month of Muharram. The actual death of Imam Husayn is recalled on Ashura, and the entire period is marked by passion plays, mourning ceremonies, fasting, and prayer recitations of profound grief.

With the exception of the final, triumphant resurrection scene, then, Holy Week as practiced by Catholics is not unlike the ten days of Muharram as commemorated by Shi'is. Catholics begin Holy Week by reading and contemplating the passion of Christ; they practice a wide variety of enactments of the Passion, ranging from recitations of the Stations of the Cross to stagings of elaborate Passion plays. The Catholic tradition of fasting and abstaining from meat on Fridays and the long vigil on Good Friday represent graphic remembrances of Christ's passion. Other special ceremonies venerate the cross—the symbol and instrument of Christ's sacrifice. Catholics have developed prayer rituals that dwell on the five wounds suffered by Christ and the seven words that He uttered while hanging on the cross during the passion, while the clergy, dressed in black vestments, dwell on the suffering and death of Christ in their sermons and homilies. Finally, the precious blood of Christ is stressed repeatedly in such prayers as the following: "Hail, Precious Blood flowing from the wounds of our crucified Lord Jesus Christ, and washing away the sins of the whole world."[31]

Shi'i Muslims maintain an equally elaborate and intense mourning season, with the entire month of Muharram given over to the commemoration of sorrow and suffering. The routinization of Imam Husayn's act of martyrdom is evidenced in the existence of such institutions as *husayniyas* (or *ma'tims*), and such ceremonies as *rawzas*, *ta'ziyas*, and processions. *Husayniyas* are designated structures (usually separate from the mosques) where Shi'is gather during Muharram to commemorate the martyrdom of Imam Husayn and his companions: *rawzas* are meetings that take place in private or public settings at

which religious leaders read emotional narrations of the tragedy at
Karbala, and give interpretive sermons concerning this very moving
event; while ta‘ziyas are passion plays that reenact the events of Karbala on stage, before huge audiences of believers.[32] The processions,
which are usually reserved for the ninth and tenth of Muharram, are
somber but emotional affairs in which mourners chant, beat their
breasts, and even flagellate themselves in commemoration of the
Karbala tragedy. Black banners and the symbolism of bloodshed are
everywhere present.

The centerpiece of the Shi‘i tradition of suffering is more complex and more obviously emotional than that of the Catholic commemoration of the passion and death of Christ. The Shi‘i
commemoration is a profound ceremony of grief, punctuated
throughout by cries of sadness and the sounds of incessant weeping.
The Catholic ceremonies are somewhat more restrained, less protracted, and do not permeate both public and private spheres in the
same way. While the events at Calvary involved the death of a God-
man, who brought victory from defeat by rising from the dead, the
tragedy at Karbala was marked by the martyrdom of a holy imam and
some seventy others, including women and youngsters, whose survivors were to have no Easter.

Despite these (and other) differences, however, the similarities
between Catholicism and Shi‘ism concerning the deaths of Jesus
Christ and Imam Husayn are noteworthy. Both Catholics and Shi‘is
believe that the martyr courageously chose death when he could have
chosen to forego it; both see the deaths as ultimately victorious; both
view these acts of supreme martyrdom as redemptive and selfless in
nature; both hold these deaths to be at the very center of their faith
systems; and both have built an elaborate scaffolding of ceremonies
around these tragedies, which both reenact and repeat on a daily as
well as on an annual basis. In this way, these sacrifices remain vivid
and essential parts of the lives of the believers. Where Catholics recite
numerous prayers and holy lamentations to the suffering Christ,
Shi‘is constantly voice supplications and exclamations to the martyred
Imam Husayn.

The redemptive deaths of Imam Husayn and Christ became the
sources and emanating symbols of martyrdom in Shi‘ism and Catholicism, respectively. Husayn's martyrdom, which was the major part of a
drama of death that included the death also of his father, Imam Ali,
was only the most significant of a long series of Shi‘i martyrdoms.
While Husayn's companions all died heroically with him, Shi‘i sources

also teach that all succeeding imams (with the exception of the twelfth, who went into occultation) died as martyrs. Likewise, most of Christ's twelve disciples are believed to have died as martyrs, including such central figures in early Christianity as the saints Peter, James, Andrew, and Bartholomew.

The early Christian Church witnessed the growth of a cult of martyrs who died for their beliefs. Over the years the Church developed a complex system of recognition of those who suffered persecution for professing Christianity. Those who were put to death were referred to as *martyrs* (that is, those who bore witness), while those who suffered much travail and were persecuted but not killed for their religion were termed *confessors*. In Christianity, the Catholic Church has preserved these distinctions and continues to this day to emphasize the place and importance of the martyrs and confessors. Roman Catholic believers revere a wide range of these saintly heroes and heroines, visit their shrines, and seek their intercession and favor. According to Catholic teaching, "a martyr is regarded as a hero, not so much for the sanctity of his life as for the heroism of his death."[33] While some Protestants may recognize the martyrs as Christian models, Catholics actively encourage the veneration of such holy personages. For Catholics, the practice involves praying through these saintly martyrs, as opposed to praying to them.[34]

In Shi'ism, there is little doubt that the martyred imams are a similar subject of veneration. Shi'is flock to their burial places on holy visits, direct their prayers directly to them, and—through their tears—attempt to purify their own lives and to thus wash a path to salvation. The Shi'i position is perhaps best summarized in the following words of an eminent scholar of Shi'ism:

> The lamentations for Husayn enable the mourners not only to gain an assurance of divine forgiveness, but also contribute to the triumph of the Shi'i cause. Accordingly, Husayn's martyrdom makes sense on two levels: first, in terms of a soteriology not dissimilar from the one invoked in the case of Christ's crucifixion: just as Christ sacrificed himself on the altar of the cross to redeem humanity, so did Husayn allow himself to be killed on the plains of Karbala to purify the Muslim community of sins; and second, as an active factor vindicating the Shi'i cause, contributing to its ultimate triumph.[35]

Both Catholicism and Shi'i Islam emphasize the central importance of sacred chains of saintly personalities who serve both as models and intercessors for the faithful. These individuals, whether saints or imams, are ultimately links to the Divine. In Catholicism, the saints "who have put on Christ" have become images of Christ Himself; when Catholics devote themselves to these saints, they are held to connect themselves with Christ. In Shi'ism, the imams represent a chain, with each imam existing as the emanation of the ones before him. Ultimately, they are extensions of the spirit and personalities of Imam Husayn, Imam Ali, and the Prophet Muhammad, who was himself of course the receptacle for God's revelations. In the words of Seyyid Hossein Nasr: "The imams are also the intermediaries between man and God. To ask for their succor in life is to appeal to the channel God has placed before men so as to enable man to return to Him. They are, in this sense, the extension of the personality of the Prophet."[36]

These sacred chains of saintly intermediaries are reinforced by a special spiritual strength that is the product of great suffering, travail, and pain. The chains have been fashioned and fired by the flames of suffering, and the major links are martyrs who consciously chose death and thus demonstrated the depth of their commitment. The stories of the suffering and death of Imam Husayn and his companions and the passion and death of Jesus Christ and his followers permeate the consciousness and beliefs of practicing Shi'is and Roman Catholics, respectively. This reality of suffering and martyrdom both strengthens the power of these sacred chains of saints and deepens their appeal to the faithful, who seek to link themselves into these powerful systems of emanation. For Catholics and Shi'is alike believe that it is here that they are likely to find assistance in their quest for redemption and salvation.

The Doctrine of Infallibility and 'Isma/Ma'sumiyyat

It is an article of faith among Muslims that such major prophets as Abraham, Moses, Jesus, and Muhammad had immunity from all error or sin (*'isam*), since if they did not, revelation itself would be in jeopardy, thus obviating God's purpose in speaking through His prophets. Some Sunnis have argued that prophets are immune only to grave sin and error, but the Shi'i view is that they were preserved even from minor sin and inadvertency.[37]

Shi'is also teach that God's gracious kindness (*lutf*) is intrinsic; that is, it is not simply a quality He chooses to manifest at times, implying the possibility of His being cruel and capricious, as some Sunni scholastics argue. No, for Shiʿis He is at all times the Lord of gracious kindness, never less. It follows, then, that since no one ordinary mortal understands all of revelation, even when it is plainly written in a scripture; and that since human beings are all too prone to error and sin, even to the point of perverting the scriptures (as Jews and Christians are held to have done with the Bible), that God would not have provided the definitive Scripture, the Quran, without also furnishing an inerrant and impeccable guide to it—and this guide is the imam. In the same way, Muhammad, having set up a Community of Muslims in obedience to his Lord's command (and knowing that he was soon to die), would not have left the Community of the Faithful without a leader. This was Ali, the first imam, endowed with impeccability to meet the rigors of the arduous task of guiding the Quranic Community in its religious and worldly affairs. It is not necessary for a Messenger of Revelation to be present in the world at all times once his message is delivered; it is necessary, however, for an imam to be present at all times, lest the entire creation fail in its purpose.

Again unlike the Sunnis, who frequently argue for predestination, Shiʿis vigorously assert that man is endowed with free will. Exercising that free will, the majority of Muhammad's companions chose to disregard his choice of a successor. This was in their power to do. Nevertheless, it is inconceivable that God would have left Muslims without an impeccable imam, and inconceivable, too, that the matter of the imamate would have been left to the Community to decide (as Sunnis argue), or that it would come to an end so long as the human race exists, since there will be no new dispensation after Muhammad.

Shiʿis also argue that every prophet leaves a legatee—for example, Moses left Aaron, and Jesus left Peter. Sinful and erring Muslims prevented the imams from ruling, but could not prevent them from being the leaders and guides of Muhammad's true Community. Finally, when the eleventh imam died under house arrest, and the Sunni Abbasid caliph proposed to murder his young son, the child was taken into occultation and is still alive. He is still the imam, and will return as the Expected Mahdi[38] to claim his rightful place and slay the Antichrist at the time of the second coming of Jesus Christ.[39]

It will be seen that in the matter of the imamate we come to the heart of Twelver theology, and that the general preoccupation of Muslims with ethical and legal questions here gives way to theology. Even the development of scholastic theology among the Sunnis took place largely in order to defend Sunnism against the reasoning of the Shiʿis and their allies, the Muʿtazila.

The twelfth imam, while not seen, is manifest in the Community as the guide of those who seek, the Pole of the Saints, and the enlightenment of the interpreters of the Law. In his absence, a fully qualified *mujtahid,* or a *marjaᶜ al-taqlid,* is the representative *(naᶜib)* of the imam.

> He is an authority over Muslims and performs the functions of the Imam as regards judgment and administration. . . . All that which belongs to the Imam should be given to the *mujtahid.*[40]

It is through this doctrine that Ayatollah Khomeini claims the right to rule the government of Iran, free from the challenge of other Iranian *mujtahids.*

Roman Catholicism also teaches that God would not have left the Church without a guide who is infallible in matters of faith and morals; that this legatee was St. Peter; and that St. Peter's successor is the bishop of Rome. Catholics believe that no one except Christ and his mother were preserved free from all sin, so that only they may be termed impeccable; it follows, then, that a bishop of Rome is not necessarily free from the possibility of grave sin and error. They believe that only when the pope speaks *ex cathedra*—that is, as leader of the Church, on matters of faith and morals—is he preserved from doctrinal error. The much more sweeping Twelver view of the ᶜ*isma* of the prophets and the imams appears to Twelvers as a logical consequence of the *logos*-nature of the Qurᵓan, the sinfulness of human nature, and human freedom.

Sunnis believe in the ᶜ*isma* of the majority of the Community of Muhammad, either restricting it to the Companions of the Prophet and their immediate disciples *(al-salaf)* as the Hanbali School of Law does, or extending it to the majority of the qualified interpreters of the Law in every period when they "join together" (the doctrine of ᶜ*ijmaᶜ*). Twelvers counter that the "qualified interpreters of the Law" could only be *mujtahids* who represent the authority of the imams themselves.

Catholic and Shiᶜi Models of Politics and the State

Although neither Roman Catholicism nor Shiᶜi Islam can be said to have simple, universally accepted models of politics and the state, there are certain accepted principles bearing on these areas that are identifiable in the teachings of both faith systems. These include an emphasis upon normative foundations of political systems and the preeminence of divine and natural law over human, manmade law. The goal of the ideal state should be to further the moral and spiritual fulfillment of the human being and the human community. In short, the form of the state should be such that it assists men and women to pursue lives of a quality that will enable them to attain everlasting union with God. Within this general framework, both Shi'ism and Catholicism have historically indicated a willingness to accept and to live within a wide variety of specific political systems.

For our purposes, we shall present a model of a state that is in fact prevalent in most Third World countries with large Catholic populations and where the influence of the Catholic Church is considerable. This model will then be compared to the most significant contemporary Shi'i state, the Islamic Republic of Iran.

The Organic-Statist Model of the State

A leading scholar of Latin-American political systems has developed a model of a state that is both based on Catholic doctrine and philosophy and prevalent in third world Catholic countries. This model is distinct from the two principal types usually discussed by political theorists—the classical liberal and the command socialist (Marxist) models. (Alfred Stepan refers to this third type as the organic-statist model.[41]) The western liberal model emphasizes the fundamental importance of the individual and stresses the pluralist nature of society; the focus is upon the autonomy and freedom of the individual, and the resultant democratic style of politics operates according to an equilibrizing system of checks and balances. The Marxist alternative, on the other hand, emphasizes class aggregations and the existence of a strong central state whose role it is to control class conflict while overseeing the development of a command socialist economy. Whereas liberal systems seek to maximize the autonomy of individuals and groups, the Marxist system seeks to eliminate this autonomy through an institutionalized program of collectivism.

Both liberal and Marxist models maintain an underlying empirical reality that is primarily descriptive in nature. In the former, it is the accepted fact that individuals are motivated by individual self-interest. In the latter, it is the stated reality that the fundamental fact is one's relation to the society's mode of production—in other words, class position. Although both liberalism and command socialism have normative concerns, their basic philosophical underpinning is empirical and descriptive in nature.

The organic-statist system is quite different from either of the two models above. Its fundamental premise is a normative one. The raison d'être of the state is moral in nature, and there is a preferred end, or *telos*. In this formulation, the end is considered to be of more importance than either the means or its justifying procedure. This runs strongly counter to classical liberalism, which is preoccupied with procedural due process.

The intellectual soil from which the organic-statist model of politics springs was sown by the writings of Aristotle and Thomas Aquinas, and invigorated by various papal encyclicals. Much of its heritage is found in the literature on divine and natural law, according to which the system of human law that guides the operation of the state is an application of natural law to the changing circumstances of social life. Natural law, in turn, is an emanation of unchanging eternal law perceived by a rational interpretation of this eternal law. Divine law, on the other hand, is that emanation of eternal law that is knowable primarily through revelation. The organic-statist model of government, therefore, is organized according to human laws that are applications of natural law which in turn is the reasonable interpretation of the overarching and unchanging eternal law.[42]

Briefly stated, this model of the state stresses the common good. The community takes precedence over the individual, since it is only in the community that human beings can attain their moral good. This necessitates a strong state—one that can not only protect the communal well-being but will also have the strength to truly promote the common good. The state, then, is what guarantees a unified society and political community.

Nevertheless, despite the preeminence of the state, this model also provides for a certain autonomy for individuals and groups within the overall framework of politics. This "principle of subsidiarity" was presented by Pope Pius XI in the encyclical *Quadragesimo Anno* in the following terms: "It is a fundamental principle of social philosophy, fixed and unchangeable, that one should not withdraw from individuals and commit to the community what they can accomplish by their own enterprise and industry."[43] This principle, which provides for the political participation of individuals and groups, represents a major distinction from Marxist models. It is the element described by the first adjective in the phrase *organic-statist*.

The organic-statist model, then, stresses the priority of the community over the individual, since the common good is the fundamental goal. This priority and this goal are guaranteed by the existence of a necessarily strong state. Yet, this state is not to usurp the power and responsibilities of individuals and groups. In this sense, the organic-statist system reserves and preserves individual and group power within the context of a strong and central state authority. As such, it is a hybrid that reflects features of both the liberal and the Marxist models (while its proponents sharply condemn both liberalism and Marxism).

Pius XI wrote that Pope Leo XIII, facing the great social and political conflict in the world of his day, had "sought no help from either Liberalism or Socialism, for the one had proved it was utterly unable to solve the social problem aright, and the other, proposing a remedy far worse than the evil itself, would have plunged human society into greater dangers."[44] In the end, the organic-statist model can perhaps be best described as a populist system dominated by a strong central authority whose primary role, ideally, is to promote the common moral good. Such a system can theoretically exist in governments of many particular forms, including monarchical, military, populist, theocratic, or civilian-authoritarian regimes.

Of course, the organic-statist system can easily slip into one of a number of perverted forms of political system. Just as the liberal model can slide into anarchy, selfish individualism, and an internal chaos of all against all; just as the socialist system can shade into totalitarian dictatorship and a tyranny of collectivism; so too can the organic-statist system move into extreme religious fundamentalism and ideological fascism. In this situation, the principle of subsidiarity is of course clearly subordinate to the principle of strong state control. In Roman Catholic political philosophy, the ingredients designed to protect against this dangerous deterioration are the rules of morality inherent in natural and divine law. These rules flow from the precept assuming man's inclination to do good and avoid evil, and involve principles of preservation, procreation, human dignity, and social justice.

The emphasis upon order and harmony within the community would seem to discount any possibilities of basic and revolutionary change. Yet the Catholic Church has been at times extremely sensitive to the dangers of the preservation of privilege and the need for radical social change. In such conditions, "the state needs power and must apply force for the sake of its own end. . . . It must forcefully change parts of the actual order which have grown unjust . . . and it must use force against the selfish resistance of the privileged interests that range themselves above the new and juster order."[45] Major examples of important papal statements stressing issues of human equity and social justice include Pope Leo XIII's *Rerum Novarum* (1891), Pope Pius XI's *Quadragesimo Anno* (1931), and Pope John XXIII's *Mater et Magistra* (1961).

Despite these important papal encyclicals, local Church authorities—either alone or in collaboration with the state—often lacked either the will or the capacity to curb the excessive preemption of power by elites who controlled the state apparatus. What happens when the powerful state does not act to redress injustice? If fundamental change can come only from above, then radical reform may in fact never be introduced. Naturally, those who control the state are often the least likely to risk any change that might jeopardize their own situation.

In Catholicism, therefore, the establishment has at times proven reluctant to initiate needed social and political transformation. In the 1960s and 1970s, this gave rise to a new theology that developed at the grassroots level of the Church and society. This populist theology has come to be known as liberation theology, and in Latin America, for example, it has sought to challenge the established order wherever that establishment's policies have clearly run counter to the precepts of natural and divine law. In this case, the Roman Catholic Church has from within itself sought to redress imbalances as they occur in the organic-statist model. Rather than waiting for the state to correct and reform itself, these elements (radical subsidiaries) have themselves led the struggle against corruption, injustice, and oppression. And since they are integral parts of the Church itself, they carry powerful credibility within the community and are a formidable force for reform of the organic-statist model.

The Islamic Republic of Iran: A Shi'i State in the Contemporary World

With the Iranian revolution of 1978–79, a new political system was established that put into power a government guided in every detail by Shi'i Islamic principles. Before the revolution, Shi'ism coexisted in many countries with secular regimes, but its principles concerning government and society remained only ideals discussed and debated among leading scholars and members of the *ulama*. Today, the Islamic Republic of Iran stands as an empirical example of Shi'i political rule. The essence of this model can be summarized by the following nine characteristics:

1. All power emanates from God, and therefore there is no distinction between church and state, between the secular and the religious;
2. The entire community of the faithful (the *umma*) takes precedence over any constituent parts thereof, whether they be individuals, families, tribes, or nation-states;
3. The divine law that has been revealed to man through the Prophet and the imams takes precedence over all human law;
4. All social, economic, and political affairs are guided by this divine law, known as the *shari'a*;
5. The interpretation and the implementation of the *shari'a* is to be entrusted to the guardianship *(velayat)* of learned jurisprudents *(fuqaha)*, themselves leading members of the *ulama;*
6. A true *faqih* must be learned, righteous, and accepted by the people; he is the authoritarian leader at the center of the state;
7. Within this context, political participation is an important right and obligation of citizens;
8. The principle of political participation is enshrined in an Islamic constitution that provides for a national representative body known as the Islamic Majlis;
9. The Islamic Republic of Iran is a system of Islamic populism in which ultimate power resides in God and His representatives *(fuqaha)* on earth, while important residual power rests with the people who have an important role both in accepting the *faqih* and in electing their political representatives.

The philosophical underpinnings of the Islamic Republic of Iran rest upon a strong condemnation and rejection of both liberal Western and socialist Eastern modes of government. Iran's political system, which can be referred to as a Populist-Shi'i model, is one whose very existence is permeated by perceived divine guidance. "All Islamic thought, including political philosophy, has one overriding goal: To insure that life is lived in accordance with the revealed program of the divine, at all times."[46] Ayatollah Ruhollah Khomeini's statements and writings are filled with references to the preeminence of divine law *(qanun-i khoda'i)*. Human law *(qanun-i bashari)*, on the other hand, is subject to the self-interested whims of man, and leads him to preoccupy himself with the material and the worldly. Therefore, only the *shariʿa* can be the guide to the straight path.

Although guardians and interpreters in the line of the impeccable imams have special authority and influence, there is room for popular participation. The relationship here is one between the *shariʿa* and the constitution. As long as the constitution is derived from and proceeds according to divine law, there is considerable room for representative government and participation. In the revealing words of Ayatollah Khomeini:

> Islamic government is neither tyrannical nor absolute, but constitu-
> tional. It is not constitutional in the current sense of the word, i.e.,
> based on the approval of laws in accordance with the opinion of the
> majority. It is constitutional in the sense that the rulers are subject to
> a certain set of conditions in governing and administering the coun-
> try, conditions that are set forth in the Noble Quran and the Sunna
> of the Most Noble Messenger. It is the laws and ordinances of Islam
> comprising this set of conditions that must be observed and prac-
> ticed. Islamic government may therefore be defined as the rule of
> divine law over men.[47]

The Shiʿi Islamic concept of leadership is circular rather than vertical and hierarchical: thus, while the leader leads and the fol-lowers follow, the leader will also take his cues from the followers. So, in this sense, the followers can be leaders and the leaders followers. Also, the followers play a definite role in the selection of leaders. With this said, it is important to note that those learned members of the *ulama* who are individuals of learning, rectitude, and popularity do carry great authority. When this authority is political in nature, how-ever, as in the case of the Islamic Republic of Iran, these leaders possess power that is significantly greater than that of the people. Ayatollah Khomeini and other leading members of the *ulama* direct the state apparatus, while the people exert influence through the National Islamic Majlis and a network of other foundations and religious organizations. In this sense, there is a principle of sub-sidiarity present in the Islamic Republic, despite the predominance of the *ulama* at the center of the system.

During the rule of the shah, the Shiʿi clerics were deeply involved at the grassroots level of society, where they worked with the masses of Iranian people. Their influence at this level was enormous, despite the fact that the shah's secular state controlled the military, the economy, and the governmental apparatus. The shah attempted to inject his regime with legitimacy by surrounding himself with a few state clerics who provided his rule with a form of establishmentarian Islam. Meanwhile, the overwhelming majority of the *ulama* opposed the oppression of the shah's state, thus promoting a kind of populist Islam that shows marked similarities with the liberation theology practiced by Roman Catholic clerics in other third world countries.

With the Safavi empire in 1500, Twelverism became establishment Islam in Iran; with the coming of the revolution, populist Islam became the new establishment Islam. It is this new system of government, with its tilted balance between a state cloaked in layers of divine garb and directed by learned charismatic jurisprudents *(fuqaha)* on the one hand and popular participation on the other, that we have described as Populist-Shi'i. Like the organic-statist principality of the Catholic variety, this Shi'i model tends to tilt more heavily toward the authoritarian center and away from popular representation, as the situation in the Islamic Republic of Iran clearly demonstrates.

The Organic-Statist and Populist-Shi'i Models Compared

Although there are certainly significant differences between the Shi'i and Catholic models of the state, there are at the same time a number of fascinating and striking similarities. One major difference concerns the line drawn between church and state. In the Catholic-inspired organic-statist system, there is no equivalent to the *faqih* within whom temporal and spiritual authority reside in the Shi'i model. (The element of papal infallibility applies only to matters of faith and morals.) Also, while the Catholic Church has increasingly concerned itself with social and economic issues, it has carefully avoided any direct attempt to involve its leaders or even the lower clergy in government and politics.

There are five areas in which the organic-statist and populist-Shi'i models of government show important similarities: (1) the rejection of both Western liberal and Eastern Marxist models of the state; (2) the preeminence of the concept of the community and the common good; (3) the fundamental normative nature of politics and a system of law derived from divine precepts; (4) the coexistence of two realms of power, including the authority of the state at the center and the participatory power of the people at the periphery; and (5) the increasing contemporary concern for the downtrodden and oppressed, as witnessed both by the growth of populism in Shiʿism and of liberation theology in Catholicism.

Both the organic-statist and populist-Shiʿi political models reject the alternatives of liberalism and command socialism. Although this is surely not true of Catholicism in general (since the latter thrives in liberal Western environments), organic-statism is the preferred system in third world countries where scarcity and anarchy threaten the very survival of society. In these countries, it is much preferred to a godless Marxist model that is seen as a system that collectivizes and crushes in order to control. In Islam in general and in the case of the Islamic Republic in particular, both liberalism and communism are strongly condemned as social and political systems. The central slogan of the Islamic Republic—"Neither East nor West"—well summarizes this position.

In the organic-statist system, the good of the community takes precedence over the well-being of the individual member of the community. In Catholicism, the emphasis upon such concepts as the Church and the communion of saints reveal this important underlying theme. The same is true of Islam and its emphasis upon the *umma*, which knows no borders and no boundaries. Union, unity, and community are stressed over individualism, dispersion, and the division of peoples into their own families, tribes, and even nation-states. In the thinking of Ayatollah Khomeini and the other theoreticians of the Islamic Republic, the emphasis upon the individual and the self *(nafs)* must never take precedence over that of the community, for the concept of the *umma* transcends territory, nationhood, and state. In this respect, it is not wholly unlike the Catholic conception of the Church, despite the institutional and hierarchical ramifications of the latter.

Both the Islamic community and the Catholic community emphasize the existence of a divine force who is the creator and the first mover. The system of law that guides and directs human political activity has its roots in the divine. In Islam, the divine law—referred to as the *shariʿa*—provides the totality of human guidelines. The *Shariʿa* is clearly superior to all human law, and its application to human law is known as the practice of *fiqh*. According to Catholic teaching in the Thomist tradition, unchanging eternal law subsumes both natural law and divine law. Natural law concerns the rational application of eternal law, while divine law emphasizes the revelational aspects. Human law, it follows, is nothing more than the application of the unchanging principles of natural law to the various and changing circumstances of human life.

In the Islamic system, the *shari'a* encompasses both natural and divine law (to use Thomist terms), and it is from this more encompassing form of divine law *(shari'a)* that human law in fact originates. Despite differences such as these, though, one cannot help but be struck by the fundamental similarity between these systems of law, both of which strongly emphasize the preeminence and dominance of a higher law originating in God. In the Islamic Republic of Iran, the state is organized according to the *shari'a*, which contains all the basic principles that activate the social and political system. In Catholicism, the emphasis upon divine and natural law exists primarily as the philosophical foundation for the social and political ideology of believers.

Given the priority of the common good, the community, and the *umma*, and the fact that the human law according to which this community is organized is derived from a higher system of law (divine law), it follows that both the organic-statist and the populist-Shi'i visions of politics emphasize the centralizing authority of the state. Central authority, however, has two checks: it must be applied in keeping with these higher moral principles, and a degree of power must be reserved for the popular element present in every society. This principle of subsidiarity in the organic-statist system is paralleled by principles of populism inherent in the Shi'i philosophy of leadership. The immediate presence of *fuqaha* and *mujtahids* in the Shi'i state provides a much stronger model of populist authoritarianism in Shi'ism than is the case in Catholicism, where the Church coexists with a wide variety of political systems.

This centralizing tilt to authoritarianism based upon a higher law can be easily abused in both types of political systems. Just as the *faqih* can counsel obedience and subservience in the face of oppression, so too can a cleric advise patience and accommodation in situations of secular tyranny. When this has in fact occurred, as in Iran during the rule of the shah, other clerics not associated with the state supported resistance movements originating in the lower and lower-middle classes. Authoritarianism laced with corruption and organized for oppression has given rise to countermovements. In Catholicism, these movements with their "preferential option for the poor," have come to be known as liberation theology while in the contemporary Islamic world they are referred to, variously, as populist Islam, Islam from below, or Islamic fundamentalism.

Shi'i Islam was the vehicle by means of which popular political mobilization took place in the overthrow of the powerful Pahlavi government in Iran. The rallying focus for this revolution (and one that still prevails in revolutionary Iran) is on the dispossessed, the alienated, and the oppressed. The term *mustaza'fin*, which carries this meaning and more, continues to be a key word in the religious and political vocabulary of Ayatollah Khomeini and other Iranian revolutionary leaders. In liberation theology, the oppressed or suffering masses are also the primary source of attention and concern, both religiously and politically. In this case, the key Spanish terms are *los oprimidos* or *las masas popularas:* "It is then to the oppressed that the Church should address itself and not so much to the oppressors."[48] In other words: "Recent theologies of liberation have stressed the role of the 'oppressed community' as the primary locus of the power for repentance and judgment. God's liberation is seen as first coming to the 'poor.' "[49]

The theoreticians of liberation theology have acted in situations where the principle of subsidiarity has proven to be ineffective and inoperative. In states where military juntas have often ruled capriciously, oppressively, and arbitrarily, Christian Catholic priests and bishops, most of whom have lived and worked with the masses, have become increasingly involved in challenging the governing establishments in an attempt to redress the imbalance that has developed between central authoritarianism and popular participation. In so doing, they have developed a sophisticated theology that insists upon a prophetic—as opposed to institutional—form of involvement of the church with the state, and this brings them closer to populist Islamic ideology. In this new interpretation of Catholicism, "any claim to noninvolvement in politics—a banner recently acquired by conservative sectors—is nothing but a subterfuge to keep things as they are."[50] The approach of liberation theology is much more scriptural than scholastic, and more historical-dialectic than philosophical.

Just as Shi'i believers emphasize the lives of Imam Ali and Imam Husayn, who are considered to have been both challengers to and victims of oppression, so too do liberation theologians stress the life of Christ, who championed the cause of the deprived and the dispossessed. Just as Imam Ali "lived in simplicity and poverty like the poorest of people" maintaining great "compassion for the needy and the poor,"[51] so too did Christ empty himself, taking the nature of a slave and being rich became poor (Phil. 2:6; 2 Cor. 8:9). Christ, like Imams Ali and Husayn, suffered and died a redemptive death. Each of these transcendental acts of martyrdom was undertaken as part of "the struggle against human selfishness and everything that divides men and enables them to be rich and poor, possessors and dispossessed, oppressors and oppressed."[52]

Based upon a powerful source of divine legitimacy that suffuses all human activity, and working within a framework of law promoting the priority of the community, both Catholic-inspired liberation theology and Shiʿi-populist political systems ideally reserve a special autonomy and dignity for the human individual and the popular masses. When such autonomy and dignity are seriously threatened, the religious leaders, whether Shiʿi *ulama* or Catholic clerics, have indicated a willingness to engage in political activism in the spirit of the imams and of Jesus Christ, respectively. This activism, which presupposes both an objective situation of crushing oppression and a strong blend of religion and politics, is increasingly evident in the contemporary world.

Christian Catholicism and Muslim Shiʿism:
Toward a Mutual Understanding

In an age of social incoherence, political crisis, and religious polemics, it is sometimes a useful exercise to attempt to improve understanding by focusing attention upon similarities of great religious traditions. Popular observers, religious practitioners, and scholars alike tend to emphasize and to magnify differences in religions. This persistent trend has been reinforced by parochial political factors and by such ideological forces as nationalism. Too little serious attention has been paid by social scientists to the important similarities among the world's great religious traditions. In this study, we have attempted to take two important religions with quite different traditions and analyze them in terms of important shared characteristics. In so doing, we have noted deep similarities in beliefs and practices as well as in critical perspectives of society and the state.

Both Catholicism and Shiʿism emphasize a monotheistic reality to which believers relate through chains of charismatic intermediaries. These intermediaries include saints and female-mother figures whose

lives exist as inspirations to all believers. In addition, belief in intercession and redemption is central to both faith systems. In both, too,
traditions of suffering, sorrow, and sacrifice are interrelated with
traditions of faith, hope, and the promise of ultimate and everlasting
happiness.

In society today, both Catholicism and Shi'ism are witnessing a
fundamental dialectical struggle between gathering forces of religious
populism on the one hand and the entrenched strength of establishment religion on the other. In both systems, religion "from the bot-
tom" increasingly confronts "religion from the top." This tension
exists in all societies where these religions are practiced, but is especially pronounced in those third world countries where socioeconomic gaps are widest and deepest. Contained with and an integral
part of this polarity is another churning dialectic. Here, political
authoritarianism at the center, designed to promote the continuity of
the community, exists in conflict with those forces driving to protect
individual freedoms and social justice.

The congruency of religion and politics is clearly seen in Shi'i
Islam. And in Roman Catholicism, the relative separation of the two
realms is slowly beginning to narrow, as third world citizens in increasing desperation turn to the intermediaries and representatives of
Christ for aid and succor. Since social and economic problems are
worldwide in scope, both Shi'i Islamic and Roman Catholic Christian
societies will confront similar challenges. The strategies that they
adopt in response will determine not only the relevance of their
religious heritages but also the capability of much of mankind to
survive.

In conclusion, since Catholicism and Shi'ism bear certain important doctrinal, structural, and sociopolitical similarities, and since both
face similar problems in the world today, they could do well to communicate with and to try to learn from each other. In this way, both
religious traditions could increase their chances to meet successfully
the challenges that they will inevitably confront.

Notes

1. Quran 2, 135.
2. *Romans* 4; 16 (Jerusalem Bible translation).
3. Paraphrase, John 1.

4. For a Shiʿi discussion of differences in *hadith*, cf. *The Right Path* (Karachi: Peer Mahomed Ebrahim Trust, n. d.), 2: 1–15. This is an exchange of letters between a former head of Al-Azhar University in Cairo and a Lebanese Shiʿi *mujtahid*, published in 1936 as *al-Muraji at*, and first published in English translation in 1959. The entire collection casts much light on the areas of Sunni-Shiʿi dispute and the terms upon which dialogue in modern times has taken place.

5. Wilferd Madelung, "Imama," *Encyclopaedia of Islam*, 2nd ed. (Leiden: E.J. Brill), 3: 1167.

6. See, for example, Muhammad Rida al-Muzaffar, *The Faith of Shiʿa Islam* (Qum, Iran: 1982), p. 38.

7. For the Zaydis of Yemen, one of the oldest Shiʿi sects, the imam may be any rational descendant of Fatima who rises to claim the imamate and is equal to its duties. He is not impeccable, and if he loses his rectitude may be deposed by another claimant. See Madelung, "Imama," p. 1166.

8. On *taqiya*, see S. Hussain M. Jafri, *Origins and Early Development of Shiʿa Islam* (Beirut: 1976, reprinted in Qum), pp. 298–300; and ʿAllamah Tabatabaʿi, *Shiʿite Islam*, tr. (and annotated by) Seyyed Hossein Nasr (Albany, N.Y.: SUNY Press, 1975), pp. 223–25.

9. Ibn Taymiya (d. 1328), the inspiration of modern Sunni revivalists, condemned the practice of visiting the Prophet's tomb to ask for his intercession. See his "Risala fi ziyarat al-qubur," in *Majmuʿat al-rasa'il* (Cairo: 1906).

10. There are, of course, important similarities other than those listed for brief analysis of this study. Each community, for example, has great respect for the mystical dimension. In each tradition there is much popular emphasis on the visitation of the shrines of the saints (also true to some degree in Sunnism), and there is also recognition of an esoteric dimension in religion by which the individual believer may, through purgation, illumination, and unitive prayer, enter into direct contact with the ultimate reality.

11. *The Documents of Vatican II*, "Declaration on the Relationship of the Church to Non-Christian Religions," p. 3.

12. Seyyed Hossein Nasr, *Ideals and Realities of Islam* (London: George Allen and Unwin, 1966), p. 162.

13. Ph. Marçais, "ʿAshura'," in *Encyclopaedia of Islam*, 2nd ed. (Leiden: E.J. Brill, 1960), 1: 705.

14. Tabatabaʿi, *Shiʿite Islam*, pp. 196–201.

15. ʿAqida of Shaykh Saduq (d. 381/991), ed. and tr. A. A. A. Fyzee as *A Shiʿite Creed* (London: 1942), p. 75.

16. S. H. Nasr, "Ithna ʿAshariyya," *Encyclopaedia of Islam*, 2d ed. (Leiden: E. J. Brill, 1978), 7:278.

17. Tabatabaʿi, *Shiʿite Islam*, p. 214.

18. al-Hakim al-Tirmidhi, *Khatm al-awliyaʿ* (Beirut: 1966), passage tr. John A. Williams in *Themes of Islamic Civilization* (Berkeley: University of California Press, 1971), p. 320.

19. Abu al-Hasan al-Hujwiri, *Kashf al-mahjub*, tr. R. A. Nicholson (London: Luzac, 1911), pp. 210–11.

20. Nasr, *Ideals and Realities*, pp. 162–63. The usual Persian name for a saint is *imamzada*, "seed of the imams."

21. al-Hujwiri, *Kashf al-mahjub,* pp. 75–79.

22. Ali Shariati, *Fatima is Fatima,* tr. Laleh Bakhtiar (Brooklyn, N. Y.: Muslim Students Council, n.d.), p. 136.

23. J. P. Christopher *et al., The Raccolta: A Manual of Indulgences* (New York: Benziger Brothers, 1957), pp. 253–54. This source, "authorized by the Holy See," contains 125 pages of Catholic prayers and devotions to the Blessed Virgin.

24. Shariati, *Fatima is Fatima,* p. 134.

25. Mahmoud Ayoub, *Redemptive Suffering in Islam: A Study of the Devotional Aspects of ʿAshuraʿin Twelver Shiʿism* (The Hague: Mouton Publishers, 1978), p. 35.

26. L. Veccia Vaglieri, "Fatima," *Encyclopaedia of Islam* (Leiden: E. J. Brill, 1965), 2:847–48.

27. Ayoub, *Redemptive Suffering,* p. 48.

28. *Ibid.,* p. 144.

29. Ayoub, *Redemptive Suffering,* p. 15.

30. *The Miracle Play of Hasan and Husain,* tr. Sir L. Pelly, (London: William Allen, 1879), as quoted in G. E. von Grunebaum, *Muhammadan Festivals* (London and New York: Abelard-Schuman, 1958), p. 94.

31. Christopher *et al., The Raccolta,* p. 80.

32. For an excellent source on the phenomenon of *taʿziyahs,* see Peter J. Chelkowski (ed.), *Taʿziyeh: Ritual and Drama in Iran* (New York: New York University Press, 1979).

33. Sebastian Bullough, *Roman Catholicism* (Baltimore: Penguin Books, 1963), pp. 240–41.

34. Protestantism diverges sharply from Roman Catholicism on this issue of the intercession of saints. John Calvin summarized the general Protestant view in the following strong words:

> It was the height of stupidity, not to say madness, to be so intent on gaining access through the saints as to be led away from him, apart from whom no entry lies open to them.
>
> But who will deny that this was consciously done in some periods, and is done even today wherever popery flourishes? To obtain God's benevolence they repeatedly thrust forward the merits of the saints, and for the most part overlooking Christ, entreat God in their names. Is this not, I ask you, to transfer to the saints that office of sole intercession which . . . belongs to Christ?

See John T. McNeill, ed., *Calvin: Institutes of the Christian Religion,* vol. 21 of the Library of Christian Classics (Philadelphia: Westminster Press, 1960), p. 879.

35. Hamid Enayat, *Modern Islamic Political Thought* (Austin, Tex.: University of Texas Press, 1982), pp. 182–83.

36. Nasr, *Ideals and Realities,* p. 163.

37. E. Tyan, "ʿIsma," *Encyclopaedia of Islam,* 2d ed. (Leiden: E. J. Brill, 1978), 4:182–84.

38. The doctrine of the Expected Mahdi (Guided One) from the family of the Prophet rests on certain *hadiths* disputed among Sunnis, but not among Shiʿis. Shiʿi sects identify the Mahdi variously, but for the Twelvers it is Muhammad ibn al-Hasan al-

ʿAskari, the twelfth imam. A collection of the relevant *hadith*s and texts discussing them will be found in Williams, *Themes of Islamic Civilization*, ch. 4.

39. Cf. the *ʿaqida* of Ibn Babuya, Shaykh Saduq (d. A.D. 991), ed. and tr. Fyzee, *A Shiʿite Creed*, prop. 35; and Shaykh Muhammad Rida, *The Faith of Shiʿa Islam*, pp. 41–42.

40. Shaykh Muhammad Rida, *The Faith*, p. 4.

41. Alfred Stepan, *The State and Society: Peru in Comparative Perspective* (Princeton, N.J.: Princeton University Press, 1978). Our discussion of the organic-statist model is drawn largely from the Stepan book.

42. Thomas Aquinas, *Treatise on Law [Summa Theologica*, Questions 90–97] (South Bend, Ind.: Gateway Editions, n.d.). Professor Jay Budziszewski has helped us interpret the Thomist taxonomy of laws.

43. As quoted in Stepan, *State and Society*, p. 35.

44. *Ibid.*, pp. 32–33.

45. Heinrich A. Rommen, *The State in Catholic Social Thought: A Treatise in Political Philosophy*, p. 293, as quoted in Stepan, *State and Society* p. 34.

46. Farhang Rajaee, *Islamic Values of World View: Khomeyni on Man, the State and International Politics* (Lanham, Md.: University Press of America, 1983), p. 54. This is a superb source that objectively and authoritatively explains the religious, political, and philosophical underpinnings of the Islamic Republic of Iran.

47. Imam Khomeini, *Islam and Revolution*, tr. (and annotated by) Hamid Algar (Berkeley, Calif.: Mizan Press, 1981), p. 55.

48. Gustavo Gutierrez, *A Theology of Liberation: History, Politics and Salvation*, tr. Sr. Caridad Inda and John Eagleson (Maryknoll, N.Y.: Orbis Books, 1973), p. 117.

49. Rosemary Ruether, *Liberation Theology* (New York: Paulist Press, 1972), p. 10.

50. Gutierrez, *Theology of Liberation*, p. 266.

51. Tabatabaʿi, *Shiʿite Islam*, p. 214.

52. Gutierrez, *Theology of Liberation*, p. 300.

Part ll

Vatican Diplomacy and the Middle East

···❧ 4 ❧···

The Catholic Church and the Middle East
Policy and Diplomacy

J. Bryan Hehir

My purpose in this chapter is to examine, more or less concurrently, the Roman Catholic Church as a religious organization and the Middle East as a politico-moral question. In contrast to other authors in this volume, I can claim neither regional expertise in the Middle East nor any concentrated scholarship concerning the role of religion in that troubled land. Therefore, this chapter will examine the Middle East as a problem of contemporary international politics and the Roman Catholic Church as an actor in the international arena.

The argument of the paper will move in three steps: the Catholic Church as a transnational actor; the shape of the policy problem in the Middle East; and the Catholic contribution to the policy problematic.

The Roman Catholic Church: Structural Characteristics as Transnational Actor

The Catholic Church has of course been a force in world affairs for centuries; yet the nature of its role has not yet been adequately analyzed. A variety of diplomatic histories describe the involvement of the Church with empires, nations, and states, but the kind of analysis that is regularly used by political scientists to examine other actors in the diplomatic arena has seldom—and, in my view, never adequately—been applied to the structure and policies of the Church.[1]

One example of a more systematic assessment of the Church's role in world affairs is the work that examines it as a *transnational actor*. In the study of international relations, the role of transnational actors is now an established element. While there are diverse approaches to an analysis of transnational actors, a consensus of their characteristics can be formulated: A transnational actor is based in one place but its presence is felt in several states, and it possesses a trained corps of personnel, a single guiding philosophy, and a sophisticated communications system. Entities with these characteristics are not new phenomena in world affairs, of course, but the growth in their scope, complexity, and significance in the international system since the end of World War II has led Professor Samuel Huntington to speak of a "transnational revolution" in world politics.[2] Clearly, such a revolution bespeaks a greatly enhanced role for these entities, although it does not mean that they have changed the nature of world politics. In the contemporary global system, sovereign states remain the central actors, after which the transnational actors occupy a status unrivaled by any other institutions.

The first person to focus on the Catholic Church as a transnational actor was professor Ivan Vallier in his 1970 essay, "The Roman Catholic Church: A Transnational Actor."[3] The value of Vallier's work stemmed from the way it went beyond the standard diplomatic history approach to the Church; Vallier identified those structural characteristics of the Church that give it the capacity to act in a unified way across national boundaries. Vallier did not intend to write a full-blown analysis of the phenomenon, but his original insight has led other authors to build upon the transnational concept to assess the Church's activity both within nations and across international lines.

There were, however, two limits to Vallier's analysis in my view. First, a conceptual problem proceeded from his failure to assign any significant role to theological ideas and themes in shaping the life of the Church. Vallier saw the Church as an organization devoid of serious theological influence; his study, then, is "the bureaucratic model" used without restraint. This would provide a distorted view of Catholicism in any age, but it made for a particularly serious deficiency in the post-Vatican II era in which Vallier wrote. The Council and the post-conciliar developments in the life of the Catholic Church cannot be understood apart from the direction provided by a very significant process of theological development, with roots in the late nineteenth century but which did not come to fruition until the 1950s and 1960s. Vallier accords the Vatican Council great significance, but deprives his analysis of the substantive vision of conciliar theology.

Second, the organizational model that Vallier used to analyze the Church as a transnational actor is excessively centrist. Precisely because Vallier does not take the theological and pastoral developments of the conciliar period into consideration in his conceptual model, his organizational description of the Church fits the pontificate of Pius XII (1939–58) but not that of post-conciliar Catholicism.[4] Pius XII brought the trend of centralization of papal authority to its climax in the postwar papacy; however, one of the central themes of Vatican II was the revival of the concept of "collegiality." The term means, of course, that the pope and the rest of the bishops of the world jointly shepherd and govern the Church. It does not in any sense undercut papal primacy, but it does enlarge the role of the other bishops. The result has been a less centralized papacy, the rise of new centers of governance in the Church (e.g., national conferences of bishops), and an authority that is a more pluralistic model of sharing than Vallier's description conveys.

The significance of Vallier's article, then, inheres in his unique application of the transnational character to the Church. Certainly, it is possible to amend the Vallier model, both conceptually and organizationally; however, the theological corrective will in fact deepen and broaden Vallier's identification of the Church as a significant transnational force. One of the principal consequences of Vatican II has been the transformation of the Church's social role throughout the world.

Precisely because of its institutional structure and moral authority, Catholicism has always had a temporal presence. Vatican II legitimated a more activist role for the Church, from the hierarchy to the parish, while revising existing ideas of how the moral authority of the Church could be fullest exercised. The classical model of Church involvement had theretofore focused on Church-state relations, seeking an ecclesiastical role in influencing the structure and use of political authority in society. Although the Church-state relationship admitted various modalities, the style remained a top-down view of the Church's role. Vatican II shifted primary emphasis to that role in the wider society—to the influence it could exercise through appeals to the consciences of its membership, and the role the Church should play as an advocate of social change and human rights.

The consequences of this shift from a Church-state to a Church-society focus involved placing less emphasis on the Church's traditional role of legitimating civil power and more stress on the need to shape the societal conditions that determine how that power will be used.[5] The mandate of Vatican II, therefore, was for more social engagement, and of a different type. The consequences of this can be seen in such diverse politico-cultural climates as Poland, Brazil, the United States, Central America, the Philippines, and South Africa. In each of these places in the 1980s, the Catholic Church has been a visible force—some would say a decisive force—in the political, social, and economic arena.

Unfortunately, Vallier's analysis of the activity of the Church does not address the roots of this changing social posture. His emphasis on the significance of the Church's social structure accounts for part of the answer, but the structure predates Vatican II and was not used in the style of the postconciliar period. The theological perspective of Vatican II has produced a posture and policy for the Church in the world with a different rationale for engagement on secular topics. In one of the principal documents of the Council, "The Pastoral Constitution on the Church in the Modern World," a direct connection is drawn between the Church's pursuit of its religious ministry and the consequences this should have for the protection of human dignity, the pursuit of human rights, and the fostering of unity in society. The teaching of the Council explicitly denies to the Church any distinctly political role, but it calls for a religious presence that understands social involvement as a mandated activity, not an optional one, at every level of the Church.[6]

While the implications of this call to ministry vis-à-vis the secular arena have become evident more or less rapidly in various parts of the world, it is clear that a systemic change has occurred in the Church. The most rapid and direct change has occurred in Latin America. Following upon the Council, the Latin American episcopate met, under the presidency of Pope Paul VI, at Medellín, Colombia, in 1968 to chart a course that has profoundly affected the social fabric of the continent from Brazil to Chile to Central America. In a vastly different political and cultural setting (and with different emphasis and method), the bishops of the United States emerged in the 1970s and 1980s with a much more public and more activist profile than had historically been their pattern. Similarly, the culmination of a long process of social engagement placed the Philippine church in the mid-1980s in the position of providing leadership in the extraordinary nonviolent revolution in that country. Each of these examples requires a full-length case study, of course, but none of them can be understood through the purely bureaucratic prism of Vallier's analysis.

A related criticism can fairly be made of Vallier's organizational model: it catches a part of the Church's life, but it does not include those key changes that have been introduced with and since Vatican II. To understand the potential and the complexity of the post–

Vatican II Church as transnational actor, then, it is necessary to examine three levels of activity, rather than place exclusive emphasis on Rome and the local church, as in the Vallier article. Leaving aside the ideological connotation that would accompany these terms in an economic analysis, I would distinguish in the Church (1) a center-periphery relationship; (2) a periphery-center relationship; and (3) a periphery-periphery relationship. In each of these combinations, Rome is the center, embodied in the pope and the Vatican secretariat of state, while the local church—specifically, the local bishops' conference—is the periphery.

Each of these relationships adds a distinct dimension to the church's potential as a transnational actor; each has its own strengths and liabilities. They coexist in the transnational community of the Church, but there is tension among the relationships—a tension that derives from distinct sources of action which, in turn, produce differing perspectives and different priorities for policy. In examining each of the relationships, we shall identify the key actor and the strengths and liabilities of each form of activity.

Center-Periphery

The center-periphery relationship is the most significant form of transnational activity within the Church. Historically and analytically, therefore, it is possible to defend the priority that Vallier gives to this relationship. In it, the initiative is with the Holy See as it shapes—through an admixture of normative teaching, pastoral activity, and diplomatic intervention—a posture for each of the local churches. The strength of this position derives from the systemic perspective of Rome and the unique position the Holy See enjoys in the international arena. Both perspective and position make it possible for Rome to formulate and project an international policy for the Catholic Church vis-à-vis the major questions in the international system. One limitation on this form of initiative from the center, however, is that the policy positions are stated at such a high level of generality that it is necessary, as a condition for effectiveness, that they be assimilated, specified, and applied by local actors functioning in divers cultural and political settings.[7] Only the center has the capacity to attract systemic attention to its position, but—in a decentralized international system marked by the continuing primacy of the nation-state—the center's need of the periphery is profound.

The dynamic of center-periphery relationships normally exhibits the characteristics of complementarity, but it can also be marked by an element of muted conflict. On issues of general policy—the arms race, internal development, support for the United Nations—the local churches follow the lead of the Holy See with varying degrees of activism, as determined to a great extent by the character of the local bishops' conference; however, a different dynamic is possible when the issue at stake directly affects the local church. In this context, differences of perspective between the center and the periphery can yield sharply diverse policy orientations. An example is the case of the Vatican *Ostpolitik.* This policy, designed to improve relations between the Church and the communist governments of eastern Europe, is conducted from the center under the subtle and skillful direction of Cardinal Agostino Casaroli, but its objective is to change the relationship between government and the local church. Since the local churches are so directly touched by the progress and outcome of any such negotiations, they have their own perception of the issues and their own calculus for assessing the outcome. It is a matter of public record that the center and periphery have not always shared the same view of these negotiations.[8]

In assessing the divergence of the center and periphery in the *Ostpolitik,* it is necessary to distinguish various levels of negotiation (that is, strategy *vs* tactics) as well as among the different local actors. At the level of long-term strategy, there is substantial agreement between the Holy See and the local churches on the need for improved Church-state relations; both center and periphery share the view that the future of the institutional Church is tied to this question. At the level of tactics, however, differences are evident. The specific problem concerns the way in which each actor (center and periphery) calculates the tradeoffs in the negotiating process between the Vatican and the various governments involved. What can appear to be a reasonable agreement from the perspective of the center, then, can be viewed at the local level as providing too much religious legitimation in exchange for too little religious freedom. The situation of the local churches in this dialogue about tactics is not unlike the problem faced by European NATO countries when the superpowers negotiate on arms control; in each case, parties feel their fate is being decided in a bargaining process they cannot control or even substantially influence.

Finally, the differences of perception and policy between Rome and the local church seem to vary in direct proportion to the relative strength of the local church vis-à-vis the government. In the case of

Poland, for example, where the Church is in a strong negotiating position, there is more reluctance to passively accept a policy directed from the center than in the case of Czechoslovakia, say, where the local hierarchy has almost no leverage against the government. It is not our purpose to adjudicate the merits of *Ostpolitik,* or to compare in detail the specific positions of the actors at the center and on the periphery. The example has been used to show how, on the one hand, the communist governments must deal with both a systemic and local source of action, and—on the other—how these two sources of Catholic presence must constantly work at the process of shaping a common position in their dealings with an adversary state.

Periphery-Center

A different form of transnational activity is produced when the initiative originates in the local church and evokes a response from the center. The strength of this kind of movement lies in the way in which a local church can bring an issue to the attention of the universal Church through the action of Rome, and can inform the perspective and activity of the whole Church. A second asset of this model is the way in which the local church, especially in periods of trouble, can be supported and sustained in its pastoral witness by the considerable systemic influence and prestige of the center. An example that illustrates both of these points is the initiative of the Brazilian church in the area of human rights. Following the military coup in 1964, which established a prototype of the authoritarian regimes that came to dominate Latin America in the 1970s, the Brazilian church was confronted with a major pastoral problem. The episcopal conference, which had been in a process of shaping a cohesive pastoral strategy over a period of years, slowly evolved a conception of ministry with substantial sociopolitical significance. The ministry was conceived in terms of a religious defense of human dignity, and it was aimed at the problem of human-rights violations perpetrated by the military regime. This strategy of ministry placed the Church in direct confrontation with a regime of the right, and produced a classical Church-state conflict. Priests, religious, and lay people working with the Church were imprisoned, tortured, and generally harassed in their work. The local church was clearly in serious trouble.

As international attention was drawn to the conflict, a key question focused on the linkage between the local church and Rome. The issue was whether or not systemic support would be extended to this aggressive pastoral posture. The exact pattern of exchanges and communications is not a matter of public record, but three results are readily demonstrable. First, the Holy See in a series of statements called attention, implicitly or explicitly, to the problem of human rights in Brazil, thereby enhancing international pressure on the regime. Second, the style and substance of the Brazilian church's approach to human dignity and human rights began to be reflected in other activities of the universal Church. (Especially significant in this regard were the statements of Pope Paul VI; the declaration of the 1974 international synod of bishops on human rights; and the study produced by the Pontifical Commission of Justice and Peace on the same theme.) Third, at a regional level the Brazilian example of pastoral ministry in the face of an authoritarian regime became a reference point for other Latin American episcopates confronted with similar patterns of repression.

The liability of the periphery-center relationship lies in the inherent potential for misperception and policy conflict. This judgment is not based on the premise that all conflict in the Church is a liability; it is rather based on the presumption that the transnational potential of the Church is affected when it becomes clear that a local church is in an isolated position on an issue because the center cannot or will not respond to its initiative or posture on an issue of central importance. Some initiatives taken by local churches on the population question have met this response, and without such legitimation from the center the local church has difficulty breaking new ground on policy issues. Moreover, the costs of periphery-center conflict are usually high for the local church, and the means of resistance unimposing. True, the local church can similarly fail to respond to an initiative of the center in a given instance, but the center can usually absorb the loss and seek support in other quarters. It is another matter indeed for the local church to find a meaningful substitute for lack of support from the center.

Periphery-Periphery

The periphery-periphery relationship is the one least commonly analyzed and—on policy issues of social ministry—the most underdeveloped transnational activity in the Church. The strength of this model of transnational action lies in the significant possibilities it opens for increased Catholic presence on issues of justice and peace.

The principal actors here are the local episcopal conferences, and the strategically critical position these conferences hold in the transnational structure of the Church confronts them with an agenda of issues that no other actor in the Church can effectively address. These are bilateral or regional issues, issues that the Holy See understandably would not engage at the systematic level but which nevertheless have significant human and moral importance in the international system.

An example of this kind of activity was the joint position taken by the Panamanian and U.S. bishops' conferences supporting a new understanding between their nations to replace the 1903 Panama Canal Treaty. The issue involved classic questions of political sovereignty and economic justice, and was a volatile matter in both countries; yet it was and would prove to be capable of peaceful resolution. The episcopal conferences played the twofold role which only they could fulfill—seeking to shape public opinion within their countries and, through this, to influence their respective governments to proceed with a just and reasonable resolution of a conflicted issue.[9] (The process of collaboration which the U.S. and Western European bishops conferences used in preparing their letters on the question of nuclear strategy and arms control provides another example of periphery-periphery interaction.)

In summary, both the theological perspective of Vatican II and the emergence of new centers of institutional action in the Catholic Church have contributed to an expansion of the scope and style of the latter's transnational activity. It is now necessary to examine the political structure of the Middle East problem, and then to ask what potential the Church has there as a religiously based transnational force.

The Middle East: The Shape of the Problem

The structure of the Middle East problem is of course not exclusively political; the region is an analyst's dream and a statesman's nightmare. In the Middle East, politics, strategy, ethics, and religion are woven into a tapestry—some might say a crazy quilt—which defies the making of any clear-cut divisions among these dimensions of the policy problem.[10] The purpose of this section is to sketch three levels of the Middle East question to illustrate the setting within which the Church, as well as the other actors, functions in the region.

The Middle East can be viewed at a systemic, regional, and local level. Each level has its own dynamic and distinct set of actors. This sketch seeks to identify each level, and to try to illustrate the linkage among them.

The *systemic dimension* of the Middle East is defined by the place the region holds in world politics. The important systemic actors, therefore, are the Soviet Union and the United States. Their relationship to the Middle East is a reflection of their adversarial relationship in the system as a whole. The relationship, in spite of the rhetoric which often characterizes it, is in fact a mix of severe competition and some measure of cooperation. The competition is easily recognized, but the limits observed are not often stressed. The principal limit—and one very relevant to the Middle East—is the care the superpowers take in avoiding any nuclear conflict or even direct conventional confrontation. The nuclear possibility inherent in the superpower relationship has of course transformed the accustomed logic of a bipolar competition. The inner logic seems to be total competition, but the actual pattern of relationships shows the superpowers setting discrete, if fragile, limits to their conflicts. The prototypical case is the Cuban missile crisis of 1962, but events in the Middle East in 1967 and 1973 also reflected the caution of the superpowers when confronted with a real possibility of open conflict. This caution provides some degree of confidence, but should not lead to complacency. The lurking spectre of superpower involvement in the Middle East is chillingly analogous to conditions in southeastern Europe in 1914. There is a striking similarity between the way in which the superpowers are tied to the Middle East and the way in which the major powers were connected to the Balkans prior to the outbreak of World War I. In each case, an intense local conflict with deep historical roots was tied in with Big Power competition. As we know, the great powers were rapidly drawn into a conflict that soon went beyond their control.

It should be pointed out that the comparison of 1914 and the Middle East seventy years later is an analogy, not an identity. One finds in the comparison cause for concern, signals to be heeded, but not a determinist scenario that should set the course for the Middle East. The relevant dimension of the analogy, of course, is the possibility that superpower confrontation in the Middle East has the real potential to be nuclear. Loss of control in this case takes on qualitatively different dimensions than the 1914 example.

In spite of the risks inherent in the superpower competition in the Middle East, though, neither the Soviets nor the United States will retreat from the region. The systemic level of the Middle East problem resides in the fact that neither of the major powers will allow the other control over the region. (Such a systemic competition exists quite apart from the historic Arab-Israeli conflict.) In geopolitical terms, the character of the Middle East makes it a permanent stake in the superpower competition. Yet, while this independent cause of the competition exists, it is factually the case that both superpowers relate to the region at one remove, through allies. The relationship is therefore neither symmetrical nor simple. The Soviet linkage is through Arab states and/or the Palestinians; the particular channel which is most viable varies over time. The United States, for its part, has not only unique ties with Israel but also substantial understandings with some of the Arab states (though no formal ties with the Palestinians).

The dynamic of the superpower-regional relationship reminds many observers of the 1914 scenario. It would appear that the local actors have a certain irreducible freedom of action which the superpowers cannot control. The influence of the Soviets and the United States, therefore, is closer to deterrence (that is, of certain actions by this or that ally) than to compulsion. Each of the big powers can exercise some measure of restraint by refusing support or cooperation, but neither holds ultimate veto power and neither can guarantee the unquestioning acquiescence of a local actor in negotiations. The evidence surrounding the 1973 war suggests that Egypt's Sadat resorted to force less from a conviction that he could win than from a belief that open conflict would bring the United States back into the Middle East picture as a full partner. The Israelis have also used the tactic of confronting the United States with a *fait accompli*, forcing their ally to react on their terms.

The systemic-regional relationship has political, strategic and moral dimensions. Politically, the superpowers are partly unwilling and partly unable to disengage from the region. Strategically, they help perpetuate the conflict by providing the means of war for both sides, but they also seek to set clear limits to their involvement, since the Middle East is one of those few places in the world (central Europe is another) where any local conflict may be said to have global and nuclear potential. Morally, there is at least an implicit tension between

the demands of systemic safety (that is, avoiding global war) and the
rights of regional actors to pursue such legitimate objectives as security, redress of grievances, and self-determination. Pursuit of these
goals can threaten systemic safety; hence the tension between regional
claims for justice and systemic safety requirements. The superpowers
are not simply honest brokers with clean hands; they are definitely
part of the problem, but they also have a distinct responsibility for the
safety of the system. Sadly, neither the history of their politics nor
their limited control over regional actors provides much confidence
that the superpowers are prepared to play their crucial role well. And
even if they do, the complexity of the regional relationships will
continue to place extreme demands on outside actors.

The *regional dimension* of the Middle East is a scenario for three
actors: Israel, the Arab states, and the Palestinians. (Some analysts—
and some governments—seek to collapse the Arab and Palestinian
terms of the problem, but I would argue that such a move fails to
illuminate either the political or the moral dimensions of the Middle
East problem.) These three actors, in turn, are in conflict over three
objectives: security, sovereignty, and territory. Moreover, the politico-
strategic problem for each actor is different.

The Israeli policy problem is defined in terms of security and
territory: specifically, how much territory guarantees security? This
has been the Israeli dilemma since 1967. One answer equates territory
and security, seeing the occupied territories as a clear benefit for
Israel's security. A second possible answer sees the territory-security
relationship in more complex terms. The case can be made that Israel
has paid a significant *political price*—internally and internationally—
for any increase in *physical security* that the territories have produced.
The territory-security debate in the first instance engages the domestic political system within Israel, but it is also a question that bears
critically on U.S. foreign policy calculations. At one point in the
post-1973 negotiations Secretary of State Henry Kissinger made the
observation that the United States was committed to guarantee Israel's
security but not its conquests. The territory-security tradeoff is thus
both a political and a moral question. Israel is a state with a very
narrow margin of safety; the determination of what constitutes the
absolute minimum and the reasonable maximum of territory needed
for security, therefore, is a fundamental consideration for Israel's
foreign policy (as well as for the United States in any Middle East
negotiations). The moral problem is that Israel's territorial claims are

made on land also claimed—also on political and moral grounds—by the Palestinians and/or by various Arab states.

The Palestinian policy problem is defined in terms of territory and sovereignty: How to guarantee both land and international acknowledgment of their right to self-determination and sovereign status. This is the maximum Palestinian diplomatic objective, but variations on this theme include land without sovereignty (or autonomy) or land and some sort of relationship with Jordan. While these other possibilities may well be the likely outcome of any negotiations on the Middle East, it is useful when defining the problem to recognize the basic objective the Palestinians are pursuing. Obviously, the Israeli territory-security problem runs directly counter to the Palestinian territory-sovereignty problem. And, since both sets of issues are defined as political and moral claims, adjudication of them is not possible though some purely political tradeoff: each actor argues that it has a moral right to territory, security, and/or sovereignty.

The third set of actors, the Arab states, are confronted by territory, security, and sovereignty issues. Some, like Syria and Jordan, have territorial disputes with Israel (Golan and the West Bank). Jordan, moreover, has a delicate political relationship with the Palestinians, since they lay competing claims to the West Bank. Syria and Israel are in persistent tension about classic security questions. Other Arab states face a "security-sovereignty" dilemma in the sense that sovereignty may well be threatened from within if any state is perceived by the populace as being insufficiently aggressive about the Palestinian question (or other unresolved issues in the Middle East). It is generally believed, for example, that Sadat went to war in 1973 due to domestic pressures, having been perceived by many Egyptians as too complacent in accepting the outcome of the 1967 war.

When these three positions—Israeli, Palestinian, and Arab—are sketched out, the regional problem in the Middle East can be seen in all its intractability: *prima facie,* the claims are irreconcilable. Possible solution lies in distinguishing between the maximal goals of each party and the minimal conditions for peaceful cooperation with its neighbors. It is the maximum statement of each case that creates the stalemate: a maximal Israeli territorial claim negates the Palestinian territorial claim, for example, while maximal Palestinian territorial claim would exceed Israel's fundamental security requirements.

The hope for a negotiated settlement lies in reconciling the minimal claims of each actor, then. Minimal claims are those that must be satisfied or the claimant will decide that peaceful pursuit of its objectives is not possible. When an actor's minimal claims are not met, resort to force is regarded as a necessary option. How the superpowers and the regional actors define and relate the minimal claims of each party to the Middle East conflict, therefore, determines the possibility for a regional settlement.

As the regional actors deal with each other, they are faced—in varying ways—with the constraints and pressures of domestic or local forces. At the *local* level, politics and religion are interwoven in a unique way in the Middle East. In addition, several of the key Arab states are passing through the rough shoals of modernization and development, with all the problems accompanying these processes. (An analysis of how politics, religion, and modernization intersect locally would require a thoroughgoing analysis of the individual states of the Middle East.)

The relationship of the systemic, regional, and local dimensions of the Middle East question makes it unique in international politics. Each level has a degree of independence, but all three must be related if there is to be any hope for a stable political settlement.

The Catholic Church and the Middle East: Points of Intersection

For the Catholic Church, the Middle East is both a politico-moral question of great significance and a pastoral question (because of the various Christian communities in the Middle East). Hence, the Church addresses the Middle East in terms of both public policy and specifically religious values and interests. Using the categories outlined at the outset of this chapter, it may now be useful to identify how the Catholic Church addresses the Middle East question.

The center of the Church, embodied in the policies of the Holy See, plays a preeminent role through the personal activity of the pope and the diplomatic network of the Vatican. It is from this position of the "center" that the Catholic Church addresses such issues as the status of Jerusalem, the Palestinian question, and diplomatic relations with both Israel and the various Arab states. Other parts of the Church touch on these questions, but the policy positions are set by the Holy See. No other voice or place in the Church can project a defined position into the policy debate on the Middle East as consistently and visibly as the Holy See.

The role of local churches in shaping the policy of the universal Church is best exemplified by the activity of the Arab Christian communities in the Middle East. The latter are both an object of the Holy See's pastoral concern and a source of information and perspective that influence—without necessarily determining—the specific positions the Holy See takes on the Middle East. Particularly in recent years, Rome's position on the Middle East and on Jerusalem and Lebanon especially has stressed concern for maintaining a Christian presence in the region. There has been a conscious effort to stress that it is the Christian communities and not just the "holy places" that is at the center of the Church's interest in the area. The interplay between the perspective of a local church and the wider policy concerns of the Holy See forms a complex relationship. On Lebanon, for example, one would have to distinguish between the Holy See's abiding interest in the survival of a free Christian community—a topic addressed repeatedly by Pope John Paul II—and its considerable care not to associate itself with all dimensions of the positions of Christians in the Lebanese conflict.

The role of local churches working together to address common problems is also visible in the Catholic Church's Middle East policy. The role of the Church in the United States is a good example of this theme. In terms of both relief and development efforts and of participation in the policy debate about American policy in the Middle East, the Catholic bishops maintain a serious policy and programmatic interest. The relief and development programs are administered by the Catholic Near East Welfare Association and the Catholic Relief Services; the policy positions are taken and represented by the U.S. Catholic Conference of Bishops.[11] On both fronts, the U.S. bishops are related to the local churches in the Middle East. While the programmatic activities have been longstanding endeavors, there has been an increasing recognition in recent years of the importance of the U.S. bishops' role in the policy debate about the Middle East. Precisely because no other outside power has such influence in the region, the role of the local bishops conference in the United States is a unique one.

Using the levels of the Middle East question outlined above, it is clear that the Catholic Church has the capability to engage the policy debate at the systemic, regional, and local levels. The transnational presence of the Church offers the possibility of a coordinated approach to the policy issues, involving such locations as Rome, Washington, Jerusalem, Damascus, and Beirut. The content of such a coordinated policy involves both internal ecclesial questions and external foreign policy considerations. Precisely because the Middle East is such a unique blend of religious and political themes, the Catholic Church brings a distinct potential to the policy debate.

Notes

1. For examples of standard treatments of the Church's diplomatic activity cf: R. Graham, *Vatican Diplomacy: A Study of Church and State on the International Plane* (Princeton, N.J.: Princeton University Press, 1959), and H. Cardinale, *The Holy See and the International Order* (London: Colin-Smythe Publishers, 1976).

2. S. Huntington, "Transnational Organizations in World Politics," in *World Politics* 25 (1973): 333–68.

3. I. Vallier, "The Roman Catholic Church: A Transnational Actor," in R. O. Keohane and J. Nye, eds., *Transnational Relations in World Politics* (Cambridge: Harvard University Press, 1972), pp. 129–52.

4. For an overview of developments, cf. P. Nichols, *The Pope's Divisions: The Roman Catholic Church Today* (New York: Holt, Rhinehart and Winston, 1981).

5. For a fuller development of the theme, cf. J. B. Hehir, "Church-State and Church-World: The Ecclesiological Implications," *Proceedings of the Catholic Theological Society of America,* 1986.

6. For a commentary on the Council's theology of church and world, cf. J. C. Murray, "Church and State at Vatican II," *Theological Studies,* 27 (1966): 580–606.

7. Examples of major papal statements can be found in J. Gremillion, *The Gospel of Peace and Justice: Catholic Social Teaching Since Pope John* (Maryknoll, N.Y.: Orbis Books, 1976).

8. For a review of Ostpolitik, cf. H. Stehle, *Eastern Politics of the Vatican 1917–1979* (Athens, Ohio: Ohio State University Press, 1981).

9. For the U.S. Bishops statement, cf. H. J. Nolan, ed., *Pastoral Letters of the United States Catholic bishops,* vol. 4 (1975–1983) (Washington, D.C.: U.S. Catholic Conference, 1984), pp. 44–46. See also G. D. Moffitt III, *The Limits of Victory: The Ratification of the Panama Canal Treaties* (Ithaca, N.Y.: Cornell University Press, 1985), pp. 143–44.

10. I have drawn on several themes for this section. Helpful overviews on the Middle East include those of A. Atherton, "Arabs, Israelis and Americans," *Foreign Affairs* (Summer 1984), pp. 1194–1209; H. Saunders, *The Middle East Problem in the 1980s* (Washington, D.C.: American Enterprise Institute, 1981); and W. Khalidi, "Regropolitics: Toward a U.S. Policy on the Palestinian Problem," *Foreign Affairs* (Summer 1981) pp. 1050–63.

11. Cf. Nolan, *Pastoral Letters,* vol. 3 (1962–1974), pp. 88, 388; and vol. 4 (1975–1983), p. 276.

5

The Holy See
and the Israeli-Palestinian Conflict

GEORGE EMILE IRANI

The Palestine question, which arose early in this century, constitutes a fundamental challenge to the interests of the Holy See. This
challenge stems from long-held misperceptions that exist between
Catholics and Jews, and from the Church's attitude towards Zionism.
The key problem faced by the Holy See is that it sees Judaism as a
"religion with a national basis and a nation with a religious mission."[1]
This factor, along with the creation of the State of Israel as a national
home for the Jewish people,[2] presents the Holy See with a dilemma of
major proportions. It is a dilemma that stems essentially from the
theocratic nature of the Jewish state, which is in diametric opposition
to the papacy's objective of drawing a clear distinction between temporal and spiritual affairs.

The other facet of the dilemma is that the interests of the Holy
See in the Israeli-Palestinian dispute include the fate and welfare of
Catholic minorities living in the Holy Land (especially in the West
Bank) and in the Arab-Islamic countries, as well as the status of
Jerusalem and the Holy Places. In light of these interests, the Holy
See has opted to pursue its interfaith relations with Islam, thereby
protecting the Catholic community. The commonality of interests
between the Holy See and the Arab-Islamic states is more pronounced
and less controversial than are the concerns the Holy See shares with
the Jewish state. Moreover, the role of the Holy See in the Palestine
question is rooted in the Church's advocacy of social justice, in addition to its concern for endangered Catholic minorities. Therefore, the
involvement is executed on two interrelated levels: a humanitarian-
religious level as well as a diplomatic one.

In the Israeli-Palestinian dispute, the Holy See has elected to

An expanded version of this topic can be found in the author's book, *The Papacy and the
Middle East, 1962–1984* (1986).

follow a policy that confirms its role as that of mediator, moderator, and conciliator between, variously, Arabs and Israelis, Muslims and Jews, Muslims and Christians, and Jews and Christians. The nature of the Holy See's intervention in the Holy Land was defined by Monsignor William F. Murphy, under-secretary to the Pontifical Commission on Justice and Peace of the Holy See, in an address delivered in Boston in May 1983. According to Monsignor Murphy, the Holy See intends

> to offer its services and good offices, such as by arbitration and mediation, in any and every way that is consistent with its spiritual misison. It does not seek to offer technical solutions outside its competence, but rather wishes to be at the service of all in finding the ways to a just and lasting peace that will guarantee the legitimate rights of all involved.[3]

In this cautiously worded statement, the Holy See elucidated a policy that revolves around three key principles: (1) the papacy intends to act as a mediator between Arabs and Israelis; (2) the Holy See, given its religious nature, does not seek to advance any practical solutions to the dispute, but will act as a facilitator of such; and (3) the Holy See recognizes the legitimate rights of both Israelis and Palestinians. However, a close reading of the text indicates the narrow path available for intervention by the Holy See. The legitimate rights of Palestinians and Israelis are in radical and apparently irreconcilable opposition. It is a matter of one people—the Israelis—denying the existence of Palestinian rights, while the Palestinians assert that their national claims are more justified by historical facts and societal realities. Therefore, in addition to the religious dimensions of the conflict, the papacy is confronted with the task of narrowing the gap between these two peoples. Furthermore, the Holy See is not an impartial actor in the dispute. It has temporal as well as spiritual interests to defend in the Holy Land, which to some degree compromise both its margin of maneuverability and its credibility as a disinterested mediator.

The Holy See and Israel

Since the early days of the Zionist movement and its stated aim to establish a homeland for the Jews in Palestine, the reaction of the

Holy See has been mostly negative. The central concern of the papacy is, of course, the fate of the Holy Places and the Catholic presence and interests in the Holy Land. Following the proclamation of the State of Israel on 14 May 1948, *L'Osservatore Romano*, the Holy See's daily newspaper, wrote that Zionism is not the embodiment of Israel as it is described in the Bible. Zionism is a contemporary phenomenon which undergirds the modern state [of Israel], which is philosophically and politically secular.[4] The Holy Land and Holy Places as they are, form part and parcel of Christendom.[5]

Since then, there has been an evolution in the attitude of the Holy See towards Israel. This evolution can be characterized as having a mixture of theological prejudice and political pragmatism. Following the 1967 Arab-Israeli War, when the Holy Places of Christianity fell under Israeli control, the Holy See opted for informal talks with the Israeli government in order to work out a *modus vivendi* regarding the status of Catholic interests in Palestine. However, despite its readiness to acknowledge the Jewish state as a political entity, the Holy See has not yet established diplomatic ties with Israel. A recent position was expressed by Monsignor Murphy in the Boston address cited earlier:

> The Holy See recognizes the factual existence of Israel, its right to exist, its right to secure borders and to all other rights that a sovereign nation posseses. The Holy See would have no problem in principle with establishing diplomatic relations. However, there are certain difficulties and problems that the Holy See would first want to have resolved. I might add that it is the common custom of the Holy See not to be the initiator of diplomatic relations with any country, although it welcomes and appreciates diplomatic relations.[6]

The reasons currently used by the Holy See to explain the absence of diplomatic relations with the Jewish state are: (1) the Israeli invasion of Lebanon in the summer of 1982; (2) the Jewish settlements on the Israeli-occupied territories of the West Bank and the Gaza Strip; (3) the fate of the Palestinians; and (4) the status of Jerusalem and the Holy Places.[7] Other explanations often mentioned can be divided into formal and substantive issues. Formal issues include the policy that the Holy See avoids establishing diplomatic relations with any state that lacks definitive and recognized borders: an example is the Holy See's position regarding the Oder-Neisse borders between Germany and Poland.[8] The substantive issues can be further divided into two categories: those that reflect the reluctance of the Holy See to recognize states in controversial and changing situations, which is manifestly the case of Israel today; and those germane to the substantial loss, beginning in the Middle Ages, of the pope's exclusive authority over all matters of consequence in Christendom. Today, the pontiff has to take into account "the global view and undoubtedly the views of the Christian churches in the Arab countries (Greek Catholic, Maronite, Copt, and so forth)."9

There exists another potential problem that would almost certainly arise from the establishment of official diplomatic relations between the Holy See and Israel. As in the case of all other countries with which it has diplomatic ties, the Holy See would require guarantees regarding the regulation of Catholic teaching and the Catholic presence in Israel proper. The Christian presence in Israel is not positively viewed by some Orthodox Jews, who are concerned about the threat of possible missionary activities.10

Notwithstanding all the problems and obstacles in the path of Holy See–Israeli relations, the papacy has taken a pragmatic stance towards the Jewish state, especially after 1967 and the Israeli occupation of Jerusalem. The apostolic delegate has frequent contact with the Israeli foreign ministry and the ministry of religious affairs. In Rome, Israeli diplomats accredited to the Italian government are often received in Vatican City. After the 1967 Arab-Israeli War, Pope Paul VI received in audience Israeli Foreign Minister Abba Eban in 1969; Prime Minister Golda Meir, 1974; and Moshe Dayan, 1978. The last two Israeli officials to visit the Vatican were Israel's Prime Minister Yitzhak Shamir, in 1982, and Shimon Peres, the Prime Minister of Israel, in 1985.

If the Holy See is handicapped by its historical stand towards Judaism and by the absence of diplomatic relations with Israel, it nevertheless has the major advantage of being in permanent contact with all the parties involved in the Israeli-Palestinian dispute. Moreover, the prestige and influence enjoyed by the Holy See in such international institutions as the United Nations clearly motivate Israeli leaders to pay close attention to the positions adopted by the Holy See.

Three important elements bear on Holy See–Israeli relations. First, Vatican City is legally recognized by the international community as the territorial base for the Holy See, but the legitimacy of Israel as a homeland for Judaism is still in doubt in the minds of both dissenting Jews and some Gentiles. Second, Israel does not want to alienate the Holy See, since the Jewish state has diplomatic ties with several countries that have important Catholic communities. Third and finally, the whole issue of the status of Israeli–Holy See relations gained a new dimension with the recommendation by Catholic and Jewish members of the United States Congress on 26 November 1984 that Pope John Paul II initiate the necessary steps leading to the establishment of diplomatic relations with Israel.[11] For the twenty-six American legislators, "the exchange of ambassadors between Israel and the Vatican would be a watershed in the history of Jewish-Catholic relations equivalent only to the Second Vatican Council."[12] In their overstatement, the American congressmen probably were not aware that the Declaration on the Jews issued during Vatican II had only a purely religious significance. In contrast, the question of the establishment of diplomatic ties between Rome and the Jewish state was more a matter of temporal politics, and one that would place the Holy See in an awkward and untenable position in the Arab-Israeli dispute.

The call by the members of the House of Representatives came at a time when disagreements were reported inside the Roman Curia between those prelates favoring the creation of a Palestinian homeland and those favoring closer ties with Israel.[13] The whole affair was the result of a leak to the media by someone in the U.S. State Department. The U.S. ambassador to the Holy See, William Wilson, had had a meeting with a personal associate of Pope John Paul II, the outcome of which was not to be revealed. In a letter to the author, Wilson wrote of these events:

> Unfortunately this matter is receiving far too much publicity and, in my personal opinion, the publicity which it is receiving and which was recently augmented by a letter to the Holy Father signed by a group of Congressmen may have the unfortunate effect of even postponing such a decision [to establish relations with Israel].[14]

The Holy See and the Palestinians

Just as there is a close relationship between Judaism and the state of Israel, so is there a close interrelationship among Christianity, Islam, and the question of Palestine. Acknowledging this important fact, the Holy See has tried to improve its relations with the Muslim world with a frank and open dialogue.

The history of past relations between the Catholic Church and Islam is troubled. In its first centuries of expansion, Islam spread rapidly into the heart of Christendom. This was followed by the European invasion of the Middle East under the pretext of religion: the Crusades. In the nineteenth century, the activity of Catholic missionaries was closely tied to the givens of colonial enterprise. It was not until after World War II that a tradition of respect for other religions became generalized in Catholic theology—a change in perspective that was officially sanctioned by the Second Vatican Council, through which Pope John XXIII generalized for all Catholics the renewal which some had already experienced. After approaching the internal questions of the Catholic Church and those of its relations with the world, the council fathers dealt with the problem of the relations between Catholics and believers of other religions.[15] In fact, with regard to Islam, the council declaration *Nostra Aetate* noted that

> although in the course of the centuries many quarrels and hostilities have arisen between Christians and Muslims, this most sacred Synod urges all to forget the past and to strive sincerely for mutual understanding. On behalf of all mankind, let them make common cause of safeguarding and fostering social justice, moral values, peace and freedom.[16]

Both the Arab and non-Arab Islamic countries and the Holy See find themselves allied against common enemies: atheism and materialism. A third common interest linking the two sides is the fate of Jerusalem. Furthermore, the Christian-Islamic dialogue has been institutionalized in the course of several meetings, and has provided the Holy See with formal channels through which it can express its views regarding the fate of Catholics in the Arab and Islamic countries: in October 1974, the Holy See established a Commission for Religious Relations with Islam which is included in the Secretariat for Non-Christians. Finally, the Holy See maintains normal diplomatic relations with a number of Arab and non-Arab Islamic countries, including Sudan, Iran, Kuwait, Morocco, Pakistan, Syria, Tunisia, Iraq, Egypt, Lebanon, and Turkey.

From the beginning of the Israeli-Palestinian dispute, the Holy See has maintained a stand sympathetic to the plight of the Palestinian people. This attitude was motivated mainly by the papacy's concern for the fate of Catholics living in Palestine on the one hand, and the humanitarian aspects of the plight of Palestinian refugees following the various wars between Arab and Israeli armies on the other. Moreover, the Holy See has remained faithful to the policy adopted after the Second Vatican Council and after the publication of Pope Paul VI's encyclical *Populorum Progressio,* which called for the consolidation of peace through justice. In the last twenty years, sovereign pontiffs have condemned acts of terrorism from all sides and have called for a just and equitable solution to the Arab-Israeli quarrel in the framework of the resolutions adopted at the United Nations.[17]

Diplomatically, however, while recognizing the legitimate rights of the Palestinians to a homeland, the Holy See believes that "this cannot happen in isolation, but a solution must be constructed with the agreement and cooperation of all the countries involved."[18] By the end of the 1960s, following the defeat of the Arab armies, the Palestinians reasserted their yearning for nationhood through a resort to guerrilla warfare and the establishment of the Palestine Liberation Organization (PLO).[19] And at least one Vatican official has drawn a parallel between the PLO and the Zionist movement.[20] Father Dubois has stated that "it is Jewish Zionism which has awakened Palestinian Zionism."[21] Palestinian guerrilla actions followed by Israeli military retaliation remains the typical pattern of the relationship between Palestinians and Israelis.

The resurgence of Palestinian nationalism was reflected in Paul VI's speeches. By the end of 1975, he declared that both peoples, Palestinians and Israelis, had to recognize each other's right to self-determination and nationhood. The pontiff's feelings were dramatized in an often quoted address he gave on 22 December 1975:

> Even if we are well aware of the tragedies not so long ago which have compelled the Jewish people to seek a secure and protected garrison in a sovereign and independent state of their own, and because we are aware of this, we would like to invite the children of this people to recognize the rights and legitimate aspirations of another people which also have suffered for a long time, the people of Palestine.[22]

Given his background in Poland, with its long history of struggle for justice and human dignity, it is not surprising that Pope John Paul II has adopted a more active and outspoken posture toward the Israeli-Palestinian dispute.[23] The pope's attitude toward the conflict was highlighted in a controversial speech he delivered on 5 October 1980 in Otranto. Noting that the situation in the Middle East had reached an explosive stage, he went on to explain his perception of the origins of the dispute between the Israelis and Palestinians:

The Jewish people, after tragic experience linked to the extermination of so many sons and daughters, gave life to the State of Israel. At the same time a sad condition was created for the Palestinian people who were in large part excluded from their homeland.[24]

The pontiff's address was stunning in its frankness. No previous pope had ventured to go so far as to publicly note Israel's partial responsibility for the plight of the Palestinians.

Not surprisingly, the controversial character of the papal speech elicited the anger of both Israeli and non-Israeli Jewish leaders, who disagreed strenuously with the pope's interpretation of historical facts vis-à-vis the Palestinian issue. Replying to the pope's address, Rabbi Joseph Sternstein, president of the American Zionist Federation, expressed his group's point of view when he said that

> the Arabs living within the borders of the newly established State of Israel fled their homes at the insistence and admonition of their Arab leaders and despite assurances of safety from the Israeli army. Moreover, the Vatican statement ignored the fact that at the same time as Arabs fled their houses in Haifa and Jaffa, Jews were forcibly driven from their homes in cities throughout the Arab world.[25]

Pope John Paul II's address can be considered as the most explicit statement yet from a sovereign pontiff regarding the Palestinians. It was also symbolic of the stand that the Holy See had decided to adopt in light of the increasing militance and expansionist policies adopted by the Israeli government in the Occupied Territories after 1967. In fact, on 10 November 1977, *L'Osservatore Romano* published an article critical of the Israeli settlement policy on Palestinian-occupied land in which it stated that

> it is clear to everyone that a massive Jewish presence in the occupied territories would make it impossible to realize their return to the Arabs. As regards the West Bank the introduction of Jewish population radically upsets the plans that are being made to set up there a "Palestinian homeland" whatever form this "homeland" may take—in order to solve the Palestinian problem, which has now become the most complex and at the same time fundamental difficulty in the whole tangle of the Middle East crisis.[26]

The "plans" referred to were those agreed upon in the Camp David Agreements of 1978 between Egypt and Israel under the supervision of the United States. In fact, the Holy See took a position not far different from that of the Carter administration as regards the future status of the West Bank and Gaza. Thus, even if the papacy remains faithful to its stated policy of offering no "technical solutions" to the conflict between the Palestinians and Israelis, it nevertheless keeps the door open to support the possible involvement of Jordan in deciding the fate of the Occupied Territories.

Having thus lightly sketched the background of the attitude of the Holy See toward Israel and the Palestinians, we are ready now to delve into the humanitarian aspects of the Holy See's intervention in the Israeli-Palestinian dispute—an intervention inspired by the papacy's commitment to the right of peoples to self-determination and the fostering of peace through justice.

The Pontifical Mission for Palestine and Bethlehem University

One of the central interests of the Holy See in the Near East is the welfare of Catholic minorities living in that area. This concern is directly linked to the plight of the Palestinian refugees, which, since the start of the Israeli-Palestinian dispute, has elicited the papacy's constant solicitude. For this purpose, and in light of papal teachings, two major institutions were established by the Holy See to oversee relief and educational initiatives in the Holy Land: the Pontifical Mission for Palestine and Bethlehem University.

The Pontifical Mission for Palestine was founded in 1949 by Pope Pius XII. Its purpose was to assist the Palestinian refugees through the provision of goods and services to meet educational, cultural, religious, and humanitarian needs. It predated the United Nations Relief Work Agency (UNRWA), an agency established by the international body for similar purposes. The main offices of the Pontifical Mission are in New York, but it has regional offices in Beirut, Jerusalem, and Amman, and a liaison office in Rome. The Holy See agency is closely associated with its United States-based sister organization, the Catholic Near East Welfare Association (CNEWA), the Holy Father's Mission Aid to the Eastern Churches.[27] CNEWA was established in 1924 to be "the sole instrumentality authorized to solicit funds for Catholic interests in these regions [Near East] and shall be so recommended to the entire Catholic population in the United States."[28]

To highlight the importance of the Pontifical Mission in its humanitarian work in the Middle East, Pope Paul VI notified its president, Monsignor John G. Nolan, by letter on 16 July 1974 that

> the work of the Mission for Palestine has been one of the clearest signs of the Holy See's concern for the welfare of the Palestinians, who are particularly dear to us because they are people of the Holy Land, because they include followers of Christ, and because they have been and are still being so tragically tried. We express again our heartfelt sharing in their sufferings and our support for their legitimate aspirations. May our paternal solicitude bring comfort and encouragement, especially to the refugees, who for years have been living under inhuman conditions. Unfortunately, such a state of affairs has produced in many Palestinians a sense of frustration and, in some, violent protest which with sorrow we have been constrained strenuously to deplore.[29]

The papal message dramatized the three-fold importance attached by the Holy See to the plight of the Palestinian people. First, they are the "people of the Holy Land," which means that they are entitled to the same rights to self-determination as any indigenous population. (There is here of course an implicit rebuttal to the Zionist claim that Palestine was a land without people.) Second, some Palestinians are Christians, and as such a fundamental focus of papal attention. Finally, the Palestinians are considered a beloved people by the pope because they have been and are still "being so tragically tried." This concern echoes Paul VI's constant theme of fostering peace through justice.

Two other very important points surfaced in the pontiff's letter. First, he expressed his "support for their legitimate aspirations," which in a sense means that the Holy See, although stopping short of explicitly stating it, backs the effort for the establishment of a Palestinian homeland. Second, Pope Paul VI gave an explanation as to why the papacy had to condemn "acts of violent protest" perpetrated by Palestinian commandos. In other words, the Holy See's condemnation proceeded from a full awareness of the factors that underlay such acts of violence.

Following Pope Paul VI's pilgrimage to the Holy Land in 1964, the Holy See became aware that immediate action needed to be taken to stem the decline of Christian communities in the area by improving the quality of education there. As a step in this direction, the Holy See's Sacred Congregation for Oriental Churches signed a contract with the Brothers of the Christian Schools (Christian Brothers) to administer Bethlehem University, which opened its doors on 1 October 1973.[30] In a memorandum prepared for Monsignor Nolan, the then apostolic delegate in Jerusalem, Archbishop Pio Laghi, wrote about the necessity and urgency of establishing Bethlehem University, pointing out that it was

> necessary to keep the elite here: otherwise there will be no leadership in any field of public or private life, religious life included. It is necessary to consolidate the Christian presence in the Holy Land and to show by example that we care not only for stones and shrines but also for people and, in particular, the youth.[31]

Together with a few other academic institutions on the West Bank, Bethlehem University has become a center for training what may become the leadership of a possible future Palestinian state. Predictably, this situation has caused some tension with the Israeli military authorities. Brother Scanlan, vice-chancellor of Bethlehem University, believes that the Israeli government is worried about the success of such educational establishments in stabilizing the population and increasing its level of education: "As we stabilize the population, we are running against the policies of the present [Israeli] government which would like to increase emigration and make annexation easier."[32] Moreover, the universities are the only substantial institutions left on the West Bank. In emphasizing this factor, Brother Scanlan stated that if "the universities were terminated, the next focus of pressure would be on the churches because they are providing many social services, committing the 'sin' that we are."[33] The Israeli government's suspicion toward Bethlehem University and other Palestinian educational institutions reflects how history can sometimes repeat itself in reverse. In 1922, almost twenty years prior to the establishment of the Jewish state, Chaim Weizmann, the most prominent Zionist diplomat, met with the then secretary of state of the Holy See, Cardinal Gasparri. Weizmann explained to the cardinal the purposes and aims of the Jewish National Home in Palestine. After having detailed what the Zionist settlers were doing (drainage, afforestation, education, etc.), Gasparri looked at his guest and observed in French: "C'est votre universite que je crains."[34]

The Holy See has demonstrated through such concrete actions its humanitarian concern for the Palestinians. The Pontifical Mission, a product of the Church's mission to help the oppressed and the downtrodden, provided for aid and relief, as well as for the religious needs of the refugees. Bethlehem University is an expression of the urgency that the Holy See feels toward the Holy Land. The papacy seems to have a sense of time running out, and a particularly keen sense of anxiety about the younger generation. Indeed, the Holy See knows that if the exodus of young people from the Holy Land is not soon stemmed, the only role left for the Church will be that of curator of museums and caretaker of "shrines and stones." What is most interesting to note here is that, indirectly, the Holy See is contributing actively to sowing the seeds of a Palestinian homeland. Moreover, given the fact that Bethlehem University is directly supervised by the Holy See, the Israeli military authority in the West Bank must at all times carefully consider the integrity of the institution. Anything that threatens the Holy See-sponsored university puts at risk the delicate *modus vivendi* that exists between Rome and Jerusalem.

Given the fact that the conflict between Palestinians and Israelis is directly linked to the fate of Catholics in the Holy Land, the Holy See could not be expected to adopt a policy of being a neutral bystander in the dispute. However, in order to be able to defend its interests and preserve the credibility of its intervention, the Holy See had to take a public stance based on impartiality.

Yasser Arafat and Pope John Paul II: 15 September 1982

To set the famous audience in its proper context, mention should be made of the fact that the pope was helped in his decision to meet with the PLO spokesman by several events related to the Arab-Israeli conflict. In their 1982 summit in Fez, Morocco, the Arab heads of state, together with Arafat, approved a resolution which, among other things, implicitly recognized the existence of Israel. This was the first time that an Arab gathering had accepted the reality of the Jewish state. The Fez Declaration was in a sense an answer to diplomatic initiatives taken at the international level, such as the European Community's Venice Declaration of 13 June 1981, which stressed the importance of PLO participation in any settlement of the Israeli-Palestinian dispute.[35] Moreover, the audience granted to the Palestinian leader was justified on the grounds that Arafat was a prominent personality with the authority to say yes or no to any decision related to his people's fate.[36] The meeting between John Paul II and Arafat also allowed the Holy See to emphatically express its stand toward the conflict in the Middle East.

The meeting between the pope and Arafat lasted for more than twenty minutes. A press communique released by the Holy See after the audience reported that

> the Holy Father—moved by his constant preoccupation to foster the difficult process of peace in the Middle East—received Mr. Yasser Arafat. . . . During the conversation the Supreme Pontiff manifested his good will for the Palestinian people and his participation in their long suffering, expressing the hope that a just and lasting solution might be reached as soon as possible for the Middle East conflict, a solution, which excluding recourse to arms and to all violence—in any form, and especially terrorism and reprisals—may lead to the recognition of the right of all peoples and in particular the right of the Palestinian people to a homeland of their own, and the right of Israel to its security.[37]

In light of this communique it appears that there are three major principles guiding the papal attitude toward the Israeli-Palestinian dispute. First, John Paul II asserted without ambiguity his opposition to acts of terrorism and the use of reprisals; this assertion is in line with the policy followed by the Holy See since the beginning of the conflict. Second, the Holy See declared without hesitation that the Palestinians are entitled to a homeland of their own. This was the expression of a new approach adopted by the Polish-born pope to grapple with the political implications of the Israeli-Palestinian dispute. Furthermore, it was consistent with earlier papal statements that, since 1973, have stressed the necessity to recognize the Palestinians as being not just refugees, but rather a people with a definite and legitimate right to self-determination.

The third principle constitutes an unequivocal statement that the Holy See recognizes the *de facto* existence of the Jewish state and its right to secure and defined borders. However, the pontiff's call to Arafat to recognize Israel's right to be secure did not have the desired impact. Some Israeli observers pointed out that as long as the Holy See stopped short of officially establishing diplomatic links with Israel, it was not in a position to impart any credible advice in that direction to anybody else. (In defending its stand, the Holy See has always said that by not establishing diplomatic ties with the Jewish state it was in a better position to contribute to a settlement of the conflict in the Middle East.)

The same day that the meeting took place in Rome, Pope John Paul II addressed the Middle East crisis in a speech. Papal concern had been heightened by the assassination on 14 September 1982 of the newly elected Lebanese president, Bashir Gemayel. In his speech, the pope restated, in unequivocal terms, the Holy See's position regarding a resolution to the conflict between Palestinians and Israelis:

> The Holy See is convinced above all that there will not be able to be *true peace without justice;* and that there will not be able to be justice if the rights of all the people involved are not recognized and accepted, in a stable mode, fair and equal. Among these rights, primordial and irrenounceable, is that of *existence* and *security* on one's own territory in *safeguarding the proper identity* of each one. It is a dilemma which is debated in a bitter manner between two peoples, the Israelis and the Palestinians, who have seen simultaneously or alternately their rights assaulted or denied.[38]

The pope's speech could not have been more explicit or balanced. Without overstatement, the papal address constituted the ultimate and clearest statement to date on the Holy See's perception of a solution to the question of Palestine. The reference to the necessity to reach peace through justice echoed papal teachings since Paul VI issued his famous 1967 encyclical on the development of peoples. Moreover, the pope defined what he meant by legitimate rights for both Palestinians and Israelis: such rights included those of "existence," of "security," and of the preservation of "the proper identity of each one." In light of John Paul II's background and the impact of his experience in Poland, it is not surprising to hear him speaking in such clear and lucid terms. In fact, in a January 1982 address to the diplomats accredited to the Holy See, the pontiff—referring to martial law in his native Poland—stated that "every people must be able to act freely in what regards the free determination of its own destiny. The Church cannot fail to give her support to such a conviction."[39]

The inescapable conclusion is that there exist fundamental objectives for the Holy See in the question of Palestine. The first objective is to preserve and maintain a Catholic presence in the Holy Land. The papacy dreads the day on which, as a result of emigration, the birthplace of Christ will be bereft of Catholics. To stem this tide of exile, the Holy See has created two important institutions referred to above—Bethlehem University and the Pontifical Mission—through which it hopes to keep local Catholic communities in place. The key reason is that the Catholic Church cannot afford to lose its credibility on a global scale with the loss of the Holy Land.

Tied to the welfare of Catholic communities is the question of the Palestinians themselves. This is predominantly a question that relates closely to papal teachings—most significantly, as these apply to the implementation of peace with the consolidation of justice. Since one cannot be achieved without the other, the Holy See's second objective—that of advocating the right to self-determination for the Palestinians—is consequently rendered more difficult by the intractable nature of the Arab-Israeli quarrel. Furthermore, the close relationship between temporal and religious matters that exists in both Islam and Judaism is another serious obstacle to the realization of the Holy See's objectives. Explicitly, there exists the deep mistrust that some Jews feel toward the papacy because of its alleged indifference during the Holocaust. The Holy See has tried to set the record straight regarding its attitudes during World War II, but it will nevertheless take several generations and a large amount of concentrated goodwill to fill the gap between the Holy See and much of the Jewish community.

Vis-à-vis the Palestinian question, the Holy See is eager to see a final settlement of the refugees in a national homeland where they could exert and enjoy their full right to nationhood. But the road toward this goal is fraught with obstacles and traps. Moreover, the Palestinian issue is now inextricably linked to the outcome of the Lebanese War, in which the Holy See intervened in an effort to maintain the integrity of that unhappy country.

In the final analysis, the Holy See's policy derives both from long- and short-term perspectives. In the long-term perspective, the Holy See strives always to maintain and support the Catholic presence; in the short-term perspective, it continues to prod both Palestinians and Israelis toward a peaceful settlement. This policy reflects a pragmatic attitude toward both Palestinians and Israelis that motivates the intervention of the Holy See. The papacy is aware that the Jewish state is here to stay, and that the best way for the Holy See to defend its interests is to accommodate Catholic interests with Israel's whenever compromise is possible. For Israel, the Holy See represents a powerful symbol, even if a partisan one, and any concession that the Israeli authorities would like to get from Rome has to be balanced against the limited means of the papacy. Israeli–Holy See relations are thus rendered hostage to the ebbs and flows of the conflict between Arabs and Israelis.

Notes

1. Personal interview with Father Marcel Dubois, Jerusalem, 10 May 1983. See also his "The Catholic View," *Encyclopaedia Judaica Year Book*, 1974 (Jerusalem: Keter Publishing House, 1974), pp. 167–73.

2. The official text of the Balfour Declaration (2 November 1917) reads: "H.M. Government, after considering the aims of the Zionist Organization, accepts the principle of recognising Palestine as the National Home of the Jewish people and the right of the Jewish people to build up its National life in Palestine under a protection to be established at the conclusion of Peace, following upon the successful issue of the war." For further details on the Balfour Declaration, see Leonard Stein, *The Balfour Declaration* (London: Vallentine, Mitchell, 1961).

3. Quoted in *The Pilot*, 6 May 1983, p. 4.

4. On the relationship between the Holy See and the Zionist movement since its inception, see Charlotte Klein, "Vatican and Zionism, 1897–1967, *"Christian Attitude on Jews and Judaism*, nos. 36–37 (June–August 1974): 11–16; Pinchas Lapide, *Three Popes and the Jews* (New York: Hawthorn Books, 1967); Raphael Patai, ed., *The Complete Diaries of Theodor Herzl*, 5 vols. (New York and London: Herzl Press and Thomas Yoseloff, 1960); Florian Sokolow, *Nahum Sokolow: Life and Legend* (London: Jewish Chronicle Publications, 1975); Esther Yolles Feldblum, *The American Catholic Press and the Jewish State, 1917–1959* (New York: KTAV Publishing House, 1977); Maria Grazia Enardu, *Palestine in Anglo-Vatican Relations, 1936–1939* (Florence: Cooperative Universitaria Firenze, 1980); and Yehoshua Rash, "Herzl, Weizmann, Leurs Papes et Leurs Cardinaux," *Sens*, 12 (December 1983): 283–303.

5. *L'Osservatore Romano*, 28 May 1948.

6. *The Pilot*, 6 May 1983, p. 4.

7. Father Marcel Dubois, a Dominican Israeli priest who is also an advisor to the Holy See's Commission for Religious Relations with Judaism, said that these reasons

were expressed in a meeting in Rome between Cardinal Achille Silvestrini, Secretary of the Council for the Public Affairs of the Church, and representatives of six Jewish organizations. Personal interview, Jerusalem, 10 May 1983.

8. On this subject see Edmund Francis Konczakowski, "Vatican Policy toward the German Oder-Neisse Line: A Study of Foreign Policy Evolution, 1945–1972" (Diss., University of Pennsylvania, 1976).

9. Personal interview with Dr. Meir Mendes, former liaison officer between the Israeli embassy in Rome and the Holy See, Tel-Aviv, 1 May 1983. Dr. Mendes is the author of a book in Hebrew on *The Vatican and Israel* (Leonard Davis Institute for International Relations, The Hebrew University of Jerusalem, 1983).

10. *Proche-Orient Chretian*, the French Greek-Catholic journal published by the White Fathers in Jerusalem, gives regular accounts of tensions between some Israeli religious groups and local Christian communities.

11. *New York Times*, 26 November 1984.

12. Liz S. Armstrong, "Catholic, Jewish House Members Urge Vatican to Recognize Israel," *NC News*, 26 November 1984.

13. *New York Times*, 22 October 1984.

14. Personal communication, 12 December 1984.

15. On the Christian-Islamic dialogue, see Pietro Rossano, "Les Grands Documents de l'Eglise au Sujet des Musulmans," *Islamochristiana* [Rome], 8 (1982): 13–23. Also see Yoakim Moubarac, *Recherches sur la Pensee Chretienne et l'Islam dans les Temps Modernes et a L'Epoque Contemporaine* (Beirut: Publications de l'Universite Libanaise, 1977), and Gaston Zananiri, O.P., *L'Eglise et l'Islam* (Paris: Spes, 1969).

16. Walter M. Abbott, S.J., gen. ed., *The Documents of Vatican II* (Piscataway, N.J.: Association Press, New Century Publishers, 1966), p. 663.

17. See, for instance, Paul VI's speech welcoming President Sadat, *Proche-Orient Chretien*, Tome XXVI, 1976, pp. 132–34; the speech delivered by Paul VI welcoming Moshe Dayan, *Proche-Orient Chretien*, XXVII, 1977, p. 341; and the speech Paul VI delivered during the visit of King Hussein of Jordan, *L'Osservatore Romano*, 30 April 1978.

18. *The Pilot*, 6 May 1983, p. 4.

19. For further details on the Palestinians and the PLO, see Hatem I. Husseini, *The Palestine Problem: An Annotated Bibliography* (Washington, D.C.: Palestine Information Office, 1980); and William B. Quandt, Fuad Jabber, and Ann Mosley Lesch, *The Politics of Palestinian Nationalism* (Berkeley: University of California Press, 1973).

20. Personal interview, Washington, D.C., 7 July 1983.

21. Personal interview.

22. *L'Osservatore Romano*, 23 December 1975.

23. See Joseph L. Ryan, S.J., "Palestinian Rights: Resonances in the Life and Themes of Pope John Paul II," mimeographed, prepared for the Fifth United Nations Seminar on the Inalienable Rights of the Palestinian People, 15–19 March 1982.

24. *Washington Post*, 6 October 1980.

25. *Jewish Telegraphic Agency*, 8 October 1980.

26. "Israeli Settlements on the West Bank of the Jordan," *L'Osservatore Romano* (English ed.), 10 November 1977.

27. From a pamphlet distributed by CNEWA's office in New York. The author is grateful for personal interviews with Brother Joseph Lowenstein, responsible for the Pontifical Mission for Palestine, Jerusalem, 25 April 1983; and Monsignor John G. Meaney, Regional Director of the Pontifical Mission for the Near East, Jall-Eddib, 27 May 1983. Monsignor Meaney told the author that former Secretary of State Alexander Haig's father was among the founding members of CNEWA.

In November 1983, a Holy See representative, Monsignor Antonio Franco, stated at the United Nations that "the Pontifical Mission's contribution to the refugees and other Palestinians in need since 1948 has amounted . . . to more than 150,000,000 dollars." *L'Osservatore Romano* (English ed.), 19 December 1983, pp. 11–12.

28. J. T. Ryan, "Catholic Near East Welfare Association," vol. 3, *New Catholic Encyclopedia* (Washington, D.C.: Catholic University of America, 1967), pp. 271–72.

29. From *Insegnamenti di Paolo VI*, Vol. 12 (Vatican City: Tipografia Poliglotta Vaticana, 1974), pp. 682–83. Also see Ed. Maxwell, "Palestine Refugees Key to Peace: Msgr. Nolan," *Troy (New York) Record*, 30 March 1970.

30. Personal interview with Brother Thomas Scanlan, Bethlehem, 27 April 1983.

31. Memorandum prepared by the Apostolic Delegate for Monsignor Nolan, 26 December 1972. Given to the author by Brother Gottwald at Bethlehem University.

32. Personal interview.

33. Personal interview.

34. See Chaim Weizmann, *Trial and Error* (New York: Harper and Brothers, 1949), p. 286.

35. Personal interview with Vatican official, 13 June 1983.

36. Personal interview.

37. *The Pilot*, 6 May 1983, p. 4.

38. *Origins*, 30 September 1982, p. 243. Emphasis added.

39. Quoted in Ryan, "Palestinian Rights," p. 13.

⠂⠦❧ 6 ❧⠦

The Jerusalem Question and the Vatican

FRED J. KHOURI

The Mandate Period

In the course of the centuries, Jerusalem became a holy city for three religions—a circumstance which has led to many clashes, notably those between Romans and Jews in A.D. 70 and 135 and between Christians and Muslims in the wake of the Crusades. Friction also developed between different Christian factions over control of certain Christian shrines, and peace was not achieved until the area's Ottoman rulers established a status quo that resolved such disputes. To avoid further friction between the opposed Christian communities, a neutral Muslim family was designated to hold the keys to the Holy Sepulchre.[1]

After World War I, the Vatican hoped that the Holy Land would be placed under the control of a Christian power that would respect the rights acquired by the various Christian churches over the centuries, and allow the major religious communities to participate in the administration of the Holy Places.[2] The Holy See was therefore pleased to see Christian Britain given the Palestine Mandate in 1922, but opposed the inclusion of the Balfour Declaration in the Palestine Mandatory Agreement, since this declaration promised the Jews a national home in Palestine. The Vatican feared that if the Jews were given a predominant position in the Holy Land through the establishment of a Jewish state, the rights of Christians—particularly, of Catholics—would not be adequately safeguarded, and peace and stability in the Holy Land would thereby be endangered.[3] Even before World War I, Vatican newspapers had criticized Zionist efforts to establish a home for Jews in Palestine, although there seemed to be no objection to the establishment of such a home anywhere else in the world. In 1919, as General Allenby's forces were entering Jerusalem, Pope Benedict XV, in his first public statement on Zionism, expressed his opposition to the establishment of a Jewish state on the ground that it would threaten the Christian community in Palestine. In June 1921, the pope again warned against changing "the sacred character of the Holy Places."[4]

During and after World War II, the Vatican continued to fear that either an Arab- or a Jewish-dominated Palestine would prejudice Catholic interests in the Holy Land, giving rise to an Arab-Jewish conflict that would endanger both the Holy Places and the lives of the Christian peoples in Palestine. The Holy See believed that its interests and the cause of peace in the area would best be served if Britain were to continue to run the Mandate (or if the Mandate were given to some other Christian nation); or, failing that, if Palestine were to be internationalized under United Nations control.[5]

Britain submitted the Palestine question to the United Nations in April 1947, and shortly afterwards announced that, whatever the outcome, it was leaving Palestine no later than 15 May 1948. In the summer of 1947, the UN Special Committee on Palestine established by the UN General Assembly recommended not only that Palestine be partitioned into Arab and Jewish states, but that Jerusalem and its environs be made into a *corpus separatum* under UN control, to guarantee the rights and interests of all religious groups and the preservation of all Holy Places.[6]

As a result of these developments, Vatican concern began to be centered primarily—though not exclusively—on the future of Jerusalem. The Holy See supported the UN Special Committee's partition plan because it provided for full territorial internationalization of Jerusalem and its environs, and because it appeared to be the best means to three desirable ends: protecting both the Holy Places and the Catholic community in Palestine; ensuring the universal character of the Holy City; and preventing the Jerusalem area at least from being swallowed up in a Jewish or Arab state. (There was also the hope that the internationalization of this area would enable the Vatican to halt the decline in the Christian population in the Holy Land.) The Vatican, therefore, solicited support for the partition plan from Catholic member states of the UN, especially those from Latin America. Several of these states consequently made it clear that their support for partition was contingent on its provision for the internationalization of Jerusalem.[7]

At the Second Session of the UN General Assembly in the fall of 1947, all Arab delegates strongly opposed the draft resolution of the proposal to partition Palestine, since they considered all of Palestine, including Jerusalem, to be an integral part of the Arab world. (Palestinian Arabs made up two-thirds of the population at that time.) The Arab states therefore advocated the establishment of a Palestinian state that would be legally obligated to protect the religious and ethnic rights of all dwellers in the Holy Land.[8]

Although the Zionists were anxious to have Jerusalem included in the proposed Jewish state, they decided to accept the draft resolution's *corpus separatum* provision for the Holy City. They reasoned that without this provision the resolution would fail to attract enough votes to pass the General Assembly, and such passage was considered essential to the establishment of a Jewish state.[9] The partition resolution was therefore passed by the UN General Assembly on 29 November, 1947. Fighting then broke out between the Arab and Jewish communities in Palestine. On 1 May 1948, in the first papal encyclical addressed to the Palestine issue, Pope Pius XII deplored the fighting and prayed that "the situation in Palestine may at long last be settled justly thereby concord and peace be also happily established."[10]

The UN Trusteeship Council met in February and March 1948 to draw up a draft statute establishing a *corpus separatum* for the Jerusalem area. The statute provided for a governor with broad executive authority, a legislative council, and various safeguards for human rights and the Holy Places. A final vote on this statute was delayed, however, due to a special session of the UN General Assembly called to reconsider the Palestine question. On May 15, 1948, following Britain's military evacuation of Palestine, Israel proclaimed itself an independent state and full-fledged war broke out between Israel and the neighboring Arab countries.[11]

Between Two Wars: 1948–1967

During the Palestine War, Israel seized the western or New City section of Jerusalem; Transjordan (later to be known as Jordan) occupied the smaller eastern sector, including the Old City, which contains most of the Holy Places. The Israeli-Transjordan Armistice Agreement that ended the war between the two countries accepted the *de facto* holdings of each party in Jerusalem without any reference to internationalization.

Despite these developments, there was considerable support for full internationalization of Jerusalem both inside and outside the UN. Faced with protracted Israeli-Jordanian occupation of Jerusalem, and fearing that continued fighting might cause great personal suffering and further damage to religious sanctuaries and institutions, the pope issued an encyclical on 24 October 1948 in which he deplored the fighting and the resultant loss of life, the damage to and destruction of religious and other properties, and the suffering of the thousands of refugees who had fled their homes during the armed conflict. He appealed to the world's leaders to

> give Jerusalem and its outskirts . . . an international character which, in the present circumstance, seems to offer a better guarantee for the protection of the sanctuaries. It would also be necessary to assure, with international guarantees, both free access to the Holy Places scattered throughout Palestine, and the freedom of worship and respect for existing customs and religious traditions.[12]

Israeli and Vatican emissaries met in late 1948 and early 1949 in an attempt to work out their differences, but their efforts did not succeed.[13] In another encyclical issued 15 April 1949, the pope renewed his call for full internationalization of Jerusalem as the best means for protecting the Holy Places and ensuring peace and stability there. He also called for international guarantees for all Holy Places throughout Palestine, and insisted that Catholic Church rights and interests acquired during the past centuries "should be preserved."[14] Despite further talks between Vatican and Israeli officials in the summer and fall of 1949, however, the two parties again failed to reach any agreement.[15]

Many Catholic members of the UN as well as representatives of other states, such as Australia and the Soviet Union, continued to insist on the fulfillment of the partition resolution's provisions dealing with the Holy City.[16] On 11 December 1948, as a result of these pressures, the UN General Assembly reaffirmed its support for full internationalization of the Holy City in Resolution 194 (III), which set up a conciliation commission for Palestine with the instruction to draw up "detailed proposals for a permanent regime for the Jerusalem area." After investigating the situation in depth, the conciliation commission submitted recommendations (A/973) that represented a major departure from the actual terms of the 1947 partition resolution. Instead of an international regime for Jerusalem, the commission proposed dividing the city into two sections, one Arab and one Jewish, with virtually all normal powers of government left in their joint hands. A UN Commissioner for Jerusalem would be appointed, with powers limited to insuring protection of the Holy Places and to supervising the demilitarization and neutralization of the city. The commission's proposal was opposed by most member states, as well as by the Vatican.[17]

Meanwhile, Israel and Jordan continued to oppose efforts to internationalize Jerusalem. Both pledged a willingness to guarantee the safety of the Holy Places under their control, and the provision of ready access to them by members of all religious groups. Starting in March 1949, Israel began moving its governmental agencies to West Jerusalem, thus serving notice that it considered Jerusalem an integral, permanent part of the country. In January 1951 Jordan appointed a custodian for the Holy Places with cabinet rank, and in 1959 East Jerusalem was proclaimed Jordan's second capital.[18]

Until early 1949, all Arabs continued to oppose both partition and the establishment of a *corpus separatum* for Jerusalem. This attitude changed after Israel not only won the Palestine War but conquered large areas beyond those allocated to it by the partition resolution while continuing to demonstrate a clear military superiority over the Arab world. Many Arab governments, after reassessing their situation, concluded that they now had more to gain than to lose from UN enforcement of the partition resolution, since it would compel Israel to give up a large part of its occupied areas, including West Jerusalem. Not only would this reduce both the size and the power of Israel, it would also enable large numbers of Palestinian refugees to return to their homes. Many Arab officials had condemned King Abdullah of Jordan for annexing the West Bank and East Jerusalem area to advance his own political ambitions at the expense of the Palestinian cause; therefore, most Arab governments concluded that they would be better off with all of Jerusalem internationalized than under joint Israeli/Jordanian control. In view of these considerations, all Arab states except Jordan began to support UN resolutions calling for the full internationalization of the Holy City.[19]

In the fall of 1949, the UN once again took up the Jerusalem question. While some proposals were made to back the conciliation commission's recommendation (or to provide limited functional internationalization for the Holy Places alone), most UN members—particularly the Arab states (other than Jordan, not yet a UN member), the Soviet bloc, and Catholic countries encouraged by the Vatican—

continued to insist upon full internationalization. On 9 December 1949, the UN General Assembly passed a resolution, introduced by Australia and strongly backed by the Vatican, that requested the trusteeship council to draw up a statute placing the Jerusalem area under the permanent international regime called for by the 1947 partition resolution. Israel not only voted against the resolution, but accelerated its efforts to move the Knesset and nearly all other government ministries and agencies from Tel Aviv to Jerusalem, in order to make the latter Israel's capital in fact as well as in name before the UN had a chance to implement its decisions.[20]

On 4 April 1950, the trusteeship council adopted an amended version of the statute originally drawn up in early 1948. Because of the practical difficulties involved in implementing this statute in the face of Israeli and Jordanian opposition, the council referred the matter back to the General Assembly. Thus, in the fall of 1950, the General Assembly found itself once again facing the Jerusalem problem. By this time, it was obvious that the actions and attitudes of Israel and Jordan had created more serious obstacles to the carrying out of UN decisions involving Jerusalem than had been anticipated. A number of UN members who had previously backed internationalization therefore began to seek a solution more acceptable to the Israelis and Jordanians. (Even the Soviet bloc dropped its support for internationalization.) In December 1950, the only two draft resolutions to receive serious consideration in the General Assembly were a Swedish proposal providing for a limited functional internationalization of the Holy Places and a Belgian suggestion that the trusteeship council give further study to the matter. Since both of these proposals failed to pass, the General Assembly ended its session without having taken any action either to enforce or to revise previous decisions. Although in succeeding years some Arab and Catholic UN members would occasionally remind the General Assembly that its existing resolutions were not being implemented, the Jerusalem question was not seriously considered again until after the 1967 war.[21]

The Vatican, however, continued to back full internationalization—and American Catholic leaders continued to give strong support to the Vatican's position. In response to an Israeli proposal suggesting limited international supervision to the Holy Places, the Vatican reiterated its view that only a "*corpus separatum*" under international administration would guarantee [their] security."[22] The Vatican continued to improve its ties with many Arab states, even establishing diplomatic relations with a number of them, and Christian Arab leaders made many trips to the Vatican to seek its support for the Arab cause. The Vatican was at all times mindful of its ties to the large numbers of Arab Christians, especially in Lebanon and among the Palestinians. During Pope Paul VI's trip to the Holy Land in 1964, he indicated clearly that it was not to be interpreted as an act of recognition of Israel, emphasizing that his visit was to "Palestine" and never referring to Israel by name. (It is also worth noting that the Vatican has never recognized Jordan or its claim to East Jerusalem.[23])

While strong differences continued to persist between Israel and the Vatican over the Jerusalem issue, the Vatican was nevertheless able to improve relations between the Catholic Church and Israel and world Jewry in general. In 1965, a Vatican council issued a Declaration on the Jews, which repudiated the long-standing charge of collective Jewish guilt for the death of Jesus, rejected anti-Semitism, and encouraged study and dialogue between Catholics and Jews. These recommendations were acted upon without delay, and helped to bring about a degree of understanding and better relations both between Catholics and Jews and between Israel and the Vatican.[24]

The Period after the 1967 War

Israel's decisive victory over the Arab states in early June of 1967 brought under its control all of the Jordanian territory west of the Jordan River, including East Jerusalem. A tremendous outpouring of emotion among Jews, not only in Israel but throughout the diaspora, was unleashed by Israel's victory and occupation of the Old City— especially by the repossession of the Wailing Wall, which many Jews believe was once part of the Second Temple and is therefore revered not only for its religious significance but also as a symbol of the ongoing history of the Jewish people. Many Israelis considered the recovery of all of Jerusalem a fulfillment of religious prophecies, and insisted that the Holy City should be completely and permanently unified under Israeli sovereignty.

The United States and Britain urged Israel not to act hastily, since they believed that annexation of East Jerusalem would weaken Israel's position within the world community and would seriously lessen the chances for achieving a durable Arab-Israeli peace.[25] The Vatican also opposed any annexation, and reiterated its support for full internationalization of the Holy City. On 9 June 1967 an official Vatican spokesman stated that the UN partition resolution of 1947 was and remained "in accordance with the wishes of the Holy See." On 23 June, the Vatican observer to the UN circulated an official document which declared that the Vatican was "concerned that the only solution which offers a sufficient guarantee for the protection of Jerusalem and its Holy Places is to place the city under international regime" and that the "term internationalization in its proper sense means a separate territory, a '*corpus separatum*,' subject to an international regime." On 26 June, the pope himself expressed this view.[26]

Israel, however, decided to disregard these admonitions and to annex East Jerusalem quickly, in order to present the world with a *fait accompli* before Western and UN pressures could build to the point where they might interfere with Israeli plans. Israel also wished to make plain that Jerusalem's future would no longer be considered a negotiable issue. Thus, on 27 June 1967, the Knesset hurriedly passed without debate a law enabling the minister of interior to proclaim Jerusalem a single city under Israeli administration. At the same time, the Knesset approved a measure providing for the protection of the Holy Places and guaranteeing freedom of access to them by all religious groups. The next day, Israel formally united the two sections of the city and extended its borders to include Kallandia Airport and Mount Scopus to the north and northwest, the Mount of Olives to the east, and several Arab villages to the south.[27]

In July 1967, the Vatican's official newspaper, *L'Osservatore Romano,* condemned Israel's annexation, rejected again Israel's proposal for a limited functional internationalization of the Holy Places, and insisted that Jerusalem be internationalized as originally called for by the UN partition resolution. Vatican sources revealed that the pope was prepared to use all his influence to promote this policy.[28] Once again, Israel sought a dialogue with the Vatican. The Israeli ambassador to Italy met with the pope, and a Vatican representative was sent to Israel to explain the Vatican's views and to hear Israel's. However, the positions of the two parties were still too far apart, and the talks failed.[29]

Israel's annexation of Jerusalem was condemned by many states, including the United States. Ambassador Arthur Goldberg presented his country's position to the UN General Assembly on 14 July 1967: "With regard to the specific meassures taken by the Government of Israel on June 28, I wish to make it clear the United States does not accept or recognize these measures as altering the status of Jerusalem [and they cannot be taken] as prejudging the final and permanent status of Jerusalem."[30] Two years later, Ambassador Charles Yost expanded the American position: "The part of Jerusalem that came under control of Israel in the June 1967 war, like other areas occupied by Israel, is occupied territory and hence subject to the provisions of international law governing the rights and obligations of an occupying power." He also reported that the United States "regrets and deplores" Israel's activities in East Jerusalem, and did not accept Israel's actions "as affecting the ultimate status of Jerusalem."[31]

On 4 July 1967, the UN General Assembly easily passed a resolution (2253-ES-4) that dismissed the annexation as invalid and called upon Israel to rescind all measures taken to alter the city's status. However, Israel ignored this and subsequent resolutions. Nevertheless, realizing that the Jerusalem issue was seriously compromising its position within the world community, Israel initiated efforts to reach agreement with the pope and other Christian leaders. Representatives of Israel met with officials of the Vatican, the World Council of Churches, and other Christian groups, as well as with delegations from various Christian countries. Israel offered an arrangement whereby it would retain sovereignty over the entire city, but would give the Holy Places extraterritorial, "universal" status, under the supervision of the religious communities themselves. Israel said it would grant quasi-diplomatic standing to the official church delegations stationed in Jerusalem, and expressed a willingness to work out the final details with representatives of the various religious organizations. It was Israel's contention that religious interests in the Holy Land could be adequately protected without internationalizing Jerusalem, that such an international regime would not be a practical solution, and that peace in Jerusalem and the safety of the Holy Places would more likely be assured by a unified city administration than a divided one. Israel won support from some Protestant and Greek Orthodox leaders. But the Russian Orthodox, the Copts, some Greek Orthodox, and certain other Christian groups, including Protestants, refused to accept the Israeli view. Efforts to win the Vatican's support also failed.[32]

On 30 June 1967, a group of Latin American states inspired by the Holy See presented a draft resolution supporting the full internationalization of Jerusalem. The failure of this resolution (A/L.523/REV. 1) to obtain the two-thirds majority needed to pass the General Assembly indicated that many UN members who had once supported internationalization no longer considered the solution viable. In fact, some Latin American states started to move their embassies from Tel Aviv to Jerusalem, thus indicating that they accepted Israel's continued occupation of the entire city as a fact of life. Israel meanwhile continued to consolidate its claim to Jerusalem, and neither the UN nor the major powers took any serious action to stop it. Israel even gained wide support among many American Catholic leaders and laymen.[33]

By late 1967 the Vatican was beginning to reconsider its position. From this point, the main change in the Vatican position was that, while it continued to call for an internationally guaranteed statute for Jerusalem and the Holy Places, it did not reiterate its usual references to the *corpus separatum* of the Holy City. In a Christmas message on 22 December 1967, the pope simply indicated those features that he considered "essential and impossible to evade" in any solution to the problem of Jerusalem and the Holy Places. He stressed two essential features:

> The first concerns the Holy Places . . . It is a matter of guaranteeing freedom of worship, respect for, preservation of and access to the Holy Places, protected by special immunities thanks to a special statute, whose observation would be guaranteed by an institution international in character, taking particular account of the historic and religious personality of Jerusalem. The second aspect of the question refers to the free enjoyment of the legitimate civil and religious rights of persons, residences and activities of all communities present in the territory of Palestine.[34]

The Pope also reiterated his concern for the people, as well as for the religious institutions, in Palestine, referring to the need to guarantee their "civil" as well as religious rights.

The concern of the Vatican, as well as of other Christian leaders, about the future of both the Christians and their Holy Places increased in the early 1970s after the Israeli government announced a "master plan" for the future of Jerusalem.[35] This plan envisaged the doubling of the Jewish population of the city by 1980, and the expansion of the Jewish population in the surrounding area. Vast housing projects were to be developed in and around the city; many Arab properties were to be sequestered; and Arabs to be removed from their homes in certain sections of the city and its environs in order to make room for immigrant Jews.[36] In repeated resolutions, the UN

General Assembly and Security Council deplored these Israeli policies and actions, and declared them null and void. The United States and other Western countries also protested. Nevertheless, Israel continued to carry out its master plan.

The Vatican assumed the leadership of the protest within the Christian world, in an effort to forestall Israeli moves to consolidate its sovereignty over Jerusalem and fundamentally alter the city's character.[37] On 14 March 1971, Pope Paul VI told a crowd in St. Peter's Square: "Not only in our name but in the name of all Christianity we have a grave duty to safeguard the recognition of the extraordinary requirements of the Holy Places in Palestine, the continued presence of Christians in that troubled country and the statute for Jerusalem."[38] In his 1971 Christmas message, the Pope reaffirmed the "necessity of a special statute, guaranteed internationally, which would take into account the pluralist and completely special character of the Holy City and of the rights of the various communities."[39] On 25 March 1974, the Pope held that "were the presence of the Christians in Jerusalem to cease, the Shrines would be without warmth . . . and the Holy Land would become like a museum."[40] In March 1971, an editorial in *L'Osservatore Romano* criticized Israeli expropriation of lands in the Arab sector, which would force out 6,000 Arabs in order to complete the "Greater Jerusalem" plan. The paper condemned these actions, which would not only change Jerusalem's historical and religious character and its universal vocation but would also make Jerusalem Jewish "at the expense of the non-Jewish population" and would compel both native Muslims and Christians "for reasons of [Israel's] urban expansion to live in ever increasingly restricted spaces and finally to look elsewhere for a future they feel they no longer can find in their homeland environment." It further contended that Israel's actions and policies confirmed "the necessity" of an international statute which would "guarantee truly the peculiar character of the city and the rights of the minority communities."[41] These actions strengthened the Vatican's determination to "oppose any proposal to make Jerusalem a city belonging to a specific nation" or coming under the control of any one religion.[42]

In January 1973, the pope met with Israeli Prime Minister Golda Meir with the hope of narrowing their differences over Jerusalem. However, their positions on the Jerusalem issue remained as incompatible as ever, even though general Israeli-Vatican relations continued to improve and fruitful dialogues between Catholics and Jews continued to take place in a number of countries, notably in the

United States and Western Europe.[43] In 1972, in an effort to promote better relations, Israel sold to the Vatican the Notre Dame de France Hospice, which had been badly damaged during the 1948 Palestine War and in 1970 had been sold to a subsidiary of the Jewish National Fund by the Assumptionist Fathers despite Vatican opposition. The Vatican subsequently rebuilt the structure for use as an international pilgrim center, thus both demonstrating its support of the Arab Christian community and affirming its continued existence in the Jerusalem area. In 1977, Israel released Archbishop Hilarion Capucci from prison at the request of the Vatican. (The archbishop had been found guilty of helping to smuggle arms to the Palestinians in the West Bank.) From time to time, top-level Israeli officials were received by the pope and Vatican emissaries visited Israel, but deep differences over Jerusalem persisted.[44]

By the early 1970s, Vatican views on the Palestinian issue and on the Palestine Liberation Organization were significantly influenced by several major developments. The world community, including Western Europe, had become increasingly aware of the plight of the Palestinians, and had become convinced that there could be no just and lasting resolution of the Arab-Israeli conflict without allowing the Palestinians their own state in Palestine. The UN General Assembly passed annual resolutions by large majorities, positing the formation of such a state as an essential part of any Middle East peace settlement.[45]

Prior to the 1973 war, the PLO refused to accept the existence of Israel and backed the goal of a single, secular state in Palestine, to be achieved by means of "armed struggle." However, both the goal and the means were rejected by most countries. After the 1973 war, moderate PLO leaders reassessed the situation and concluded that not only was their goal unrealistic, but that continued stress on it and on the threat of "armed struggle" was preventing the PLO from winning wider support within the world community. Consequently, PLO leaders began to indicate a readiness both to accept a smaller Palestinian state made up of the West Bank (including East Jerusalem) and the Gaza Strip, and to concentrate on the use of diplomatic and political means for achieving this limited objective.[46] These changes in policy led the UN General Assembly and the great majority of the nations of the world, including many of those in Western Europe, to recognize the PLO as the legitimate representative of the Palestinian people. In late 1974, the UN General Assembly invited Yasser Arafat to make a statement before that body and gave the PLO official observer status.[47]

As indicated earlier, the Holy See's concern about the Palestinians was rooted in a desire to promote the Christian presence in the Holy Land as well as by humanitarian considerations. Therefore, the Vatican repeatedly insisted on the need to protect the civil as well as the religious rights of all groups in the Holy Land, while continuing to refuse to extend official diplomatic recognition to Israel until such time as the Palestinian, Jerusalem, and other basic Arab-Israeli issues had been fairly and finally resolved. Meanwhile, the Vatican continued to extend substantial aid to the Palestinian refugees.[48]

The Vatican, like most of the world community, saw a just and lasting solution to the Palestinian question as the only way to peace in the Middle East and the preservation of human lives and the Holy Places. Moreover, the Vatican feared that, unchecked, Middle East conflicts could trigger a superpower confrontation that would threaten the entire world. Consequently, it began to speak more forthrightly about the need to recognize the rights and legitimate aspirations of the Palestinians, including their right to a homeland, and to urge both the Israelis and the Palestinians to recognize the other's right to coexist in peace and security. The moderate position taken by the PLO under Arafat enabled the Vatican to hold direct and open talks with PLO officials, and in 1982 Pope John Paul II met with Arafat. Nevertheless, the talks with PLO representatives, as well as those with Israeli representatives, did not imply formal diplomatic recognition by the Holy See; rather, these colloquies were held for the purposes of reaching understanding and eventual reconciliation.[49]

In October 1979, Pope John Paul II visited the UN. In a speech before the General Assembly, he reiterated the "hope for a special statute that, under international guarantees . . . would respect the particular nature of Jerusalem."[50] The Vatican's UN observer presented a very detailed note reaffirming the call for such a special statute and stressing the need to recognize the existing "historical and religious pluralism" of Jerusalem and the civil and religious rights of religious communities. At the same time, it called for "suitable guarantees" for all Holy Places throughout Palestine, and insisted that all rights be internationally guaranteed, rather than granted unilaterally by one state.[51]

On 30 June 1980, the Knesset passed a bill that formally made "complete and united Jerusalem" the *de jure* capital of Israel, signalling to the world that Israel would never give up the city, even as part of an overall peace settlement. This move evoked strong protest, not only in the Arab and Muslim worlds but also in the United States, Western Europe, and the UN. American officials publicly criticized the Israeli action, and insisted that the United States would not accept "any unilateral national legislation dealing with Jerusalem" but would continue to consider Jerusalem as occupied territory, under both Security Council Resolution 242 and the canons of international law. President Carter reiterated the long-standing American position that the future of Jerusalem "can only be decided through negotiations" between the parties, and not by any unilateral actions.[52] Later, the Reagan Administration supported the traditional United States position on Jerusalem, opposing efforts initiated in Congress in 1984 to force the government to move the American embassy from Tel Aviv to Jerusalem.[53]

Israel's actions were also condemned overwhelmingly by the UN. On 20 August 1980, the Security Council declared Israel's action null and void, and urged those UN members who maintained embassies in Jerusalem to withdraw them to Tel Aviv. Nearly all of these member states, especially those from Latin America, complied with this resolution. Similarly, the Vatican and a number of Christian leaders also condemned Israel's annexation.[54] While the Knesset was still considering the bill on annexation, the Vatican submitted to the UN Security Council a detailed statement reiterating its position on Jerusalem and the Holy Places.[55]

In the 1980s, the Vatican continued to urge that Jerusalem's status be reviewed by the world community. While no longer insisting on a *corpus separatum,* the Holy See continued to stand fast on a number of points:

1. Jerusalem should be protected by a special, internationally guaranteed statute that would ensure that no one religious group would dominate and discriminate in any way against other religious groups.
2. The statute should recognize Jerusalem's unique status and character, especially as a religiously pluralistic community, and this character should not be changed by any unilateral action.
3. The Holy Places throughout the Holy Land, not only those in Jerusalem, should be protected by international guarantees.
4. The complex rights acquired in the course of centuries by the various religious communities relative to the shrines and other religious institutions in the Holy Land should be protected.
5. The continuance and development of relgious, educational, and social activity by each religious community should be ensured.
6. Both the civil and religious rights of all religious communities throughout the Holy Land should be protected on an equal basis.

7. Peace and stability in the Holy City and Holy Land being essential to protect both human lives and the Holy Places, there can be no true, lasting peace and stability until there is a just solution to the Arab-Israeli and Palestinian-Israeli conflicts, a solution that provides for the mutual recognition of all parties' rights and legitimate security needs.

8. Failure to bring true and durable peace in the Middle East will inevitably lead to more strife and war, endangering the peace not only of the Middle East but ultimately of the entire world.[56]

Conclusion

While most of the principles enunciated above are reasonably clear, some—such as those calling for an internationally guaranteed "statute" and "civil" (as well as religious) rights—remain vague and imprecise. Moreover, the Holy See has not tried to spell out how any or all of these principles are to be implemented. This vagueness has been largely due to the uncertainties of the situation, and to the Vatican's desire to retain some flexibility in its position. Nevertheless, it is clear that Israel's position—continued Israeli sovereignty over all of Jerusalem, with only limited religious rights for the Holy Places and quasi-diplomatic status for religious officials operating within the Holy City—is greatly at variance with the position of the Vatican and the majority of the members of the world community. Further, as long as Israel controls Jerusalem, potential differences between the Vatican and the Arabs over the future of Jerusalem have been and will probably remain muted.

In the years prior to the 1967 war, when the Arabs and Israelis shared control over the Holy City, the Jerusalem issue played a less important role in the Arab-Israeli conflict than did such more pressing problems as the plight of refugees, water, and borders. However, Israel's occupation of East Jerusalem in 1967 and her claim to the entire city brought the Jerusalem question to the fore once again, and it remains one of the most dangerous bones of contention between Israel and the Arabs.

Most countries opposed Israel's annexation of East Jerusalem and called upon Israel to withdraw from that area (as well as from nearly all territories occupied as a result of the 1967 war), in return for Arab acceptance of a peace settlement. The Vatican feared that Israel's plans to "Judaize" the city and its environs would weaken the position of the Christians living there and lead to a Christian exodus. Moreover, the Vatican and most other states became convinced—as moderate Arabs had warned—that no Arab or Palestinian leader would be able to make a peace with Israel that did not include the return of at least a substantial part of East Jerusalem, and especially the part containing the major Muslim Holy Places. The recent spread of Islamic fundamentalism has generated stronger pressures than ever before within the Arab and Muslim worlds to win back East Jerusalem. On the other hand, almost all Israelis, including most of the Israeli "doves" who have advocated major concessions on the Palestinian and territorial issues, oppose yielding any part of the Holy City.

Because of this incompatibility, it has been widely contended that the Jerusalem question should be put on a back burner until all other issues have been resolved. While there is some justification for this contention, it is unwise to ignore the issue altogether. Even if, by some miracle, the Arabs, Palestinians, and Israelis were able to negotiate a solution to their other problems, such a solution could not be finalized until an acceptable agreement had been reached concerning the future of East Jerusalem. Although the Jerusalem dispute remains the most difficult to resolve, the world community should make every effort to discourage any of the parties, particularly Israel, from taking actions that might further diminish the chances of reaching a mutually acceptable solution.

It has been suggested that only a united city under Israeli control can ensure freedom of access to all religious shrines by all religious groups. Actually, however, Israel's retention of all of Jerusalem is not essential to ensure such freedom of access. It was the lack of a peace settlement before the 1967 war, not the mere political and physical division of Jerusalem, which resulted in barbed wire along the armistice demarcation lines and interference with the right of Jews to visit those Holy Places under Jordanian control. Many urban centers are split by international borders, such as those along the United States' Canadian and Mexican borders, without impeding freedom of movement.

After the 1967 war, however, the problem of access was reversed: all Jews were now free to visit their shrines, but millions of Muslims and Christians living in Arab and Muslim states that did not recognize Israel and consequently forbade their citizens from traveling to Israel found it impossible to visit their sacred shrines. Therefore, only the conclusion of a just and durable peace between Israel and her neighbors could effectively ensure freedom of access for all religious groups to all Holy Places, not only in Jerusalem but throughout the Holy Land.

Besides, while Jerusalem is now united physically, it remains divided in other critical ways. Studies by Meron Benvenisti, a former deputy major of Jerusalem, and Israeli professor Alex Weingard show that, although there are no physical barriers in Jerusalem, the Arab and Jewish inhabitants remain sharply divided economically and socially, with little communication between them outside the marketplace. According to Benevisti, they live within "two separate systems with little integration," and with widespread discrimination against the Arabs: "Take away Israeli coercive powers, and the city splits on the ethnical fault line." And according to Professor Weingard, Jerusalem, despite nearly twenty years of Israeli rule, is not a truly "united city."[57]

In short, merely maintaining the physical unity of the Holy City will not promote a just and durable solution to the religious, political, and human problems involved in the Jerusalem question, much less to the overall Arab-Israeli conflict. Such a solution would ultimately require not only division of the Holy Land between the Israelis and Palestinians, but the political division of Jerusalem itself. For example, Israel's control could be extended at least to the Wailing Wall and to the old Jewish sector of the city (with the possibility of other mutually agreeable border changes), while the remainder of the Old City could become the capital of a Palestinian state, voluntarily united with Jordan in some acceptable form. An internationally guaranteed statute could be negotiated that would, as the Vatican has proposed, recognize Jerusalem's unique status and character; ensure the protection of and ready access to all Holy Places throughout the Holy Land; guarantee the rights acquired in the past by the various religious communities; prevent any one religious group from dominating or discriminating in any way against other religious groups; and ensure equal civil and religious rights for all religious communities.

Of one fact we may be sure: No religious group or state will benefit in the long run if, because of the failure of the contending parties to make sufficient concessions, the City of Peace continues to be a critical obstacle to peace in the Middle East and a major source of strife, bloodshed, and wars in that important area of the world.

Notes

1. Constantine Rackaukas, *The Internationalization of Jerusalem* (Washington, D.C.: The Catholic Association for International Peace, n.d.); Richard P. Stevens, "The Vatican, the Catholic Church and Jerusalem," *Journal of Palestine Studies* (Spring 1981): 105; and Fred J. Khouri, *The Arab-Israeli Dilemma* 3d ed. (Syracuse: Syracuse University Press, 1985), p. 102.

2. Rackaukas, *Internationalization*, p. 9.

3. Pincas E. Lapide, *Three Popes and the Jews* (New York: Hawthorne, 1967), pp. 269ff, and Stevens, "Vatican," pp. 102ff.

4. Lapide, *Three Popes*, pp. 269ff, and Rackaukas, *Internationalization*, p. 9.

5. Silvio Ferrari, "The Vatican, Israel and the Jerusalem Question (1943–1984)," *Middle East Journal* (Spring 1985): 317.

6. UNSCOP Report to the UN General Assembly (1947) 1: 40ff, 59ff.

7. Ferrari, "Vatican," pp. 318ff, and Meron Benvenisti, *Jerusalem: The Torn City* (Minneapolis: University of Minnesota Press, 1976), pp. 3ff, 53.

8. UN, Official Records of the Second Session, UN General Assembly Ad Hoc Political Committee, 3d meeting, 29 September 1947, pp. 5f; 6th meeting, 6 October 1947, pp. 26ff; 8th meeting, 8 October 1947, pp. 44f; 18th meeting, 15 October 1947, p. 122; and Khouri, *Arab-Israeli Dilemma*, p. 49.

9. Khouri, *Arab-Israeli Dilemma* pp. 44, 49f.

10. Claudia Carlin, comp., *The Papal Encyclicals: 1939–1958*, (Raleigh, N.C.: McGrath Publishing Company, 1981), pp. 157ff.

11. Khouri, *Arab-Israeli Dilemma*, p. 103.

12. Carlin, *Papal Encyclicals*, pp. 161f.

13. Ferrari, "Vatican," p. 321.

14. Carlin, *Papal Encyclicals*, pp. 163ff.

15. Ferrari, "Vatican," p. 321.

16. UN Conciliation Commission for Palestine, A/838, 19 April 1949, pp. 4ff; Rackaukas, *Internationalization*, pp. 38, 47ff; and Khouri, *Arab-Israeli Dilemma*, p. 104.

17. Khouri, *Arab-Israeli Dilemma*, p. 104.

18. Ibid., pp. 104ff, 111; *New York Times*, 23 October 1962; *UN Survey of Opinion*, 4 October 1949, p. 3; 18 October 1949, p. 12; 25 October 1949, p. 12; and UN Documents A/838 (19 April 1949) and A/927 (23 June 1949).

19. UN, Official Records of the Fourth Session, General Assembly, Ad Hoc Political Committee, 44th meeting, 25 November 1949, pp. 257ff; 45th meeting, 25 November 1949, pp. 268ff; 46th meeting, 26 November 1949, pp. 277ff; and Khouri, *Arab-Israeli Dilemma*, p. 106.

20. Khouri, *Arab-Israeli Dilemma*, pp. 107ff.

21. Ibid., pp. 109ff; Stevens, "Vatican," p. 107; and UN, Official Records of the Fifth Session, General Assembly, Ad Hoc Political Committee, 73d Meeting, 7 December 1950, pp. 469ff.

22. Lapide, *Three Popes*, p. 288; Stevens, "Vatican," p. 107; and Rackaukas, *Internationalization*, pp. 49f.

23. Khouri, *Arab-Israeli Dilemma*, p. 111, and *Middle East International*, September 1978, p. 27.

24. *Jerusalem Post*, weekly ending 6 July 1985; Lapide, *Three Popes*, pp. 345ff; *Commonweal*, 3 March 1978, p. 133; and *The Tablet*, 17 September 1983.

25. *New York Times*, 29 June, 14 July 1967; and Khouri, *Arab-Israeli Dilemma*, pp. 112f.

26. Ferrari, "Vatican," p. 323; *The Tablet*, 15 July 1967; and Benvenisti, *Jerusalem*, p. 264.

27. *New York Times*, 30 July 1967, and Khouri, *Arab-Israeli Dilemma*, p. 113.

28. *The Tablet*, 15 July 1967.

29. Benvenisti, *Jerusalem*, pp. 265ff.

30. Department of State *Bulletin*, 31 July 1967, p. 149.

31. Ibid., 28 July 1969, p. 76.

32. Khouri, *Arab-Israeli Dilemma*, pp. 115f, and *New York Times*, 21 December 1967.

33. Ferrari, "Vatican," pp. 324f, and Stevens, "Vatican," pp. 108ff.

34. Ferrari, "Vatican," p. 325, and O. Kelly Ingram, ed., *Jerusalem: Key to Peace in the Middle East* (Durham, N.C.: Triangle Friends of the Middle East, 1978), p. 30.

35. Editorial, *L'Osservatore Romano*, 22–23 March 1971, quoted in *The Tablet*, 3 April 1971, and *New York Times*, 25 July, 1 November, 1971.

36. *The Middle East and North Africa, 1982–83* (London: Europa Publications, 1982), pp. 63f, and *The Tablet*, 3 April 1971, quoting *L'Osservatore Romano* for 22–23 March 1971.

37. *New York Times*, 25 July 1971.

38. *The Tablet*, 3 April 1971.

39. *New York Times*, 24 December 1971, and Ingram, *Jerusalem*, pp. 30f.

40. *The Church in the Holy Land (Nobis Animo)*, 24 March 1974 (Washington, D.C.: U.S. Catholic Conference, 1974), p. 3.

41. Quoted in *The Tablet*, 3 April 1971.

42. *New World*, 3 May 1974, p. 18.

43. Benvenisti, *Jerusalem*, p. 269; *Israeli Digest*, 4 February 1972, p. 8; Ferrari, "Vatican," p. 328; and Golda Meir, *My Life* (New York: Putnam's, 1975), pp. 406ff.

44. *The Tablet*, 18 March 1972; Ferrari, "Vatican," pp. 326ff; and *New York Times*, 7 November 1977.

45. Khouri, *Arab-Israeli Dilemma*, pp. 360ff, 415, 420ff, 446ff, 483ff; *New York Times*, 7 July 1974; and *Washington Post*, 6 October 1980.

46. Khouri, *Arab-Israeli Dilemma*, pp. 374ff, 415, 447ff, 483ff; *New York Times*, 9 June 1974; and *Le Monde*, 6 November 1973.

47. Khouri, *Arab-Israeli Dilemma*, pp. 377, 420ff, 447.

48. Ferrari, "Vatican," pp. 328ff; Stevens, "Vatican," pp. 109ff; and *New York Times*, 22 October 1984.

49. *Origins:* NC Documentary Service, 30 September 1982, pp. 242ff; *New York Times*, 7 July 1974, 22, 23 December 1975, 14 February 1978, 26 March 1979, 11 November 1980, 28 June 1982, and 22 October 1984; *Washington Post*, 6 September 1982; Stevens, "Vatican," pp. 109ff; *Middle East International* (September 1978): 26; *Middle East Perspective* (October 1979): 1; and *The Church in the Holy Land*, pp. 1, 6.

50. The full text of the speech is to be found in *New York Times*, 3 October 1979.

51. UN Document S/13679, 4 December 1979.

52. *Presidential Documents XVI*, 20 October 1980, pp. 2194, 2305, and 3 November 1980, p. 2462.

53. Statement by Undersecretary of State Lawrence Eagleburger before the Senate Foreign Relations Committee, 23 February 1984. Quoted by *Mideast Observer* (Washington, D.C.), 1 March 1984, p. 2, and *New York Times*, 11 March, 29 March, 2 April 1984.

54. Stevens, "Vatican," p. 110, and *Saudi Report* (16 April 1984): 7.

55. *New York Times*, 1 July 1980, and *Testimony Before the Senate Foreign Relations Committee* (Washington, D.C.: U.S. Catholic Conference, 1984).

56. *Testimony* . . .

57. Meron Benvenisti, *Jerusalem: Study of a Polarized Community*, quoted in *Palestine Congress of North America, PNCA Monthly* (May 1984): 8f, and *The Other Israel: Newsletter of the Israel Council for Israeli-Palestinian Peace* (February–March 1984): 6.

··✦◀☙ 7 ☙▶✦··

The Holy See and Jordan

JOSEPH L. RYAN, S.J.

Introduction

In the context of "The Vatican, Islam, and the Middle East," an exposition of the relations between the Holy See and the Kingdom of Jordan is certainly appropriate. Jordan is a country with a predominantly Muslim population, but with a small though significant number of Christians (approximately 4 percent, according to some estimates), whose history goes back to earliest Christian times.

While Jordan is not, in comparison with other Arab countries, outstanding in terms of either population or natural resources, it is strategically located, bordering on Saudi Arabia, Iraq, and Syria, and lying very close to both Egypt and Lebanon. Because of its strategic relationship with Palestine and Israel—the West Bank and East Jerusalem, which had been under Jordanian control since 1948 under an arrangement legalized in April 1950, were occupied by Israel during the June 1967 war—Jordan has been deeply involved in the Palestine problem. And, in view of the 11 February 1985 accord between Jordan and the Palestine Liberation Organization, the country seems likely to continue to play a role of prime importance in the future. Jordan is also significant, if hardly unique, finally, for its ties to the West, especially for its close relationship with Great Britain since the First World War.

The continuity of King Hussein on the throne from 1952 to the present is also pertinent. In his long tenure, unequaled among the other Arab countries of the Middle East, one can study the effect of extended political leadership. In fact, it is through the prism of comparison with the other Arab countries that the significance of the special relationship between Jordan and the Holy See can be most clearly seen.

When Jordan became independent in 1946, it contained only the area on the east bank of the river.* In 1948, as a result of the decision to set up the state of Israel, a war ensued, after which East Jerusalem and the West Bank became part of Jordan. After the June 1967 War, Israel occupied the West Bank and Jerusalem, but its sovereignty over these areas has never been recognized. In the Rabat Conference of 1974, the Arab states officially declared the Palestine Liberation Organization to be the sole representative of the Palestinian people, a decision which was accepted by Jordan. On 11 February 1985, the PLO and Jordan made what was then regarded as a historic agreement on a common approach to a peace process, which would involve, after the achievement of peace, a special relationship between Jordan, East Jerusalem, the West Bank, and Gaza.[1]

The background thus sketched in, we are ready to review the contacts, particularly at a high level, between the Holy See and Jordan from 1953 to the present. It remains for the political and diplomatic historian to examine these events in the wider political context, as well as to attempt a detailed analysis of the significance of each contact.

1953: King Hussein Visits Pope Pius XII

Hussein, proclaimed king by the national assembly on 11 August 1952, had been crowned on 2 May 1953, a regency council having been constituted for the interval until the king reached his majority. In October 1953, King Hussein went to the Vatican. Although he had never met Pius XII before, he knew of the pope's sympathy and active concern for the Palestinian people and for Palestine. In 1946, for example, Pius XII had received a delegation of Christian and Muslim Palestinians seeking his assistance in the conflict they saw about to take place. In addressing them, the pope recalled that on several occasions he had condemned the persecution of Jews by fanatical anti-semites. Nevertheless, he went on to say, he would exert himself to the end "that justice and peace in Palestine will become a beneficient reality of the commonweal, creating . . . an order which guarantees to each one of the parties of the conflict the security of existence."[2]

Later, on 1 May 1948, before fighting had actually broken out,

---

*In any discussion of Jordan, it is important that one be scrupulous about area and date: Is one referring to the East Bank or the West Bank alone, or to both together? Is the time-frame after 1948, after 1967, or in the future? The writer will strive for such clarity and precision in the pages that follow.

Pius XII issued his encyclical *Auspicia Quaedam*, touching on peace in the world including a solution of the Palestinian question.[3] He brought up the Palestine problem again in his address to the college of cardinals on his feast day (2 June 1948).[4] On October 24 of the same year, he addressed the issue of Palestine in another encyclical, *In Multiplicibus Curis*.[5] And on 15 April 1949, in his encyclical *Redemptoris Nostri*,[6] the pope spoke strongly and movingly of the conditions among the Palestinians as a result of the fighting, alluding to "the well-founded complaints of those who very legitimately deplore the profanation of sacred buildings, holy images and of welfare homes, as well as the destruction of peaceful convents of religious communities." The pope spoke also of "the ardent appeals of very many refugees of all ages and every condition who have been forced by this disastrous war into strange areas where in transient camps they lead a life of exiles, exposed to misery, to contagious disease and to all kinds of dangers."[7] Early in 1949, the Pope had established the Pontifical Mission for Palestine to provide immediate and generous assistance of all kinds for those Palestinians who had been forced from their homes as a result of the 1948 fighting and its aftermath.[8]

Further, in 1950 Pius XII had received warmest Christmas greetings from Abdullah, king of Jordan and grandfather of the future king Hussein.[9] (Seven months later, while entering al-Aqsa Mosque in Jerusalem with Prince Hussein at his side, Abdullah was shot and killed by assassins.) Before any personal meeting between the pope and King Hussein, then, there were numerous reasons to expect favorable relations between them.

Upon King Hussein's arrival at the Vatican, Pius XII received him in a papal library with the greatest cordiality. The pope commended to his royal visitor both his loyal Catholic subjects and the institutions of the Catholic Church within his kingdom.[10] Thus, in the first year of his reign, this young king of the line of Muhammad the Prophet met the seventy-seven-year-old leader of the Catholic Church, the pope who had guided the Church through World War II and beyond. Although Jordan did not have then—nor has it had since—formal diplomatic relations with the Holy See, this would be the first of many personal contacts between the king and a pope.

January 4–6, 1964: Pope Paul VI Visits the Holy Land

The pope's 1964 visit to the Holy Land was an extraordinary spectacle, full of color, pomp, and religious sentiment, a journey with important (and delicate) ecumenical, interfaith, and political implications.[11] The first word of the pilgrimage had come at the end of the address Pope Paul gave to conclude the second session of the Second Vatican Council on 4 December 1963: "We have decided to make a pilgrimage to the land of Jesus Christ, . . . to go to Palestine . . . to honor the first mysteries of our faith, the Incarnation and Redemption."[12] This momentous announcement, which came as a complete surprise, evoked enthusiastic applause within St. Peter's Basilica—and, outside, raised enormous world-wide expectations.[13] In Jordan, a central preparatory committee with several subcommittees was set up to plan for the pope's coming. Although the committee was to be chaired by the prime minister, the king himself presided personally over several of the sessions, inspiring the preparatory work for this extraordinary event with his dynamic interest and regal presence.[14]

On January 4 the pope arrived at the Amman airport where he was received by King Hussein and welcomed by the patriarchs and clergy. He then travelled by car to the Jordan River, crossed it to visit Jericho, and then drove to East Jerusalem, at that time under Jordanian sovereignty. All the while, King Hussein flew above him in his helicopter.[15] As the papal cortege approached Jerusalem, its arrival announced by the appearance of the king's helicopter, the enthusiasm of the dense throngs of people was unbounded. The pope's car turned in at the Damascus Gate, where elaborate welcoming ceremonies had been carefully planned for this historic event. However, the enormous crowd, surging forward in an outburst of joyful, noisy welcome, broke through the barriers and surrounded the car, preventing any further movement. The other dignitaries were engulfed in this human wave and scattered, since any thought of proceeding with the ceremonies was out of the question. Finally, police and guards were able to free the pope's car and allow him to take refuge nearby in the sixth station of the Way of the Cross. After a short while, order was restored and the pontiff continued his approach into the city.[16]

In Jerusalem, the Pope venerated the Holy Sepulchre and met with Orthodox and Catholic patriarchs. On 5 January, he was driven north to Samaria, through Nablus and Jenin, where again he received such an extraordinarily enthusiastic reception, from Muslims and Christians alike, that his cortege was delayed an hour in reaching the Israeli border. Crossing it, the pope went on to Megiddo, where he was greeted by Israeli president Zalman Shazar. After visiting Nazareth and Carpharnaum, the Pope returned by way of Mount

Tabor, Naim, and Ramleh to Jerusalem, crossing from Israeli West Jerusalem into Jordanian East Jerusalem at the Mandelbaum Gate. That night, the pope had his first meeting with Patriarch Athenagoras of Constantinople. On 6 January the pope visited Bethlehem, then returned to Jerusalem where he met Patriarch Athenagoras again and was greeted by the civil, religious, and consular authorities of East Jerusalem, including a delegation of Muslims.[17] The pontiff then drove from East Jerusalem to Amman, with the king again escorting him by helicopter. At the airport in Amman, finally, the pope and king exchanged cordial farewells.

The statements of both the king and pope relative to this visit are of more than a little interest. On 2 January—two days before the Pope's arrival—King Hussein held a press conference in Jerusalem for the journalists who had come to cover the pope's visit. In his prepared statement, the king welcomed the journalists, and assured them that all of Jordan awaited "this holy visit with enthusiasm, respect, and warmest affection."[18] He also said that, in the face of changes in life and thought in our time, changes such as the world had never before seen, it was necessary that religious leaders make clear, amid worldwide confusion, the simple and immortal truths of existence as incorporated in the great religions. Modern progress, he went on, was an accomplishment, not a negation of our spiritual heritage. Faith in God, the dignity and equality of men, the intrinsic value of the individual, love, peace, charity, mercy, and the essential unity of the human race—these are the invaluable legacy of our religious beliefs.

We rejoice, the king continued, that the pope's pilgrimage will awaken· anew the flame of faith in God in the hearts of all believers. And that pilgrimage had another deep meaning, too, underlining as it did the fundamental affinity of the two great religions, Islam and Christianity. He allowed that one of the most unfortunate of all historical deformations is the false idea that such irreconcilable differences exist between Christianity and Islam that it is impossible to resolve them. He pointed out that few people realize that these two great religions owe much to one another. Thus, the king said, Islam believes in and venerates the divine nature of Jesus Christ as emanating from the spirit of God, and its Quran has only veneration for and faith in the divine message of Christ.

So, too, the king pointed out, few people realize that more than a thousand years ago, when Islam and Christianity were seriously threatened by the shadows of nonreligious and even antireligious philosophic thought, it was Averroes, Avicenna, and other eminent Muslim theologians and scholastics who reconciled religion and philosophy and had an impact on the Christian theologians who faced the same kind of attacks, an influence evident in the prodigious works of St. Thomas Aquinas. There was, he continued, a fundamental affinity between the two great faiths, and the violent conflicts of the past could not and did not represent the true spirit of either. Rather, these conflicts had to have been the harvest of ignorance, intolerance, and human ambitions—the weakest elements of human nature, and alien to the sublime spirit of the two great beliefs.

It is our most lively hope, the king said, that, as the Vatican makes its laudable efforts to unite the Christian family, the visit of the pope to the Holy Land will begin a new epoch of authentic understanding and fruitful cooperation between two great religions, facing and overcoming the scepticism and indifference that have proceeded from the modern scientific revolution and the accompanying materialism. The king stated it as his ardent hope that religious men of the two great faiths would work toward this historic and blessed objective.

King Hussein assured the media representatives that during their stay in Jordan they would see the faithful of the two great religions living side by side as good citizens of a united people:

> We do not preach tolerance, we live and suppose it. Such has been our inalienable history and tradition despite all the vicissitudes which have shocked this part of the world all these long centuries.

The king recalled the example of the seventh century Caliph Omar, who on entering Jerusalem refused to pray in the Church of the Holy Sepulchre for fear that certain fanatics, misinterpreting their religion, might profit from the occasion to build a mosque on this great Christian site.

Finally, the king spoke of the despoliation of the Palestinian people and of his hope that the conscience of the Christian world, once made aware of this human tragedy, would not fail to give support to this just cause.[19]

Two days later, on 4 January, addressing the pope after the latter had deplaned at Amman airport, King Hussein, speaking in English without a text, warmly welcomed the pope:

May I, on behalf of all members of the Jordanian family, the united family, Muslims and Christians alike, and on behalf of all Arab peoples as well as of all people believing in God, express our deepest gratitude and sincere welcome to Jordan, the Holy Land. This is a great occasion which we will always remember and wish it to be a success in every way. . . . We hope that the members of the Jordanian family will be able to show in a very little way . . . our admiration and respect to you as a man, as a great leader in the service of humanity, the service of peace and the service of humanity striving to attain a better future. As a man of God, we welcome you, Sir, to Jordan, the Holy Land.[20]

The Pope replied in English:

Your Majesty! We are most appreciative of your kindness in coming to welcome us personally on our arrival in your Kingdom. Our visit is a spiritual one, a humble pilgrimage to the sacred places. . . . At each of these venerable shrines, we shall pray for that peace which Jesus left to his disciples. . . . Your Majesty, we know, ardently desires peace and prosperity for all peoples, and for all the nations of the world.[21]

The pope then cited the first Epistle of Peter: "Search for peace and pursue it; honor every one, love your brothers, fear God, honor the king," before concluding:

May God grant our prayer, and that of all men of good will, that, living together in harmony and accord, they may help one another in love and justice, and attain to universal peace and true brotherhood.[22]

On January 6, his brief but exhilarating journey over, the pope again met King Hussein at the departure ceremonies at Amman airport. The king, speaking in Arabic for which an English translation was provided, said that he hoped that the pope's great heart had been enkindled with warmth by the outflowing affection of the entire Jordanian family:

You have asked me to work with you and with other governments for the peace of the world; my response is that I shall do it with all my heart and strength, working for justice as well, for no peace is durable without justice.[23]

The king said that, for centuries, pilgrims to the Holy Places had been welcomed in the spirit of the caliph Omar, who, on his arrival in Jerusalem, accorded religious liberty to all: "It is in this spirit that we welcome your Holiness, the greatest of pilgrims." The king went on to assure the pope of his determination to protect the Christian Holy Places, on which converge with special predilection the hearts of Christian pilgrims from the whole world.[24]

Paul VI, speaking in English, thanked the king profoundly for his welcome and wished him, in the words of the pope's patron, the Apostle Paul, "grace, peace, and prosperity."[25]

The exchange of farewells completed, Paul VI flew off to Rome,[26] carrying with him a joyful memory of Jordanian hospitality which he would be happy to recall later. Some indication of his concern that his visit to the Holy Land be not readily forgotten is evidenced by several initiatives he took in the form of the following permanent establishments:

- The Institute at Tantour, for theological research for Christian scholars of all countries and religious groups;
- The House of Abraham, for poor pilgrims and later also a center of renewal for bishops, priests, and seminarians;
- The Institute of Paul VI "EPHPHETA" for deaf-mute Arab children;
- The University of Bethlehem, for young Arabs desirous of undertaking higher studies in their own land. This university was a product of the Vatican's preoccupation with Palestinian emigration, which weakened the presence of the Christian community in the Holy Land. This concern was poignantly expressed in Paul VI's apostolic exhortation *Nobis in Animo*, 25 March 1974;
- The Arab Housing Society at Beit Hanina, for young Arab families looking for homes in the vicinity of Jerusalem which they might eventually come to own;
- The Notre Dame Center of Jerusalem, a "home of the pope," to give Christians remaining in the homeland of their ancestors a center of unity and resources, of life and culture, where Orientals and Latins might meet fraternally together in complete equality; and to provide priests and religious a place of retreat.[27]

Paul VI's visit to the Holy Land also provided him an occasion to confirm his interest in the Pontifical Mission for Palestine. One of the prelates who accompanied him on the pilgrimage was Monsignor Joseph T. Ryan, president of the Pontifical Mission for Palestine and national secretary of the Catholic Near East Welfare Association. On 6 January, at the Apostolic Delegation in Jerusalem, the pope gave Monsignor Ryan a gift of $5,000 for the work of the pontifical mission. He also recalled how, when he had been pro-secretary of state at the Vatican, he had actively cooperated in the creation of the pontificial mission.[28] Ten years later, on the twenty-fifth anniversary of the mission, Paul VI would recall, in a letter to the new president of the mission, Monsignor John G. Nolan, that the action of the mission had "constituted one of the most eloquent witnesses of the interest which the Holy See bears for the well-being of the Palestinians who are particularly dear to us." The pope went on to speak of the new task awaiting the mission in view of the changing circumstances.[29]

1964: King Hussein Visits the Vatican

On 11 May 1964, King Hussein came to the Vatican on an official visit, in return for the pope's trip to Jordan. The king was received with great cordiality by Paul VI, who said: "We shall never forget the royal welcome you accorded us on your recent pilgrimage to the Holy Land . . . ." Then, after commenting on the development of Jordan under the king, the Pope added:

> Your Majesty can be sure that the Catholics of Jordan will loyally do everything possible to promote the progress of the country, especially in the initiatives in the domain of education and social work, hoping that they will always enjoy their civil rights and the favor of Your Majesty . . . ."[30]

The warm memory of the affectionate Jordanian hospitality was recalled again, a little less than a year later, when Pope Paul was on his way to Bombay for the Eucharistic Congress there in December of 1964. Pausing at Beirut, the pontiff addressed the people assembled to greet him and spoke of the Arab world having "shown to us on our journey to the Holy Land its characteristically spontaneous welcome, joyous popular enthusiasm and religious veneration, which have stayed with us and will remain forever in our memory."[31]

1967: King Hussein Visits the Vatican

The next visit of King Hussein to the Vatican took place under very different circumstances, and was clouded by an atmosphere of sadness and tension. The Arab-Israeli War of 1967, preceded by intense international agitation, had brought almost instant humiliation to the Arab states involved. With the Israeli occupation of East Jerusalem and the West Bank, Jordan had lost all effective control over its lands west of the Jordan. On 8 June 1967, Pope Paul VI sent telegrams to the heads of state of Egypt, Jordan, Iraq, Israel, and Syria:

> . . . We beg you to adhere to the request of the United Nations for an immediate cessation of hostilities, in order that hopeful reasonable and honorable negotiations may replace the violence of arms, and that peace, so greatly desired, may be reestablished.[32]

The war was followed by intensive international diplomatic and political activity. At the United Nations, the General Assembly discussed possible action. King Hussein arrived to present his country's case on 24 June. Ten days later, the General Assembly voted on two propositions, neither of which could have brought any satisfaction to the Arab states.[33]

On his return home, the king visited British Prime Minister Wilson on 3 July, French President De Gaulle the following day, and Italian President Saragat the day after that. That same day he was granted an hour's audience with Pope Paul VI, but no account of their meeting has been published.[34] However, in the years immediately following the war of June 1967, the Vatican and Jordan were similarly engaged in protesting conditions brought about by the Israeli government in the occupied territories, including Israel's efforts to "Judaize" the city of Jerusalem.[35]

1978: King Hussein Visits the Vatican

When the king was received in audience on 29 April 1978, the pope extended a most cordial welcome, recalling once again the warm and spontaneous welcome accorded him by the king and the people of Jordan during the papal pilgrimage to the Holy Land. The pope expressed the hope that the social and economic development being undertaken in Jordan would always be accompanied by "a deep religious and moral spirit in all citizens, and especially in the younger generation, from the first moment of their education." Paul VI then reiterated a frequent papal sentiment that "the Catholic community of Jordan will make its contribution to that progress."[36]

Referring to the Holy See's preoccupation with peace in the Middle East, the pope acknowledged the king's efforts on behalf of peace and expressed his hope that the leaders involved might

> come decisively to grips with the crucial issues of the conflict, and through wisdom and good will find a speedy solution to them. . . . In particular, we once again express the hope that a just end may be put to the sad situation of the Palestinians, and that Jerusalem, the Holy City for the three great monotheistic religions . . . may really become the "high place" of peace and encounter for peoples from every part of the world, who, in spite of their diversity, are joined in brotherhood by the worship they offer to the one and only God.[37]

In reply, King Hussein spoke of the satisfaction of renewing with the pope "a strong and old tie," and alluded to the pope's wisdom and inspiration.[38]

> Your historic pilgrimage to the Holy Land, fifteen years ago, acquainted you with my country and people directly and opened new horizons of understanding and spiritual association between us. We have always had, deep in our culture and national heritage, a profound and sincere respect for the values you embody, the message you carry and the role you undertake in the world and for mankind.
>
> In my country, Jordan, as in the larger Arab region, Islam and Christianity have interacted positively and creatively to mold our history and enrich our spirit. The brotherhood of Muslim and Christian Arabs has been fostered and reinforced by the special place that the Christian religion occupies in the Islamic doctrine as well as by the trials and sufferings through which both Muslim and Christian Arabs have gone in their long history.
>
> Nowhere has this been more strikingly reflected than in the suffering of the Palestinian Arabs. To their uprooting and dispossession has been added now the suffering of occupation for over eleven years. They have watched with their own eyes, and with them the

whole Arab world and the world at large, the mutilation of their beloved and holy Jerusalem.

The message of peace which Your Holiness carries extends to the Middle East. All the peoples of this religion need and want peace. But a lasting and viable peace must be rooted in justice and human dignity, not in military imposition and suppression.

Your Holiness is an inspiration of peace and of justice. Jordan cherishes its association with what you represent and serve. We wish to strengthen this tie and sincerely cooperate in the service of the Almighty and of mankind.[39]

At the close of the meeting, the pope presented King Hussein with an olive branch as a testimonial of their common desire for peace. The branch was from an olive tree the pope had received during his visit to the Holy Land, and which now grew in the garden of the pope's villa in Castel Gondolfo.[40]

This was to be the last encounter between Paul VI and King Hussein. On his next visit to the Vatican, King Hussein would call on Pope John Paul II.

1978: King Hussein Meets Pope John Paul II

King Hussein traveled to Europe in December 1978, and on 15 December, he visited Pope John Paul II. *L'Osservatore Romano* carried no statements by the pope or the king on the occasion of their meeting, although photographs of the two seated together were published. However, the chief of the Royal Jordanian Court, Abdul-Hamid Sharaf, declared that the king had examined with the pope various world problems, especially those of the Middle East. There had been agreement that the area could not know stability and a just peace until such time as there was a complete and just settlement for all parties in the conflict, including the Palestinian people. The situations of Jerusalem and Lebanon were also examined, it was revealed.[41]

1979: Jordanian Minister Ibrahim Meets Cardinal Casaroli

On 7 May 1979, Mr. Hasan Ibrahim, Jordanian minister of state for external affairs, who was attending the Arab meeting in Fez, visited Rome. At the Vatican, he met Secretary of State Cardinal Casaroli, and discussed with him the matter of Jerusalem and the Holy Places.[42]

1 September 1980: King Hussein Visits Pope John Paul II at Castel Gondolfo

January 1982: Vatican Mission Visits Amman

The good relations between the Holy See and the government of Jordan, including the closeness of their positions on Jerusalem and the Palestinians, were affirmed, according to the Italian paper *Corriere della Serra*, by the visit to Amman of a pontifical mission headed by Archbishop Mario Brini, secretary of the Congregation for the Oriental Churches. This Vatican delegation took part in the installation ceremonies of the new Latin-rite auxiliary bishop in Amman, Bishop Selim Sayegh, and met with King Hussein on 19 January. A Vatican communique reported that Archbishop Brini described to King Hussein the Holy See's efforts toward realizing a just solution of the crisis in the Middle East, including its extensive investment in education and in the areas of social and humanitarian work, which were "intended to encourage Palestinians to remain in their native country and to preserve their own identity."[43]

King Hussein thanked the pope for sending the mission, and for handwritten letter (the pope sent to the king) which, the king said, he had read with emotion. The king also spoke of the Arab position regarding the problem of Jerusalem, "underlining the importance of the Holy See's point of view, that the Holy City become a place for the fraternal encounter of the members of the three monotheistic religions." The king also expressed his appreciation for the persevering efforts of Pope John Paul II for peace.[44]

June 1982: Muslim-Catholic Consultation in Amman

On 7–10 June 1982, a Muslim-Catholic Consultation took place in Jordan. At the invitation of the Crown Prince Hassan, a delegation from the Holy See, headed by Archbishop Jean Jadot, president of the Secretariat for Non-Christians, came to Amman. Also taking part were Monsignor P. Rossano and Dr. M. Sabanegh of the secretariat, and Monsignor Ceirano of the Apostolic Delegation in Jerusalem. The Jordanian delegation included Crown Prince Hassan; Sheikh Abdul Aziz al-Khayyat, dean of the Shari'a College; Sheikh Ibrahim al-Qattan, chief justice; Dr. Nasser al-Din al-Assad, president of the Al al-Beit Foundation; Dr. Walid Tash, director general of the ministry of foreign affairs; and Dr. Taysir Toukan, Jordanian ambassador to Italy.

Both sides detailed their interest in developing relations with the other, and discussed possibilities of further meetings. The Vatican delegation was cordially received by King Hussein.[45]

John Paul II Receives Joint Jordanian-Palestinian Delegation

The most recent high-level contact between the Holy See and Jordan took place on 1 July 1985, when a joint Jordanian-Palestinian delegation briefed Pope John Paul II on the 11 February 1985 Jordanian-Palestinian accord and on moves to achieve a just and durable peace in the area, in accordance with international legitimacy. According to Petra, the Jordanian News Agency, the pontiff supported the joint move. The delegation, headed by Deputy Prime Minister Abdul Wahab al-Majali, included Foreign Minister Taher al-Masri, PLO executive committee member Jawid Ghussein, and PLO central committee member Khaled al-Hassan.[46]

Afterwards, the delegation—which had already had talks with Italian and French leaders—met Cardinal Casaroli, the Vatican secretary of state. According to Petra, the cardinal expressed the Vatican's support for the Jordanian-PLO moves, and pledged to increase its international contacts to promote Jordanian-Palestinian efforts for peace in the Middle East. The week before, the Palestinian news agency Wafa announced that PLO Chairman Yasser Arafat had sent a letter to the pope about living conditions in Palestinians refugee camps in Lebanon.[47]

The Vatican support for the Jordanian-PLO accord was publicly mentioned again later in the same month by Mr. Taher al-Masri, Jordan's foreign minister. Speaking on Jordan's foreign policy at a conference of Jordanian expatriates, Mr. al-Masri lauded the position of the EC (European Community) countries and the pope's enthusiasm for the 11 February 1985 accord, saying that the positive response of these countries "strengthens our position with the United States, since they are allies."[48]

September 1985: Vatican Representatives Participate in Muslim-Christian Conference in Amman

At the invitation of Crown Prince Hassan, Cardinal Francis Arinze, president of the Vatican Secretariat for Non-Christians, led a second delegation from the Vatican to Amman on 28–30 September 1985 to participate in a Muslim-Christian conference. Other Catholic participants included the Reverend Thomas Michel, S.J., of the office of Islam in the Secretariat for Non-Christians, and the Reverend Mourice Borrman, P.B., a Catholic scholar who has written extensively on Islam.[49] This was a continuation of a previous conference held on 15–18 November 1984 at St. George's House, Windsor Castle, England, in which Archbishop (later Cardinal) Arinze and Cardinal Franz Koenig took part.[50]

Possibilities for Diplomatic Relations Between the Holy See and Jordan

The Holy See has formal diplomatic relations with a number of Arab and Muslim countries. In some cases, this involves an ambassador at the Vatican; in others the ambassador is resident elsewhere.

The question of official diplomatic relations between the Holy See and Jordan, however, appears to be inextricably linked with the question of possible diplomatic status between the Holy See and Israel. Closer Vatican ties with Israel have of course been constantly and publicly urged for years by some Christians as well as Jews, particularly in the United States. Pope Paul VI met with Israeli President Zalman Shazar at the Israeli border in January 1964. Later, the pope received at the Vatican the Israeli Foreign Minister Abba Eban, in 1969; Prime Minister Golda Meir, in 1973; and Foreign Minister Moshe Dyan in 1978. In addition, Pope John Paul II met with Israeli Foreign Minister Yitzhak Shamir in 1982 and Prime Minister Shimon Peres in 1985. None of these meetings with Israeli officials, however, has seemed to awaken any readiness in the Holy See to establish formal diplomatic relations with Israel.

The difficulties thereof were treated publicly in May 1983 at an American National Workshop on Christian-Jewish Relations. Monsignor William Murphy, undersecretary in the Pontifical Commission on Justice and Peace, stated at that time that "the Holy See would have no problem in principle" with establishing diplomatic relations with Israel; however, there were certain "problems that the Holy See would first want to have resolved."[51] Paramount among these, of course, is the problem concerning Israel's permanent borders.

Were it not for these obstacles to Vatican-Israeli relations, including the question of borders, it would seem that the Holy See would have no difficulty in accepting a request by Jordan for diplomatic status. Certainly, Jordanian-Vatican contacts have been far more cordial than comparable Israeli-Vatican contacts. As to the latter, one need only recall the great sensitivity in Israel to some Vatican statements and actions. The visit of Prime Minister Golda Meir to the Vatican, for example, was surrounded with Vatican caution and Israeli concern. After the visit, Meir herself revealed that Paul VI, early in their conversation, had remarked that "he found it hard to understand how the Jewish people, which should be merciful, behaves so fiercely in its own country."[52] And after Pope Paul II received Yasser Arafat on 15 September 1982, Israeli—and other Jewish—reaction was immediate and fierce. A Vatican communique of that time described an angry outburst of an unnamed Israeli official (believed by some to have been Prime Minister Begin)—in which the speaker described himself as having "little regard for the person of [the] Pope."[53]

A later statement by the Holy See relevant to the possible recognition of Israel was made on 25 June 1985, when the Vatican commission for religious relations with Jews issued a paper entitled "Notes on the Correct Way to Present Jews and Judaism in Preaching and Catechesis in the Roman Catholic Church."[54] The text referred to Jews in the Diaspora—that is, those outside the original land of Israel—as "preserving the memory of the land of their forefathers at the heart of their hope." The document then invited Christians "to understand this religious attachment which finds its roots in Biblical tradition, without however making their own any particular religious interpretation of this relationship." It also declared that "the existence of the State of Israel and its political options should be envisaged not in a perspective which is itself religious, but in their reference to the common principles of international law."[55]

Not surprisingly, the "Notes" drew immediate and strongly negative criticism from several leading Jewish organizations. The International Jewish Committee on Interreligious Consultations, for example, branded the above-mentioned passage as emptying "modern Israel of any possible religious significance for Christians," while "nothing is said about Israel's right to exist or the justice of her cause."[56]

Certainly, the text was a disappointment to those who shared the view, expressed shortly beforehand, that Vatican diplomatic recognition of Israel should be a goal of Catholic-Jewish dialogue.[57] Yet, as knowledgeable observers have pointed out, the establishment of Vatican-Israeli diplomatic relations is a matter that requires more than goodwill on the part of the Holy See.[58] The Holy See's views and actions regarding Jerusalem, the Palestinians, and Lebanon illustrate the Vatican's wider priorities, and the serious obstacles to Vatican-Israeli diplomatic recognition that these pose.[59]

Jordan, for its part, would strongly favor diplomatic status, and there is clear evidence of Jordanian initiatives in this direction. In 1972 and again in 1973, the question was informally raised by the government of Jordan with the apostolic delegate, and in 1973 Jordan was ready to name an ambassador to the Holy See.[60] Nevertheless, the absence of diplomatic relations does not mean that Jordan lacks opportunities for high-level contacts with the Holy See. The Greek Catholic archbishop Saba Youakim and the Latin auxiliary bishop and vicar general, Selim Sayegh, both reside in Amman, and the Latin partiarch James Beltritti, who resides in Jerusalem, regularly visits the Latin parishes in Jordan and occasionally meets with King Hussein.

The apostolic delegation in Jerusalem also provides opportunities for contact. Created by Pope Pius XII on 11 February 1948, the delegation represents the Vatican in Israel, Jordan, and Cyprus. Although also pro-nuncio to the government of Cyprus, the apostolic delegate represents the Holy See to the Catholic churches in Israel and Jordan, *not* to their governments. The current apostolic delegate, Archbishop Carlo Curis, lives in Jerusalem but maintains contact with Jordanian officials though his secretary, Monsignor Raouf Najjar, who resides in Amman and who, as president of the Catholic court, has many contacts in Jordan.[61] In addition, the government of Jordan also has access to the Vatican through the Jordanian ambassador to Italy.

Formal diplomatic relations between Jordan and the Holy See, then, seem to be blocked indefinitely because of the obstacles to official Vatican-Israeli relations. Despite these obstacles, however, ample opportunity exists for other Vatican-Jordanian contact short of formal recognition.

The Unique Character of Vatican-Jordanian Relations

In addition to Pope Paul VI's historic visit to Jordan, there have been seven visits of King Hussein to the Vatican, two ministerial-level Jordanian visits to the Vatican, and three high-level Vatican visits to Amman. Given this amity, one might reasonably ask why Jordan would be interested in cultivating pro forma relations with the Holy See? There is more than one answer.

First, most of the world is desirous of having good relations with the Holy See. It has worldwide moral authority; it represents in some very real—if somewhat difficult to define—sense Roman Catholics everywhere; it has a long history of far-sighted diplomacy; and it has shown, especially since World War II and most particularly since Vatican Council II, a remarkable openness to the world. Further, because of the Holy See's extensive and constant communication system, involving bishops, priests, and lay Catholics everywhere in the world, the Vatican has constant access to a wealth of grassroots information, a knowledge of which is of obvious value to many states.

Second, Arab countries have traditionally cultivated the Vatican. Thus, in the early 1950s, for example, those Arab states that wished to have UN resolutions regarding Jerusalem implemented recognized the important influence of the Pope on certain Catholic countries. Thus, a Palestinian Arab delegation visited Pope Pius XII in the summer of 1946, and in 1947 Lebanon and Egypt became the first Arab states to establish diplomatic relations with the Holy See.[62]

Further, Jordan has very special reasons for wishing to have good relations with the Holy See. The Palestinian question and the issue of Jerusalem are preeminently the concern of Jordan, more so than of any other single Arab country. Hence Jordan, above all other Arab states, would and does look to any international institution with the potential of assistance and support for Jordanian imperatives. Since 1948, few other non-Arab countries have given the consistent and conspicuous support to the Palestinian cause and the issue of Jerusalem as has the Holy See. (This is not to say, of course, that the interests and policies of the Holy See and of Jordan are identical, or even necessarily similar.)[63] A striking case in point was the dramatic visit of Pope John Paul II to the United Nations headquarters in New York City on 2 October 1980. With the eyes of the world on him as he addressed the community of nations gathered before him, John Paul singled out for special mention, apart from the Argentinian-Chilean dispute, only three specific international issues: the Middle East crisis, Lebanon, and the Palestinians.[64]

Further, from the beginning of the rise of Zionism, both the Holy See and Jordan have been concerned, each from the point of view of its own interests, with the establishment of an exclusive Jewish state in Palestine, and with the possible effects of that state's policies on Palestinians and the city of Jerusalem. When Catholic—or other—Palestinians are oppressed or dispossessed, the Holy See is quickly informed. An apostolic delegate in Jerusalem told me once how he would begin his talks to visiting groups of Christian pilgrims to the Holy Land by pointing out that the Catholic Church in the Holy Land is overwhelmingly Arab and Palestinian.[65]

Precisely because Palestine *is* the Holy Land, Jordan has since 1948 shared with Christians a common concern over that troubled territory—a concern that is at the very heart of Jordan's central internal and external strategic problem: Jerusalem and the Palestinians of the West Bank. While Jerusalem has an extraordinary importance for all Arabs and Muslims, that is not the issue; what are at issue internationally are the other aspects of Jerusalem, including its Christian heritage vis-à-vis the Jewish state and international Christian concern, of varying intensity, about that heritage. Hence, in this matter Jordan seeks Christian support from every quarter—from the Orthodox patriarch in Constantinople, for example, and from the Archbishop of Canterbury, and especially from the Holy See, due to its extraordinary position and international prestige.[66]

Finally, there is the character of King Hussein, and a background, including an education abroad, that disposes him, perhaps more than most other Arab leaders, to an active, confident, and effective demeanor in presenting his country's case before the bar of the world. His impact in addressing audiences in the West over many years is one example; another is the image of the young, energetic monarch receiving Pope Paul VI at the Amman airport, and then, by helicopter, escorting the Pope's motor cortege to Jerusalem. King Abdullah's open and frankly favorable views of Christianity must also have deeply influenced his royal heir and grandson.

These personal relations and contacts between the Holy See and Jordan in the course of thirty-two years are all the more impressive when one compares Jordan in this respect with all other predominantly Muslim Arab countries of the Middle East (Lebanon being a special exception). Not only has the personal leadership of these countries not been continuous, but—apart from President Sadat of Egypt, who visited the Vatican twice in 1976 and 1978, and King Hassan II of Morocco, who visited there in 1980—no national leader of Egypt, Syria, Iraq, Saudi Arabia, the Gulf, or North Africa has had similar personal contact with the Holy See (or, for that matter, had the same deep reasons for having it). Both Paul VI (in 1967) and John Paul II (1979) have visited Turkey,[67] but no other Arab country in the Middle East has been visited by a modern pope, except for Lebanon, where Pope Paul briefly touched down at the Beirut airport en route to India, and, of course, Morroco, where John Paul made his spectacular visit to Casablanca on 19 August 1985.[68]

If it is in Jordan's interest to cultivate good relations with the Vatican, though, surely the converse is true: it is very much in the interest of the Holy See to establish and maintain good relations with Jordan, not only because of Jordan's special role regarding Jerusalem and the West Bank, but also because of the Christians—and particularly the Catholics—living on both sides of the Jordan.[69]

Further, the character and attitudes of Pope Paul VI have been an important factor. He was a person of great personal sensitivity, with an extraordinary receptivity to other cultures and modes of thought and religious sentiment. His active interest and initiatives as Pope regarding Islam are astonishing, if not entirely surprising.[70] He had contacts with scholars sympathetic to Islam, and a long-standing and profound friendship with Professor Louis Massignon, the eminent French Islamic scholar whose spirit had such great influence in the Catholic Church before and during the Council.[71] Further, the Pope had shown a personal interest in Islam when he was substitute in the secretariat of state in the Vatican, and afterwards, when he was archbishop of Milan.[72] As pope, Paul VI wrote the famous encyclical on dialogue, *Ecclesiam Suam,* and even before the end of the Council, he founded the Secretariat for Non-Christians, in which the only specialized section, begun under his direction, is that devoted to Muslims.[73] Further, the text on Muslims in the Vatican II declaration on the Church bears a striking resemblance to the wording on this matter in Pope Paul's encyclical, *Ecclesiam Suam.*[74]

On many occasions, Pope Paul spoke of Muslims with great warmth and sensitivity. He met Muslim leaders on his various travels, and during his pontificate welcomed the establishment of diplomatic relations with many countries with a majority or significant numbers of Muslims.[75] And Muslim leaders were cordially received at the Vatican.[76]

The spirit of Pope Paul VI continues. His successor, Pope John Paul II, while receiving the members of the Secretariat for Non-Christians a few months after his election, spoke of Pope Paul VI's love for non-Christians and his interest in their concerns, and added that he was sure some people were wondering if this new pope would pay as much attention to them as did his predecessor.[77] And the record shows that Pope John Paul II has indeed continued the initiative of his predecessor regarding Islam. His first remarks on Islam were given in his address to the Catholic community in Ankara on 30 November 1979; and in the next fifteen months he gave no fewer than seven other discourses to Muslim communities in various parts of the world. One commentator has observed that "never, in so short a time, has any Pope demonstrated so much interest in Muslims,"[78] and another that "no Pope in history has devoted so much attention to the relations between Christians and Muslims as has Pope John Paul II."[79]

Further, John Paul II has been remarkable not only in the number of contacts he has made but also in the quality of the detailed, positive reflection he has brought to bear regarding Islam. His Ankara address has been called "the principal document of the Church with regard to Islam after paragraph three of *Nostra Aetate* [the statement from Vatican Council II]."[80] Too, on the issue of the Palestinians and Jerusalem, John Paul has continued to vigorously articulate the policies of Paul VI.[81] Finally, in an event that would provoke much controversy, he received Yasser Arafat, chairman of the Palestinian Liberation Organization, on 15 September 1982.[82]

Conclusion

From the perspective of both Jordan and the Holy See, there have been several reasons of substance and of personality to account for the many cordial and fruitful contacts made during the long reign of King Hussein. The extraordinary visit of Pope Paul VI to the Holy Land and the seven visits of King Hussein to the Vatican, along with other high-level visits to the Vatican and to Jordan—the totality of these personal contacts makes Jordan, in its relations with the Vatican, unique among all the predominantly Arab Muslim states of the Middle East. To the simple fact of these exchanges must be added the personal cordiality involved and, more fundamentally, the basic political sympathy of the Holy See to Jordan, as compared with the uncertain and sensitive nature of Vatican-Israeli relations.

Since the absence of Vatican diplomatic relations is a serious public issue with regard to Israel, it is clear that, until the obstacles to Vatican-Israeli diplomatic status can be resolved, Jordan and the Holy See will have to continue to have contacts at other levels.

Notes

Abbreviations

AAS:	Acta Apostolicae Sedis	OM:	Oriente Moderno
DC:	Documentation Catholique	POC:	Proche Oriente Chretien
MD:	Moniteur Diocesain		

1. "Palestinians will exercise their inalienable right of self-determination when Jordanians and Palestinians will be able to do so within the context of the formation of the proposed confederated Arab states of Jordan and Palestine." Text of the Jordanian-PLO agreement reached on 11 February 1985, as released by the Jordanian government 23 February 1985. (*Jordan Times*, 24 February 1985.)

[On 19 February 1986 King Hussein announced that he would no longer be able to "coordinate politically with the PLO leadership in seeking a negotiated peace in Israel." Hussein attributed the collapse of the talks to Arafat's refusal to accept UN Security Council Resolution 242, which recognizes Israel—Ed.]

2. Fred J. Khouri, *The Arab-Israeli Dilemma*, 2d ed. (Syracuse: Syracuse University Press, 1976), p. 111, and *DC* (1946), col. 1117. For the text of the pope's talk to the Arab High Committee of Palestine on 3 August 1949, see *DC* (1948), cols. 1185–86. The pope refers to this visit in his encyclical *In Multiplicibus Curis* (*DC* [1948], col. 1474).

3. *AAS* (1948), 169–72 (Reference is to pp. 170–71), and *DC* (1948), cols. 705–8.

4. *DC* (1948), col. 774.

5. *AAS* (1948), 433, and *DC* (1948), cols. 1473–78.

6. *AAS* (1949), 161–64, and *DC* (1949), cols. 641–44.

7. *AAS* (1949), 162, and *DC* (1949), col. 642. See also *Le Pape et la Tragedie Palestinienne* (Mission Pontificale pour la Palestine, 1950).

8. For an early account of the work of the Pontifical Mission for Palestine, see *POC* 1 (1951): 119–24.

Even before the establishment of the Pontifical Mission for Palestine, Monsignor Thomas J. MacMahon, who would be its first president, was active on behalf of Palestinian rights. In 1947, he presented a letter to the General Assembly of the United

Nations on behalf of Cardinal Spellman of New York, asking that in the settlement of the Palestinian question the secular rights of the Christians of the Holy Land be clearly guaranteed. (*Catholic News of New York*, 17 May 1947 and *DC* (1947), cols. 911–16.)

The pontifical mission has offices in Jerusalem, Beirut, and Amman, and a liaison office in Rome in addition to its headquarters in New York. Monsignor John G. Nolan is its president. Monsignor Antonio Franco, head of the delegation of the Holy See at the United Nations, stated before the Special Political Committee of the General Assembly on November 9–18, 1983 that, since 1949, the Pontifical Missions for Palestine has distributed more than $150,000,000 in aid. (*L'Osservatore Romano* [English edition], 19 December 1983, pp. 11–12.)

9. A. M. Goichon, *Jordanie Reelle*, 2 vols. (Paris: G. P. Maisonneuve & Larose, 1967, 1972), 1:360, 30.

10. *L'Osservatore Romano*, 21 October 1953, p. 1, and *POC* 3 (1953): 371–72. The king received in audience the Latin patriarch of Jerusalem and the Melkite archbishop Assaf, who were able, "in an atmosphere of complete understanding, to discuss different questions concerning the life of religious institutions in the country." *L'Osservatore Romano*, 22 October 1953, p. 1, contains a photograph of the pope and the king with the king's entourage.

11. *Jerusalem: le Moniteur Diocesain du Patriarchat Latin de Jerusalem*, January–February 1964, Nos. 1–2, Annee XXX. *Paul VI en Terre Sainte* (Jerusalem: Imprimerie du Patriarchat Latin). This double issue contains a very detailed description of the entire papal visit, with many texts. *POC* 14 (1964): 1–71 also provides extended coverage of the pope's visit, also with many texts. See also Ludwig Kaufmann, S. J., *Recontre en Terre Sainte* (Lausanne: Editions Rencontre, 1964).

12. *MD*, p. 2.

13. Ibid., p. 3.

14. Ibid., p. 14.

15. Ibid., pp. 26–33.

16. Ibid., pp. 34–38, and *DC* (1964), col. 164.

17. *MD*, 101–4.

18. *POC* 14 (1964), pp. 48–52.

Note: In the absence of the original text, which was in English, this free translation from parts of the French text in *POC* is used temporarily.

19. Ibid.

20. *MD*, p. 28.

21. *AAS* (1964), pp. 159–60, and *MD*, p. 29.

22. *MD*.

23. *MD*, pp. 107–8. The text given here is a translation from the French.

24. Ibid.

25. Ibid., p. 109, and *AAS* (1964), 179–80.

26. *MD*, pp. 110–14. On his return to Rome, the pope received as enthusiastic a welcome as he had received at the Damascus Gate in Jerusalem.

27. *Annuaire de l'Eglise Catholique en Terre Sainte* (Jerusalem: Franciscan Printing Press, 1984), p. 10.

28. *MD*, p. 104.

29. The letter is dated 16 July 1974. *L'Osservatore Romano*, 29–30 July 1974 (English ed.), and *DC* (1974), p. 758. See also Paul VI's Apostolic Exhortation, *Nobis in Animo*, on the needs of the Church in the Holy Land (*DC* [1974], pp. 351–54).

30. *AAS* (1964), 446–47; *POC* (1964), p. 243; *DC* (1964), cols. 709–10; *L'Osservatore Romano*, 11–12 May 1964 (English ed.); and *OM* (1964), p. 326. Papal decorations were given to members of the king's entourage. (*AAS* [1964], 479.)

31. *DC* (1965), col. 3.

32. *AAS* (1967), 642.

33. Khouri, *Arab-Israeli Dilemma*, p. 274.

34. *AAS* (1967), 642; *OM* (1967), p. 499; Goichon, *Jordanie Reelle*, 2:675; and *Le Monde*, 8 July 1967.

35. Thus *L'Osservatore Romano* of 22 March 1971 wrote that "a very grave state of affairs is being created against legality on the basis of the logic of the 'accomplished facts' . . . It is impossible to avoid experiencing a profound apprehension towards such grave charges."

36. *AAS* (1978), 335–36; *L'Osservatore Romano* 30 April 1978, 11 May 1978 (English ed.), p. 2; and *DC* (1978), p. 456.

37. *DC*, p. 456.

38. *L'Osservatore Romano*, 11 May 1978, p. 2.

39. Ibid.

40. Ibid. (for a photograph of this presentation).

41. *OM* (1979), p. 570, and *ar-Ra^y* (Amman), 16, 21, 22 December 1978.

42. *OM* (1979), p. 584, and *ar-Ra^y* (Amman), 15 May 1979, pp. 8–12.

43. *Servizio informationi*, SICO, Rome, March–April 1982; and *Corriere della Serra*, 21 January 1982.

44. *Corriere della Serra*, 21 January 1982.

45. Report of meeting.

46. *Jordan Times*, 2 July 1985, p. 1.

47. Ibid.

48. Ibid. 21 July 1985, p. 1.

49. Ibid. 29 September 1985, p. 3.

50. Report of the meeting.

51. *Boston Pilot*, 6 May 1983. Cited in George E. Irani, *The Papacy and the Middle East: The Role of the Holy See in the Arab-Israeli Conflict, 1962–1982* (Doctoral thesis, submitted to the Graduate School, University of Southern California, December 1984, p. 66. To be published by the University of Notre Dame Press.)

52. *Jerusalem Post*, 21 January 1973, and Irani, *Papacy*, p. 85.

53. Irani, *Papacy*, p. 88.

54. *L'Osservatore Romano* 1 July 1985 (English ed.), pp. 6–7.

55. Ibid.

56. *New York Times*, 25 June 1985.

57. *N.C. News Service* (Rome), 19 April 1985, "Vatican Recognition of Israel Called Goal of Catholic-Jewish Dialogue."

58. One of the most recent public rumors occurred in October 1984. It was reported from Rome that a group of Roman Catholic prelates, mainly Polish, headed by Archbishop (later Cardinal) Andrzej Deskur, a Pole and personal associate of Pope John Paul II, was urging the Pope to grant diplomatic recognition to Israel. (E. J. Dionne, Jr., "Ties to Israel Urged in Vatican," *New York Times*, 22 October 1984, p. 4.) The article also points out the reasons why such recognition is unlikely.

59. Irani, *Papacy*, pp. 51, 74, 78, 96.

60. Memorandum 27 November 1973, Apostolic Delegation, Jerusalem.

61. *Annuaire*, p. 9.

62. Khouri, *Arab-Israeli Dilemma*, p. 111.

63. For a comparison of the positions of the Holy See and the Arab states on Jerusalem, see Pietro Pastorelli, "La Santa Sede e il problema di Gerusalemme," *Storia e Politica*, Fasc. 1 (1982): 57–98.

64. *DC* (1979), p. 875. The pope's phrasing is worthy of particular attention. While not explicitly naming the Egyptian-Israeli peace moves (which the Holy See supported), he makes a clear reference to them and a strong comment on their limitations:

> It is my fervent hope that a solution also to the Middle East crisis may draw nearer. While being prepared to recognize the value of any concrete step or attempt made to settle the conflict, I want to recall that it would be of *no value* if it did not truly represent the "first stone" of a general overall peace in the area, a peace that, being necessarily based on equitable recognition of the rights of all, cannot fail to include the consideration and just settlement of the Palestinian question. (italics added)

65. Personal comment to the author.

66. King Hussein sent letters to the pope, the Maronite patriarch, and the Archbishop of Canterbury concerning the Judaization of Jerusalem. *OM* (1971), p. 333; *Le Monde*, 17 April 1971; and Goichon, *Jordanie Reelle*, 2:963.

67. Pope Paul visited Turkey 25–26 July 1967. (*DC* (1967), cols. 1377–91.)

68. Pope John Paul's visit to Morocco on 19 August 1985 is an event of extraordinary importance in the development of Muslim relations with the Catholic Church.

> The Pope received one of the most enthusiastic welcomes of his papacy last night from the Muslim youth of Morocco when the main football stadium in Casablanca erupted in delight at his arrival. . . . Hardly a Catholic country had greeted him as warmly.

(Clifford Longley, "Pope makes appeal for unity to Muslims," *Times* (London), 20 August 1985, p. 1.)
An English translation of the pope's address, which was delivered in French, may be found in *Origins*, 29 August 1985, pp. 174–76, or in *L'Osservatore Romano* (English ed.), 16 September 1985, pp. 6–8.

69. For a detailed discussion of the Holy See's policies regarding Jerusalem and the Palestinians, cf. Irani, *Papacy*, p. 96.

70. For articles on Pope Paul and the Muslims, see: Maurice Borrman's, "Le Pontificat de Paul VI et les Musulmans," *Islamochristiana* 4 (1978): 1–10; Michel Lelong, "Le Pontificat de Paul VI et l'Islam," in *Paul VI et la Modernite dans l'Eglise: Actes du Colloaue*

Organise par l'Ecole Francaise de Rome (Rome, 2–4 juin 1983), (Rome: Ecole Francaise de Rome, Palais Farnese, 1984), pp. 837–49; Thomas Michel, "Christianity and Islam: Reflections on Recent Teachings of the Church," *Encounter* (Documents for Muslim-Christian Understanding) (Rome: Pontifical Institute for Arabic and Islamic Studies), February 1985, no. 112; and Yoakim Moubarac, "La Papaute et l'Islam de Paul VI," in *Recherches sur la Pensee Chretienne et l'Islam* (Beyrouth: Publications de l'Universite Libanaise, Section des Etudes Historiques XXII, 1977).

71. Borrmans, "Le Pontificat," p. 1, and Moubarac, "La Papaute," p. 394.

72. Moubarac, "La Papaute," p. 394.

73. Borrmans, "Le Pontificat," pp. 3–4, and Moubarac, "La Papaute," p. 396.

74. Borrmans, "Le Pontificat," p. 5.

75. Ibid., pp. 1–10.

76. Lelong, "Le Pontificat," p. 848, and Borrmans, "Le Pontificat," pp. 9, 19.

77. Lelong, "Le Pontificat," pp. 848–49, and *L'Osservatore Romano,* 7 May 1979 (English ed.), p. 4.

78. Rossano, p. 19.

79. Michel, "Christianity and Islam," p. 6.

80. Rossano, p. 18.

81. See Pope John Paul II's apostolic letter, *Redemptionis Anno* ("On the City of Jerusalem, the Sacred Patrimony of all Believers and the Desired Meeting Place of Peace for the Peoples of the Middle East"), *L'Osservatore Romano,* 30 April 1984, (English ed.), p. 6. See also Joseph L. Ryan, S. J., "Palestinian Rights: Resonances in the Life and Themes of Pope John Paul II," *Fifth United Nations Seminar on the Inalienable Rights of the Palestinian People* (New York: United Nations, 15–19, March 1982), pp. 147–59, and Robin Wright, "Strange Bedfellows: The Pope and PLO," *Washington Post* ("Outlook" section), 2 January 1982, pp. D1, D3. The latter discusses Palestinian-Vatican contacts before Arafat's visit.

82. *DC* (1982), p. 921, 1. For some reactions, see *DC* (1982), pp. 947–49, 1081.

··◄❧ 8 ❧►··

Egypt's Diplomatic Relations with the Holy See

Tahseen M. Basheer

The relationship between Egypt and the Vatican is unique. Its special quality stems from the fact that Egypt represents two great religious traditions, being both the historical center of Muslim learning in the Arab Islamic world and the seat of learning and practice of Orthodox Coptic Christianity. Egypt has the largest Muslim population of all Arab countries, as well as the largest number of Christians; however, sheer numbers and quantity do not wholly represent Egypt's crucial role as the continuous center of Muslim learning and practice, with such great religious institutions as the Azhar Mosque, nor its place in the Orthodox Christian Coptic tradition of "the church of Alexandria and the five cities"—the long historical and ideological evolution of Christianity in Egypt through a rooted national church.

Egypt's relationship with the Vatican (which of course represents the temporal and spiritual authority of the Roman Catholic world) seems to have solidified in the twentieth century after a period of fluctuations. Egypt and the Vatican established diplomatic legations in 1947, and full embassies in the 1960s. During this time, there have been no great problems, and such differences as have arisen have been resolved through courteous and patient diplomacy.

The Egyptian-Vatican relationship reflects the historical equilibrium in Egypt between the realm of Christianity and the realm of Islam. It also echoes "the unwritten entente cordialle" between the Coptic Orthodox Church and the Vatican, which led to the strife that had divided the Orthodox Church in Egypt and the Melkites since the Council of Chalcedon in A.D. 451. The Egyptian-Vatican relationship has also relieved any tensions between the Roman Catholic orders and churches in Egypt and the native Egyptian Orthodox Copts. Intense proselytism on the part of the Roman Catholics has given way to a spirit of respectful coexistence, in which both sides acknowledge that true charity is rooted both in fidelity to Christ and a respectful recognition of the other's traditions. In short, in a world challenged by the threat of nuclear holocaust, famine, and social and racial injustice, Egypt and the Vatican have learned that more joins them in the common destiny of a free and stable world than divides them in the area of differing religious beliefs and practices, differences long overshadowed by the stern imperatives of history.

Mode of Research

Little has been written or published in any language on the historical relationship between the Vatican and Egypt. The reason for this would appear to reflect the diplomatic *modus operandi* of quiet and patient relations. There have been no sharp exchanges between the two states, and minor problems are handled with sensitivity and finesse. Each side keeps the issues raised in strict confidentiality, and when a problem eludes immediate solution it is consigned to protracted discussion over time. This *modus operandi* is very effective, but it leaves but little documentary material for the scholar to work with. In order to collect data, I conducted off-the-record interviews with most of the Egyptian ambassadors who had served in the Vatican, as well as in-depth interviews with a number of Orthodox, Catholic, and Muslim religious leaders. I also consulted the reports of the Egyptian Foreign Ministry, which represents the Egyptian side of this diplomatic exchange.

The Vatican also has interaction with Egyptian institutions outside the government, including the Catholic Coptic Church of Egypt, the various Catholic orders operating in Egypt, the Coptic Orthodox Church of Egypt, Al-Azhar University, and the Muslim community in general. This Muslim-Christian dialogue and Orthodox-Catholic dialogue, although non-governmental, have an impact upon official relations.

The Egyptian-Vatican diplomatic relationship floats on the ever-changing currents of history. I will deal with some of these currents as lurking perceptions of the past.

Some Past Perceptions

In Egypt, with its ancient recorded history, the past is always present; nevertheless, in a dynamic society, even deeply entrenched perceptions undergo change in relevance, emphasis, and impact. I will now cite some of these past perceptions and review some of the modifications they have undergone in modern times.

The Continuous Crusades

The complex intermittent wars known as the Crusades, with their purpose of controlling Jerusalem and conquering Egypt, left Muslims with a deep feeling of unease regarding the Vatican and the various Roman Catholic missionary orders that penetrated the Egyptian countryside. Their activities were seen by some Muslims as an unwelcome attempt to Christianize the believers of Islam—as a new form of assault by an imperial power bent on changing the Islamic mind and "reforming" the Islamic value system. Coptic Christians shared this feeling, for all Egyptians, irrespective of their religion, tend to be suspicious of foreign activities geared at altering Egyptian belief systems. This attitude is ironic, since both Islam and Christianity came to Egypt from the outside, but Egypt has developed its own Muslim and Christian institutions, which have assumed an Egyptian character, gained deep respect, and are jealously defended against any outside intrusion. Historical changes have pretty much pushed to the sidelines this negative conception of the Vatican, but it is reactivated, at least to a degree, in times of misunderstanding.

Between The Coptic Orthodox Church and the Catholic Church: Ideological Differences

In the nineteenth century, the Coptic Orthodox Church reacted to the incoming Catholic Church with ambivalence, welcoming the support and understanding of fellow Christians on the one hand, but fearing the conversion of Orthodox Christians to Catholicism on the other. The Coptic Orthodox tradition of Egypt had been born out of long struggle and suffering, and suffered for years under the pressures of Rome. The Church of Egypt is very much a "church of martyrs," and has paid in blood for its resistance to outside pressures throughout its history. The spectre of theological quarrels and a smoldering hostility between Monophysites and Melkites still casts a certain negative light on the relationship between Orthodox and Catholics in contemporary Egypt. In particular, the issue of intermarriage tends to awaken these old fears.

One also senses the existence of lurking suspicions concerning the role of the several Catholic orders in Egypt, particularly the suspicion that the Jesuits have attempted to interfere in both political matters and in the affairs of the Orthodox Church. Such clouds of suspicion, however, cannot overshadow the long-established historical relationships between Egypt and its Catholic orders. A Franciscan library and church were founded in the seventeenth century in the heart of Gammaliya district, only a few yards from Al-Azhar University. A visit to that district, with the rumble of its intense trading activities, gives the visitor a taste of the basic tolerance of Egypt: mosques and churches of different denominations exist harmoniously side by side. Similarly, when one concentrates on mainstream attitudes, one finds many areas of shared beliefs and concerns. This has led, in time, to an equilibrium and dialogue between Muslims and Christians, as well as to dialogue between the Coptic Orthodox Church and the Catholic Church.

Historical Equilibrium Between Islam and the Catholic Church in Egypt

The hostilities that existed between Islam and the Catholic Church in medieval times have given way to a new equilibrium between the followers of these two great religions. Egypt is a Muslim country with a strong Orthodox community, and conversion to Catholicism is not common. Out of this realization has come a new understanding—an existential reality, if you will—as past fears have given way to new openness to dialogue. Egypt has welcomed Catholic schools, hospitals, medical services, and especially the devoted nurses of many Catholic orders. The initiation of diplomatic relations with the Vatican in 1949 (Egypt was the first Muslim country to do so) reflects the practical side of this new equilibrium.

Setting aside theological differences over the message of Christianity and the role of Christ, there is an inclination to respect and understanding for Christianity in the typical Muslim mind. This is perhaps easier to understand when one recalls that belief in Christ is an inseparable part of Muslim faith. The Quran states: "Thou wilt surely find the nearest of them in love to the believers are those who say 'We are Christians'; that, because some of them are priests and monks, and they wax not proud. We gave unto him [Jesus] the Gospel. And we set in the hearts of those who followed him tenderness and mercy *(ra'fatan wa rahma)*".

In addition, since the early 1960s there has been new understanding of Islam in the Catholic Church. This ecumenical spirit is reflected in *Nostra Aetate:* "The Catholic Church rejects nothing which is true and holy in these religions. She looks with sincere respect on those ways of life and conduct, those rules and teachings which, though differing in many particulars from what she holds and sets forth, nevertheless often reflect a ray of that Truth which enlightens all men." The declaration of the Second Vatican Council stated:

Upon the Muslims, too, the Church looks with esteem. They adore one God, living and enduring, merciful and all-powerful, Maker of heaven and earth and Speaker to men. They strive to submit wholeheartedly even to His inscrutable decrees, just as did Abraham, with whom the Islamic faith is pleased to associate itself. Though they do not acknowledge Jesus as God, they revere Him as a prophet. They also honor Mary, His virgin mother; at times they call on her, too, with devotion. In addition they await the day of judgment when God will give each man his due after raising him up. Consequently, they prize the moral life, and give worship to God especially through prayer, almsgiving, and fasting. Although in the course of the centuries many quarrels and hostilities have arisen between Christians and Muslims, this most sacred Synod urges all to forget the past and to strive sincerely for mutual understanding. On behalf of all mankind, let them make common cause of safeguarding and fostering social justice, moral values, peace, and freedom (*Nostra Aetate*).

The Egyptian nationalist movement asserted Muslim-Christian dialogue as a basis of nationalism. In the 1960s, President Nasser said: "We obviously encourage and welcome contacts between peoples of the whole world with a view to realizing humanity's goals. We view the present situation favorably, being a people attached to religion: in our country religious instruction is obligatory—for Muslims and Christians alike. All religions preach the same noble principles; and rapprochement between the Catholic Church and other religions will, I hope, have humanitarian results—provided there is no mixing of politics and religion."

Many learned Muslim scholars, including Sheikh Shalttout, director of the Al-Azhar Mosque, supported this call to dialogue. An association called *al-ikha al-dini* [religious fraternity] was created to promote understanding, and a number of meetings took place. In March 1965, Cardinal Koenig of Vienna was invited by the late Sheikh

El-Bakkoury, director of the Al-Azhar University, to chair a public conference on the subject of "monotheism in the world today." In 1974, Cardinal Pignedoli and Monsignor Rossano accepted an invitation of the Higher Council for Muslim Affairs in Cairo, and in 1978 President Sadat visited Pope Paul VI to enlist his support for a just and comprehensive peace in the Middle East.

Interreligious dialogue involves serious and sensitive exchanges of belief, of course, and the writer feels that dialogue is most productive which concentrates on issues of potential agreement and cooperation, including such international issues as peace, justice, tolerance, and human development. Dialogue should also be free of missionary zeal in such places as Africa, inclining both Muslim and Christian teachers to conduct their activities in a friendly and harmonious manner. The recent speech by Pope John II to a Muslim audience in Casablanca gives testimony to the great potential of Muslim-Christian dialogue.

The Unwritten Entente Cordialle between the Catholic Church and the Coptic Orthodox Church

The schism of Chalcedon in A.D. 451 and its resulting hostilities have subsided in the course of centuries of historical interaction. The 1973 joint declaration by Pope Paul VI and Pope Shenouda III reflects this new spirit:

> Paul VI, Bishop of Rome and Pope of the Catholic Church, and Shenouda III, Pope of Alexandria and Patriarch of the See of St. Mark, give thanks in the Holy Spirit to God that, after the great event of the return of relics of St. Mark to Egypt, relations have further developed between the Churches of Rome and Alexandria so that they have now been able to meet personally together. At the end of their meetings and conversations they wish to state together the following: We have met in the desire to deepen the relations between our Churches and to find concrete ways to overcome the obstacles in the way of our real cooperation in the service of our Lord Jesus who "has given us the ministry of reconciliation, to reconcile the world to Himself" (2 Cor. 5: 18–20).

As a result of the visit of Pope Shenouda III to Pope Paul VI, a joint Catholic-Coptic commission was founded. The mandate of this commission is "to guide common study in the fields of church tradition, patristics, liturgy, theology, history and practical problems, so that by cooperation in common we may seek to resolve, in a spirit of mutual respect, the differences existing between our churches and be able to proclaim together the Gospel in ways which correspond to the authentic message of the Lord and to the needs and hopes of today's world."

The meetings of this commission have led to the adoption of certain general recommendations for example: "It is strongly urged there be avoided all words, articles, homilies, instructions and attitudes which wound each other's Churches, in their leaders or in their faithful."

This dialogue demonstrates that concentration on practical measures to solve concrete human problems fosters an atmosphere of cooperation. Theological arguments over points of doctrine still stir deep suspicion, but it is to be hoped that greater understanding and respect for the other's position may eventually lead to greater spiritual harmony. There is, meanwhile, evidence of the existence of an unwritten understanding that I call an *entente cordialle,* which brushes aside past fears to achieve better cooperation in the present.

The Relationship between the Vatican and Egypt

Both the Vatican, with its limited territory, and Egypt, with its dual historic role as both Arab-Afroasian power and leading center of Islam and Orthodox Christianity, extend their influence far beyond their territorial borders, with the result that their serene diplomatic relationship has benefitted both states. The Vatican has supplied Egypt with schools, hospitals, and humanitarian aid, but—above all—with support on humanitarian issues. During the difficult days of the 1967 Arab-Israeli war, for example, the Vatican gave medical supplies to Egypt and, along with the International Red Cross, played an important role in helping the Egyptian prisoners of war rescued from the inhumane conditions of the Sinai. Although Egyptian internal developments have affected prevailing conditions on such issues as the taxing of Catholic schools, nationalizing some hospitals, and modifying the law regarding marriage and divorce, patient diplomacy has been applied to and has effectively dealt with these problems.

Egypt faces the challenge of rapid change. It has to cope with the problems incident to the growth of a population which increases by more than a million every year, while continuing to try to meet the rising expectations of its population, which demands the best that life can offer in the shortest time possible. These are tremendous challenges, of course, but the will of the Egyptian people, undergirded by their belief in God and their trust in humanity, should be a potent factor in the struggle to answer them. Both Muslims and Christians (Catholic and Orthodox) must work to make human life more tolerable and human fraternity a living reality.

The Vatican, The Palestinians, and The Middle East Problem

The Vatican's stand on the Middle East problem and the right of Palestinian people to achieve self-determination is of great concern to the Muslims and Christians of Egypt, as it is to many people elsewhere. Egypt appreciates the Vatican's endorsement of the right of the Palestinian people to a national home, and endorses the Holy See's refusal to establish diplomatic relations with Israel until such time as there is a peaceful settlement to the Palestinian problem and an equitable resolution of the status of Jerusalem. There is great support for Pope John Paul II's April 1984 pastoral message on the Palestinian problem, as well as for the Vatican's position that any peaceful settlement to the Lebanese problem must safeguard the independence and sovereignty of Lebanon.

The feeling of millions of Arabs is echoed in this joint statement by Pope Paul VI and Pope Shenouda III carried in *L'Osservatore Romano*, 23 May 1973:

> As we rejoice in the Lord who has granted us the blessings of this meeting, our thoughts reach out to the thousands of suffering homeless Palestinian people. We deplore any misuse of religious arguments for political purposes in this area. We earnestly desire and look for a just solution for the Middle East crisis so that true

peace with justice should prevail, especially in that land which was hallowed by the preaching, death and resurrection of our Lord and Saviour Jesus Christ, and by the life of the Blessed Virgin Mary, whom we venerate together as the Theotokos. May God, the giver of all good gifts, hear our prayers, and bless our endeavours.

Dialogue Between the Vatican and Jewish Leaders

The Vatican's dialogue with Jewish leaders, which has among other things exonerated the Jews from responsibility for the death of Jesus Christ, raises three concerns among Arabs:

1. The fear that political considerations will lead to a review of the historical beliefs of the Eastern churches vis-à-vis the Jews. This is a matter of biblical interpretation, which must be distinguished from the mutual respect that should now exist between the Eastern churches and Jewry.
2. The concern that dialogue between Catholics and Jews may undermine the crucial Vatican stand on the rights of the Palestinians, the occupation of the holy city of Jerusalem by Israel, and the attempt by Israel to bypass its responsibility as the occupying power of Jerusalem, the West Bank, and Gaza.
3. Concern that dialogue between the Vatican and the Jews has not touched on the responsibility of Israel and Jewry for the Palestinians and their political rights, or the end of Israeli occupation of the West Bank, Gaza, and the holy city of Jerusalem. It is the feeling that any serious dialogue between Christians, Jews, and Muslims must focus on these issues. The last report by the Vatican commission for religious relations with the Jews (June 1985) included the following paragraph: "The existence of the State of Israel and its political options should be envisaged not in a perspective which is in itself religious, but in their reference to the common principles of international law." It is to be hoped that the moral responsibility of Jews regarding the rights of the Palestinians will be discussed in more detail, for this consideration represents the best test of any living dialogue among Arabs and Jews; Muslims, Chris-

tians, and Jews; and, ultimately, Israelis and Palestinians. Then and only then would we be able to say that spiritual values have had a successful application.

Conclusion

The diplomatic relationship between Egypt and the Vatican is a living example of what can be achieved by tolerance, human understanding, and the opening of serious dialogue. It is a constructive and positive force, on both the political and the spiritual level. May the different streams that flow into its main channel enrich and bless this relationship.

Part III

The Vatican and Muslim-Christian Relations

··◄◄§ 9 §►►··

Eastern Christians in
Contemporary Arab Society

Robert M. Haddad

The Arabic-speaking Christians of geographic or Greater Syria—
that area bounded by the Taurus Range, Sinai, the Mediterranean,
and the Syrian Desert, and consisting today of the states of Syria,
Jordan, Lebanon and Israel—are the principal subject of this study.
The followers of the Nazarene in contemporary Iraq, the easternmost
nation of the Arab world, comprise mere fragments: non-Chalcedonians whose forebears, from the fifth through the twelfth century,
cast their shadow over the entire Fertile Crescent; and Chalcedonians,
Orthodox and Uniate, most of them relatively new to the Mesopota-
mian scene. None of them, singly or together, is capable of playing
any historically meaningful role in the heavily Muslim society (variously Sunni and Shiʻi, Arab and Kurdish) in which they dwell. The
more substantial and influential non-Chalcedonians of Egypt, the
Copts, will be remarked on briefly toward the end of this presentation, but I leave any detailed discussion to those who know them
better. I shall hazard that, because the Copts and their Greater Syrian
coreligionists have not been shaped by quite the same historical circumstances, their respective futures may differ, although their roles
in determining the future may be similarly restricted.

As for the Arab world west of Egypt, Christianity in those regions
has long since shriveled into dust, there to mingle with the remains of
Tertullian, Augustine, and Donatus, whose devotees dealt Christianity
in western North Africa blows perhaps as damaging as those administered by the Vandals and later by the Muslims. In any case, the
absence of a numerically significant and historically continuous Christianity in North Africa west of Egypt keeps Arabic-speaking Christians from being a general issue (one hesitates to say "problem")
throughout the Arab, much less the Muslim, world. Christian concentration in the East, its notorious denominational disarray, and the

extra-Arab affinities of Arabic-speaking Muslims deprive arabophone Christians of a universal Arab relevance.

In a long essay published in 1970,[1] this author sought to place within a conceptual construct the Christians of the Fertile Crescent, with special emphasis upon the Christians of Greater Syria in early modern and modern times. I shall not deviate from the main outlines of that construct, for I remain convinced of its validity as well as its utility in understanding the events of the last fifteen years.

The Christians of Greater Syria may be described as "marginal communities," a status foisted upon them by the Islamic invasions of the seventh century and the establishment of a political order sustained by Muslim arms and dedicated to Muslim—or, in any event, non-Christian—ends. The history of these Eastern Christians, subsequent to the Muslim conquests, may be divided into four phases. The first can be labeled "The Twilight Age of Creative Christianity in Islamic Lands," and spans the years between the conquests and the mid-eighth century. Dominated for the most part by the Umayyad dynasty (661–754), this phase featured the rapid development of Islamic political organization—at the center of which stood the caliphate—but only the beginnings of the institutionalization of an Islamic theocracy which, in the opinion of neophyte non-Arab Muslims, was clearly implied by the Quran and the experience of the Medinan period (622–61). The Arab Muslims burst from their barren homeland provisioned with prophetic utterance deemed to be divine decree, but lacking the developed law and theology that alone could make explicit the implicit Quranic mandates and thus secure the bases for genuine theocratic institutions. It was precisely the embryonic nature of Islamic definitions that helped undermine the theoretic theocracy of the Medinan caliphate and, during the Umayyad era, lulled John of Damascus (d. 750?), the last Syrian Christian theologian with any strong claim to original achievement, to catalogue Islam as yet another Christian heresy—something of a latter-day Arianism. One may even assert that Islam's want of an intellectually distinct identity allowed the latitudinarian milieu in which the Melkite Damascene doctor could flourish and the Monophysite Arab poet al-Akhtal (d. 710?) display around his neck, ostentatiously and with impunity, a large cross as he recited his much-acclaimed verses before the caliph.[2]

The undoing of the Umayyad dynasty in Syria came around 754 at the hands of the Abbasids, whose rise to political preeminence owed more than a little to a burgeoning Muslim sentiment that had slowly rendered anachronistic the Umayyads' narrow Arab basis of power. Whatever else the Abbasid advent meant, it signified an imminent, deliberate attempt to create the Islamic theocracy, and could only presage the end of the creative age of Christians in the Muslim empire and the initiation of the second phase of their life under Islamic hegemony. This, "the First Age of Transmission" (*c.*750–*c.*950), saw a battery of Christian translators deliver up to their Muslim conquerors most of Hellenistic philosophy and science. Among Eastern Christians the creative vitality of John of Damascus yielded to the imitative intelligence of the Nestorian Arab, Hunayn ibn Ishaq (d.873), translator and compiler and symbol of a marginal community on the defensive, losing its struggle against a politically dominant Islam that was well on its way toward becoming the faith adhered to by a majority of the Middle Eastern population. The Greek thought earlier expropriated by Eastern Christianity would, with certain qualifications, become part of the Islamic patrimony and help to spawn many of the characteristic definitions of Islamic civilization. With these definitions articulated (the *shariʿa* before the tenth century, the so-called "medieval synthesis" before the close of the twelfth), meaningful participation in the intellectual and aesthetic as well as the political life of the Middle East and North Africa assumed fidelity to the faith of the Arabian Prophet, principally in its Sunni formulation.

Eastern Christians then entered the third phase of their history under Islam: "The Age of Intellectual Irrelevance" (*c.*950–*c.*1850), a period of unrelieved retreat before Islam and further atrophy of the creative instinct as all energy was directed toward preservation of the diminishing remnant—a remnant fated never to replenish itself, if only by virtue of laws (born of political dominance) that forbade proselytizing among and apostasy by Muslims.

The Christians' role during The First Age of Transmission testifies to the ability of a marginal community to influence the intellectual development of the politically dominant community when the latter's characteristic definitions are in the process of formation. The emergence of these salient definitions, however, further marginalized the politically subordinate community because of its inability to fully accept them. But although the Islamic definitions made more emphatic the marginality of Eastern Christians and served to progressively deplete their numbers and resources—for the experience of the Muslim centuries made it clear that marginality could be dissolved only by emigration or through conversion to Islam—the same definitions, in confirming the qualified legitimacy accorded Christians by the Quran, helped to ensure Christian survival. Survival in turn ensured that Christians would seize any opportunity to induce Muslims to discard those definitions that pronounced non-Muslims marginal. However, such an opportunity presents itself only when the definitions of the dominant community seem no longer adequate to its political survival. Not until the late eighteenth century did a few Muslims begin to suspect that the institutions grounded in the traditional definitions were failing to preserve the political integrity of Dar al-Islam before the accelerating Western Assault.

Thus, the fourth phase of Eastern Christianity in the Islamic Middle East: "The Second Age of Transmission" (*c.*1850–*c.*1950), a period during which Arabic-speaking Christians, notably in Greater Syria, once more assumed the role of conduit between an alien culture—this time the civilization born of Western Christendom—and Islam. During the First Age of Transmission, the Christians helped to provide much of the material and method with which the Muslims would phrase their own characteristic definitions and, in the process, formalize and deepen the marginality of Christians. The Second Age of Transmission, by contrast, found the Christians striving to destroy many of the same definitions, which bore upon both the nature of polity and membership in it, and which for a millennium had affirmed Christian marginality. The times appeared to demand radical redefinition to meet a radical threat, and Christians inevitably sought to steer Muslims toward those redefinitions that would end forever the marginality of non-Muslims.

In a sense, the parts played by different Eastern Christian communities during The Second Age of Transmission were assigned to them by the Church of Rome. When Ottoman forces drove the Manluks from Syria and Egypt in the second decade of the sixteenth century, the Maronites and the Greek Orthodox (whom we shall refer to as Melkites) were the two largest and most important Christian communities in Greater Syria. The Maronites were and are Uniates, in communion with Rome from roughly the era of the Crusades; although the Melkites were not, they did not share the inveterate hatred of the papacy so openly displayed by ethnic Greeks, virtually all of whom embraced the Ottoman imperium and preferred the turban of the sultan to the tiara of the pope. In contrast to the Greeks of the ecumenical see, the almost universally Arabic-speaking Melkites of the patriarchates of Antioch and Jerusalem had been shielded by Islamic hegemony from most of the bitter combat with the Latin West that led to the Great Schism. Indeed, a patriarch of Antioch in the first half of the sixteenth century admitted to a papal envoy that he had never heard of the Council of Florence.[3]

Nor can one exaggerate the practical effect of communion with Rome on sixteenth-century Maronites. The turmoil of Reformation Europe had deflected serious papal concern from the mountaineers and permitted them a *de facto* independence that would not be theirs again until perhaps our own day (and then on a political rather than ecclesiastical level). Consider that remarkable union of the Maronite and Melkite churches, concluded by their respective patriarchs around the year 1540: a union dictated by purely local circumstances, arranged without consultation with Rome or Constantinople, sublimely oblivious of doctrinal issues, and quickly aborted by Constantinople (with Ottoman support) while Rome remained unaware that anything at all had happened.[4] The long-term effects of such a union, had it taken hold, would obviously have altered subsequent Syrian history beyond recognition. A united Maronite-Melkite Church—wholly indigenous to Greater Syria, claiming the loyalties of the vast majority of Syrian Christians, and not controlled by Rome or Constantinople—would have been in a position to confront a fragmented Syrian Islam. By forcing the Maronite vision beyond the mountain to encompass all or most of Greater Syria, the union of 1540(?) would likely have precluded, among other things, the emergence of the modern Lebanese state.

But Maronite and Melkite independence of Rome and Constantinople was not to be. Indeed, the contest between the First and Second Rome would constitute one of the determining factors in the history of Eastern Christians in the Islamic Middle East before and during the Second Age of Transmission. Renewal of the Vatican's active involvement with Syrian Christians commenced early in the seventeenth century, as the impetus generated by the Counter Reformation carried the papal forces eastward. Before the second half of the seventeenth century, contingents representing various Latin religious orders could be found in Mt. Lebanon and in such key Syrian cities as Aleppo, the great northern entrepot; Damascus, then as ever the political heart of Syria and an important center of trade; and Sidon, the chief port for Damascus. The principal Christian element in all three cities was—or, in the case of Aleppo, would soon be— Melkite. Missionary aims included binding the Maronites more closely to Rome and "returning" to obedience the Melkites and other Eastern Christians. From the outset, the Latins enjoyed the diplomatic protection of France, Eldest Daughter of the Church and enthusiastic par-

ticipant in Ottoman commerce. Firm establishment of a French consul
and factory in Aleppo and Sidon more or less coincided with the
advent of the missionaries to the two cities. Although it would be some
time before Damascus, that bastion of urban Sunni Islam, could bring
herself to suffer a comparable French presence, Latin missionaries,
under the protection of the Catholic monarch's consul in Sidon, took
up residence in the City of Praise and, before the end of the seventeenth century appear to have been tolerated as yet another piece of
the Damascene mosaic. It is to be noted that Melkites in Damascus
could boast blood and trading ties to Sidon's Melkite community, and
so were never entirely removed from French consular and factory
connections.

The Latins encountered few obstacles in confirming and deepen-
ing Maronite allegiance to Rome. Nevertheless, this effort—like the
much more formidable one of creating numerically significant Uniate
communities among the Melkites, and among the Jacobites and Armenians in Syria—would have been considerably more complicated
had it not transpired during the period (c.1650–c.1750) that saw
Christian Europe seize from Ottoman Islamdom the economic, military, and political balance of power—proof, were any needed, of the
West's glaring superiority in science and technology. Only when the
Syrian Christian subjects of Latin proselytism could conclude that
surrender to the papal embrace would afford them opportunities
greater than those offered by their traditional confession did many of
them declare in favor of Rome and, implicitly, association with that
civilization busily establishing world hegemony. By 1700, elite elements of the Melkite hierarchy, lower clergy, and laity had drawn
precisely that conclusion and, for the first time in a millennium, a
Syrian Christian seeking, as marginal man will, an added measure of
advantage could see an alternative to apostasy or emigration—the
latter, of course, a virtual impossibility in any case before the late
nineteenth century. Nor was the multiplication of Uniates without an
economic cause, for the French king's consuls left the Syrian Christian
lay notables—most of them men of commerce—little room to doubt
that the road to Rome was also the way to affiliation with a French
factory or consulate, and hence to broadened trading opportunities
and reduced customs duties. The Franco-papal connection also offered the only hope for restoration of goods seized by European
corsairs plying the eastern Mediterranean.[5] Economic possibility thus
conspired with diplomatic patronage to militate against fidelity to the

ancestral confession. So did the superior learning and, often enough, the spiritual qualities of many of the Latin missionaries.

With certain variations, the forces operative among the Melkites also agitated the Jacobites and Armenians. So, in the course of some one hundred years, Rome succeeded in all but doubling the number of Syrian Christian Churches and destroying the will toward communal accommodation to which the Maronite-Melkite union of 1540(?) attests. In the eighteenth and nineteenth centuries, the bitterness separating non-Uniate from Uniate often flared into violent confrontation (and, to be sure, has yet to be entirely dispelled in our own day). The fractionalization of Syrian Christianity ended any possibility of unity of action and gravely impaired the Christians' position vis-à-vis the dominant Muslims. Where two churches, the Maronite and the Melkite, distinct but not notably hostile to one another, had claimed the loyalty of perhaps ninety percent of all Syrian Christians, by 1724 (the year marking the creation of an unambiguously Uniate-Melkite patriarchate) there stood three. The Latins seemed to have tipped the scales of Syrian Christianity in favor of the Uniates, albeit Uniates under different jurisdictions.

I emphasized earlier the capacity of the marginal community to influence the characteristic definitions of the ruling community during the formative phase of the latter's civilization. The marginal community's ability to significantly influence the majority manifests itself again only when the same definitions give evidence of flagging vitality, when their elimination or restatement appears to be essential. Both tendencies came to dominate the official Ottoman agenda in the nineteenth century. The period of the Tanzimat witnessed the severe weakening or even destruction of the traditional Ottoman institutions, the theoretic theocracy included, for their impotence in preserving the Empire's political integrity had been amply demonstrated by the eighteenth-century Ottoman retreat. But Ottomanization, the policy designed to substitute a secular Ottoman identity for the political primacy of the religious identity, fared no better, its promise of political equality between Muslims and non-Muslims breaking upon the twin reefs of Muslim resistance and Balkan Christian nationalism.

By the late nineteenth century, nationalism, that originally Western virus, had spread beyond the Balkans and into the largely Muslim areas of the Fertile Crescent and British-occupied Egypt. In the Ottoman Empire (and elsewhere), the rise to preeminence of the national consciousnes had often been signaled by literary revival—an integral part of a process whereby the political primacy of the religious identity yields to the centrality of territoriality and ethnicity, principles underpinned by common language. The first attempts to transmute the Arabic literary productions of Syrian Christians from the almost purely ecclesiastical into the mundane belonged to a coterie of Aleppine Uniates. Melkite as well as Maronite, they had been quickened by Latin mission schools and association with Europeans in Aleppo but perhaps energized most by their inner need, as Uniates, to rationalize their Roman religious allegiance—new for Melkites, renewed for Maronites—in light of their own Eastern traditions. Toward that end, the Aleppine Uniates wrote not only apologetical works but also historical chronicles that frequently reached beyond exclusively Church history. Then, curiosity aroused and Arabic skills sharpened, these Christians began incursions into Arabic poetry, employing classical forms that had long been almost the exclusive possession of Arabic-speaking Muslims.

Significantly, the Uniate Melkites' aversion to the pervasive ecclesiastical influence of Greek Constantinople led them to dwell upon their specifically Syrian, even Arab, ethnicity.[6] Their posture, however, could not be perfectly analogous to that of the Maronites. Although the Uniate Melkites were and would remain a minority within the total Melkite community, they tended to share with their Orthodox brethren a Greater Syrian outlook, born of the fact that the boundaries of geographic Syria and those of the Melkite patriarchates of Antioch and Jerusalem were roughly conterminous. By contrast, the Maronites, pondering the history of their church (as they did with increasing frequency after the late seventeenth century), could scarcely avoid seeing it largely with the context of Mt. Lebanon—the fastness that enveloped, in the past as in the present, the greater part of the Maronite population. The political implications seemed clear, and only a few Maronites have questioned them since.

Uniate Melkite attitudes underwent notable changes in the late eighteenth and nineteenth centuries. The patent inability of the Melkite see of Antioch to contain the Uniate advance prompted the ecumenical see to discard her policy—pursued since the Ottoman conquest of Syria in 1516—of occasional and almost always Antiochene-inspired intervention in the patriarchal affairs of Antioch in favor of direct governance, exercised by a Greek hierarchy appointed by the Great Church and fastened upon the Syrians without regard for their wishes. By 1724, the Eastern See found herself divided into an abbreviated Orthodox patriarchate, bound on the one hand to

Constantinople as a shield against further Uniate penetration and Roman control, and on the other hand an unstable Uniate patriarchate that viewed Rome, Paris, and certain local powers (particularly though not exclusively the Lebanese *amirs* who, like the Uniates, skirted the edges of Ottoman legitimacy) as its only hope against Greek control and an enforced reversion to Orthodoxy.

Syrian Antioch watched helplessly as her autonomy—ecclesiastical and, in the case of the Uniates, cultural—withered. Greek and largely Greek-inspired Ottoman hostility heightened European patronage of the Uniate Melkites and this, together with Rome's penchant for latinizing Eastern rite,[7] helped to gradually subvert the Uniate Melkites' sense of security in their Eastern heritage and, with it, awareness of themselves as a community sharing with wider Syrian society a common destiny. Sporadically subjected to official Ottoman pressures in the cities of Syria, many Uniates sought refuge either in the Lebanon, where they created the modern towns of Zahlah and Dayr al-Qamr, or in an Egypt which, even prior to the British arrival, stood well beyond the effective control of the Ottoman government and could provide a comfortable base for Uniate Melkite merchants studiously seizing control over Syro-Egyptian costal commerce and simultaneously moving into the European trade. The Uniate Melkite bourgeoisie, often educated in Latin mission schools and occasionally in Europe, trafficking to some of the great ports of the Christian and Muslim Mediterranean and, particularly after the mid-eighteenth century, able to avail themselves of European nationality, became, like their Latin-educated clergy, increasingly oriented toward the West that had spawned and sustained them. Ottoman legitimation of the Uniate Melkite patriarchate in 1839 served merely to deepen the devotion of her faithful to Rome and Paris, for it was plain to all that only massive French (and Austrian) pressure had wrung from the sultan his reluctant recognition. In level of prosperity, education, and awareness of the world beyond the Middle East, the Unitate Melkite elite in the nineteenth and first half of the twentieth century compared favorably to their analogues in any religious community in Greater Syria, not to mention Egypt. Nevertheless, they resembled less a bridge between their native society and an ascendant Western civilization than a neophyte band distracted from their specifically Eastern heritage by beacons beamed from Europe.

The Orthodox Melkites evolved in a different manner. While direct Greek control over Orthodox Antioch from 1724 to 1899 did much, even in the estimate of Melkites, to preserve Orthodoxy in

Syria, impatience with Greek autocracy mounted as the decades passed and a certain stability in ecclesiastical affairs was achieved. The Greek presence helped nudge the Orthodox Melkites into the national awareness evinced earlier among the Uniates. Indeed, as Syrian-Arab national sentiment dimmed among the Uniate Melkites (and never quite superseded Lebanese particularism among the Maronites), it waxed among the Orthodox Melkites. But reaction against Greek ecclesiastical control constitutes only one explanatory factor: demography must be counted as another. For the Orthodox Melkites enjoyed the widest geographic distribution of any religious community in Syria, Christian or Muslim. They could be found in the Maronite ramparts of Mt. Lebanon. They lived among the Druze in the southern reaches of the Mountain, and were represented in some strength in the villages of the Anti-Lebanon. Established in the villages and towns of the Syrian steppe, the Orthodox Melkites were also located in the principally Alawi region around Latakia. Perhaps most significantly, they usually comprised the most important Christian element in the largely Sunni urban centers—excepting Aleppo and Sidon, of course, where, by the early eighteenth century, the Uniate victory was nearly complete.

Although located everywhere, however, the Orthodox Melkites were everywhere a minority and, unlike the Maronites, could entertain no fantasies of future political dominance in a substantial portion of Greater Syria. In addition to being spread thinly throughout their homeland, they lacked a European patron as staunchly and effectively committed to them as was France to the Uniates. (It was not until the 1860s, or almost two hundred and fifty years after the appearance of the Latins and French, that Russian activity in Syria extended much beyond the Holy Places.) Consequently, the Orthodox Melkites clearly understood the necessity of accommodation with the Syrian Muslim majority. They saw that their interests would best be served by the development of a non-Islamic principle of authority, but one to which Muslims as well as Christians could subscribe with something like equal enthusiasm.

Until the mid-nineteenth century, the hallmark of the Arabic literary revival among Christians had been rediscovery rather than innovation—a tendency that culminated in the work of the Uniate Melkite Masif al-Yaziji (1800–71), perhaps the era's master practitioner of classical Arabic verse. The step from rediscovery to invention would be taken by Maronite turned Protestant Butrus al-Bustani (1819–82), and before the turn of the century even Muslims had to acknowledge the accomplishment of certain Syrian Christians in the language that had been universalized by the Quran.[8] Between the age of al-Bustani and World War I, most Christian literary luminaries, essayists as well as poets, continued to be drawn from the ranks of the Uniate Melkites. Almost without exception, however, these men, either by virtue of recent conversion, membership in clans that remained predominently Orthodox, or education at such institutions as the Syrian Protestant College (progenitor of the American University of Beirut), swam outside the Uniate mainstream. None of them matured in that Franco-papal milieu that so enveloped the Uniate Melkite clergy and bourgeoisie, the truly representative leaders of their community.[9] They failed, moreover, to perpetuate their kind. Few Uniate Melkite voices after World I were raised in behalf of cultural and political aims calculated to win the endorsement of Syrian, let along other Arab, Muslims.

For its part, the Orthodox Melkite intelligenstia could see no alternative to reaching out toward the Muslims. Given their geographic distribution, the Orthodox Melkites could muster little fervor for the Lebanese parochialism that enthralled the Maronite imagination, nor could they afford the partial alienation, evinced by the Uniate elite in general, from a Syrian culture permeated by Islam. And ambivalence marked the Orthodox Melkites' attitude toward the West. Certainly, they understood that Western political ideology—specifically, a nationalism grounded in the secular categories of territoriality, ethnicity, and language—might be turned to their advantage. But they could develop neither the Uniates' infatuation with virtually every cultural manifestation of the West nor the Uniate tolerance (tending toward enthusiasm) for the hardly concealed political ambitions of France vis-à-vis the Middle East as the demise of the "Sick Man of Europe" appeared imminent. Finally, the Orthodox Melkites were unable altogether to forget or forgive either the Latins, the West's first emissaries, or later the Protestants for directing their missionary efforts primarily against them while judging them deficient to the degree that they persevered in their peculiarly Eastern "errors."

The tardy entry of Holy Russia onto the Syrian scene has been noted. But enter at last the Russians did, establishing in Syria, between the 1860s and the outbreak of World War I, a modest network of primary and secondary schools. In part because the Third Rome sought elimination of Constantinople's control over Orthodox Antioch, and in part because Orthodox tradition itself prescribes employment of the vernacular for liturgical purposes, the Russian schools in Syria, in stark contrast to their Latin counterparts, emphasized proficiency in Arabic, thereby fostering the Syrian and Arab awareness of their Orthodox Melkite wards.[10] As this emergent consciousness wedded itself to Western notions of secular nationhood, the way was prepared for the singular role to be played by the Orthodox Melkites in developing political ideologies intended no less for Syrian and other Arab Muslims than for Syrian and other Arabic-speaking Christians.

The Second Age of Transmission, then, occupied itself with two related activities: first, an Arabic literary revival that brought forth new literary forms, often devoted to themes and subject matter theretofore unrelated directly to the traditional Arabic literary culture of the Muslims; and second, the production and nurture of secular nationalist ideologies, particularly by Orthodox Melkites striving to provide a post-Islamic basis of political authority in Syria (and even within Arab society generally). But the assertive inventiveness of the important Christian writers and political ideologues should be understood for what it was—an attempt (not always conscious) by members of marginal communities to undermine the historic Muslim-dominated intellectual and political culture that had defined their marginality. It was a means toward a new set of definitions to which Arabic-speakers, non-Muslim as well as Muslim, could assert equal claim. In his writings, Jurji Zaydan (d. 1914) conceived an Arab history inclusive of but somehow transcending Islam.[11] An Orthodox Melkite resident in Egypt, his career perhaps signaled the imminent eclipse of Uniates by Orthodox Melkites in modern Arab Christian literature. Zaydan's views would be refined into political ideology by such later Orthodox Melkites as Antun Saʿadah (d. 1949), founder of the Syrian National Party; Michel ʿAflaq, chief ideologue and cofounder of the pan-Arab Baʿath party; and, I would suggest, George Habash, avowedly Marxist creator of the Popular Front for the Liberation of Palestine. Vastly different in their visions of the future, these men unite in insisting upon the necessity—indeed, the inevitability—of a politically secular tomorrow that includes an end of political definitions that limit non-Muslims to second-class citizenship.

In his advocacy of a politically unified Greater Syria, Saʿadah, ever the adamant secularist, demonstrated in a backhand manner a striking fidelity to his religious tradition, for the borders of Saʿadah's Greater Syria correspond almost exactly to those of the Melkite patriarchates of Antioch and Jerusalem. Even Saʿadah's hallucination about binding "Syrian" Cyprus, with her predominantly Orthodox (though hardly Arabic-speaking) population, to her proper mainland, reminds one faintly of the abortive attempt by the Melkite Patriarch of Antioch, Joachim ibn Ziyadah (1593–1603), to extend his jurisdiction over the same island.[12] The appeal of the Syrian Nationalist Party remains limited, confined mainly to Orthodox Melkites but with some following among Melkite Uniates and such heterodox Muslims as the Druze and ʿAlawis—all of whom see most of their respective co-sectaries concentrated within Greater Syria, and none of whom can realistically expect to create and dominate politically a viable independent state. The Party commands virtually no allegiance from the Maronites who, with French connivance, did in fact create and—until 1975, sustain—a state dominated politically by themselves, despite their status as a minority among minorities within the Republic of Lebanon.

Nor did Saʿadah's Party gain a substantial following among either Sunni or Twelver-Shiʿi Muslims. Although the Sunnis would boast a majority in a Greater Syrian state, it would not be of a size sufficient to ensure the dominance to which four hundred years of the Sunni Ottoman imperium had accustomed them. Sunni Muslims were unprepared to relinquish all hope of inclusion within a larger Arab (and more emphatically Sunni) state. Few of them, moreover, were ready to swallow whole the undiluted secularism prescribed by Antun Saʿadah. Neither were the Twelver Shiʿi, almost all of whom dwelt in southern Lebanon. Led by their landed class, they could see little advantage in rejecting a Lebanese state in favor of a Greater Syria in which their minority position would be only further emphasized. Fundamentally, however, the Greater Syrian nationalists found themselves wedged between the Lebanese particularism of the Maronites and the more catholic political aspirations of the Sunni Muslims. Nothing better illustrates Saʿadah's dilemma than the circumstances of his demise: extradition from Sunni-dominated Syria at the behest of Maronite-dominated Lebanon, and there, on his native soil, execution by firing squad. (Saʿadah declined the blindfold.)

The quite circumscribed appeal of Greater Syrian nationalism inspired other elements of the Orthodox Melkite community to help sponsor a different effort at accommodation with Sunni Muslims: Baʿath pan-Arab nationalism. The Sunnis' legacy of religio-political universalism, so resistant to the restraints of Lebanese and Greater Syrian nationalism, might, it was thought or intuited, adjust to a broadly-based Arab nationalism. The latter, although officially secular, would nonetheless feature a Sunni majority of overwhelming proportions. The ideological offspring of the Damascene Orthodox Melkite, Michel ʿAflaq, Baʿthism was calculated to appeal to the Sunni Muslim. Indeed, it carried some risk to those of ʿAflaq's native confession as well as to other minorities. These included the Christian minority in particular, but also the non-Sunni Muslims, precisely because of the magnitude of the Sunni majority in the pan-Arab state to be summoned into reality under the Baʿath aegis. In the mind of the doctrinaire Baʿathi, of course, Sunni preponderance would be of small consequence, since the Party's secularism would guarantee equal citizenship and the distributive justice of socialism to all those speaking Arabic and declaring themselves Arabs.

Today, neither of the two states formally professing Baʿathism embodies the Baʿath ideal as enunciated by the principle founding father of the Party. Iraq is a military dictatorship under the unsparing Saddam Husayn, while Syria is a military dictatorship controlled by an ʿAlawi minority directed by the harsh but infinitely subtle Hafiz al-Asad. Nevertheless, neither government may be accused of wandering too far from the strict secularism—or, for that matter, the pragmatic socialism—dictated by Baʿath doctrine.

Still, the future of the Baʿath in an Iraq of latent Sunni-Shiʿi and not so latent Arab-Kurdish hostility, and currently torn by a debilitating war with Iran, is at best uncertain. So too is the assumption that the Baʿath would continue to hold Syria were Hafiz al-Asad or, more likely, his ʿAlawi successor overcome by a Sunni reaction, evidence of which is not lacking. Nor has Baʿath ideology penetrated, to any appreciable degree, the rest of the Arab world. A pan-Arab Baʿath whose power remains restricted to two nations at daggers drawn in the Fertile Crescent may simply decay and die, a victim of the Party's internal disarray and the discrepancy between its grandiose pretensions and its modest achievements. From his residence in Baghdad, Michel ʿAflaq himself, persona non grata in his native Syria, appears to have been stunned into silence. His (and others') dream of an Arab nation extending from the Atlantic eastward to Iran notwithstanding, it is a distinct possibility that the political boundaries now separating the Arab world will endure, despite their bastard birth, into the distant future. (Likely exceptions are the borders of those states strewn along the Gulf coast of Arabia, and those huddled uneasily within the western arc of the Fertile Crescent.) Should the nearer future yield, within that western arc, something resembling a Greater Syrian state, it is hard to see how it could remain untouched by the pluralistic secularism advanced by the Syrian National Party.

One thing at least is certain. The Maronite illusion—shared after World War I by more and more Uniate Melkites—of a Lebanese state, pluralistic but forever biased politically by Maronites facing firmly westward, is gone beyond recall. That Lebanon would almost certainly have fallen sooner or later in any case, undone by demographic shifts unfavorable to the Maronites and to the Christians generally. The end was, of course, hastened by a series of developments attendant upon the creation of Israel: the expulsion of the Palestinians, some eighty percent of whom were Muslims, from their immemorial homeland; the Palestine Liberation Organization's loss of freedom of action in Jordan; and the PLO's subsequent transfer of its base of operations to Lebanon. The Palestinians' creation of a quasi-state on the soil of the state that reluctantly hosted them—a Lebanon whose military weakness reflected the strength of her religio-political divisions—precipitated an increasingly open alliance between the Maronite leadership and the Israelis. This, in turn, drew a predictable reaction from the Sunni Muslims, most of whom, in any case, felt a profound sympathy for the Palestinian plight. The Israeli invasion of Lebanon, which replaced the Palestinians with more fearsome Israeli occupiers in the Shiʿi south, succeeded brilliantly in diverting Shiʿi hostility from the Palestinians to the Zionist warriors and their Maronite collaborators. The fragile vessel is burst, and if the nightmarish division of Lebanon along confessional lines is ever to be checked, it is difficult to see an alternative to a strong Syrian-Lebanese connection. The end product of this may, after all, remind one of a Greater Syrian secular state modified, at least in the short term, by the subtraction of Jordan and all or most of what was Palestine. Antun Saʿadah may yet have his day, though perhaps not quite the day he envisioned.

It is clear, too, that the Second Age of Transmission has run its course. The educational edge that Eastern Christians (especially the Uniates) had enjoyed over Muslims since the introduction of those very modest Latin mission schools into seventeenth-century Syria, has measurably diminished. Likewise, the Christians' intellectual influence on the Muslims, manifested first through the Arabic literary revival they dominated in the nineteenth and first half of the twentieth centuries, and then through the political movements discussed above, is now of little weight. Like most of a confused contemporary humanity, Arab Muslims today count themselves beneficiaries and victims of the universalization of Western thought and require Eastern Christian intermediaries no more than they did after Islam's selective assimilation of Hellenistic philosophy and science ended the First Age of Transmission. Should Eastern Christians finally come to rest in states of secular constitution, it is doubtful that they will have been instrumental in creating them. The confessional heterogeneity of Muslims as well as Christians in the Fertile Crescent would seem to preclude establishment there of Islamic regimes a la Khomeini's Iran. However, even a formally secular regime, made of stuff spun first by Sa'adah and 'Aflaq, may tend to revert to a more traditional rhythm and tone—may tend, that is, to adopt a pattern of political behavior that is more supportive of Muslim than of non-Muslim. Though the burden of the Muslim defintions be formally lifted from them. Arabic-speaking Christians may still have to endure a political and cultural marginality, the more so of course in an Arab state that encompasses but extends beyond the borders of geographic Syria. One suspects that descendants of those central and eastern European Jews who, in an effort to end their historic marginality, labored assiduously to usher in the Marxist millennium, might testify that new, formal political definitions do not always translate easily into new political realities.

If that pessimistic prognosis carries validity for Christians in geographic Syria and, indeed, throughout the Fertile Crescent, it applies with greater force to the Copts. However, it must be admitted at once that the history of Egyptian Christians under Islamic hegemony differs in important respects from that of their coreligionists to the northeast. The First Age of Transmission and the resultant elaboration of the classical Islamic definitions were phenomena associated less with Egypt than with the Fertile Crescent—particularly, its eastern arc. Egypt, unlike geographic Syria before or after the Islamic conquest, has not been characterized by great religious heterogeneity. For many centuries, Sunni Muslims (mainly of the Shafi'i school) and Coptic Christians have made up virtually the entire population. Nature has denied Egyptian Christians as well as Muslims the kinds of natural refuge areas wherein to harbor and perpetuate heterodox and frequently martial communities that found themselves out of phase with the power prevailing over the river and its narrow banks. Latin Christian penetration of the Coptic Church began late and produced nothing akin to the dislocations and fermentation associated with Rome's effort in Syria. Despite the British sojourn in Egypt, the historical ties of the Monophysite Copts to Chalcedonian Europe are seen to be weak, particularly when compared to those connecting the Uniates of Syria to Rome and France.

It is true that when the opportunity first presented itself in the nineteenth century, the Copts, like the Syrian Christians, availed themselves of Western education with few qualms, and so for a period enjoyed an advantage over the understandably more reticent Muslims by grasping some of the new knowledge. Still, I think it fair to say that, in attempting to reshape Egyptian Muslim attitudes in conformity to Western intellectual and political norms, the Copts were less influential than the Syrian Christian intelligentsia resident in Egypt. The latter were most active between 1875 (the year marking the founding in Cairo of the newspaper *Al-Ahram* by the Uniate Melkite Taqla brothers) and 1914 (the year of the death of the Orthodox Melkite Jurji Zaydan). Most of the members of this intelligentsia, together with the older Syrian Christian trading elements, are now departed the Nile Valley. The economic position of the commercial was undermined by the "Arab Socialism" introduced by Gamal ʿAbd al-Nasir in the mid-1950s, and the position of the intellectuals weakened as the Muslim audience they aspired to command turned to less alien sources for its instruction and lead in responding to even more alien ideologies.

At all events the Christians of Egypt, like their Syrian counterparts, can now provide Muslim society with little intellectual sustenance that Muslims cannot and would not prefer to provide for themselves. The Second Age of Transmission done, the historically decisive role once more devolves upon the Muslims. It is they who will determine for themselves and, ipso facto, for the non-Muslims in their midst, the characteristic political and cultural definitions of tomorrow's Middle East. In Egypt, obviously, the sheer weight of Sunni Muslim preponderance at least suggests a political future more Islamic than anything easily contemplated in Greater Syria, or even in Iraq with its Sunni-Shiʿi cleavage. While Arabic-speaking Christians will not and certainly should not resign themselves to political and intellectual passivity, theirs is not to mold a world quite round but only to patch it as they can.

Notes

1. Robert M. Haddad, *Syrian Christians in Muslim Society: An Interpretation* (Princeton, N.J.: Princeton University Press, 1970).

2. Philip K. Hitti, *History of the Arabs,* 8th ed. (London: Macmillan, 1963), p. 196.

3. C. Karalevskij, "Antioche," vol. 3, *Dictionnaire d'Histoire et de Geographie Ecclesiastiques*, col. 639.

4. Joseph Nasrallah, "Chronologie des Patriarches d'Antioche de 1500 a 1634," *Proche-Orient Chretien*, 7:34–35.

5. For a discussion of the "economy" of schism, see Haddad, *Syrian Christians*, pp. 32–49.

6. Ibid., pp. 52–54.

7. A policy much more prominent in the nineteenth century, as one approaches Vatican I, than it had been in the century before. See Constantin G. Patelos, *Vatican I et les eveques uniates* (Louvain: Editions Nauwelaerts, 1981), pp. 21–22, 39–40, 71–77, 162–63, et passim.

8. For more on al-Yaziji and al-Bustani, see ibid., pp. 70–72.

9. Ibid., pp. 75–79.

10. Ibid., pp. 83–85.

11. Ibid., p. 88.

12. Nasrallah, "Chronologie," 7:292–93.

··◄⊰ 10 ⊱►··

The Lebanese Experience
and Muslim-Christian Relations

Yoakim Moubarac

Introduction

In order to address the problem of Muslim-Christian relations in Lebanon, assess the stake that the Vatican, France, and the United States have in the Lebanese experience, we will examine five aspects of that experience:

1. The concept of "minority" as univocally—and incorrectly—applied to the Muslim and Christian peoples of the Middle East;

2. The role of prototype communities—that is, the specific communities that have *created* Lebanon, as distinct from the many ethnic-religious groups that make up the region;

3. The formation of the Maronite Plan, as expressed in a major work by Patriarch Istifan Duwayhi[1] in the seventeenth century and in the undertaking of Youssef Bey Karam[2] in the last century.

4. The harmony of the Maronite Plan with the "oriental aims" of the Vatican since the Renaissance, and with the Muslim and Arab policy of France since the Capitulations; and

5. The practical incomprehension of the Maronite Plan by the government of the United States.

The Concept of Minority as Applied to Lebanon

It is common knowledge that Lebanon is composed of no fewer than seventeen ethnic-religious communities. This fact is often acknowledged as a way of emphasizing Lebanon's pluralistic and democratic character, and, justifiably, of comparing it favorably with the other countries of the Middle East. When friction threatens the harmonious coexistence of these communities, however, as has been the case since 1975, the confessional character of the Lebanese state is also blamed. Since "confessionalism" is at the root of the conflict, the reasoning goes, the confessional system must be destroyed.

Without propounding any subtle theories and wishing to offend no one, I will attempt to show that the numerical and not the qualitative concept of minority is unevenly applied to all the Lebanese communities. The image of Lebanon as a beautiful mosaic is a popular one, but is nevertheless particularly inadequate to describe the communities that, religion aside, actually created Lebanon.

The Armenians, for example, are a minority in Lebanon. They have their own language and culture and, as a people, are distinguished from other peoples or nations by a history that includes centuries of conflict. Outside of Armenia, however, whatever their numbers, the Armenians are a minority. They form a community that necessarily claims kinship with an Elsewhere. To the extent that the Armenians renounce this Elsewhere and their special cultural and religious identity, their political integration will cause no problem.

The Muslim Kurds, like the Christian Armenians, are also a minority—not only in Lebanon, but everywhere in the Arab, Iranian, and Turkish world. And they will remain a minority until such time as they are able to recover their national identity in a renascent Kurdistan. As with the Armenians, numbers do not affect this status. The Kurdish language and culture, even leaving aside the ambiguous factor of race, give them a national identity. Unless these things are renounced and the people assimilated, the Kurds can reclaim their national identity only with the recovery of Kurdistan.

In contrast to the Armenians and Kurds, there are in Lebanon the *unionists,* a term preferable to "indigenous people." They include both Christians (Greek Orthodox and Greek Catholics) and Muslims (Sunnis). Whatever the numbers of each group or the nature of the animosities that exist among them, all share an intense feeling of being—and of always having been—the people of the country. The great majority live in the port cities or inhabit the oldest settlements in the mountains. This fact, without doubt, has profoundly marked their political behavior. Despite differences of religion, they have worked together in the administration of the state and in the arts, trade, and commerce. Even when they choose their identity, whether Lebanese, Syrian or Arabic, they have worked well together despite the antagonisms which characterize all differentiated societies.

Three Prototype Communities

Between the minorities and the unionists, there are those whom we might call, superficially, irredentists. They are minorities in an absolute sense, and in some ways irretrievably so. Even when they possess a particular language and dialect, they claim their environment's language and culture as their own, sometimes even maintaining that they pioneered it. Because they are jealous of their special character (and in this way differ from the unionists), they are anxious to share their ambitions with the world to which they consciously belong. In this they also differ from the minorities: their Elsewhere, when they have one, is not geographic. But whether a country of origin or an original mission, their Elsewhere, in the context of the Lebanese *hegira,* lies in the permanence of their settlement, not in their race, language, or religion. For this reason, they are prototype communities. I refer to the Shiʿa, Druzes, and Maronites. Let us look at each briefly in turn.

The Shiʿa

It is difficult to speak of the Shiʿa as a Muslim minority if one is aware of the Shiʿa plan for all of Islam and, indeed, the world—a plan that is constantly being reshaped according to the latest Shiʿa vision of unity. Certainly, though, diverse historical factors and the burden of time have made Shiʿism appear as a minority religion in particular regions or eras. One may even think that such an esoteric understanding of Shiʿism necessarily limits it to such a role. As the resurgence of Iranian Shiʿism clearly demonstrates, however, since the time of Ali Shiʿism has had a "revolutionary" plan for the entire Muslim world, and indeed for the world as a whole. This explains the emergence in Lebanon of such a man as Imam Musa al-Sadr.[3] Those who do not recognize this dimension of Shiʿism regard Sadr's program as only another minority claim, not a plan which sides wholeheartedly with the mass of disinherited people. His is not only a plan for Lebanon, but also for the whole Arab-Muslim world. Under these circumstances, then, it is not surprising that Sadr has been forced to remain "hidden from view."

The Druzes

Historically, Druzism is a prime example of a religious sect which has been condemned to minority status. Indeed, the current behavior of certain Druze factions in Lebanon, Israel, and Syria reinforces this interpretation. However, the esotericism of birth that for the Druze is the same as *da'wa* or universal mission in principle, must not be overlooked. In spite of the fact that *da'wa* is transmitted through the male initiates and is then closed, the Druze plan corresponds to the rise of Fatimism, or universal Shi'ism, and can never be considered as closed. Two major facts of modern Lebanese history are cited as proof:

• The political plan of modern Lebanon was formed, beginning in the sixteenth century, in the Druze environment. (It is striking that the emirs of Druze Lebanon were Sunnis in the beginning and Maronites at the end.)

• It is with Kamal Jumblatt[4] and his philosophical understanding of Druzism that the most generous, if not the most coherent, plan of Arab Socialism developed. Whatever Jumblatt's family origins, university education, and political variations, Druzism found in him the seeds of a Lebanese and Arab plan so forceful that, as in the case of Imam Musa al-Sadr, its promoter could only be suppressed.

The Maronites

With the Shi'a and Druzes of Lebanon, the Maronites form the third prototype community of the East.[5] The Maronites, too, are often incorrectly identified as a minority. Although they protect their independence and are noted for their ambition, their uniqueness should not be considered a source of envy. They appeal to neither race, religion, language, nor culture to differentiate them from the other religious groups of their environment. Like the Shi'a and the Druze, the Maronites also have a plan, and it is the subject of our next section.

The Maronite Plan in the Work of Patriarch Duwayhi and the Defense of Youssef Bey Karam

Patriarch Istifan Duwayhi[6] was a contemporary and correspondent of Louis XIV of France. Professor Kamal Salibi of the American University of Beirut has devoted a number of prominent studies to Duwayhi since 1954. For Salibi, a non-Maronite, as for numerous other historians of the Arab East, Patriarch Duwayhi is a pioneer of Lebanese history as well as the so-called father of Maronite modernity. His works contain the essentials of what appears to be the basis for the Maronite identity.

Maronitism is built on the attachment to Peter, prince of the Apostles and rock of faith in Christ. The head of the martyred Peter was placed in Rome, where it remains still, testimony to his martyrdom. From this comes the ecclesial primacy of Rome, and the indestructable attachment of the Maronites to this primacy. Before sealing his testimony by blood in Rome, however, Peter established his chair in Antioch. Rome and Antioch, therefore, are two Churches in one. Together, they are responsible—the one in the West, the other in the East—for the development of authentic Christian faith. The Maronites, who guarantee Catholic continuity in the East, are mindful of their place in the forefront of this mission.

The attachment of the Maronites to Rome opened their church to vast ecumenical horizons. It concurrently committed them to a modernity for which Europe had been the focus of development and diffusion since the Renaissance. Although fully engaged in the process of modernity, the Maronites do not give allegiance to any hegemony. On the contrary, they discovered in the European-type modernity a greater attachment to their Eastern identity. Furthermore, the Maronites regard it as a part of their mission to make the East known to Europe as well as to infuse European modernity into the East.

The Eastern identity of the Maronites is Syrian. Geographically, linguistically, and culturally, the Church of Antioch is deeply rooted in Syria. According to Duwayhi, Syria is the homeland of God's prophets and the Apostles, and where, in the fullness of time, His only Son was born of the Virgin Mary. Syriac was the language spoken by our Lord Jesus Christ, and as such the first language of mediation between the ancient and Christian worlds. It is, then, not only closely related to the Semitic and Greek worlds but actually transcends them.

Since the Arab conquest, the Church of Antioch has undergone a great number of difficulties, including severe limitations of its liberties. The church, however, has condemned only those whom Arab historians have condemned, and praised those whom these same historians judged to be righteous. Meanwhile, the Arabic language has progressively superseded Syriac. The Maronites did not accept the predominance of Arabic in their liturgy or on the scientific and cultural levels, but neither were they imprisoned by Syriac. They welcomed the language of the conqueror, which eventually became the language of the people, and even modernized and promoted Arabic among other languages and cultures of the world. The Maronites proved that the sons of Arabism by adoption had the same duties and rights as sons by birth. Syriac actually proved essential to the cultural completion of Arabism, however, since it was through Syriac that the wisdom and knowledge of the Greeks passed into the language and culture of the Arabs, and through them into Europe. Arabic, Syriac, and Greek thus constitute three inseparable links in the chain of universal culture.

Antiochean Maronitism presides over a privileged territory between Europe and the Arab-Muslim East. It is wary of overtures from whatsoever quarter, and systematically refuses alignment. Although a recipient in the cultural encounter, it defends the rights of the individual without which there can be no creative encounter. Consequently, Maronitism regards Mount Lebanon as a bastion that has no equivalent. For the Maronite, it is a privileged place of contemplative life, cultural symbiosis, and, consequently, of political liberties that must and will be defended at all costs.

Youssef Bey Karam came from the same land of Ihden as Patriarch Duwayhi. From the age of Louis XIV, however, we move to that of Napoleon III, and to the dramatic events that followed upon the tragedies of 1840 and 1860 in Lebanon.[7] Karam's *Memoirs*,[8] addressed in 1871 to "the leaders and nations of Europe," defended positions that are particularly significant for the Maronite identity—that is, somewhere between minority behavior and its opposite. Although times and perspectives have changed, his positions, summarized below, are relevant today.

The Lebanese Homeland

For Karam, Mount Lebanon had always been a refuge for the Christians of Syria, and Christians had a natural right to this sanctuary in times of misfortune. This refuge, however, is not a Christian but rather a Lebanese homeland. Lebanon, therefore, should never be governed by a foreigner, Christian or otherwise.

The Lebanese Identity

The identity of Lebanon derives from history, geography, and the right of nations based on natural law. It is *not* based on race, religion, or self-interest, regardless of the importance of these factors in the historical formation of Lebanon. Lebanon's identity depends, therefore, on the free consensus of the Lebanese, since this is the only consensus that conforms to the rights of those individuals and collectivities that claim kinship with Lebanon.

The Territorial Integrity of Lebanon

The partition of Lebanon into two *qaimqamates* (prefectures) and the further subdivision of the *qaimqamates* into *mudiriyye* (administrative districts) between 1840 and 1860 was, according to Karam, the basis of the ruination of the country. Partition fostered tribalism, and enabled foreign powers with selfish interests to intervene in Lebanon by sponsoring particular communities. Lebanon's territorial integrity, therefore, must be upheld.

The Maronite Attachment to France

Karam believed that the traditional Lebanese Maronite attachment to France was historically legitimate. This did not mean, however, that the Maronites would not oppose any French plan that compromised Lebanese liberties. Karam agreed to exile himself to Algeria, and then to Paris, at the invitation of the French Government; however, after a disagreement with the French Minister of Foreign Affairs, he left France for Rome. It was from the latter city that he addressed his petition to the European nations and their leaders, convinced that all the great questions of the world, of which the Lebanese question was then first, needed concerted international action.

Karam's defense of the Lebanese cause—and it is important to note that he specified Lebanese, not Christian—was primarily concerned with establishing a consensus between the Sublime Porte and the Great Powers. He was convinced that such a consensus would be useless unless it took into consideration the liberty of the Lebanese people and the permanence of the Lebanese entity in the heart of the Arab nation.

The Maronite Plan and Its Correspondence with the Islamic-Christian Policy of the Vatican

A great deal might still be said about Youssef Bey Karam's commitment to Arabism and to Lebanon, as evidenced by his correspondence with another famous exile, the Algerian Emir Abd-el Kader. His testimony, however, supplies sufficient material to evaluate the convergence of the Maronite plan in Lebanon with the Islamic-Christian plan of the Vatican.[9] The Vatican seeks to promulgate from Lebanon, principally through the Maronites, an ecumenical, cultural, and political undertaking for the Levant. Evidence of this plan stretches from the foundation of the Roman Maronite College in 1584 to the 1985 mission to Lebanon of Cardinal Roger Etchegaray, president of the Vatican's Commission for Peace and Justice.

Since the time of Francis I, France has followed a convergent plan. Breaking the traditional pattern of European Christianity, France dealt directly with the Ottomans to obtain the capitulations which provided for the protection of the Christian interests in the East.[10] This treaty's effect on the Maronites increased when the French ambassador to Constantinople, Savary de Breves, submitted to Louis XIII a report on France's Muslim policy that imparted to the Christians, and particularly to the Maronites, an essential role. The Roman and French undertaking in the Levant, and the Maronite contribution to it since the end of the sixteenth century, was, first of all, an ecumenical undertaking.[11] Its primary goal was the unity of the Eastern Christians, but that ended, and quite quickly, with the rise of Uniatism—that is, with the establishment of Eastern Christians united with Rome, though in separate churches. Viewed from the current ecumenical perspective, the formation of the Uniate churches was an error: it set back by at least two centuries the unity and sentiment of belonging which, despite schisms, the Antiochean Church had preserved since the first Christian millennium. It is difficult to say what would have happened had the Romanizers of the past centuries, with the cooperation of the French consular agents, not awakened the Eastern Christians from their Ottoman somnolence. It should be noted that the Catholic hierarchy of Antioch has been indigenous from the beginning, whereas the Orthodox liberated themselves from Greek dominance only during the last century.

In addition to the ecumenical undertaking, however, the Roman and French plan had a cultural aspect: the educational missions. These represented the most important and successful aspect of the dual plan, although also the most disputed. It is possible, therefore, to accuse the Maronites of collaborating with Rome and Paris in a colonialist undertaking—"Orientalism"[12]—in which knowledge was placed at the service of power. It must be clearly understood that this means European knowledge in the service of European colonial power. But before orientalism became European knowledge imposing itself on the East in the form of political and economic domination, it had been, at least as practiced by the Maronites, an Eastern penetration of Europe. This was a matter of free choice on the part of the Easterners themselves—and not only by Christians and Lebanese. Muslims, and especially Egyptians, tried to find in Europe's modernity the secret of their own renaissance.[13] It was by choice, therefore, that the East took from Europe the tools of scientific research that it saw as the means of recognizing its origins and recovering its cultural identity.

The cultural choice of the Maronites that began with the foundation of the Roman College in 1584, would become the choice of all Eastern intellectuals in the nineteenth and twentieth centuries. Despite the recriminations of the postcolonial era, this cultural choice enabled Taha Hussein, the greatest Arab and Muslim author of his generation, to resuscitate, in *The Future of Culture in Egypt,* the entire history of his country and to link it freely to Cartesian and Greek philosophy. Hussein, who was French-speaking and married to a Frenchwoman, was one of the greatest guiding lights that the Mediterranean cultural landscape has produced.[14] (It should not be surprising, given the current wave of fanaticism and obscurantism that followed the postcolonial era, that Taha Hussein, along with classical humanism, is no longer recognized as a cultural model.)

The third undertaking that the Maronites helped to promote under the aegis of the Vatican and with the help of France was a political design. This design also had a very precise starting point. It was Maronite students in Rome, acting as advisers and agents of the

Emir Fakhr al-Din, the prince of Lebanon in exile in Florence, who assisted him with the technology and manpower necessary not only to regain his power in Lebanon but to extend it from Antioch to Jerusalem.[15]

Because the ten thousand men whom the Grand Duke of Tuscany had promised had to be dispatched instead to Spain, Emir Fakhr al-Din returned to the East with only the techniques of the European Renaissance. He succeeded, nevertheless in establishing in Lebanon the seeds of modernization. Eventually of course, he was captured by the Ottoman expeditionary force, taken to Istanbul, and executed.

What were these seeds of modernization? Essentially, there were three, and it is their effects which are today exploited by those waiting to undermine the basis of Islamic-Christian coexistence. As the Lebanese political plan, freely conceived and progressively realized, sprang into action, the three essential factors which came into the play were as follows:

Technology

The emirate borrowed from Europe the technical means of its own renaissance not only culturally but also in the areas of agriculture, industry, and commerce. It was at this time that the beginnings of agriculture management appeared in Mt. Lebanon: for example, terracing, an agricultural technique well-known in Tuscany, would become equally well-known in Lebanon. It was also at this time that students from Rome and Paris returned to Lebanon and Syria (Aleppo), where, with the help of the religious and educational missions, they were instrumental in raising the literacy rate of Mt. Lebanon. The printing press was also introduced, thereby facilitating the spread of books throughout the entire East.

Mixing of Populations

The Maronites, known as good peasants, soldiers, and accountants, were transplanted during the emirate to the Druze areas of the Mountain. This policy would eventually lead to the massacres of the last century and to the conflicts with which we are so familiar today. What is not always stated, however, is that, of itself, jealousy between populations does not spark massacres. These must be fanned and fueled by outside powers, and by the large landowners in their employ. The common interests of the populations, however, were expressed in the emergence of a new dynamic in Lebanese society, and neither the feudal landowners, outside powers, nor the massacres of the last century were able to diminish the phenomenon engendered by the emir's policy of mixing the populations. Yet, because such a society carries so many risks, such as the revolutions and resistance we see today, it is a frightening and unwanted phenomenon. During the last century, however, Lebanese society was so dynamic that not even the most knowledgable foreign visitor could distinguish at first sight between a Maronite and a Druze horseman.

Autonomy

The third element of the emirate's modernization plan—and the one that was to legitimize politically the introduction of modern technology and pluralism into Lebanese society—was the movement toward autonomy. Two centuries before Muhammed Ali in Egypt, one can find in the Lebanon of Fakhr al-Din the first movement toward emancipation and autonomy in the very heart of the Ottoman Empire. If I did not fear the ambiguity of applying terms of one era to another, I might say that Fakhr al-Din inaugurated the movement for national liberation and independence in the East. Regardless of the terms used, however, it is certain that the movement he launched continues to this day. Fakhr al-Din anticipated the ferment that gripped the Ottoman Empire after the First World War, not only in Lebanon but throughout the Arab world. The principle of the nation-state asserts itself even today, despite the numerous attempts at unity which have been proposed between the Arab principalities.

The political plan of the Maronites, more so than the ecumenical plan and at least as much as the cultural plan, converged successfully with the other national emancipation movements in the Near East. First, Lebanon's uniqueness among the nation-states of the Arab East was made clear. Lebanon is still the one country, not only in the Arab East but in the whole world, where Christians who so desire can engage in dialogue on an equal footing with their Muslim compatriots. Also it is Lebanon alone where Christians and Muslims together have instituted a regime based on liberty, equality, and fraternity. The motto of the 1789 revolution is invoked in recognition of France's decisive role in the years between the founding of "Little"

Lebanon in 1860 and "Greater" Lebanon in 1920. In this national undertaking, Lebanon was fortunate to find people of the caliber of Patriarch el-Hoyek and President Edde.[16]

It goes without saying that the Vatican was at the heart of the movement that engendered modern Lebanon, and that, having supported the undertaking from its inception, continues to follow events there with great interest. Even when, as currently seems to be the case, Lebanon is abandoned by everyone else, the Vatican still insists upon its unity. It does so precisely because Lebanon is a unique experiment, both politically and in the spirit of the Islamic-Christian entente. Besides Cardinal Etchegaray's 1985 mission to Lebanon, the Vatican's continuing interest is evidenced by three letters, dated 1 May 1984, that Pope John Paul II addressed to the Maronite patriarch, the Lebanese people, and the bishops of the world.[17] The letters expressed the pope's commitment to the Lebanese formula, and asked that everything possible be done to safeguard and develop for everyone's benefit the totality of Islamic-Christian relations.

The Lebanese Model and the United States

The final consideration of this paper is of the role of the United States in the last phase of the Maronite Plan.[18] In this regard, attention should be called to the great number of friends of Lebanon among the American intelligentsia, particularly among the churches. Prominent among these were the late Cardinal Cooke, archbishop of New York, who was in the forefront of the defenders of Lebanon, and the late Malcolm Kerr, a colleague in Arab and Islamic studies and president of the American University of Beirut at the time he was killed. Nor should the many Americans, both civilian and military, who have given their lives in defense of Lebanon be forgotten.

I mention Malcolm Kerr to point out that no matter how much I have emphasized the Vatican's inspiration for and France's participation in the triple ecumenical, cultural, and political plan of Lebanon, I have not forgotten that for more than a hundred years a Syrian Protestant college was laying the foundation for what was to become the greatest scientific institution in the Near East, the American University of Beirut. Initially, this institution created by American Presbyterians not only differed from the Roman-French undertaking, but was openly antagonistic to it. In time, however, it developed, along with the French Jesuit university, into one of the principal foci of the

Arab Renaissance. Today, both institutions suffer as a result of Lebanon's misfortunes; nevertheless, along with the Lebanese University, they remain bastions of national resistance.

Despite the many happy associations of the past, it is necessary to bring the history of United States–Lebanese relations up to date with the following facts. According to the former president of Lebanon, Sulieman Frangieh, the government of the United States not only did not defend the Islamic-Christian model of Lebanon, but actually planned to install the displaced Palestinians in Lebanon, so that Lebanon would become an Arab country like the other countries in the Middle East. Raymond Edde, former cabinet minister and leader of the Lebanese National Front, while unable to supply actual proof of the existence of such a plan, confirms that, previous to 1975, former Secretary of State Henry Kissinger favored the partition of Lebanon into a Christian mini-state north of the Beirut-Damascus highway and a Muslim state in the south where the Palestinians would be settled. This, according to Edde, would fulfill the Israeli partition plan revealed in an exchange of letters between Ben Gurion and Moshe Sharett in 1954, and which provided for Israel's annexation of all Lebanese territory south of the Litani River.

Throughout, I have attempted to show that an egalitarian and modern Islamic-Christian Lebanon was to have been a prototype for the nation-states of the Arab East. One might also add that Palestine was meant to be a model derived from this prototype—a place where Christians, Muslims, and Jews would have realized more completely the benefits of modernity derived from the European Renaissance and the Arab Awakening. However, despite the best efforts of American intellectuals and their colleagues, both in the field and at home, the government of the United States has done nothing to promote this model. On the contrary, the government of the United States has done everything possible to sacrifice both the Palestinian model and its Lebanese prototype to the success of the Israeli model. As a consequence, it has guaranteed the unconditional supremacy of Israel—an entity composed of religious and ethnic groups from Europe—over all the various Muslim and Christian societies of the Near East.

Since World War II, the government of the United States has maintained the best of relations with conservative Islam, notably Wahhabite Arabia. Most assuredly, this is a legitimate American economic and strategic interest. But when one has sown the wind, one should not be astonished to reap the whirlwind. In other words, if the

United States favors religious fundamentalism in one country, it should not be surprised to see it arise forcefully in another, threatening not only conservative governments but also the more liberal regimes of the region.

The drama of Lebanon is, after all, only the price thàt is being paid to the agents of conservatism and reaction for the rejection of the Palestinian model. Beginning with the Lebanese plan, then, the United States should reflect on its overall options within the framework of Islamic-Christian relations. More precisely, the sincere compassion which the United States has demonstrated for Lebanon's fate should permit it to act more consistently with its ideals of democracy · and human rights. If this were to occur, the United States could consider in a more equitable way the differences between the Islamic and Israeli models, and—in undiminished opposition to both—the Lebanese prototype model.

Conclusion

The spontaneous approval by President Reagan of the Israeli bombing of PLO offices and homes in Tunisia in October 1985 is yet another example of the United States' policy of rejecting the Lebanese prototype and the Palestinian model.[19] This rejection stands in stark contrast to the Vatican's Oriental policy and France's Muslim and Arab policies.

The testimony of two prominent Maronites (Raymond Edde, deputy of Byblos, and the former president of Lebanon, Sulieman Frangieh, who was delegated by all the Arab heads of state to plead the case of the Palestinians at the United Nations in 1974) regarding the United States' intentions in Lebanon has already been mentioned. These disastrous intentions, I am convinced, were thwarted only by protests of the Catholic hierarchy in Lebanon, supported by the Catholic Church in the United States and, especially, through the efforts of that tireless friend of justice and peace, and of Lebanon, Father Bryan Hehir of the United States Catholic Conference.

However utopian the Lebanese prototype of Muslim-Christian coexistence in the Middle East and the Palestinian model of Christians, Muslims, and Jews living peaceably together in the Holy Land, no American administration since World War II has shown any interest. On the contrary, American policy of the past fifty years has resulted in the domination of the Middle East by Israel, which today occupies all of ancient Palestine and—by its own army or with mercenaries—parts of Syria and Lebanon. It cannot be denied that the predominance of Zionism in the Arab Middle East has exasperated Muslims the world over, and moved them to react to the Jewish state by favoring the reestablishment of a Muslim state. At this point, Lebanon is caught in the middle, bled almost to the death between Zionist designs and Islamist factions.

The Lebanese experiment of coexistence concerns not only Christians and Muslims, but also various political groups. Lebanon is currently being torn apart. Its people, when they are able to escape massacre, are transferred, debased and humiliated from one region to another. No serious consideration of Muslim-Christian relations can long ignore this situation.. Furthermore, Judeo-Christian as well as Muslim-Christian relations must be reexamined. Continuing to ignore these matters constitutes tacit agreement to allow a country like Lebanon to be destroyed without protest. Lebanon, in fact, represents more than a prototype: it is a challenge to the cruelty of renewed sectarian fundamentalism. Consequently, the future of Muslim-Christian relations in Lebanon must be postulated on three factors:

First, the option for modernity must be left open in opposition to any sectarian fundamentalist revival. This option is implicit in the French declaration of 1789, the San'Francisco charter of the United Nations, and the Second Vatican Council's declaration, *Gaudium et Spes,* regarding freedom of conscience. Modernity, in this sense, signifies the evolution of men toward the right of equality, and the right of peoples to independence, regardless of religious or racial differences. It rejects any government which relies on a divine right to occupy territory by force, or that practices discrimination in that territory. It does not question the legitimate right of peoples to a social life in accordance with their religious traditions. Moreover, the state is obliged to preserve the "right to differ," and to acknowledge the legitimacy of divers religious traditions. Since no state can cleave to a particular religion—or even to the militant nonreligion of atheism—without threatening both harmony between communities and peace between nations, the legitimate claims of various societies to live according to their beliefs must be supported. In short, the "laicity of the state" must be strongly affirmed. Only in this way can harmony be promoted and justice ensured between the legitimate claims of "homo religiosus" and the definitive achievements of "homo laicus" in modern times.

Second, regarding the particular case of Lebanon, I should like to invoke the ideals which gave birth to the American nation. There is no future for Lebanon as long as it remains dominated by its neighbors, and regional conflicts are fought on its territory at great cost to its people. Several Lebanese leaders have proposed that Lebanon be removed from the arena of armed conflict in the region, suggesting for it a status in the Middle East somewhat analogous to that of Austria in Europe. A group of Paris-based Lebanese university professors presented such a proposal in the form of a UN resolution to President Carter and asked him to communicate it to his successor.[20] This proposal called for the disarmament of Lebanon and the formation of a multinational protective force guaranteed by the five permanent members of the UN Security Council. It also constituted an appeal to the American people and their churches to support these recommendations.

Third, no lasting peace in Lebanon or elsewhere in the Middle East can be achieved without resolving the problem of Palestine. Whatever its nature, the only efficacious solution to the problem depends on direct dialogue between the interested parties—namely, Israel and the Palestinians.

Abrahamism Perverted

It is a perversion of Abrahamism when innocent blood is shed in the Middle East without reference to the Abrahamic heritage. For the intellectual as well as the believer, this is an intolerable situation. Abrahamism, as both the Quran and the Bible teach, represents three basic values: obedience to God in *faith*, and, if need be, in sacrifice; the primacy of *prayer* in adoration and intercession; and the sacred duty of *hospitality*. These three values, as defined by their eponym, were experienced by him as an expatriate who recognized the desert as a spiritual condition. This condition is what the Bible calls *exodus* and the Quran *hegira*.

It is difficult to identify these values in the principles and practices of the present generation, which nevertheless continues to call itself Abrahamistic. Furthermore, many members of the three monotheistic religions pervert Abrahamism when they exploit the notion of a chosen race with an inherited set of privileges, the possession of land by force on the pretext of some divine right, and the founding of a state through claims to a divine assignment. Abuses in the name of Abrahamism include not only state exactions, spoliations, and discrimination, but also the kind of "toleration" of other beliefs and minorities practiced by the ascendant power. This type of tolerance is merely a form of discrimination that seeks to disguise the domination of the strong over the weak, and illustrates a contemptuous disdain for the principle of the equality of all men before God.

Another abuse of the Abrahamic legacy is the talk of a so-called reconciliation between Israel and Ishmael. Basically, such reconciliation places the universalism of Islam in the context of the Arab-Israeli conflict. Quranic Islam, however, refers to Abraham's faith in the context of prayer and the promotion of the Meccan pilgrimage, and not the actual condition of the Abrahamic ascendance of any one people, such as the Arabs. Besides, in this context reconciliation between Israel and Ishmael would confer upon the state of Israel a political status and legitimacy which can hardly claim to be rooted in faith. It is perhaps significant that the latest Vatican declaration concerning interchange with the Jews has carefully omitted any reference to faith in the establishment of contemporary Israel in Palestine.[21]

On a practical level, one should be wary of any ecumenical attempt that aims at reconciling monotheists before meeting the justified demands of the most oppressed among them. I am thinking here in particular of the joint project of building a synagogue, a mosque, and a church on Mount Sinai. No project of this sort can be justified until the rights of the Palestinian people are met. This was the conviction of Judah Magnes, founder of the Hebrew University, as well as by his Ihud group.[22] First among their demands was the right of the Palestinians to return to their homeland.

(I might add that, great spiritualist that he was, Magnes tried to solve the ambiguity inherent in any reference to Abrahamism by adjoining it to three necessary connotations: devotion to the love of God, as suffered through the martyrdom of Hallaj; openness to universal brotherhood, as experienced by St. Francis and Charles de Foucauld; and the nonviolence of Gandhi. To simplify matters, let it be said that nothing in the Abrahamic heritage can be saved if it is inconsistent with the Gandhian ideal of *satyagraha*.[23])

Finally, I should like to call the reader's attention to the meeting at Casablanca of 19 August 1985 between Pope John Paul II and King Hassan II of Morocco, at the latter's invitation and in the presence of

80,000 young people. Noting that he often speaks to young people, the pope welcomed the opportunity to meet for the first time with Muslim youth. He urged them not to be passive in the face of war, hunger, racism and injustice, for they "are responsible for the world of tomorrow." He said that Christians and Muslims have "many things in common," that "Abraham is the model for us all of faith in God," and that "the dialogue between Christians and Muslims is more necessary than ever today." Although he is bishop of Rome, the pope said that he came to them "as a believer" and as a member of the church which "shows particular concern for Muslim believers in view of their faith in the one God."[24]

To emphasize the importance of this meeting, and to preclude any ambiguity or exploitation, we should keep in mind that Peter's successor as bishop of Rome and universal pastor can in no way be considered a political *commandeur des croyants*, much less an *Ayatollah des Roumis:* John Paul does not claim temporal power over anything but Vatican City, and that only to guarantee his freedom as head of the Catholic Church. He is also a stubborn defender of the rights of man and the freedoms of peoples. In his speech at UNESCO on 2 June 1980, in which he refered to culture as the foundation of national identity, John Paul declared that a nation's right to independence, as in the case of his native Poland, is not founded on religion, however fundamental that may be to the identity of a nation; the *culture* of the nation is the deciding factor, the pontiff said.[25] John Paul II's speech, along with the three papal letters favoring coexistence in Lebanon,[26] therefore constitute the basis of the case for Lebanon and the cause of Muslim-Christian relations.

Draft of a Resolution to be Presented by the Lebanese Government to the Security Council of the United Nations, on the Proposal of the National Reconciliation Committee

Resolution:

The Security Council:

On the basis of the Memorandum received from the Lebanese Government dated _____.

On the basis of previous decisions of the Council concerning Lebanon,

Given that the dangers threatening the existence of the Lebanese Republic and the integrity of its territory constitute a danger for the peace and security of the world,

Concerned about avoiding the repetition of similar situations in the future which are contrary to the spirit and letter of the United Nations Charter,

Decides the following:

Article 1: The Council confirms that the borders of the Lebanese Republic as defined by the Constitution of the country are definitive and fixed and solemnly reaffirms the prohibition of the use of Lebanese territory for any military action by a third party.

Article 2: The Council demands that the unconditional withdrawal of Israeli forces from the entire Lebanese territory be initiated forthwith and that the Syrian and Palestinian military occupation be brought to an end.

Article 3: The Council reaffirms that the Armistice Agreement between Lebanon and Israel signed in 1949 under the United Nations is still in force. The Council takes cognizance of the official announcement of the Lebanese Government in which the latter affirms that the Cairo Accord signed in 1969 is null and void; the Council also takes cognizance of the reaffirmation by Lebanon of its adherence to the League of Arab States and of the suspension of its participation in the Inter-Arab Defense Treaty.

Article 4: By means of this decision the Council constitutes a peace-keeping force in which nations not directly involved in the Arab Israeli conflict will participate, and puts at the disposal of this force all the means necessary to carry out its mission.

Article 5: The mission of the peace-keeping force includes support to the legal Lebanese authorities for the realization of the following objectives:

a. Dissolution of all armed militias and incorporation of their qualified individuals into the Lebanese army, with the understanding that the Lebanese army must play the role of a unified national force working towards national integration, the defense of the borders and constitutional institutions, as well as the socio-economic development of the various regions of the country.

b. Organization of free legislative elections for the purpose of establishing a new parliament which will have as its mission making the necessary modifications to the functioning of the institutions, in order to insure adequate guarantees to the various groups and communities, as well as to the citizens as a whole, based on the principles of liberty, democracy and equality.

c. Return to their homes of all persons displaced by the war since 1975, and protection of the entire civilian population.

Article 6: This resolution is to be considered a new International code of the Lebanese Republic; the permanent members of the Security Council guarantee this new code as well as the immediate implementation of this resolution through any and all means provided by the United Nations Charter.

[Paris, November 1983]

Notes

1. Istifan Duwayhi, *Ta'rikh al-Ta'ifah al-Maruniyyah,* ed. Rashid al-Khuri al-Shartuni (Beirut, 1890). Cf. Philip Hitti, *Lebanon in History* (New York: St. Martin's, 1957), p. 402.—ED.

2. Youssef Bey Karam (1823–89) was a Maronite leader from Ihdin in northern Lebanon and champion of the Christian cause in Lebanon.—ED.

3. Imam Musa al-Sadr was born in 1928 in Qom, Iran, of a prominent Shi'a family with branches in Iran, Iraq, and Lebanon. In 1969, Sadr became the first head of the Higher Shi'a Islamic Council in Lebanon, and in 1974 he created the "movement of the deprived" to protest the Lebanese government's failure to protect south Lebanon against Israeli attacks. He later established a resistance movement to defend south Lebanon. Called *Afwaj al-Muqawama al Lubnaninyya* ["Battalions of the Lebanese Resistance"], the movement is now better known by its acronym Amal. Sadr disappeared in 1978 while on a visit to Libya.—ED.

4. Kamal Jumblatt (1917–77) was the leader of one of the two most prominent Druze families in Lebanon. He studied law at the Sorbonne and the Jesuit University in Beirut. He played a central role in the Lebanese civil war as leader of the Lebanese National Movement until his assassination on 16 March 1977.—ED.

5. I have purposely avoided mentioning particular Maronites by name in this section.

6. Istifan Duwayhi (1630–1704) was born at Ihdin in northern Lebanon. He was educated at the Maronite College in Rome and ordained to the priesthood in 1656. He became bishop of Nicosia in 1668, and was elected patriarch of the Maronites in 1670. Duwayhi's works include a history of the Maronite community, *Tarikh al-Taʿifah al Maruniyyah*, whose theme is the perpetual orthodoxy of the Maronites and their early connections with the Church of Rome, and *Tarikh al Azmininah*, a general Middle Eastern chronicle devoted to the events affecting the Maronites and their local history. For more on his ideas, see Iliya F. Harik, *Politics and Change in a Traditional Society, Lebanon, 1711–1845* (Princeton, N.J.: Princeton University Press, 1968), pp. 131–34.—ED.

7. Karam was deeply involved in the civil war of 1860. He opposed the 1861 settlement imposed by the international powers when it became clear that, under the Muttasarrifiyyah system, Maronites could not hold the office of governor of Mount Lebanon. He was exiled for his opposition to the newly appointed Ottoman governor, Dawud Efendi, an Armenian Catholic, residing first in Istanbul, then in Algeria, France, and finally Italy, where he died. See Kamal S. Salibi, *The Modern History of Lebanon* (London: Weidenfeld and Nicolson, 1965), pp. 112–13.—ED.

8. Joseph Karam, *Reponses a des Attaques Centre l'Auteur et Contre d'Autre Chretiens du Liban* (Paris, 1863), and *Aux Gouvernements et Nations de l'Europe: Situation du Liban* (Rome, 1877).—ED.

9. In addition to the references which I have sprinkled my paper, the reader will find in my *Pentalogie antiochienne* very extensive material on both subjects. In fact, the first volume (which runs to more than a thousand pages) is largely dedicated in its opening section to the relations of the Maronites with Rome, and in its second part to the situation of Lebanon vis-à-vis France, Islam, and the Arab world.

10. According to Hitti, regulations for privileges and responsibilities of foreign citizens were gradually embodied in commercial and judicial treaties drawn in chapters ("capitulations," <Lat. *capitula*). In 1535, Francis I obtained the first capitulations for France, laying the basis for the French trade. In 1740, Muhmud I signed a treaty with Louis XV that put under French protection not only French pilgrims to the Holy Land but all other Christians visiting the Ottoman Empire. These concessions laid the foundation for the French claim to protect all the Catholic Christians of Syria. See Hitti, *Lebanon in History*, pp. 362–63.—ED.

11. Naturally, I cannot go into detail about the intentions of the various agents and the successive and at times incredible (but more often tragic) states of this joint Franco-Roman plan for the Arab and Muslim East. Neither will I attempt to justify the various contributions of the Maronites, who have in the past suffered tribulations which they remedied as best they could with the means at their disposal. Stripped of all complexes in this respect, and not being disposed to do penance for my ancestors (but not uncritical either), I fully accept my heritage and present and defend it as an undertaking whose success or failure constitutes precisely the current stake of the relations between Christians and Muslims and Jews. The defense which I make in favor of this undertaking, therefore, brief though it may be, is an invitation, if not a summons, to the reader to adopt a free and personal position. It is clear that the misfortunes which have seemed to spare no one in the Middle East do not give us either the time or the leisure to indulge in purely academic dissertation. The reader should not be surprised, there-

fore, if—as an impotent witness of the misfortunes, not alone of the Maronites but of Lebanon, of Palestine, and of the whole Arab world—I sometimes stray beyond strict historical analysis (though not, it is hoped, beyond the bounds of proper restraint) in an effort to make the bitterness more bearable.

12. According to the well-known work by Edward Said. See his *Orientalism* (New York: Random House, 1978).—Ed.

13. The same process took place in the course of the modernization of Japan.

14. According to Albert Hourani, Taha Hussein (1889–1974) was "the writer who has given the final statement of the system of ideas which underlay social thought and political action in the Arab countries for three generations." Hussein was born in a small town in Upper Egypt. Blind since an early age, he was educated first at an Islamic *kuttab* and then, at age thirteen, at the Azhar, where he came into contact with the ideas of Muhammad Abduh. (He also studied in France from 1915 to 1919.) At the Azhar he obtained a thorough knowledge of the Arabic language, and later became a pioneer in developing the modern Arabic novel. In 1938 he published his most important work of social thought, *Mustaqbal al-thaqafah fi Misr [The future of culture in Egypt]*, in which he stressed the fact that "the Egyptian mentality has been exposed to Mediterranean influence from its earliest days, and . . . has been cross-fertilized in every domain by the peoples of the Mediterranean." For an analysis of Hussein's thought, see Albert Hourani, *Arabic Thought in the Liberal Age: 1798–1939* (London: Oxford University Press, 1970), pp. 324–40.—Ed.

15. Fakhr al-Din II (1573–1635) was the Ma'nid Druze Amir of the Shuf. After the death of his father in 1585, his mother placed him under the protection of the Maronite Khazin family. He later returned to the Shuf, where favorable circumstances enabled him to extend his rule over all of Mount Lebanon, Sidon, and Galilee, and into Syria. He was responsible for the Maronite-Druze entente which established Lebanon as an autonomous Ottoman province and laid the foundation for modern Lebanon. His challenge to Ottoman domination and his desire to modernize Lebanon attracted the attention of the European powers, especially of the Grand Duke of Tuscany, Cosmo II, who himself had ambitions for an empire in Syria. His negotiations with European powers, the development of a formidable military machine, and his favorable attitude toward the Christians, however, alarmed the Ottoman authorities, who sent an army against him. Fakhr al-Din was defeated, captured, taken prisoner to Istanbul, and strangled. See Hitti, *Lebanon in History*, pp. 371–85, and Salibi, *Modern History of Lebanon*, p. 3.—Ed.

16. Elias el-Hoyek was the Maronite patriarch who led a delegation to the Versailles Peace Conference in 1919 to press for a separate and enlarged Lebanon under French protection. Emile Edde was a prominent Maronite lawyer who was president of Lebanon from 1936 to 1941. An ardent Lebanese nationalist and Francophile, Edde regarded Lebanon as primarily a Christian homeland. For more on Edde's political career and personality, see Salibi, *Modern History of Lebanon*, pp. 171–78.—Ed.

17. In his address to the Lebanese people, the pope said: "Freedom, understanding, hospitality and openness of heart are the values on which the Lebanon of yesterday stood. These values are the basis of the Lebanon of tomorrow. A society animated by the democratic and pluralistic ideal is a precious patrimony which cannot be permitted to disappear." (John Paul II, "Toward Peace in Lebanon," *Origins* 14 (24 May 1984): 29–30.

18. I will begin by calling on a certain number of witnesses. I do so, not to excuse the severity with which I am obliged to speak of the American role, but to justify it. First, I call upon the American people of liberty who insist that when one is obliged to keep silent in other lands, one can say openly in the United States what one thinks—certainly not against the people, but against the errors of their leaders. Next, I call upon the great number of my own people, members of my family as well as of the country of my birthplace, who, for more than 100 years, have made the land of liberty their own. Finally, I call upon the Americans of Lebanon, whether they be Lebanese by birth or only Lebanese in their sympathy.

19. On 1 October 1985, Israel attacked the PLO headquarters near Tunis with American-built F-15s, killing at least sixty-one Palestinians and a dozen Tunisians. According to the Israelis, the raid was in retaliation for a series of terrorist attacks—in particular, the killing of three Israelis in Cyprus. President Reagan first characterized the raid as a "legitimate response," but the White House later said that although the raid was "understandable" a bombing in which scores of people were killed "cannot be condoned."—ED.

20. The text of this proposal may be found at the end of the article.

21. "Notes on the Correct Way to Present Jews and Judaism in Preaching and Catechesis," issued 24 June 1985 by the Vatican's Commission for Religious Relations with the Jews.—ED.

22. Judah Magnes (1877–1948) was chancellor and first president of the Hebrew University in Jerusalem. The Ihud (Union) Association in Palestine was a Jewish group which was convinced that the Palestine problem could only be solved through Jewish-Arab cooperation. According to the statement of Magnes and Martin Buber to the Anglo-American Committee of Inquiry, "The Ihud (Union) Association stands for the union of Jews and Arabs in a bi-national Palestine based on the parity of the two peoples; and for the union of the bi-national Palestine with neighbouring countries. This Union is to be a Regional Union under the auspices of the U.N.O." Magnes was chairman of the Ihud Association. See Judah Magnes and Martin Buber, *Arab-Jewish Unity: Testimony before the Anglo-American Inquiry Commission for the Ihud (Union) Association* (1947; reprint ed., London: Victor Gollancz, 1976).—ED.

23. Al-Husain ibn Mansur al-Hallaj (A.D. 857–927), considered one of the greatest Muslim mystics and saints, was martyred in Baghdad. He recognized that the way of union with God was through love and suffering. In accepting his torture and condemnation, he sought to transcend the judicial framework of his community and offer himself as a sacrifice for it by submitting voluntarily to its law. He is the subject of a famous two-volume biography by L. Massignon, *La Passion d'al-Hallaj, martyr mystique de l'Islam* (1922).

St. Francis, is of course, St. Francis of Assisi (1182–1226).

Charles de Foucould (1856–1916) was born in France and, in the tradition of St. Francis, renounced a military career and became a hermit at Beni-Abbes in the Sahara. His unique apostolate depended not so much on "good works" as upon bringing the "presence" of Christ to the desert tribes. He was murdered by tribesmen on 1 December 1916, but his spiritual writings provided the inspiration for the founding of the Little Brothers of Jesus in 1933 and, three years later, of the Little Sisters of Jesus.

Satyagraha was the Sanskritic combination Gandhi used to describe his way of life and action—namely, "truth and force." It has been famously translated as "passive resist-

Yoakim Moubarac

ance," but this has been elaborated upon by Erikson and others "as [not only] implied action based on the refusal to do harm, but also as a determination not to violate another person's essence." See Erik K. Erikson, *Gandhi's Truth* (New York: Norton, 1969), pp. 410–18.—ED.

24. "John Paul II in Morocco, Dialogue Between Christians and Moslems," *Origins* 15 (29 August 1985): 174–76.—ED.

25. "The Pope's UNESCO Address: The World as an Environment for Humanity," *Origins* 10 (12 June 1980): 58–64.—ED.

26. The pope's letter to the world's Catholic bishops stated that "we do not forget" the Christians of Lebanon, but "count on them and on their presence in a democratic Lebanon." Both the pope and the universal church, he said, are aware that "the development of Christianity in Lebanon has an effect on the presence of Christian minorities in the Middle East" and that "the Christians of the Arab world have always felt at home in this region where they have contributed to the spread of a message of culture and progress beneficial to all." The pope closed his letter by expressing "our esteem for the non-Christian Lebanese, and we ask God to enlighten them so that they will be able to resist the temptation to yield to partition and to the mistrust which it so easily engenders." ("Toward Peace in Lebanon," *Origins* 10 (12 June 1980):30.—ED.

··◄⦂ 11 ⦂►··

Christian-Muslim Relations in Egypt

WILLIAM SOLIMAN KILADA

Past writers of various nationalities have described the everyday life of Egyptians as one of religious harmony. Thus Professor Nadav Safran of Harvard University: "There is virtually unanimous agreement among observers of all nationalities that the uprising of 1919 [in Egypt] was universal. The literature on the reawakening of Egyptian nationalism is so vast and so repetitious that we cannot and need not list . . . all the works."[1] A well-known English visitor to Egypt during the last century, Lady Duff Gordon, wrote in her *Letters from Egypt:* "The thing that strikes me most is the tolerant spirit that I see everywhere . . . Muslims and Christians appear perfectly good friends. . . ," and she went on to recount some incidents she had witnessed in one of the cities of Upper Egypt.[2] Likewise, the earl of Cromer, the British high commissioner after the occupation, stated that "the only difference between the Copt and the Muslim is that the former is an Egyptian who worships in a Christian Church, whilst the latter is an Egyptian who worships in a Mohammadan Mosque."[3] And well before any of these observers, *Description de l'Egypt* had noted: "The Copts form part of the nation in a conquered land; their . . . community, due to some organizations derived from the Gospel (moral) give Egypt a picture of unity and harmony; it is a picture rare indeed in these regions devastated by tyranny and oppression."[4]

It would be remarkable to speak about unity and harmony at this moment in Egypt's history. For this reason, one must emphasize the importance of Egypt's historical experience in the course of the last millennium in order to understand the great possibilities for peaceful Muslim-Christian relations when mutual goodwill predominates in a society.

My theme in this chapter, in the words of Professor Afaf Lutfy al-Sayed Marsot of the University of California, is "based on a rational premise; that, since something does not arise out of nothing, there must be a historical pattern of continuity and an integral framework for studying Egypt that would allow us to find reasons for events in historical terms."[5]

Broadly speaking, the fundamental bases for this phenomenon are three: *conceptual*, as it refers to the concept of man both in Christianity and in Islam; *objective*, as it refers to the place of the land and the people of Egypt in the Christian and Islamic traditions, and *historical*, as it refers to the constant endeavors of the Egyptian people—excluded for centuries from exercising authority in their land— to regain power and independence, and to implement their national, political, economic, social, and cultural aspirations. A fourth consideration, of course, is *the course of Muslim-Christian relations*. Although not without occasional setbacks, Muslim-Christian relations in Egypt have a strong, positive basis. Thus, the question is whether the previous phases of their relationship can provide a guide to new prospects.

Conceptual

Christianity teaches that man is made in God's image, after His likeness (Gen. 1:26). St. Paul said in Athens: "In Him we live and move and have our being. . . . We are also of his race" (Acts 17:27,28). "In Jesus Christ men acquired the power to become Sons of God" (John 1:12). The high position of humankind was also deeply expressed in Patristic works. According to St. Athanasius of Alexandria, the human soul can behold as in a mirror the Image of the Word of God (*Against Heathens*, 34.3).[6] In his *Incarnation of the Word*, Athanasius said that the Word of God was made man that we might be made God (54.3).[7] St. Antonius, the great Egyptian father of monks, said in his third letter: "He who knows himself knows God, and he who knows God, knows also the dispensations which he makes for his creatures."[8] St. John, too, had a bold vision for man. Dissatisfied by what man had acquired, he ventured to discern greater prospects, saying in his first epistle: "Here and now, dear friends, we are God's children, what we shall be has not yet been disclosed. . . . Everyone who has this hope . . . purifies himself" (1 John 3:1–3).

This self-consciousness of human dignity cannot exist without affecting both personal and social life. Although the Church did not exercise coercive state authority, its teaching and practice created an atmosphere that changed the actual legal and social system to make it compatible with this conception of humankind. In this regard, one can cite such historical examples as the abrogation of slavery. St. Paul's epistle to Philemon demonstrates how the dissemination of such ideas paved the way to adopting total legal liberty and equality between all human beings. The transformation of promises unaccompanied by the formalities prescribed by ancient law into binding legal contracts was achieved under the Christian ethic, which prohibited lying.[9] Egyptian historical precedents include the struggles of the Coptic church to safeguard its faith, independence, method of selecting its hierarchy,[10] monastic standards of communal life, and the regulation of fasting.[11]

Islam elevates the dignity of humankind and offers two important concepts. First, according to a *hadith* considered valid by Ahmed Ibn Hanibal, man was created by God in His image, the image of the merciful. Imam al-Nisaburi said that God granted to man, feeble as he is, a share of his glorious character.[12] In addition, the Quran dictates the dignity of man and the superiority of his creation. Its esteem for man is indicated by the *sura* that God, after creating man, ordered the angels to prostrate to him; the devil refused, and in so doing negated man's dignity. According to Quranic interpreters, man's creation in the image of God and his superiority to the angels are attributes of all human persons, of whatever religion or creed, by virtue of fatherhood in Adam.[13]

The second Islamic concept is that man, in the Quran, is God's *khalif*—His representative on earth and the guardian of His trust in the world. Hence, man is responsible for world welfare and prosperity.

From these two Islamic concepts emanates the basic principle in interreligious relations: there can be no coercion in religion. The legality of other religions rests on the dignity of the human person, which excludes any assault against a person's free will. Moreover, respect for the individual extends bridges of mutual understanding and authentic dialogue. Scholars consider this protection not only a right of man, but a necessity inherent in his personality, and thus a part of Islamic creed.[14]

The concrete historical course of the Islamic state since the Umayyads, however, has caused another concept to take precedence—that of the khalif as ruler. Professor Hassan Hanafi of Cairo University asks: "Why is the concept of man absent in the ancient Islamic

heritage?" Then he answers: "Because the study of the Imamate, that
is, the khalif as ruler, places emphasis upon man as governed, or man
as such."[15] The history of the Islamic state, both internally and exter-
nally, obliged legal scholars to exhaust their talents in safeguarding
the head of state, regardless of whether he fulfilled the prerequisites
of the khalifate, and to put forth arguments that justifed acceptance
of the status quo and submission to whomever had the mightier
hand.[16]

On the other hand, a new direction in political theory was taken
after the resurgence of the governed, who demanded the return of an
authentic khalif of God who would penetrate the realm of authority
and implement what their religion had guaranteed them. In Egypt,
this was achieved by the common endeavor of all elements of society.
One cannot understand relations between the religions without pursuing the course of Egyptian history.

Two ancient documents are essential to illustrate the extent to
which the concept of man could be implemented concretely in a
pluralistic society. First is the Islamic text which dates from the *higra*,
the first constitution promulgated by the Prophet on his arrival at
Yathreb.[17] Three groups constituted the society of Medina: the emigrants (muhaghareen) who came with the Prophet from Quraysh; the
Ansar, those Medinan believers who welcomed him; and the Jews. The
document regulates the relations between these groups and, most
significantly, uses the same terminology to designate the community
of *muhaghareen* and Ansar and the community of Muslims and Jews:
"They [Muslims of Quraysh and Yathrib] are a single community. . . .
The Jews . . . are a community with the believers. To the Jews their
religion, and to the Muslims their religion." The text calls all the
partners "the people of this document." From this we can trace, in an
accurate and precise manner, the basic principle of a genuine pluralistic society: one community with members from diverse religions.

Details of the participation of these constituents in political, financial, and defensive resolutions and activities affirm that every action is
taken collaboratively and conjointly:

Between them [Muslims and Jews] are counsel and advice and
honorable dealings, not treachery.

Between them there is help against whoever wars against the people
of this document.

The Jews bear expenses along with the believers so long as they continue at war.

The Valley of Yathrib is sacred for the people of this document.

Between them is help against whoever suddenly attacks Yathrib.[18]

The second document is a Christian letter from the second century that is attributed to the dean of the theological school of Alexandria. Its content is a clear prohibition against segregation and withdrawal from social life; its teachings encourage integration of all parts of society in one community:

The Christians are distinguished from other men neither by country nor by language nor by the customs which they observe. For they neither inhabit cities of their own, employ a peculiar form of speech, nor lead a life which is marked by any singularity. . . . But, inhabiting [among societies] and following the customs of the people in respect of clothing, food and rest of their ordinary conduct, they display to us their wonderful and confessedly striking method of life. . . . They obey prescribed laws, and at the same time surpass the laws by their conduct.[19]

Objective

From the time Muslims first came into contact with Egypt, Islamic thought has cherished the land and its people. Abd al-Rahman Ibn ʿAbd al-Hakam's ninth century account, *The History of the Conquest of Egypt, North Africa and Spain*, the earliest surviving Arab record of this event, extolls the merits of Egypt in its first pages.[20] Thus began a long tradition which was followed by an unbroken chain of such historians as Omar Ibn Yusuf al-Kindi, whose tenth century work is revealingly entitled *The Merits of Egypt*.[21] Of special note is the objectivity of the accounts, which reflects the ancient religious attitude of the Coptic consciousness. For example, one of the rivers of paradise mentioned in the book of Genesis is Gihon (2:13), which is the name of the Nile in Coptic liturgical prayers.[22] (In fact, the Coptic liturgy is preoccupied with the waters of the Nile.) Al Kindi also mentions Christ's visit to Egypt in his book.[23]

Egyptians were nutured in the values and understanding of Egypt through the rituals and institutions of the Coptic church many centuries before Islam. Schooled in this system and fortified by these values, they were able to fight in defense of their identity, independence, and dignity. Despite Egypt's varied religious history of Pharaonism, Christianity and Islam, the sense of belonging to the land of Egypt is a unifying bond that guarantees the continuation of a unique Egyptian world view. For example, the names of the months in the calendar used by the Egyptian *fellah* to calculate the agricultural seasons are the same as those used in ancient Egypt. They are also identical to the liturgical calendar used by the Coptic church. The Egyptians' love of the land thus has been a source of consolation during Egypt's occupation by foreign governments.

Besides the merits of Egypt cited by Muslim authors, there is also a special emphasis on the Copts, who are described as the most generous, virtuous, and hospitable people living outside the Arabian peninsula. Many of the sayings of the Prophet Muhammad also esteem the Copts.[24]

The historic meeting between Amr ibn al-As, who conquered Egypt in A.D. 642, and Benjamin, the thirty-eighth Coptic pope, has two versions, one Islamic and the other Coptic. Ibn Abd al-Hakim, writing two centuries after the event, noted

> in Alexandria a Bishop for the Copts called Abu Benjamin. Learning of the arrival of Amr ibn al-As in Egypt, he wrote to the Copts to inform them that Roman authority [in Egypt] was at an end.

Ibn Abd al-Hakim described the Copts as assistants to Amr.[25]

The second narrator is Severus ibn al-Muqaffa‘, historian of the Coptic patriarchs:

> Senutius, the believing duke, made known to Amr the circumstances of their militant father, the Patriarch Benjamin, a fugitive from the Romans. The Amr then wrote a letter to the provinces of Egypt in which he said: "There is protection for the place where Benjamin, the Patriarch of the Coptic Christians is, and peace from God; therefore let him come forth secure and tranquil and administer the affairs of his church, and the government of his nation." When the holy Benjamin heard this, he returned to Alexandria with great joy, clothed with the crown of patience because of the conflict which had

befallen the orthodox people through persecution by the heretics and in exile for thirteen years. Amr gave orders that Benjamin should be brought before him with honor, veneration and love. When Amr saw the Patriarch, he received him with respect and said to his companions and close friends: "Verily in all the lands of which we have taken possession hitherto, I have never seen a man of God like this man." For Father Benjamin was beautiful of countenance, excelled in speech, and discoursed with calmness and dignity. Then Amr turned to him and said: "Resume the government of all thy churches and of they people, and administer their affairs." Then the holy Benjamin prayed for Amr and pronounced an eloquent discourse (which made Amr and those present marvel), which contained words of exhortation and much profit for those that heard him. Afterwards he departed from Amr's presence honored and revered.[26]

Amr adopted an economic policy in favor of the indigenous population. He refused to raise taxes *(kharaj)*, and took a firm stand against the claims of the khalif, a fact which eventually caused his removal from his post.[27] Moreover, in opposition to the Caliph Omar's intention to create a military oligarchy that lived on the periphery of Egypt and specialized in military activities, Amr ordered the soliders to make periodic visits to rural areas. As a result, the conquerors were absorbed within the vast ocean of the Egyptian people and civilization. In time, those who came to Egypt identified, not with their original clan in Arabia, but with the district in which they lived during their occupation of Egypt.[28]

The Coptic historian Yoannis an-Naquiusi, who lived during the conquest, said that Amr respected church property, behaved honorably, and put the church under his protection.[29] The book containing the lives of the saints that is read during the Coptic mass honors Amr's memory, and states that the hearts of the Copts hailed what Amr had performed and thanked him.[30]

The first encounter between Islam and Christianity in Egypt, therefore, did not involve the elimination of one creed by another; rather, it was characterized by mutual respect and coexistence. In this way, a people emerged with a common language and continued its course in literature, art, folklore, history, and the religious sciences, both Islamic and Christian. Thus united, this people encountered the challenges from within as well as those from abroad. From this common life slowly emanated an authentic dialogue that started, not from theory, but from general practical attitudes that influenced each religion's view of the other.[31] Since the course was full of struggle and suffering, the third base of the Egyptian phenomenon, the historical, must be considered next.

Historical

Historically, Egyptians have sought to regain their dignity, both as a people and as a country. A look at the Medinan constitution and the epistle to Diognetus reveals the basis of Egyptian common life and religious integration. In the constitution, Muslims and the Peoples of the Book live together; in the epistle to Diognetus, Christians are forbidden to live in segregated areas. The influence of these documents on Egyptian society is striking: to this day, no Egyptian city or village is devoid of religious integration.

The epistle, which prohibits the wearing of distinctive clothing, attests to the integration of the religious communities. (A certain al-Hakim gave a ridiculous order determining the clothing of Christians, but these orders were disobeyed. According to scholars, this is further evidence that Egyptian society staunchly rejected religious segregation.) According to the Medinan constitution, both Muslims and the Peoples of the Book are to participate in the rights and duties of citizenship. The epistle to Diognetus teaches that Christians should not only obey the regulations of their society but should try to surpass the limits of these laws in their conduct.

There are five successive stages of Egyptian history: the preliminary uprisings; the administrative phase; the institutional phase; the revolutionary phase; and the seal of blood. We shall discuss each in turn.

Preliminary Uprisings

Three uprisings had a great impact on the political liberty of Egyptians. The first, in 1736, as recorded by al-Jabarti, occurred under the leadership of Shaykh al-Arab Hamman, a prince of the Hawara tribe.[32] The rebellion was crushed in 1769, but continued to have a lasting value in that it had begun in the region of the scholar and historian Rifaa al-Tahtawi. In France during the 1830 revolution, he noted the similarities between the Sa'di and French movements. Al-Tahtawi said that citizens cannot be both ruled and rulers; it is incumbent upon them, therefore, to relegate authority to those whom they choose. Such, according to al-Tahtawi, was the example of Egypt under the rule of Hammanis. The princedom of As-Sa'id, Upper Egypt, became *Iltizamia* Republic: *Jumhuria Iltizamia.*[33]

In 1795, before the arival of the French, the second uprising took place in Cairo. According to al-Jabarti,[34] it occurred when some villagers from the eastern region of the Delta complained to Shaykh al-Sharkawi of the injustice of those in authority. The people and their religious leaders demanded justice from the ruling Mamelukes; the Mamelukes declared their repentance and accepted the ruling imposed by the religious leaders. The judge was present and recorded the declaration, and the pasha issued a decree which the Mameluke leaders signed. Although the document was not respected because actual authority was in the hands of the Mamelukes, it was an important step forward because it recorded the demands of the ruled in a document signed by the representatives of a legal authority. Subsequent events would give the required institutional and compulsory guarantees to the document.

The final confrontation in this preliminary phase took place in 1805, after the 1801 withdrawal of the French from Egypt. Three powers then contested for authority: The Turks, the English, and the Mamelukes. The reader of al-Jabarti's third volume will understand how much the people of Cairo and the provinces suffered from strife and injustice in this period. Reacting to these hard conditions, the people formed a new movement, and—though the circumstances were similar to those in 1795—the results of 1805 were far more impressive, as the people at last succeeded in causing drastic changes in governmental institutions.

According to al-Jabarti,[35] the leaders of the people presented to the kadi the demands listed by al-Rafi'i:[36] henceforth, no tax was to be imposed without the consent of the *ulama* and the leaders of the people, and regulations were to be imposed upon soldiers. (These demands invite comparison with the bill of rights decreed by the British parliament in 1868.) For the first time in Egypt's political history, the *ulamas* and Omar Makram issued a decree which deposed the wali, the envoy of the Turkish sultan, and selected another in his stead. The will of the people, now backed by jurisprudential arguments, crystallized in the rejection of the concept that existing authority can extort obedience based on religious texts, and emphasized the right of the people to depose unjust rulers.

Hence, Egypt faced a new, more effective confrontation between the khalif of God and the khalif-ruler, who loses his legitimacy when he loses the approbation and the khalif of God. The sultan succumbed to the will of the khalif of God and issued a decree that designated Muhammad Ali as wali, seeing that he was desired by the people and the *ulamas*."[37]

The administrative phase is linked to the project of the new ruler, Muhammad Ali: to seek redress from the Ottoman state and/or build in Egypt a state for himself and his family.[38] Muhammad Ali concentrated on the army and, after many trials, concluded that it should be made up of Egyptians. Once Egyptians were admitted to the army, other barriers began to crumble and Egyptians entered the corridors of governmental administration.

Bowring, the British envoy, wrote in 1837 that the appointments of Christians in government offices had reached a high level. Moreover, he noted a new tolerance.[39] Kamil Saleh Nakhla, a Coptic historian, mentions that from the beginning of his rule, Muhammad Ali considered all Egyptians, of whatever creed, to be equal. He accorded the service of the homeland to those worthy of it, each according to his capabilities.[40] The advancement of the governed to positions of power was accompanied by a fresh political outlook that brought together both new constitutional concepts and the inherited legacy. Two shaykhs from al-Azhar fulfilled this task; Hasan al-Attar, who became shaykh of al-Azhar during Muhammad Ali's rule, and his disciple, Rifa'a al-Tahtawi.

Al-Attar (1766–1835) proclaimed that "our country must change its conditions and renew its sciences in order to achieve what it has not."[41] He was close to the ruler, who let him select an al-Azhar man to guide the first group of students to be sent to France. Al-Attar chose al-Tahtawi (1801–73), who had an intense, long-term impact on the Egyptian regime, from the era of Muhammad Ali to Ismail.[42] When he left for Paris in 1826, the Egyptians had risen in revolution and, as previously mentioned, had for the first time deposed a ruler, secured the appointment of another, and begun to share in the institutions of government. Al-Tahtawi, perceiving the similarity between the Hammani revolution and that of France in 1830 and deeply interested in the political and constitutional life of the latter country, translated and published important French documents of the periods.

From the first pages of his book describing his stay in Paris, al-Tahtawi declared his strict adherence to his religion:

> I have taken God the Almighty for a witness that I will not waver at all in what I say from the path of Truth. It is known that I only approved of that which was not in opposition to the Mohammedan Shar.

Al-Tahtawi presented a theory of authority in which two strong powers are needed, the ruler and the ruled. His translation of the French constitution posited that both rulers and ruled submitted to it, and that as a result the country prospered and no one complained of injustice. Upon his return to Egypt, al-Tahtawi showed his book to al-Attar who, pleased with it, presented it to Muhammad Ali. The latter ordered the book to be translated from Arabic into Turkish and distributed to government offices and officials, and that it be read in all Egyptian schools.[43]

By 1843, after al-Tahtawi's return, the high council was re-structrued to permit the representation of Egyptians from the provinces. As a result, the people of each province sent a shaykh to the council. Muhammad Ali also entrusted al-Attar to choose two religious leaders to sit on the council.[44] It should be noted that the decrees of the high council remained advisory; as a result, the popular constitutional movement in a subsequent phase demanded that the council's decisions be made obligatory.

Meanwhile, the regime's difficulties, both internal and external, continued to accumulate. As a consequence, the amendments were abolished in 1837 and Muhammad Ali's project ended.[45]

The Institutional Phase

The khedivate of Ismail—especially the formation of Egypt's first parliament, *maglis shura al nouab*, in 1866—marks the institutional phase of Egyptian history. Two noteworthy incidents, however, happened during the reign of Ismail's two predecessors. The first was the decision of Khedive Abbas I to expel all Christians from Egypt and banish them to the Sudan. Abbas sent for Shaykh al-Bagoori, shaykh of al-Azhar, to ask for a religious justification for this plan. The

shaykh, however, is supposed to have frowned and said: "Thank God
that no blemish has stained the conscience of Islam that you turn
treacherous to those who are under its guardianship until the last day.
Why this order banishing them?" Furious, Abbas dismissed the
shaykh. The incident demonstrates that Muslims insisted on the presence and protection of Christians, which affected all aspects of Egyptian life.⁴⁶

In 1855 Khedive Said abolished the last vestiges of religious
discrimination, the *jizya*. In Egypt there were two kinds of *jizya*: the
general tax paid by the nation to the Ottoman state, which applied to
Muslims as well as Christians (since both communities were excluded
from military service); and the special tax paid only by Christians.
Egypt continued to pay the general tax a century after the abolition of
the special tax, further demonstrating the equality of both commu-
nities.⁴⁷

The constitutional movement in Egypt grew to maturity as it
confronted two challenges: the decline of the Ottoman state and
Europe's financial and military expansion. Because the Egyptian government (the khalif-ruler and his wali) failed to defend the state and
look after the welfare of its subjects, the ruled (God's khalif on earth)
came forward. Just as Muhammad Ali was obliged to rely on the
Egyptians to fulfill his project, so too was Ismail as he faced Egypt's
financial crisis. Thus, Ismail formed the first parliament, in which
deputies were assembled from all the constituents of the Egyptian
community.⁴⁸

The Council was preoccupied with the interests and the integration of the community at large. For example, a proposal that special
schools be opened by the patriarchate for Coptic pupils was vehemently rejected. The Coptic community, the Council said, is part of
the nation. Copts, therefore, should be educated by the state, although priests may enter the schools to teach Coptic students their
religion. The history of Egyptian education proves that schools established by the government or by Coptic and Muslim associations were
the womb in which the consciousness of Egyptian citizenship was
bred.⁴⁹ The official organ, *al-waquai al-misra*, in its issue of 29 January
1875, hailed the inauguration of the first Coptic seminary.⁵⁰

European interference in Egyptian affairs reached its peak in
1879; an attempt was made to dismiss the parliament, but its members
refused to disband and insisted on discussing the budget and the
financial crisis.⁵¹ The notables and leaders of the people held several
meetings and decided on a financial program that would both thwart

the British and enable the country to guarantee the payment of its debts. They also demanded formation of a council of ministers composed entirely of Egyptians, and the promulgation of a constitutional order stipulating a cabinet responsible to parliament whose resolutions would be binding, not advisory.

On 2 April 1879, this "national assembly" presented a National Project that declared: "We have resolved, in our persons, and as deputies of the children of the homeland, to expend every effort to pay the debts of the government." They further resolved to implement the resolution "in complete union in word and deed." The declaration had more than three hundred signers, representing all elements of society, including the shaykh of the Azhar, the Coptic patriarch, and the chief rabbi.[52]

The project was accepted and implemented by the khedive. National celebrations followed, and the khedive received the national notables and leaders on 8 April 1879. The first to be received were the shaykhs *(ulama)* and the patriarch of the Copts, who were accorded great respect and honor. The next day a prominent Islamic religious notable hosted a banquet that was attended by statesmen and other important persons, including the khedive and the patriarch.[53] These endeavors were aborted when, on 26 June 1879, the sultan deposed Ismail and installed Tawfiq in his place.[54] The Egyptian people, nevertheless, continued their quest. Military officers under the leadership of Ahmed Urabi continued to demand constitutional reform and the end of autocratic rule.[55]

The confrontation between the khedive and Urabi in Abdine Square on 9 September 1881 revealed the conceptual basis of the revolution. The khedive rejected Urabi's demands for reform with the words, "To all these demands I have no right. I inherited the rule of this country from my father and grandfathers. You are nothing but the slave of our bounties." Urabi replied: "God has created us free. He did not create us a heritage or a possession. By Allah Who is the One and Only God, we shall not be legated or enslaved after today."[56]

Urabi's revolutionaries formed the first purely political party in the history of Egypt. The Nationalist Party, according to article 5 of its program, "is a political party, not a religious one. It is composed of men of different creeds and denominations, and all the Christians and Jews and whoever tills the earth of Egypt and speaks its language, are part of it." According to Shaykh Muhammad Abduh, this article showed that all are brothers with equal rights under the law. He declared that the al-Azhar shaykhs readily accepted this equality and supported the party because authentic Islamic teachings prohibited hatred and regard all persons as equal."[57]

With the British Navy in Alexandria and ready to occupy Egypt, the khedive deposed Urabi. A national assembly composed of five hundred members convened on 22 July 1882 to condemn the khedive's decision. It declared that his orders must be rescinded "because the Khedive has transgressed *al-shar* and the respected principles." Members of this assembly included the supreme judge of Egypt; the muftis of Egypt; many of the *ulama;* the Coptic patriarch; the chief rabbi; and representatives of the Orthodox, Greek Catholic, Armenian, and Maronite patriarchates, as well as the religious constituents of the assembly.[58]

The most important political constitutional decree of nineteenth century Egypt—that deposing the representative of the khalif-ruler—was issued by the entire Egyptian community. This marked the second time since the population had deposed the wali and nominated Muhammad Ali in 1805 that a decree was issued expressing the authority practiced by the ruled, God's khalif. The second decree, however, went further than the first, as it included a call for the participation of all members of society. In the ensuing conflict, peoples of all classes and religions, Copts as well as Muslims, rose to defend the nation and assist the army. Thus, the ruled, God's khalif on earth, rushed to implement his mission and prove his faithfulness.

The Revolutionary Phase

Counselor Tarek al-Bishri's voluminous study, *Muslims and Copts in the National Community,* describes the feelings of the Egyptians during the 1919 revolution:

> The Egyptians were sure of themselves and of the remoteness of the movement from any suspicion of sectarian dissidence. In fact, this was firmly controlled. What could be called a "secretarian problem" was absent from political life and action. The people proceeded joyfully, in confidence, as a person who has found himself and was self-confident. They were proud of what had been achieved. Even after the realization of independence, mutual confidence and optimism in the future of national life prevailed.[59]

With the shock of defeat and the occupation, Egyptians began their efforts to regain independence. One lesson of this difficult period was that the Egyptians themselves were their most effective ally. Since the rule of Muhammad Ali, Egyptian leaders and politicians had maneuvered for assistance from such contemporary great powers as France, Britain, and Turkey. But the nationalists became convinced that self-reliance was essential;[60] without solid unity, any national effort was doomed to failure.[61]

Immediately after the First World War, Egyptian politicians began their contacts with the British occupation authority in Cairo. A representative delegation of Muslims and Copts was formed to give legitimacy to the national movement.[62] According to the *Morning Post* of 9 April 1919:

> The Copts are more enthusiastic than the enthusiasts. They were among the foremost zealots in defending the nationalistic aims. The priests urged love of nation from the pulpits in the mosques and in al-Azhar, and the *ulama* and Shayks spoke in the Churches. One of the most rousing sights was the flag on which hung the Crescent and the Cross. The phenomenon is nothing but a politico-religious revolution.[63]

The most relevant expression of this classical national movement was the "new flag" or the "flag of the revolution," representing Egypt's millennary history. Similar symbols can be seen on lamps dating from the twelfth and thirteenth centuries and preserved in Egyptian museums.[64]

Two articles of the 1923 constitution crystalized the national revolution. Article 3 states: "All Egyptians are equal before the law, enjoy civil and political rights, and bear public duties and obligations. No discrimination exists between them as to race, religion or language." Article 149 states: "Islam is the religion of the state and Arabic its language." No contradiction between the two articles seems to have appeared in any one's mind at the time. The Copts did not feel anxious, since both Islam and Christianity dictate the dignity and equality of man. The experience of their common life, attachment to the land of Egypt, and national devotion were concrete proofs that guaranteed the common cultural heritage of Muslims and Christians.

Moreover, Egyptian thought from the late eighteenth and early nineteenth centuries, led by al-Tahtawi, accepted modern formulations of constitutional principles and saw no contradictions between them and traditional Islamic concepts. According to al-Tahtawi, all rational deductions elaborated in civilized nations and considered the basis of their laws are within the domain of the rules and criteria of *usul al fiqh*. He considered equality in rights and duties between the members of the community as natural, and advocated freedom of religion and the principle that citizenship is based on one's relations to a country, nation, or fatherland *(watan)*. According to al-Tahtawi, it is not possible to exclude the population from authority. He formulated the important modern principle of citizenship:

> All that is binding on a believer in regard to his fellow believers, is binding also on members of the same fatherland *(watan)* in their mutual rights. There is an obligation on those who share the same *watan* to work together to improve it and perfect its organization in all that concerns its honor, greatness and wealth.[65]

Phrases such as *minority complex* and *hegemony of the majority* disappeared from the Egyptian lexicon, to be replaced by *national fraternity*. In fact, the term *minority* in subsequent political literature lost any religious connotation, being applied strictly to economic and political matters. As a result of periods of oppression, Egyptians regarded religion as an individual matter, one whose function was to give consolation, inspiration, and courage. The events of 1919, therefore, became a gauge by which to measure the future course of Muslim-Christian relations.

The Seal of Blood

This phrase united the Egyptian people from Urabi to the 1919 revolution and through three successive wars in the Sinai. In the 1973 war, texts from the Quran and the Gospel were cited side by side.[66] Examples of valor on the part of those of all faiths filled the register of these national battles. A slain Copt general was the first to be decorated by the president of the republic in parliament, in 1973. Muslim and Coptic names are inscribed on the sides of the artistic pyramid forming the shrine of Egypt's Unknown Soldier, which states: "none can fix the rank of religion of this dear symbol; he is no more than an Egyptian soldier."[67]

The Course of Muslim-Christian Relations

The Egyptian phenomenon is a Muslim-Christian achievement in which both communities collaborated theoretically and practically. The Islamic elaboration, in which *ijma* or consensus is the source of rules, prescribed a mode of living in the Egyptian community which is compatible with the Quranic concept of man and the earliest Islamic political document. (It is also consistent with the Biblical concept of man and the Patristic legacy.) This is not to deny that there were difficulties and friction between Copts and Muslims, as noted by such Egyptian historians of the middle and modern ages as al-Maqrisi, Ibn Iyas, Severus, and al-Jabarti. With this conflict in mind, the following points can be postulated:

1. Discrimination in Egypt was between the ruled and rulers; it was never based on religious differences between Copts and Muslims. The rulers were not only of a different economic and social class than the ruled, but typically were of foreign origin. Egyptian Muslims, as well as Copts, were excluded from the realm of authority, although in due time both entered it.

2. The Egyptian experience shows that religious friction occurs when society at large is confronted by a general crisis, be it economic, social, or political. Philosophical, religious, and ethical discussions may be a substitute for the actual cause of the crisis.[68]

3. Religion is a global phenomenon. However, it has been observed that, in Egypt, certain concepts and modes of life have been imported from other countries, and may be incompatible with the nature of Egyptian society.

4. The contemporary religious situation in Egypt cannot be understood without taking into consideration the fact that the country was not free to develop its institutions until the first years of the nineteenth century. Its strategic geographical position repeatedly attracted the attention of the Great Powers. Muhammad Ali began to create modern Egypt in 1805, but Turkey and the European powers obliged him to desist in 1840. The same situation was nearly repeated

forty years later, when the British occupied Egypt. As a result, the Egyptian liberal experience was not allowed to develop and reach maturity, and it has been similarly stunted in the period since 1952.

In the nineteenth century, conflicts took place every forty years on the average; since 1952, there has been a conflict every ten years. As a result, essential resources for the development of science and technology have been lost.

The interpretation of these recurrent failures took on a religious cast. The remedy, in the minds of many of the new, frustrated generation, the one most keenly touched by the resulting economic and social difficulties, was a return to religious standards.

5. It is now evident that the solution to these problems is not religious extravagance, but lies rather in an honest confrontation. Once this is accomplished, religious masks will disappear, easing communal tensions, and new patterns of social, political and cultural life will emerge.

The historical course of Muslim-Coptic relations is an achievement for Egypt. The current generation may be in a better position than its predecessors, for Egypt now has an experience of national life and unity that was lacking when efforts began to remake modern Egypt, and to realize the marvelous combination of Crescent and Cross.

Notes

1. Nadav Safran, *Egypt in Search of Political Community* (Cambridge: Harvard University Press, 1961), p. 276.

2. Duff Gordon, Lady, *Letters from Egypt*, ed. Gordon Waterfield (London, 1969), p. 56.

3. Evelyn Baring Cromer, *Modern Egypt*, vol. 2 (London, 1908), p. 205.

4. *Description de l'Egypte*, 2d ed. (Paris, 1826), 28: 16.

5. Peter Gran, *Islamic Roots of Capitalism, Egypt: 1760–1840*, foreword by Afaf Lutfy al-Sayed Marsot (Austin, Tex.: University of Texas Press, 1979), p. viii.

6. *Nicene and Post-Nicene Fathers*, 2d series (Michigan, 1957), 4: 22.

7. Ibid; p. 65.

8. *The Letters of St. Anthony the Great*, tr. Dewars Citty (Oxford, 1975), p. 11

9. Chevallier, "Inexecution du Contract Synallgmatique" (Cours de Doctorat, Universite du Caire, 1944–45), p. 4.

10. See William Worrel, "A Short Account of the Copts," in *Dictionnaire d'Archeologie Chretienne et Liturgie* (Paris; 1940), cited by Sylvestre Chauleur in *Historie des Copts* (Paris, 1960), p. 20; and Scott-Moncriff, "Coptic Church," in the *Encyclopedia of Religion and Ethics*, (New York, 1912), 4: 113. See also William Soliman Kilada, "Currents of Christian Thought," *al-Taliᶜa* (Cairo, December 1966 and idem, "The Elections of the Patriarch and the Egyptian Democratic Heritage," *al-Taliᶜa* August 1971.

11. Asis Suryal Atiye, "Egyptian Monasticism," *Madaris al-Ahad* (November 1947), and p. 19, (December 1947), p. 13. See also Hakim Amin, *Studies in the History of Egyptian Monasticism* (Arabic) 3d printing, Cairo, 1963.

12. Al-Bahi al-Khawli, *Adam, Peace be Upon Him* (Arabic)(Cairo, 1974), p. 143.

13. Huwaydi Fahmi, *Muwatinun Lazimiyyun* (Cairo, n.d.).

14. Muhammad Imara, *Islam and Human Rights: Necessities not Rights,* (Arabic)(Kuwait, 1985).

15. Hasan Hanafi, *Islamic Studies* (Arabic) (Beirut, 1982):229ff.

16. Ibrahim Hasan Hasan, *The Social, Cultural, Religious and Political History of Islam,* (Cairo, 1979), and Muhammad Mahmud Rabiᶜa, *Ibn Khaldun's Political Theory* (Cairo, n.d.) (both in Arabic).

17. Quoted by Abdu Muhammad Adb al-Malik ibn Hisham, *Ibn Hisham's Biography of the Prophet* (Arabic)(Cairo, 1329 H.), pp. 94ff. See Montgomery Watt, *Mohammed at Medina* (Oxford, 1962), pp. 22ff, and Mohammed Hamidullah, *Le Prophete de l'Islam* (Paris, 1959), pp. 133ff.

18. The translations of both Watt and Hamidullah are inaccurate.

19. "The Epistle of Mathetes to Diognetus," *Ante-Nicene Fathers* (Michigan, 1956), 1: 63.

20. Abd al-Rahman Ibn ᶜAbd al-Hakim, *The History of the Conquest of Egypt, North Africa and Spain,* ed. Charles Torrey (New Haven, Conn.: Yale University Press, 1922). See also, *Studies on Ibn ᶜAbd al-Hakim* (Arabic) (Cairo, n.d.)

21. Umar Ibn Yusuf al-Kindi, *The Merits of Egypt,* ed. Ibrahim Ahmad al-Adawi and Ali Muhammad Umar (Cairo, 1971).

22. *The Book of Yearly Holy Blessings,* (Printing of the Association of the Church Renaissance (1949): 567.

23. Al-Kindi, *Merits of Egypt,* p. 64.

24. Ibn ᶜAbd al-Hakim, *History of the Conquest,* pp. 4–5.

25. Ibid., p. 74.

26. *History of the Patriarchs of the Coptic Church of Alexandria,* Arabic text., tr., and ann. B. Evetts, 2: "Benjamin I".

27. Ibn ᶜAbd al-Hakim, *History of the Conquest,* pp. 158ff. See also Ibrahim Ahmid al-Adawi, "The Description of Ibn ᶜAbd al-Hakim and the Financial and Administrative Reorganization in Egypt," in *Studies on Ibn al-Hakim [al-Hayᶜa al-Misriyya lil-Kuttab],* (Arabic), (1975), p. 131.

28. Ibn ᶜAbd al-Hakim, *History of the Conquest,* p. 139. See also Jamal Hamdan, *Egypt's Personality,* pt. 2 (Cairo, 1981), p. 306.

29. "Chronique de Jean, Eveque de Nikiou" (Ethopian), tr. and publ. M. H. Zotenbert, in *Notices et Extraits des Manuscrits de la Bibliotheque National et Autres Bibliotheques* (Paris, n.d.), 24: 584.

30. *The Book of the Upright and Trustworthy, Concerning Information on the Saints,* (Arabic) Used in the Churches of the Missionary Province of St. Mark (the Coptic Patriarchate), publ. Hegumen Philotheus al-Maggari and the Priest Michael al-Maqqari. Part I, (Alexandria, 1629), 1:281.

31. William Soliman Kilada, *Conversations between the Religions (Arabic)* (Cairo, 1976), pp. 182ff.

32. Abd al-Rahman al-Jabarti, *The Wonders of the Ancient Monuments* (Arabic) (Cairo, n.d.)

33. Muhammad Imara, *Complete Works,* (Arabic) (Beirut, 1973), p. 201.

34. Al-Jabarti, *Wonders,* p. 25.

35. Ibid.

36. Al-Rafi'i, *History of the Nationalist Movement,* (Arabic) (Cairo, n.d.), p. 302.

37. Al-Jabarti, *Wonders,* p. 26.

38. Amani Abd al-Rahman Salih, "The Roots of the Nationalist Idea for the July Revolution," in *al-Mashru' al-Qawmi li-Thawrat Yulyo* [The national plan for the July revolution], (Arabic) (Cairo, 1984), p. 50.

39. Muhammad Fuad Shukry, Abd al-Mansur al-Inati, and Sayyid Muhammad, Khalil, *The Permanence of a State: The Egypt of Muhhammad Ali* (Arabic) (Cairo, 1948), pp. 632, 692–93. See also Tariq al-Bashari, *Muslims and Copts in the National Community,* (Cairo, 1980), pp. 9ff. (Both in Arabic.)

40. Kamil Salih Nakhla, *Series on the History of the Patriarchs of the Alexandrian See,* (Arabic) pt. 5 (Cairo, 1954), p. 177.

41. Muhammad abd al-Ghani Hasan, *Hassan al-Attar* (Cairo, 1948) and Sami Badrawi, "Shaykh Hasan al-Attar," *Majallat al-Majalla* (Cairo journal) (March 1965) (both in Arabic)

42. Ahmad Badawi, *Rifa'a al-Tahtawi* (Cairo, 1958) and Mahmud Fahmi Hijazi, "The Origins of Modern Arab Thought in Rifa'a al-Tahtawi," *Alam al-Fikr* (Kuwait, April–June 1973) (both in Arabic).

43. Muhammad Imara, ed., *Rifa'a al-Tahtawi, The Complete Works* (Arabic), pt. 1, p. 46; pt. 2, p. 11.

44. William Soliman Kilada, "Muhammad Ali as Ruler," *al-Tali'a* (Cairo), p. 56.

45. Ibid.

46. Riyad Suryal, *Coptic Society in the 19th Century* (Cairo, 1981), p. 260. See also al-Bashari, *Muslims and Copts,* pp. 40–41. (Both in Arabic.)

47. Samira Bahr, "The Copts in Egyptian Political Life During the Period of the British Presence" (Arabic) (diss., faculty of Economics and Political Science, Cairo University, 1976), p. 167, and al-Bashari, *Muslims and Copts,* pp. 30–31.

48. Abd al-Aziz Rifa'i, *The Dawn of Parliamentary Life in Modern Egypt* (Cairo, 1964), pp. 9ff. See also Louis Awad, *History of Modern Egyptian Thought, From the Age of Ismail to the 1919 Revolution,* pt. 2 (Cairo, 1983), p. 34. (Both in Arabic.)

49. Anwar Abd al-Malik, *The Renaissance of Egypt* (Arabic) (Cairo, 1983), pp. 249ff.

50. Nibih Kamil Dawud, "The History of the Clergy in the 19th Century," *Majallat Madadaris al-Ahad* (Arabic mag.), nos. 1–3 (January–March, 1974), pp. 78–79.

51. Al-Rafiʿi, *The Age of Ismail* (Arabic) (Cairo, n.d.), pp. 177ff.

52. Ibid., p. 180–84.

53. Ibid., p. 191.

54. Ibid., p. 230.

55. Muhammad Husayn, *Nationalist Trends in Contemporary Literature* (Arabic) pt. 1 (Cairo, 1980), p. 134.

56. Abd al-Rahman Al-Rafiʿi. *The Urabi Revolt and the English Occupation* (Arabic) (Cairo,1937), pp. 127–28.

57. Ibid., p. 147. See also Muhammad Imara, *The Complete Works of Imam Muhammad Abduh,* (Arabic), pt. 1 (Beirut, n.d.), p. 107.

58. Al-Rifiʿi, *Urabi Revolt,* p. 402.

59. Al-Bashari, *Moslems and Copts,* pp. 141–53.

60. Husayn, *Nationalist Trends,* p. 142, and Awad, *Modern Egyptian Thought,* p. 124.

61. Ahamd Muhammad Al-Hawfi, *The Patriotism of Shawqi* (Cairo, 1978), p. 418. See also Faruq Abu Zayd *The Crisis of Nationalist Thought in the Egyptian Press* (Cairo, 1979), pp. 81–97. (Both in Arabic.)

62. Abd al-Azim Muhammad Ramadan, *The Development of the Patriotic Movement in Egypt from 1918 to 1936* (Cairo, 1968), p. 90, and Ramzi Mikhail Jayid, *Patriotic Unity in the 1919 Revolution* (Cairo, 1980), p. 19. (Both in Arabic.)

63. Mustafa Amin, *From One to Ten* (Cairo, 1976), pp. 130–90. See also al-Bashari, *Moslems and Copts,* pp. 150–52, and Abbas Mahmud Al-Aqqad, *Saʿad Zaghlul* (Cairo, 1936), p. 231. (All in Arabic.)

64. Muhammad Imara, ed., Rifaʿa al-Tahtawi, *Complete Works* (Arabic) pt. 2, pp. 433–76 See also al-Bashari, *Moslems and Copts,* pp. 207–25.

65. William Soliman Kilada, "On the Foundations of the Egyptian Model for Patriotic Unity," in *The People are One and the Fatherland is One* (Arabic) (Cairo: Center for Political and Strategic Studies, 1982), 30ff.

66. *Al-Akhbar* (Cairo), October 1977.

67. Hamdi Lufti, "Egyptian Soldiership Over Sinai" (Arabic), *al-Hilal* (October 1976), pp. 205, 325.

68. Saad al-Din Ibrahim, *Egypt Reconsiders* (Arabic) (Cairo, 1983).

··•◀§ **12** ᴽ▶··

Christian-Muslim Relations in the Sudan
Peaceful Coexistence at Risk

Abdullahi Ahmed An-Na'im

Introduction

In a recently published article, Dr. Hans Küng said that "there can be no peace among nations without peace among religions."[1] I fully agree, and add that there can also be no peace within a nation without peace among the religions adhered to by the population of that nation. It may be argued, of course, that the people who inhabit a given territorial unit are not a nation. Some of the inhabitants of present-day Sudan, for example, dispute that the Sudanese are a nation, and seek to justify secession on this ground.[2] As it is the view of the vast majority of Sudanese that they are a nation, however, and in light of their obvious determination to maintain the unity of their country, I will proceed on the assumption that Sudan is a nation—but not without noting that secessionist claims may be more widely asserted if such problems of national integration as the question of minority rights discussed in these pages are not addressed properly and soon.

Sudan was first united under the Turco-Egyptian administration of 1820–84. Mohamed Ahmed *(al-Mahdi)* then succeeded in overthrowing foreign rule, and established a native government, the Mahdist or *Mahdiyya*, which lasted until 1898.[3] In that year, Egypt reconquered the country, with strong British support. As Britain was occupying Egypt at the time, the British factor was dominant in the condominium (partnership) Administration that governed the Sudan until 1956, when full independence was achieved.

On the eve of independence, however, a civil war started in the predominantly non-Muslim southern part of the country. This phase of the civil war lasted, intermittently, until it was settled through a grant of regional self-government under the Addis Ababa Agreement of 1972.[4] When former Sudanese president Nimeiri sought to revoke

the agreement and impose traditional Islamic law *(Shari'a)*, the civil
war resumed in the south and continued to rage after his overthrow
in April 1985. One of the major demands of the rebels, who call
themselves the Sudanese People's Liberation Army, is the repeal of the
laws introduced by Nimeiri in 1983–84.[5]

The north-south conflict is clearly due to a variety of social,
economic, and political causes, but religion plays a significant role. If
the insistent claims of both sides that the unity of the Sudanese people
and the territorial integrity of the country must be maintained are to
be meaningful, the underlying causes of the conflict must be addressed. The goal of this chapter, then, is to identify some aspects of
the religious dimension of the north-south conflict, with its political
and legal implications.

Although Christians constitute a small minority of the country as
a whole, they are the educated leaders of tribes and communities in
the south.[6] There are also some Christians in the north, especially in
the Nuba Hills of central western Sudan. It is therefore possible to see
some of the country's problems in terms of Christian-Muslim relations, provided that one continues to be aware that this is but one
aspect of an extremely complex situation.

Historical Background

Sudan has always been greatly influenced by Egypt.[7] When Christianity came to Upper Egypt in the second century, it naturally
followed the Nile south into northern Sudan, the area sometimes
called Nubia. By the time of the Muslim-Arab invasion of Egypt in
A.D. 640, Christianity was well established in northern Sudan.[8] Instead of immediately pushing south, the Muslim armies continued to
advance to the west, into North Africa and Spain. A series of re-
ciprocal raids on the Egyptian-Nubian border led to the conclusion of
the Abdalla Abi Sarh peace treaty of 646. The subsequent centuries of
peace enabled Muslim Arab tribes to gradually migrate south from
Egypt and North Africa, and to spread Islam in the process. Reasons
of trade and cultural ties also contributed to the gradual Islamization
of northern Sudan. In due course, the Muslims challenged the political power of the Christian kingdoms of north and central Sudan, and
succeeded in replacing them with Muslim kingdoms that would last
until the nineteenth century.[9] This era of Islamic kingdoms, common

to the whole region of sub-Sahara Africa, ended in Sudan with the Turco-Egyptian invasion of 1820, which was succeeded, in turn, by the Mahdists, Anglo-Egyptian rule, and finally independence in 1956.

Little is known about southern Sudan prior to the nineteenth century, since that region had little contact with the outside world.[10] Its political isolation was broken by the Turco-Egyptian invasion, which extended the influence of the sultan over most of the areas now known as southern Sudan. Under the provincial governorship of Europeans, notably General Gordon, who would later become the governor-general of the whole Sudan, Christian missionary work started in southern Sudan in the mid-nineteenth century.[11] The advance of Christianity in southern Sudan was interrupted by the Mahdist victory in 1884, but the Anglo-Egyptian administration that followed the Mahdists allowed the missionary work to resume in the south.[12]

Except for a few Copts and pockets of Christianity in the Nuba Hills, the northern Sudanese are today predominantly Muslim. In contrast, the southern Sudanese remain largely animist, continuing to subscribe to a variety of traditional African beliefs despite their Christian leadership. It is therefore more accurate to describe the conflict in the Sudan, insofar as it is a religious conflict, as one between the predominantly Muslim north and the predominantly non-Muslim—rather than "Christian"—south. The Christians, however, are the leaders of the south, and their education and access to international resources help to define the conflict in terms of Christian-Muslim relations.

In concluding this historical overview, it may be helpful to note that Christian northern Sudan coexisted peacefully with Muslim Egypt for many centuries, and that Islam came to Sudan through gradual migration and conversion rather than military conquest. To put it another way, transfer of political power to the Muslims in northern and central Sudan was the consequence rather than the cause of the conversion of the population to Islam. During these periods, Muslims and Christians were able to live in accordance with their respective beliefs while coexisting with each other. This suggests that it was only when the Muslims sought to impose the totality of their own religious law, *Shariʿa*, upon Sudan as a whole that this peaceful coexistence was threatened.

The peaceful coexistence may also have been due to the fact that neither Christians nor Muslims adhered to their beliefs strongly enough that they felt disposed to fight with each other. It has been suggested that

historians have emphasized both the Christian character of medieval
Nubia (northern Sudan) and the Islamic aspects of its culture following the conversion of the rulers to Islam. There is evidence, however, that both religions rested lightly over an indigenous African
culture of rather a different character.[13]

During the only previous Sudanese experience with Islamic fundamentalism,[14] the Mahdist state of the late nineteenth century, all
Sudanese suffered, Muslims and non-Muslims alike.[15] The question
is now whether the current Islamic "fundamentalist" drive will succeed in imposing *Shariᶜa,* and the likely consequences of such imposition.

Islamization Politics

In modern times, Muslims tend to see an assertion of the ethical
and legal aspects of their religion as legitimate exercise of their right
to self-determination. On achieving independence in 1956, the question immediately arose of whether the proposed permanent constitution was to be Islamic or secular.[16] The country had inherited a legal
system based on English common law, due to the British dominance
of the Condominium administration.[17] The transitional constitution
of 1956 was therefore based on British constitutional practice, providing for a multi-party parliamentary government and guaranteeing
the fundamental rights developed within liberal tradition.[18] Some
Muslim Sudanese started to challenge that system as "alien" and
"inappropriate" to conditions in Sudan, and demanded an "Islamic"
constitution. Non-Muslim and even some Muslim Sudanese objected
to the very idea of such an "Islamic" constitution, and insisted on
maintaining the secular system, in one form or another.

Before the issue was settled with the adoption of a permanent
constitution, the army took over in November of 1958, postponing
the debate indefinitely.[19] When military rule was terminated in October of 1964, however, the issue was revived. The constituent assembly was in the process of adopting what may be described as an Islamic
constitution when the army seized power again in May of 1969. The
new regime enacted its own constitution, called the Permanent Constitution, in 1973. This constitution, which lasted for eleven years,

provided for a secular, one-party state, with some guarantees against discrimination on grounds of religion. The Addis Ababa Agreement of 1972, and the Regional Self-Government Act that implemented that agreement, were incorporated into article 9 of the constitution, and thereby safeguarded against amendment or repeal, except by constitutional amendment. Under these guarantees, and given the favorable political climate that prevailed for ten years, all hostilities ceased in the south. Later developments, unfortunately, revived the civil war.

Opposition to Nimeiri, who led the 1969 coup and became the first president of Sudan in 1971, was effectively suppressed in a series of confrontations in 1970, 1971, and 1973. The proponents of the Islamic constitution of the 1960s were either imprisoned or driven into exile in neighboring Arab-Muslim countries. In view of their continued opposition to his rule, culminating in the armed invasion launched from Libya in July 1976, President Nimeiri sought and achieved "national reconciliation" with his opponents in 1977. Imprisoned opposition leaders were released, and those living abroad were allowed to return. The proponents of the Islamic constitution, notably the Muslim Brothers, were given a prominent role in various political and executive organs. Most significantly, a national committee for the revision of Sudanese law in accordance with *Shari'a*, headed by Dr. Hassan At-Turabi, leader of the Muslim Brothers, was established in 1977. Moreover, Nimeiri encouraged the implementation of the so-called Islamic banking system, which was largely controlled by the Muslim Brothers.[20]

It is difficult to identify the exact causes of what might be described as the Islamic fundamentalist coup of August/September 1983, led by President Nimeiri himself.[21] Whatever his reasons, Nimeiri in any case suddenly decided to play the fundamentalist trump card and claim credit for implementing *Shari'a*.[22] This coup—and Nimeiri's earlier move to dismantle regional self-government in the south, in violation of both the constitution and the Addis Ababa Agreement—led southern Sudanese to retaliate in open armed revolt. If Nimeiri's moves were designed to strengthen his hold on the country, as most observers seem to agree, he couldn't have been more wrong-headed. Both moves proved tragically counterproductive. The revival of the civil war in the south both created a profound negative political reaction and intensified the country's economic problems. Moreover, the repressive and hasty manner in which *Shari'a* was applied generated wide-scale dissatisfaction, notwithstanding the support of the Muslim Brothers and a few traditional *sufi* (mystic) sects. In March/April 1985, a series of demonstrations and street riots, followed by a crippling general strike, forced the army to overthrow President Nimeiri.

Sudan in Transition Once Again

Although the overthrow of Nimeiri reintroduced the transitional state of the 1950s and 1960s, it was a transition with a difference. The laws that purported to transform the nature of the constitutional and legal system of Sudan from a common law–oriented secularism into a *Shari'a* Islamic state remained in force. The transitional military council, which is supposed to hand over power to an elected government by April 1986, said that it would leave the question of the principle and manner of implementation of *Shari'a* to the proposed parliament.[23] Nimeiri's "permanent" constitution of 1973 was repealed and his administration and political organizations were disbanded, although the *Shari'a* laws he had imposed remain intact.

This, I submit, tends to load the dice in favor of the proponents of *Shari'a*. The burden is now on opponents of *Shari'a* to have these laws repealed—a difficult task indeed. Whatever Muslim Sudanese think of Nimeiri's efforts to implement *Shari'a*, they will find open opposition extremely hard. Muslims have a religious duty to implement Islamic law,[24] and traditional *Shari'a* is the only view of Islamic law most Muslims have. True, some Muslims advocate basic reform in that law, but the move to develop a modern version of Islamic law is appreciated by only a small, persecuted minority. The leader of this group, the late Muslim reformer *Ustadh* Mahmoud Mohamed Taha, was executed by Nimeiri in January 1985 precisely because of his opposition to total and immediate implementation of traditional *Shari'a*.[25] In the view of this author, *Ustadh* Mahmoud's approach—seeking to reform *Shari'a* from within the Islamic tradition itself—offers the best hope for resolving the potentially explosive religious situation in Sudan today. This is not a view shared by the majority of Muslim Sudanese, however, The advantage apparently remains with the proponents of *Shari'a*, the traditionalists and "fundamentalists," until such times as there is a change in the thinking of the Muslim majority.

Other opponents of the total implementation of *Shari'a* are the secularists. Some of the liberal and traditional political parties, in the center and to the right of Sudanese politics, are somewhat ambivalent with regard to *Shariʿa*, and see great problems in its total implementation. They are unable to opposes *Shariʿa* openly, however, for fear of retaliation from their political bases. It is most likely, therefore, that these parties will be swept into open support for *Shariʿa*, or at least neutralized until *Shariʿa* takes strong hold of the country.

Recent developments tend to support this analysis. Despite its election pledge to repeal Nimeiri's laws, known as the September laws of 1983, the current government of Prime Minister Saddiq Al-Mahdi has been slow in implementing that pledge. Both parties of the coalition government, the *Umma* and Unionist parties, are bound by their supporters to a commitment to the same principles of *Shariʿa*. Any alternative legislation introduced by the current government, or by any new government constituted under the present prevailing view of Islamic law, will therefore not be able to redress the serious objections of non-Muslims outlined below. What is needed is not simply a change of political regime, whether democratic or otherwise, but a change in the Muslim understanding of Islamic sources and reformulation of *Shariʿa*.

On the left of the political spectrum are the Marxists, Arab nationalists, and similar groups. Their line of thinking, however, suffers the handicap of an association with atheism, in addition to the negative impression of secularism which seems to prevail among Muslims.[26]

With their numerical strength—one quarter of the total population; their location in the relatively inaccessible tropical equatorial part of the country; and their ability to obtain arms from and find training in neighboring countries, the southern Sudanese pose the most serious challenge to the proponents of *Shariʿa*. To understand why the non-Muslim Sudanese are so opposed to *Shariʿa*, however, we need to look into some of the implications of total application of that ancient legal system in a modern national state like Sudan.

Implications of Total Islamization

Shariʿa has always been applied in the Muslim parts of Sudan as the personal law for Muslims—that is, family law and inheritance. The debate over Islamization relates to the claim of the proponents of *Shariʿa* that it should be the *sole* basis of Sudanese law and constitution.

The opponents of *Shari'a* are not opposed to the application of *Shari'a* as personal law for the Muslims; their opposition is directed to the total application of *Shari'a*, since, as non-Muslims, they will be relegated to the status of second-class citizens under *Shari'a* rule.

As historically developed, *Shari'a* classifies its subjects in terms of their religious belief.[27] The limitations imposed by *Shari'a* on Christians, one of the Peoples of the Book *(Kitabyyn)*, are less severe than those imposed on polytheists *(Mushrikyyn)*, including those Sudanese who still follow traditional African beliefs. If the Christian Sudanese are entitled to object to their status under *Shari'a*, then non-Christians are entitled to even stronger objection. To illustrate the point, I will cite some of the less serious limitations that *Shari'a* imposes on Christians.[28]

As one of the Peoples of the Book, Christians fall under the compact of *dhimmi*, whereby they are a "protected community," enjoying security of person and property in exchange for payment of *jizyah*, or a poll-tax. Members of a *Shari'a* community, however, suffer a variety of civil limitations. For example, they have no access to certain types of public office, such as high-ranking executive office, general judicial office, and service in the armed forces of a Muslim state. *Dhimmi* status also involves a variety of other consequences flowing from the notion that non-Muslims, even the People of the Book, enjoy less legal competence *(ahliyah)* than the Muslims. Hence, a Christian would lack competence to testify in certain types of judicial proceedings.

Proponents of *dhimmi* object to describing a *dhimmi* community as a "tolerated" community, because of the derogatory connotations of this term. They say that *dhimmi* is in fact a privileged position, since it is a compact guaranteed by *Shari'a*. But since the rights of the members of a *dhimmi* community are inferior to those of Muslims—and since, further, a non-Muslim has no choice in the matter—*dhimmi* is inherently derogatory, irrespective of the particular term used to describe it. How can a Christian be said to be in a privileged position while assigned, by law, to an inferior status?

It is not surprising, therefore, that non-Muslim Sudanese, particularly educated Christians, strongly object to being made second-class citizens in their own country. They also resent being subjected to the *hodud* penalties, the strict punishments provided by *Shari'a* for certain offenses, such as theft and highway robbery. A Muslim may submit to these penalties out of a sense of religious obligation, believing that enduring such penalties in this life relieves him from eternal suffering in the next. But for non-Muslims with no such religious motivation, *hodud* is an abomination. Similarly, on the economic side, non-Muslims see no justification for restricting banking and commerce in the country in accordance with *Shariʿa's* prohibition of *riba*, interest and *gharar*, speculation. Again, the motivation is religious for the Muslims, and as such resented by non-Muslims.

Christians and other non-Muslim Sudanese have not hesitated in expressing their objections to *Shariʿa* rule. On 23 September 1983, the Sudanese Catholic Churches issued a statement entitled "We Prefer To Call God The Merciful."[29] In September 1984, another protest statement was issued by the Sudanese Catholic bishops and leaders of the Episcopalian Church, the Sudanese Church of Christ, the Presbyterian Church in the Sudan, and the Sudan Council of Churches.[30] Both statements strongly objected to the total imposition of *Shariʿa* in Sudan, although neither suggested any measures to be taken in opposition. The clear implication of the position taken by Sudanese Christians, however, seems to be that stronger action will follow if their grievances are not quickly addressed. A more militant and violent line was adopted in the south, for example, when the civil war resumed in earnest in 1983.

It is therefore clear that the total imposition of *Shariʿa* in Sudan will have drastic consequences for all non-Muslim Sudanese—and equally clear that non-Muslim Sudanese will not submit to *Shariʿa* docilely. The Muslims will either have to suppress the non-Muslims, by force if necessary, or the country will collapse again into civil war, this time probably on a scale never witnessed before. In either case, the human suffering and loss to the country as a whole will be considerable.

Finally, it must be noted that Sudan is a strategically important country. Besides bordering eight African countries in a sensitive part of a sensitive continent, it has a vital importance in the security of Egypt. Moreover, countries facing similar Muslim–non-Muslim conflict, such as Egypt, will view Islamization of Sudan as a dangerous precedent. It therefore seems extremely likely that any Sudanese conflict will invite external intervention, thereby threatening the region with the horrors of an international war.

Conclusion

The obvious conclusion is that Muslim–non-Muslim relations in Sudan face a potentially explosive situation. The Islamization debate—whether or not to implement total Shariᶜa—is accelerating to a heated conclusion, with both sides determined to settle the issue once and for all. The only hope, in my view, lies in the reformulation of Shariᶜa to achieve complete equality for all the citizens of a nation-state such as the Sudan. A promising way of achieving this degree of reform may be found in the work of the late Sudanese Muslim reformer, Ustadh Mahmoud Mohamed Taha, whose proposed reform methodology would give both sides what they want: an Islamic law, implemented by the Muslim majority, which fully safeguards the rights of the non-Muslim minority.[31] The Muslims seem, at the moment, unwilling to listen to this compromise. But as the intensity of the conflict grows, and all other hopes for an escape diminish, Ustadh Mahmoud's position will no doubt be appreciated by more and more Muslims until, let us hope, it achieves the necessary degree of support for its implementation. In the meantime, we can do little more than hope that the human cost will be kept to a minimum.

Notes

1. *Christian Century*, 102 (9 October 1985): 894.

2. Peter Russell and Storrs McCall, "Can Secession be Justified? The Case of the Southern Sudan," in Dustan M. Wai, ed., *The Southern Sudan, The Problem of National Integration* (Frank Cass: London, 1973).

3. For general background, see P.M. Holt, *The Mahdist State in the Sudan, 1881–1898* (London: Oxford University Press, 1958), and A. B. Theobald, *The Mahdiyya* (London: Longmans, 1951).

4. Mohamed Omer Beshir, *The Southern Sudan, Background to the Conflict* (London: C. Hurst, 1968), and idem, *The Southern Sudan: from Conflict to Peace* (New York: Barnes and Noble, 1975).

5. This is the common demand of all non-Muslim political parties and armed groups in the Sudan.

6. Statistics, when used to substantiate political claims or assess the relative strength of religious factions, are usually controversial. A variety of sources, however, suggest that 70 percent of the Sudanese are Muslim, 23 percent follow traditional beliefs, and 7 percent are Christians.

7. For a general background, see William Y. Adam, *Nubia: Corridor to Africa* (London: Allen Lane, 1977), and A. J. Arkell, *A History of the Sudan from the Earliest Times to 1821* (London: Athlone Press, 1949).

8. John Vantini, *The Excavations at Faras, A Contribution to the History of Christian Nubia* (Editrice Nigrizia, 1970), pp. 37–153, surveys many pre-Arab, Arab, and medieval Western sources to this effect.

9. Jusef Fadl Hassan, "Sudan Between the Fifteenth and Eighteenth Centuries," in Jusef Fadl Hassan, ed., *Sudan in Africa* (Khartoum: Khartoum University Press, 1971), p. 76.

10. As so rightly pointed out by Douglas H. Johnson, this is not to say that southern Sudan had no history or that its past is not worth knowing. The problem has simply been one of lack of historian interest, coupled with the difficulty of having to draw on oral traditions and other unwritten sources. As Johnson indicated in his article, "The Future of the Southern Sudan's Past" (*Africa Today*, 28: 33), we can now hope to learn more about the history of that part of the country.

11. Mohamed Omer Beshir, *The Southern Sudan: Background to Conflict*, pp. 13–14.

12. Not without some initial difficulties, however, since the new administration was at first preoccupied with political and security considerations, and feared that missionary work might interfere with the pacification and administration of the region (Ibid., ch. 3.)

13. R. S. O'Fahey and J. L. Spaulding, *Kingdoms of the Sudan* (London: Methuen, 1974), p. 17.

14. This term is used here in accordance with current popular usage. Otherwise, many modernist Muslim movements advocating the reform of *Shariʿa*, such as that of the late *Ustadh* Mahmoud Mohamed Taha referred to below, would also claim to be Muslim fundamentalists. In this sense, fundamentalism connotes adherence to the fundamental principles of Islam rather than the literal application of the ancient codes, as demanded by what I would describe as *negative fundamentalism.*

15. So much so that the word *Mahdiyya*, referring to the Mahdist rule of the last century, is now popularly used in Sudan to describe any situation of extreme injustice and disorder.

16. For a general discussion, see C. Thompson, "The Sources of Law in the New Nations of Africa: A Case Study of the Republic of the Sudan," *1966 Wisconsin Law Review*, p. 1146, and J. A. Lutfi, "The Future of the English Law in the Sudan," *1967 Sudan Law Journal and Reports*, p. 219.

17. For a general review of the process of reception of English common law in Sudan, see Zaki Mustafa, *The Common Law in the Sudan* (Oxford: Clarendon Press, 1971).

18. Independence was attained on the basis of a transitional constitution, with the understanding that a "permanent" constitution would be drafted at a later stage. See Mohamed Omer Beshir, *Revolution and Nationalism in the Sudan* (New York: Barnes and Noble, 1974), p. 182, and Muddathir Abd al-Rahim, *Imperialism and Nationalism in the Sudan* (London: Oxford University Press, 1969), pp. 226–27.

19. Mohamed Omer Beshir, *Revolution and Nationalism in the Sudan*, chap. 12.

20. See *The Middle East* (August 1984): 43–44. This system claims to conduct banking operations without violating *Shariʿa*'s prohibition of interest and speculation. Close scrutiny of the operations of the Fidal Islamic Bank, the first "Islamic" bank to receive tax exemptions and other advantages for five years in Sudan, clearly shows that it was not as Islamic as it claimed to be.

21. For a survey of the process of total Islamization started on that date, see Carey N. Gordon, "The Islamic Legal Revolution: The Case of Sudan," *International Lawyer*, 19: 793. I think the term *coup* is more appropriate than *revolution*, given the single-handed and swift manner in which these laws were imposed.

22. Recent events in Sudan, leading up to and including the overthrow of Nimeiri and its immediate aftermath, are discussed by Ann Mosely Lesch in *Universities Field Staff International (UFSI) Reports*, 1985/No. 9-Africa (ALM-2-'85).

23. The transitional military council's decree no. 5 of 9 April 1985 stated that all laws in existence as of 6 April 1985 (the date of the overthrow of Nimeiri) shall remain valid until repealed or amended. In subsequent announcements, however, the council indicated that it would leave the issue to be settled by the duly elected parliament.

24. See, for example 5:44–45 and 24:51 of the Quran. (The Quran is cited here by the number of chapter followed by the number[s] of verse[s].

25. On the circumstances of the trial and execution of *Ustadh* Mahmoud, see A. A. An-Naᶜim, "The Islamic Law of Apostasy and its Modern Applicability: A Case from the Sudan," in *Religion* 16 (1986): 197. On 18 November 1986, the Sudanese Supreme Court ruled that the trial and execution of *Ustadh* Mahmud, were completely null and void, having been in total violation of established legal norms and procedure.

26. G. Wanburg, *Islam, Nationalism and Communism in a Traditional Society—The Case of Sudan* (London: Frank Cass, 1978), ch. 1 and 2.

27. See, for example, the Quran, 5:9 and 9:29, and see also Majid Khadduri, *War and Peace in the Law of Islam* (Baltimore: Johns Hopkins University Press, 1955), chs. 14 and 17.

28. For full discussion of these aspects of *Shariᶜa* and their historical practice, see ibid.; A. S. Tritton, *The Caliphs and Their Non-Muslim Subjects* (London: 1930); S. D. Goitein, "Minority Self-Rule and Government Control in Islam," *Studia Islamica* 31 (1970): 101; and H. A. R. Gibb and J. H. Kramers, *Shorter Encyclopaedia of Islam* (Leiden: E. J. Brill, 1953), pp. 16–17, 75–76, 91–92.

29. *Mashrek International*, February 1985, pp. 28–30.

30. *Origins*, 6 September 1984, pp. 180–81. Also published in *Al Montada*, Sept–Oct. 1984.

31. All of *Ustadh* Mahmoud's writings have been published in Arabic. An English translation of his principal work, *The Second Message of Islam*, prepared by the present author, was published by Syracuse University Press in 1987. I have also discussed the implications of *Shariᶜa* for non-Muslims and women and the prospects of Islamic law reform in a number of articles, including the following: "The Elusive Islamic Constitution: The Sudanese Experience," *Orient* 26 (1985): 329; "Religious Freedom in Egypt: Under the Shadow of the *Dhimma* System," in Leonard Swidler, ed., *Religious Liberty and Human Rights in Nations and Religions* (Philadephia: Ecumenical Press, 1986); and "Religious Minorities under Islamic law and the Limits of Cultural Relativism," forthcoming in *Human Rights Quarterly* 9 (1987).

Part IV

**Resurgent Islam
and Christian-Muslim Relations**

··◄❧ 13 ❧►··

The Christian Minority in an Islamic State
The Case of Pakistan

JOSEPH CARDINAL CORDEIRO

This is not a theoretical expose of the philosophy of history, as the title may suggest, but rather an attempt to describe how a Christian minority has tried to live the Gospel message in an Islamic state—its successes and its failures. As an historical essay, I have divided it into three parts: background, evolution, and the task ahead.

Background

The Muslim Component

Pakistan occupies the greater part of the Indus Valley and the adjacent mountains, where once flourished the ancient Buddhist civilizations of Harraqa and Mohen-jo-daro. Islam entered this land in the wake of Bin Qasim's seaward invasion in the eighth century A.D. Through all the political changes and vicissitudes of the next twelve hundred years, the Islamic faith has maintained a steady hold.

After roughly one hundred years of exposure to British rule and British institutions, Pakistan became independent in 1947. This event was marked by a mass exodus of Hindus and Sikhs to neighboring India, which left the land more solidly Muslim than before. In 1971, the eastern wing of the country was wrenched away to from Bangladesh, and a large chunk of the minority population went with it. This left Pakistan with a population of ninety million, of which 95 percent are Muslim and 1 percent Christian.

There are two denominations of Muslim origin, showing a basic faith in the Quran and the prophet Muhammad: the Sunnis, with a population of approximately 75 percent, and the Shiʿas, with a popu-

lation of approximately 25 percent. There is also a small but influential group known as the Qadianis, who hold the possibility of post-
Quranic prophets. A closely knit and well-educated body of 104,244,[1]
the Quadianis have established mission centers in many parts of the
world. They do not concede Muhammad to be the final "seal of the
prophets," and were consequently ousted form Islam and declared a
minority by legislation in 1974.[2]

The Christian Component

In the last quarter of the nineteenth century, Protestant and
Catholic missionaries began to evangelize with some success among
the depressed classes in the Punjab. These folk spoke Punjabi, the
regional language, and later Urdu, the national tongue. The second
and third generations of these Punjabi converts, educated in Christian
schools, built up a faith-conscious community. In their eagerness for
work and earning power, the Punjabi Christians spread to the other
provinces, especially to the urban centers, carrying their faith-com-
munity with them. The *pax Britannica* also drew sizable numbers of
Westernized Christians from other parts of the subcontinent, including Anglo-Indians, Goans from Portuguese India, and Tamils from
further south. These peoples were well educated, and used English in
their conversation, including liturgy.

The Christian Picture Changes

At the dawn of independence, as the new flag was raised and the
Union Jack lowered, what we must conclude was a kind of euphoria
led Pakistanis to maintain the British nomenclature, departments of
state, democratic processes, and educational system, as well as perpetuate the privileged position of the English language. In this Anglo-
phile mood, which would last fifteen years, the English schools run by
the Christian church became favorites of the public, as such reaping a
harvest of prestige and prosperity that saw them expanding to other
parts of the country. But the euphoria soon died. Muslims strove to
recover their Islamic identity, and adverse feelings toward Christian
schools and Christian missionaries began to surface. Such schools
were now said to cater to the elite, and the Christian church was
identified, along with the English language, as a hangover of imperialism. Hostile statements in the press and on political platforms led to

a large migration of English-speaking Christians to the United Kingdom, Canada, and Australia, causing a severe blow to the country in terms of intellectual substance. Those Christians who remained identified with Punjabi culture, and Urdu came into its own in Christian consciousness and usage. Minorities such as the Kohlis, Bhils, and Balmikis, nomadic agrarian tribes of vaguely Hindu or animistic origin, also began to tilt toward Christianity, and may help to further transform the Pakistani church in the long run.

The Catholic Church in Pakistan, with a membership of approximately 600,000,[3] is ruled by six bishops (one a cardinal)—four of Goan, and two of Punjabi, origin. The Protestant Church of Pakistan has six dioceses with a membership of approximately 600,000, also.

Evolution

Before we examine how this tiny Christian component fits into the vast Islamic milieu, let us explore a modern phenomenon that has affected both the Christian and Islamic communities: the intense search for new and expanded spiritual meaning. At roughly the same time that Pope John XXIII convened the Second Vatican Council to update and renew the Catholic Church, Islamic reformers—dissatisfied with the spiritual and economic conditions of this faith—sought to recapture the original spirit of the Quranic revelation in the modern world. In this process of renewal, neither the Catholic Church nor the community of Islam has been monolithic: Just as the Vatican Council has struggled with a wide spectrum of opinion, tensions, and compromise (and with post-council dissension and deadlock even at the parish level), so has the process of Islamization been struggling to gain momentum in Pakistan.

To give some idea of the nature of this process within Islam, let us examine the standing of Christians in an Islamic state, at least in theory. Father M. Geijbels has written an article that appraises the findings of four writers on this topic: Mawlana Abdul Ala Maudoodi, a fundamentalist and extreme conservative; Dr. Parveen Shaukat Ali, an Islamist who is yet sensitive to the need for tolerance; Professor Rafi Ullah, a moderate; and Riaz Ahmed, a progressive who questions the whole idea of projecting one's religious identity in civic affairs.[4] Let us review their perspectives in turn.

Maudoodi, for his part, states that Christians are to be classed as *dhimmis*, or protected citizens—protected in life and property, and subject to the same penal laws as Muslims. In matters specifically Christian, however, they are to be subject to their own laws. In the missionary arena, Christians may convert a non-Muslim to their faith, but not a Muslim. Finally, in government service Christians are entitled to any positions except head of state and those involving public policy.

Dr. Parveen Shaukat Ali is openly sensitive and sympathetic to the plight of Christians. She admits that, both constitutionally and in practice, "the treatment of minorities is one of the most perplexing dilemmas of human civilization." She assures Christians that they can count on the continued tolerance of Islam, which in the past has been widely recognized as remarkably tolerant—albeit with some deplorable exceptions.

Father Geijbels points out, however, that mere tolerance or protection is not what Christians—or anyone else, for that matter—is striving for these days; people of all creeds and colors are insisting that their human dignity be recognized, and that equal rights be extended to all, as per article 19 of the 1947 United Nations Declaration of Human Rights. And indeed, when this article was formally interpreted to include the freedom to *change* one's religion or faith, Arab Muslim delegates first objected and then abstained from voting. However, the leader of the Pakistan delegates, S. M. Zafrullah Khan, *backed* the resolution, with a quotation from the Quran: "He who wishes to believe let him believe, and he who does not wish to believe let him also be free therein" (18:27/28), and voted in its favor.

Unfortunately, though, official thinking on this matter has changed in Pakistan. In a 1978 meeting in Karachi, for example, 200 delegates from twenty-seven Muslim countries, including Pakistan, unanimously agreed to a plan aimed at counteracting Christian missionary practices and activities.

Professor Rafi Ullah states flatly that the same rights and obligations apply to both Christians and Muslims. He is preoccupied, however, with a Pakistani banking venture called Profit Sharing, which is experimenting with workable alternatives to the taking of interest on capital, a practice banned by the Quran. Ullah holds that once this profit-sharing system is satisfactorily implemented, Christians as well as Muslims will be prohibited from entering into interest-bearing transactions.

Rias Ahmed, finally, see it as the duty of the Islamic state to seek a way to ensure the happiness of every sector of Pakistani society. He posits two factors that will be familiar to the Catholic reader: fidelity to the original content of (Quranic) revelation and the practical requirements of modern times. He also states that, in purely civic matters, there is no need to maintain a Muslim identity or a Christian identity. Muslim identity has already been achieved in the world and in Pakistan, and there is no need to prove it through legislation. This may compel Christians to look at their own identity as "the salt of the earth," and to ask the vexing question: How does the salt fulfill its functions—by preserving its identity as salt, or in losing itself in the seasoning of the whole?

The Dialogue of Life

To appreciate more concretely the Christian component of Pakistan, one must bring into relief what is known as the dialogue life. For more than ten years, Muslims and Christians have breathed the same air; eaten the same food; shared the same typical third world breakdowns of electricity, telephone, and water supply; rejoiced at the same weddings; sorrowed at the same funerals; shopped at the same bazaars; shared the common anguish of parents unable to get their children into a decent school; tended their sick; experienced meanness and discrimination, kindness and generosity; and received—or been denied—preferential treatment in housing. For Muslims and Christians are joint heirs of British standards in government, as well of the distinctly British notions of fair play and sportsmanship. In moments of jingoism or frustration, many Muslims are apt to publicly berate the colonial era, but in their sober moments they are wont to admire the *pax Britannica,* and to expect Pakistani achievement to measure up to the British yardstick. This link with the British past is perhaps reinforced by the large number of Pakistani emigrants to the United Kingdom, who come home periodically for holidays to attend such personal events as funerals and marriages.

Reasons for Pessimism

In the Christian response to the Islamic state, it is not difficult to find excuses and reasons for pessimism, fear, and defeat. This pessimism has afflicted many Pakistani Christians, for three principal reasons: the threat of numbers; the threat to Christian education; and the threat of mixed or apostate marriage.

The Threat of Numbers

Many Christians are so overwhelmed at the idea of being a micro-
scopic minority in a huge population that it paralyzes them. "As
Christians we cannot be strong unless we are numerous"—this is the
kind of thinking to which they are liable to cling. This has produced
an inferiority complex in the Christian community, with the concomitant desire to seek refuge in a ghetto—whether in the home, in
politics (opting for separate rather than joint electorates, for example), in business, in the classroom, or even on the athletic field. To be
sure, such Christian fears are reinforced by such very real episodes as
the antimissionary campaign in the press in the late 1960s, outbursts
of mob violence in Hyderabad in 1965 and again in Rawalpindi in
1980, and the highly publicized progress of Islamization. Some missionaries with an eye to witnessing could be excused for asking: If
Maudoodi's brand of Islam will not permit a Muslim to convert to
Christianity even of his own free will, then why are we wasting our
time here as a missionary church?

The Threat to Christian Education

In the days of the British raj, Christian schools by and large
served to meet the needs of the relatively few education-conscious
Christians. These schools had an overwhelmingly Christian student
body, staff, and management. They took over the religious education
of the children, leaving their parents little or no responsibility in this
regard, and hence totally unprepared for the events that followed.

With the birth of a free Pakistan, there was a stampede for
admission to these Christian schools—first by educated Muslims flee-
ing Hindu India, and later by unlettered Muslim and Christian
Pakistanis. I have mentioned earlier that Christian schools enjoyed a
certain prestige and expansion, which carried with them the handicap
of having to give in to public demand in the matter of admissions. As a
result, the student bodies of the prestigious Christian schools became
largely Muslim. With the emigration of many Christian teachers to the
West, positions became filled with qualified Muslims. The Christian
character of such schools thus became highly ambiguous. And while
Christians are still admitted by preference to these schools, regardless
of intelligence or socioeconomic status, Muslim students are selected
based on the results of a competitive test. Thus, many Christian

students find themselves inferior as students to their Muslim peers, which confirms their negative self-image.

Finally, the varied demands of a government-prescribed syllabus have relegated the teaching of the Christian faith to a marginal position. True Christian identity must therefore be sought in the parishes and in the home.

The Threat of Mixed Marriage

This poses a grave problem within the Christian community. Church legislation has ruled out marriages between Muslims and Christians, specifically a marriage between a Muslim man and a Christian woman, which would see the latter accompany her new husband into a male-dominated Muslim society. In such a situation, rarely if ever can the inviolable condition of rearing the children as Christians be observed. Church prohibition, however, has not prevented a large number of women from marrying out of the Church (actual statistics are not available) and being lost to the Christian community.

While this "frontier phenomenon" is common enough in most parts of the world, there are two factors which exacerbate the situation in Pakistan. The first bears on the nature of Christian education there. Ironically, partly due to the dedication of religious sisters, Christian women are largely better educated than Christian men. A woman of superior intellectual attainments must therefore often settle for someone less fortunate in order to remain in good standing in both the Christian faith and in the community. Ambitious women are therefore confronted with the classical *angustia loci* of the Code of Canon Law, and a Muslim of polish, standing, education, and earning power easily fills the vacuum.

Second, there is also much greater freedom of movement between the sexes in the Christian community. Muslim social taboos tend to keep women fenced in and reserved. Thus, when a Muslim young man meets a Christian woman socially, he becomes the *unconscious* target of an equally unconscious stimulation—something he does not find in his own circle. And as if all this were not enough, there are two avenues of employment in which male and female professionals are actually thrown together—nursing and airplane hosting, jobs eagerly sought by Christian women and shunned by their Muslim counterparts.

The configuration of the two communities thus accelerates mixed marriage, and consequently the steady erosion of the Christian community.

The Second Response

Having dealt with the response of pessimism and defeat in the Islamic state, I wish now to talk about the signs of hope. It took a flow of external events in the 1960s and 70s, a good deal of reflection, and the frequent nudging of the Holy Spirit before Christians realized the vast potential of their position in Pakistan—a potential that was part and parcel of what they had considered handicaps. Christians were first called to cut the umbilical cord tying them to the colonial past, and to cease whimpering for the loss of those petty advantages they had enjoyed in that area. Thus liberated, they were able to see themselves clearly as a small church, perhaps, but a church in their own right.

The Small Church

As the idea of a small church was pressed into the Pakistani Christian consciousness, the more acute were astonished to see the resemblances between their position and that of the Church of Jerusalem as related in the Acts of the Apostles. Christ's mandate to the Church of the Acts—to carry the Good News beyond Jerusalem to Judea, Samaria, and the uttermost parts of the earth (Lk 1:8, Mt. 28:16)—is equally valid for the Church of Pakistan; is, in fact, its *raison d'être*. Christians thus rejected the idea that a local church needs either great longevity or great numbers before it can realize that it has a mission to fulfill. As the Second Vatican Council noted, the Church is missionary by its very nature.

Once Christians rooted themselves in the concept of a New Testament Church, other pieces of biblical perspective began to fall into place. The less they looked upon Islam as hostile to Christians (a heritage of the Crusades), the more did the Islamic milieu appear as a magnified version of the Old Law and Covenant. The month of Ramadan is an annual exercise for Christians to behold at first hand an Old Testament community at vigil, at prayer, and at fasting. (It has been humorously said that many Christians—who are notoriously ignorant of the Old Testament—learned its lessons more from observation than from reading.) The Islamic milieu was therefore recognized as possessing spiritual values reminiscent of the forgotten roots of Christian faith.

As Pakistani Christians began to study the Scriptures, the very smallness of their church began to be recognized for the supreme advantage it is. That God works through humble minorities, rather than through arrogant majorities, is a persistent teaching of the Bible. A sample of this teaching is found in the struggle of Gideon versus the Midianites.[5] When Gideon received the call to rescue Israel from the Midianite enemy, he protested in words that have been echoed by minorities ever since: "How can I? My clan is the weakest in Manassah. I am a nobody in my own family." God's reply was characteristic (and the driving message of the whole Bible): "I will be with you. You will crush them *as though they were one man*."[6] But when Gideon had marshaled his thousands on the field of battle, the Lord—at the sign of such numbers—was displeased. "Far too many for me to give you victory!"[7] For God, numbers are an obstacle: they have a habit of getting in his way. He therefore devised two stratagems for whittling down Gideon's contingent to a skeleton 300: "Now attack, and the victory is yours!"—and so it transpired.

To the extent that the Church was prepared to accept its smallness and take its stand on littleness, expectant of that "power from on high" which the Lord would supply, so would God use the weak and the foolish ones of the earth to confound the wise and the strong.[8] The nationalization of the schools was regarded by most Christians as a deep humiliation and setback for Christianity in Pakistan. When this was followed in 1979 by the announcement of the full Islamization of the country, Christians felt that their cup of disappointment was just about full. But this loss of power and prestige brought in its wake a subtle change in the attitude of many Muslims. Almost imperceptibly, charismatic prayer groups were approached to pray for the healing of sick Muslims, in home and hospital. In a few years, this spread to other parish and *basti* groups. Priests and religious given to this kind of spontaneous prayer were both amazed and edified by the reaction of Muslims. When Pope John Paul II landed on the Karachi tarmac in February 1981, President Zia asked him to pray over his family. Those engaged in the ministry of praying over Muslims for healing found themselves healed—of the congenital fear of Islam—and became relaxed enough to pray boldly in the name of the Risen Christ and the Holy Trinity. These droplets of blessings found their apotheosis in the downpour of goodwill that accompanied the Pope's visit in 1981.

The Pope's Visit

The Pope's visit, although it lasted scarcely three hours, was a spirit-filled event of nationwide impact. In the course of weeks of preparation, various committees received enthusiastic cooperation and expressions of goodwill from government departments, the press, and other agencies. Christians from all over the country were offered half-fares to Karachi by road, rail, and air. For the first time, Christians found themselves gathered together in the National Stadium of Karachi in a eucharistic celebration with the Holy Father and the bishops of the country.

President Zia met the pope at the airport and escorted him to the stadium, where he had ordered the celebration to be televised. The effect on the largely Islamic populace was remarkable. The young country had had so many visiting dignitaries—kings, presidents, religious leaders—but few had knelt to kiss the soil of Pakistan, as the pope did. The pontiff addressed the nation as a whole, praising "the rich cultural tradition of faith." He told the local Christians that they had "the vigour of a young missionary church. But what perhaps most impressed Muslim viewers was the atmosphere of profound piety. It was a new experience for Muslims (who separate sexes in worship) to see vast numbers of men, women, and children responding together to a native liturgy. In the weeks that followed, messages poured into Christian homes and religious houses, indicating touchingly that the Muslims had identified with the event. The local church was no longer a foreign pot plant, but now a mustard tree sprouted from the soil of Pakistan.

The Task Ahead

My stance on Pakistan has been based on three convictions: first, that Pakistani Christians, although a minority, are of Pakistan, and not conquered strangers; second, that since ninety-nine percent of the Christian population are natives of Pakistan, they have the right to be acknowledged as equal citizens; and third, that the Christians of Pakistan must make every effort to be fully integrated into the country, in its present form and given its present way of life. Contemporary history has taught that Christian minorities in similar situations have dwindled away as a result of attempting to live aloof from the mainstream in a ghetto ambience.

In the future, Christians will have to reemphasize some of these convictions and deemphasize others. I believe that this stand is based on truth, and that the truth will prevail. Truth calls for four elements, however: witness, preparedness, dialogue and cooperation. I would like to examine each briefly in turn.

Witness

Witness can be either individual or institutional. Individual witness, however unconscious, has been in existence in Pakistan from the very beginning. Of late, there has been a growth of consciousness, leading to specific efforts of witness. The Little Brothers, for example, who live in meager quarters by the labor of their hands and who practice a neighborly hospitality toward the poor, find their inspiration in their little Chapel of the Blessed Sacrament. Or, there is a sister who supervises a leper clinic far from priest and church—the solitary Christian in an area of 300 square miles. In the future, individual witness will depend on the activities of ordinary lay Christians, however. The opportunity for witness is favored by two prevailing conditions, neither of which is specifically Pakistani, certainly: secularism and moral corruption. There is no doubt that Pakistan is a land of believers, and the emphasis on Islamization has repeatedly put before the people a vision of God. The distinction between the sacred the profane is something that hits home. If Christians, open to the influence of the West, indicate that the sacred is no longer as important as the secular, their entire position becomes weakened. Secularism invites Christians to be more Christian than ever. Moral corruption is a world-wide disease, and Islamic countries are not immune. It is a challenge for the Christian to be sincerely honest and utterly upright in the face of corruption, but it is a challenge that must be met.

Institutional Witness

Firmly woven into the fabric of Pakistani civic life are the Christian schools and hospitals. It is impossible to estimate the impact of these institutions on all sectors of society. So highly are the schools valued by the general public that many of them have a majority of Muslim students, and pressure on heads of schools for further admissions are so heavy as to actually pose a real threat to health. In addition, many leaders of industry, government, and the armed forces are alumni of these schools.

The influence of hospitals and clinics perhaps goes even deeper, since they reach out to the unlettered in the small villages, where maternity care often entails both counseling and spiritual advice. Worthy of special mention in the realm of personal and institutional witness is the leprosy work undertaken by a group of sisters with the generous assistance of foreign funding agencies. Twenty-five years ago, these sisters discovered a group of lepers near the railway station, and began to treat them in a shack. Today, the Marie Adelaide Centre at Karachi is the hub of a vast network of clinics and rehabilitation centers, with technicians and social workers active in virtually every corner of Pakistan, including the remote tribal areas in the mountains.

Institutional witnessing must be continued, particularly in the area of education for the common people—the poor and the illiterate. During a recent synod of bishops in Rome, one bishop asked: "How is it that a small church of 1 percent in a Muslim majority of 95 percent is still considered as a rival institution and is feared? How is it that [a] majority of such proportions can conceivably feel threatened by a minority?" This question should make Christians wonder whether they appear as a power structure rather than as the font of deep spiritual values.

Preparedness

If truth is to be lived and proclaimed, one must be prepared to study the truth of one's faith wherever it prevails. Besides being a lived experience of one's own faith, preparedness also requires that the minority be ready to face obstacles with determination and without compromise of principles. By and large, however, the attitude of Christians in Pakistan is one of unreadiness and unpreparedness. The main cause is the sudden increase of the Muslim population in the last thirty years, which has left the Christians a tiny, bewildered minority. The most visible expression of this unpreparedness is seen in Christian children in schools with large Muslim majorities who are unable either to understand the Muslim faith or to explain their own faith. Christians must better educate the Christian community, as well as the Muslim. Until a few years ago, practically nothing was available to present Christianity to Muslims in a manner understandable to them—and the situation is now only slightly better.

Perhaps more urgent is the preparation needed to face obstacles. The greatest obstacle is that some of the Islamic laws enforced since 1979 seem to discriminate against non-Muslims. The fact that at least four Muslim male witnesses are required to give evidence of the proof of *zina* (adultery) makes it impossible for a witness to be a non-Muslim, except in the case of a non-Muslim victim. This raises the question of whether non-Muslims are subject to specifically Muslim laws. The Christian community must be prepared to stand up against any discrimination on the grounds of religion.[9]

To give an example of how quickly minority feelings can be aroused, last year a decision was given by a lower court and confirmed by the Shariat bench that a Christian couple accused of *zina* were to be publicly flogged. As a result of public protest in the press as well as through ecclesiastical channels, the chief minister of the province suspended the sentence. It would have been the first case of flogging a woman, and possibly the first case of flogging a Christian.

Dialogue

The truth, like goodness, calls for dialogue and cooperation. I referred earlier to the dialogue of life. It is this aspect of dialogue that I consider most important, because professional dialogue needs scholars, and there is a paucity of Christian scholars in Pakistan.

In regard to the dialogue of life, there are progressive signs of improvement, notably in the area of social cooperation and aid during such catastrophes as floods, earthquakes, and riots. An insular Christian mentality still prevails, but both the Church Universal and the Church in Pakistan try to preach the Gospel fully, and Pope John Paul II, in the context of his travels to various Islamic countries, has attempted to lay the basis for a Christian-Muslim dialogue and to set forth the principles of coexistence for the followers of these two monotheistic faiths. As the pontiff declared at Ankara:

Faith in God professed by the spiritual descendants of Abraham—Christians and Muslims—attains its lived sincerity when it penetrates life, is a sound foundation of the dignity of men, and a principle of uprightness for moral conduct and life in society.

Besides professional dialogue and the dialogue of life, there is a third but indirect dialogue in the area of worship, termed *incultura-tion*. By its terms, Christians must study local culture, including forms of worship and devotion. Of particular help will be the Jesus mysticism of the Sufis, the poetical forms for expressing veneration or mourning, and musical assemblies. The Christian community in this Muslim country must be urged "to express themselves and their faith within the local cultural context, but always in such a way that inculturation does not imply loss of identity." When Mahatma Gandhi was asked by a missionary what would make Christianity appear as a native to this soil, his answer was: "Your Gospel is perfect; nothing need be added to it or extracted from it. It has only to be practiced."[10] This is a good description of inculturation.

Conclusion

I have shared many of the experiences of the Christian minority in the Islamic Republic of Pakistan, and sought to place all the cards on the table, the trumps Christians hold, their vulnerable suits, their discards. I do not know what the future holds, but I do know who holds the future: "the power of the Spirit speaking to the Churches."[11] As long as one is not deaf to that voice, but keeps listening in and out of season, the wind of the Spirit will keep one on an even keel.

Notes

1. *Al-Mushir* (Rawalpindi), 27 (1985): 61.
2. By amendment to the constitution of 1973.
3. Vatican Secretariat, *Annuarium Statisticum* (Vatican City), 1983.
4. M. Geijbels, *Al-Mushir* (Rawalpindi), 22 (1980).
5. Judges, chs. 6 and 7.
6. Judges 6:15.
7. Ibid, 7:2.
8. 1 Cor. 1:28.

9. A. D'Souza, "Muslim Revival in Asia," *Church and Islam: A Report of a Consultation* (Varanasi: Office of F.A.B.D.).

10. M. Geijbels, "Some Aspects of Popular Islam," *Church and Islam: A Report of a Consultation* (Varanasi: Office of F.A.B.C.).

11. Revelation 2 and 3.

··◄▓ **14** ▓►··

Christian-Muslim Relations in India[1]

CHRISTIAN W. TROLL, S.J.

Christians and Muslims in India: Some Basic Facts

In the Republic of India the vast Hindu majority, along with Muslim, Sikh, Christian, and other smaller minorities, are called to strive together for a better future within the democratic, secular framework of the constitution of January 1950. Islam in India finds itself in a peculiar, if not unique, situation. The Muslims of the Indian Republic today number about 80 million, and constitute between 11.5 and 12 percent of the total population.

The partition of the Indian subcontinent in 1947 was an event whose consequences cannot be overestimated. It not only brought about the Islamic Republic of Pakistan, but in 1971 led to the birth of a third nation on the subcontinent, the People's Republic of Bangladesh. At the same time, the partition of 1947 drastically decreased Muslim influence in politics and other areas of social life within the Indian Republic. The Muslims of India lost their eminence as well as their leadership, and became suspect in the eyes of the majority community—especially when prominent Indian Muslims switched their allegiance to Pakistan, a phenomenon that continued into the 1950s and resulted in the reemergence of a largely inward-looking leadership with pietisic leanings, with a concomitant weakening of open-minded dynamic forces. The decisive fact for today is that the Muslims in India are co-citizens of a modern, pluralistic, and secular state that they share with a majority shaped by radically different linguistic, cultural, and religious traditions. The Muslims of India must face the challenge of religio-cultural pluralism and modernity—the fact that they share political power in a democracy as legally equal citizens.

This situation, which is without parallel in the past, raises fundamental questions as to the meaning of human life, the norms of social behavior, the place and importance of revelation and truth, and, finally, the relationship of one's faith to that of others. The Muslims of India are being asked how they intend to contribute to the common good of the nation and how they view their relationship with non-Muslim Indians. Their answer is of importance not only to themselves, but to the *umma*—the world community of believers. All Muslims must consider how they, an important minority in today's secular world, can contribute to the general progress and well-being of humankind.[2]

The Christians of India are a much smaller minority than the Muslims, numbering approximately 3.9 percent of the total population, or about thirty million people. The Christian population, less evenly distributed than the Muslims, is concentrated primarily in the southern states of Kerala and Goa. It reaches higher numbers in some of the larger urban centers (Bombay, Madras, Poona, Hyderabad, Calcutta), and in the tribal areas of northeastern India and South Bihar.

The Indian Christian community was hardly affected by the partitions of 1947. Most Christians neither actively encouraged nor actively opposed the struggle for independence, accepting the democratic and secular character of the Indian Republic, as outlined in the constitution, more readily than did the Muslims. Indian Christians, like their European and American counterparts, had long entertained the concepts of democracy and secularism, and did not find the new constitution alien to Christian thought and experience. Furthermore, minority status was less problematic for Christians than for Muslims. The history of Christianity, especially in its first 300 years, provides an accepted model of dynamic Christian life of faith in community without the support of a "Christian" political structure or state. The case of Islam is totally different: the decision for the Medinan state and its development belong to the formative and normative period of early Islamic history.

In the decades since independence, the chief endeavor of mainline Indian Christianity has been to strengthen its sense of community, coherence and identity. To this end it has tried to shed the traces of its colonial and foreign dependence; "indigenize" church personnel; Indianize Christian life, expression, and thought; strengthen the community by means of educational and social services; and to witness Jesus Christ both by preaching the word and by providing the social services referred to above. Significant new membership for the Church had been won among the various tribes, the Harijan, and the Hindu lower castes.

During the nineteenth and twentieth centuries, the powerful Protestant missionary movement led to a number of conversions from Islam, and many Indian Protestant churches still contain substantial elements of both Urdu culture and the great Indian Muslim heritage. The Catholic Church, however, has no such tradition of outreach to Muslims. Catholic missionary activity—and thinking—during the nineteenth and twentieth centuries was predominantly in the tradition of Robert de Nobili (1577–1656), with conversions of upper-caste Hindus and among the scheduled Hindu castes and the Advasi populations.

Catholic Forerunners of Dialogue

From the sixteenth century, Christians have made a number of well-planned efforts to come into closer contact with the Muslims of India. Christian missionaries have included the Jesuits at the court of the Mughals from 1579 onward, and such great evangelical missionaries as the Anglican Henry Martyn (1781–1812) and the German Lutheran C. G. Pfander (1803–65), the author of the classical tract *Mizan al-haqq*. All of these efforts were shaped by the traditional concept and methods of mission. Paramount was the aim of convincing the Muslim of the inadequacy of his religion and of moving him to receive baptism and to join the church.

During the 1860s, however, conditioned by the new political configuration under the British crown, there occurred the unique and courageous endeavor of the influential Muslim reformer Sayyid Ahmad Khan (1817–98). He pleaded for recognition by Muslims of the text of the Bible as used by Christians today, and tried, in his irenic yet clearly Islamic exegesis of Genesis 1:12 and Matthew 1:5, to lay the foundation for a Christian-Islamic ecumenism.

The Belgian Jesuit Victor Courtois (1907–60) worked and published his appraisal of Muslim-Christian relations years before the Second Vatican Council. Courtois saw as his foremost task making the Indian church aware of the Muslim dimension of its apostolic mission. From September 1946 until his death in December 1960, he almost singlehandedly edited and wrote *Notes on Islam: A Bulletin of Information about Islam with Special Reference to India,* whose subtitle was *A Help to a Better Appraisement of Islamic Culture.* Courtois looked with admiration to the great Ramon Lull (1232–1315), who, he said, studied Islam trying always to discover not what divides but what unites. This is the spirit that must be revived today, a spirit of intellectual fairness and charity. Indeed and sadly, prejudice is still common among both Christians and Muslims. Untrue and grossly distorted statements disparaging the other's religious beliefs and practices are still to be found in books of recent date or heard in conversation in Christendom as well as in the world of Islam.[3]

In reference to the detailed "curriculum of Islamic studies" for Christian seminaries that he had proposed in his *Notes,* Courtois said:

> Insistence should always be made, not on what separates Christians from Muslims but on what may . . . bring them closer to each other and to the heart of Christ. We study them not as enemies but as Brothers. To study we shall add much prayer.[4]

Later he said, "The discrete fruit of mutual understanding and knowledge must needs be mutual friendship."[5]

Courtois believed that what is needed is a sustained effort toward "a friendly exchange of views with the idea of bringing about mutual understanding or concord."[6] This, however, must not be confused with

> the tendency of some well-intentioned speakers to slip over difficult problems: to ignore the differences between Islam and Christianity is not to solve them, nor is it a step towards better mutual understanding. These difficulties must be faced squarely in order to be understood and appreciated.[7]

The mainspring for Courtois's call for a wide ecumenism between the religions, and especially Christians and Muslims, lay in a clear perception of what unites all men most deeply—the common Fatherhood of God—which he saw as the basis in turn for the brotherhood of all. He also stressed the heart of Christ as the center of the hearts of humans and the fulfillment of their deepest and best aspirations.

The very first pages of the *Notes* show a remarkable openness to "the riches of those [Muslim] hearts." This openness led Courtois to wish

> that in them we may recognize the features of our Heavenly Father and love them as Brothers. Were they better known, they would surely be better loved, and where there is love there is God. *Ubi caritas et Amor, ibi Deus est.*"[8]

With Courtois's untimely death in 1960, a unique voice on the Indian church fell silent.

The Henry Martyn Institute

By the beginning of the 1960s, the Protestant churches in India, with their traditional ties to Muslim religion and culture, began to attune their pastoral and theological outlook to a truly dialogical appoach. During these years, the Henry Martyn Institute in Hyderabad became a study and resource center for Christian-Muslim dialogue. In collaboration with Muslims, it offered courses on Islam to houses of religious formation, colleges, and parishes; published a quarterly in Urdu, the language of most Indian Muslims; and organized correspondence and summer courses about Islam and Christian-Muslim relations—all this in collaboration with Muslims. (For years, a specially trained Catholic has belonged to the teaching staff of the Institute.)

Since 1963, the Henry Martyn Institute has promoted formal Christian-Muslim dialogues. On the Muslim side, there was the understandable suspicion that the missionaries, as of yore, would continue to work towards conversions while disguised in the friendly garb of dialogue. One Muslim journal called the Institute's efforts a "new trap of the old trappers." Nevertheless, there have been a number of fruitful encounters with Muslim organizations and institutes, dealing with such subjects as faith and works, religions and the modern age, the nature and destiny of man, salvation, God and secularism, social justice, and the role of women in the great religions.

Catholic Initiatives

An overall effort by the Catholic Church in India to examine its response to Vatican II (which closed in 1965) culminated in 1969 with an All-India Seminar in Bangalore. This seminar led to the Indian church's recognition of the need for large-scale dialogue on the great Indian religious traditions. The following areas were singled out for special concern: 1) the change in the Church's attitude toward other religions, and education toward this goal on various levels; (2) a demand for a theology of dialogue; (3) the need for experts in dialogue training and research, as well as for the promotion of dialogue on the scholastic level and for advising the Christian community at large; (4) the setting up of dialogue centers; (5) the publication of suitable literature; 6) development of the Christian ecumenical dimension of this work; (7) and cooperation with non-Christians in the secular field.

The report of the general workshop on dialogue and evangelization urged that "scholars be set aside to study the Muslim religion, social life and culture in India, hoping by this means to come to a better understanding of this great people."[9] The first step for the Indian Church was getting to know its Muslim neighbors—no easy task given the rich, multi-faceted nature of Indian Islam.

Four years later, the All-India Consultation of Patna of October 1973 published concrete resolutions concerning Christian-Muslim relations. The need was stressed for courses, especially in seminaries, on Islam and on the approach to Muslims and Islam. The founding of a Catholic Institute to provide such courses was recommended. Finally, a note of caution was sounded against any Indianization of the church "that tended to be exclusively Hinduization."[10]

The Research Seminar on non-biblical Scriptures held in Bangalore in 1974 again organized a special workshop on Islam. Its report expressed the conviction that Islam has a positive religious message, and that special significance for the Christian church in India is

The self-communication of God . . . partially recorded in the Quran which is acknowledged as normative in Islam. . . . Therefore, there are traces of divine influence in it. In some sense, Islam in India may even be said to have been entrusted with the continuation of the Old Testament task of conveying its experiences of the transcendence and majesty of God, shown so distinctively in the deep sense of reverence for God by Muslims in their prayer life. We Christians have something to learn from this attitude which may lead us to a new awareness of God's greatness and power.[11]

From January 1973 onward, the dialogue commission of the Catholic bishops' conference on India (CBCI) in the person of its full-time secretary, Father Albert Nambiaparambil, vigorously worked to prepare the Catholic community on all levels for dialogue. It took its inspiration from Pope Paul VI's address delivered in Bombay in 1964 on the occasion of the Eucharistic Congress:

> We must meet, not only as tourists, but as pilgrims who set out to find God, not in buildings of stone but in human hearts. Man must meet man, nation meet nation, as brothers and sisters, as children of God. In this mutual understanding and friendship, in this sacred communion, we must also begin to work together to build a common future of the human race. . . . Such a union must be built on a common love that embraces all and has its roots in God who is love.[12]

Realizing "that a good deal should both be done and undone, if a dialogue worth the name is to be carried on between Christians and Muslims,"[13] the commission has organized, with the help of the Henry Martyn Institute, a number of three-day courses in different parts of the country, covering the basic tenets of Islam as well as areas of misunderstanding and convergence. Wherever possible, participants in the courses visited mosques during prayertime. These courses were meant for all Christians, and participants were from various churches. Muslims took an active part in these courses, as teachers as well as witnesses to their faith.

Dialogue get-togethers brought together participants and delegates from different dioceses for two or three days to study the nature, scope, demands, difficulties, risks, and concrete possibilities of interreligious dialogue in a particular region.

> They try to relate the call to proclaim the Gospel to the call to be dialogue-pilgrims on earth. They hear leaders of other religions expound their own ways of life or their own religion as a way of life, share their feelings and hear the opinions of Christians. . . . In the "live-together," Christians and followers of other religions come

together in prayer, meditation, and shared reflection. They share
the same life-style, share the costs of the occasion. They discuss
topics of common concern. . . . Much time is spent in prayer, songs,
and *bhajans* [religious songs in the Indian tradition] . . . Topics are
personal and the emphasis is always to keep it at that level.[14]

A report on one such "live-together" notes that

> The experience of dialogue ran into three days, through seven
> sessions. Each session began with a prayer and ended with prayers
> said by participants from each religion. The topics proposed for
> shared reflection and prayer were: "What does my religion mean to
> me?" "Challenges to my religion." "Religion and social concern."
> "Prayer in my life." "The hope that is in me." "Steps to foster unity,
> understanding and collaboration among religions."
>
> Some salient features which characterized the meeting are
> worth recording here. There was on the part of all a return to their
> own religious traditions and inheritance to draw light, inspiration
> and motivation for social concern, for hope, for meeting challenges
> of the day. There was, as in previous bilateral live-togethers, a con-
> scious effort to focus on those elements which are common and unite
> the various religious traditions, and to go beyond the divisive sepa-
> rating factors. It took some time in fact, to realize that the differen-
> tiating elements, too, can and must contribute to mutual enrichment.
> Towards the end of the meeting the participants having moved away
> from the reflex of self-defense, the focus slowly shifted to the terrible
> gap that exists in all of us between theory and practice, to a heart-
> searching confession of common guilt. These were, perhaps, the
> richest moments of the live-together. Preoccupation with the self had
> given way to a common awakening of religious experience. Again,
> while at the early state of the dialogue some seemed to conceive the
> aim set before us as the search for a universal religion, all slowly
> moved to the realization that dialogue must spring from each part-
> ner's deep commitment to his own tradition, an attitude to be con-
> stantly maintained even at the cost of disagreement on dividing
> factors.[15]

More recently, Catholics who have long been actively engaged in
Christian-Muslim dialogue founded the *Islamic Studies Association*
(ISA) (registered in Delhi on 29 March 1984). The objectives on the
ISA include: (1) in the name of God and His ever greater service, to
promote national integration of all Indian cultural, social, and reli-

gious groups and support government programs for this purpose; (2) to work toward harmonious relations among Muslim, Christian, Hindu and other religions and social communities in India; (3) to promote study, research, and teaching regarding the history, religion, culture, socioeconomic conditions, and other aspects of Islam; (4) to promote the teaching and knowledge of languages, especially Urdu; and (5) to give lectures and courses for students, teachers, and others in subjects pertaining to Indian Muslim culture.

Regional branches of ISA have been established in Karnataka and Tamil Nadu, and one hopes other regions will follow this example in due course. ISA publishes *salaam*, a quarterly bulletin to promote Christian-Muslim understanding. Every second year ISA organizes a convention; in 1983 it was held in Lucknow, and in 1985 in Calcutta. The conventions dealt with the Christian and Muslim family, with speakers from both communities. ISA also organizes an annual Urdu summer course, alone or in collaboration with the Henry Martyn Institute.

The Islamic section of Vidyajyoti Institute of Religious Studies in Delhi, under the direction of the author, has published, since 1982, the series *Islam in India: Studies and Commentaries*. The editorial board of this publication comprises Muslim and Christian scholars who live in India. "It aims at a presentation of distinctive religio-cultural aspects of Indo-Muslim life and thought, past and present. It hopes to mirror the various views and experiences of Muslims from different regions of India thereby contributing to a greater awareness and understanding which are prerequisites for harmonious living."[16] Two volumes have been published and a third is in press.

Muslim Initiatives

The previous paragraphs should not convey the mistaken impression that the Muslims of India have been solely passive partners in dialogue. Earlier, we mentioned Sayyid Ahmad Khan's contribution, and The Islam and the Modern Age Society, founded by the late Dr. Abid Husayn (d. 1978) in 1970, kept up a strong commitment to dialogue on the intellectual level. The quarterly of the society introduced itself in its first issue (May 1970) as the organ of a group.

persons in the East and the West, who are in search for a philosophy
of life calculated to reconcile the conflict between individualism and
collectivism and between material and moral values

who aim at a

new synthesis of region and revelation. . . . They feel it to be the
most pressing need of the modern age and a challenge to all the
great religions, to find in their respective ways, and if possible, in
cooperation with one another, to work out a synthesis.[17]

Under number 4 of its program of the society includes: "Discussions of the way in which Islam and other religions can cooperate to
meet the challenge of the growing scepticism and unbelief
throughout the world." Motivated by such preoccupations, the society
has organized a number of important national and international seminars—for example, the Seminar on Inter-Religious Understanding
(17–20 October 1971, New Delhi). The quarterly also produced a
detailed report and reprinted most of the papers of the famous
Christian-Muslim Consultation in Broummana, Lebanon, July 11–18,
1972.

In October 1978, not long after its transfer to the magnificent
campus on the outskirts of southern New Delhi, the Indian Institute
of Islamic Studies (IIIS) hosted a meeting of twelve Muslims and
twelve Christians hailing from various parts of India. The aim was to
explore, in the light of the message of the Bible and the Quran, the
possibilities of a common commitment to harmony and reconciliation,
not only between Muslims and Christians but among all religious and
ideological groups in India.

The IIIS, the Henry Martyn Institute, and the Dialogue Commission of the CBCI jointly organized a seminar entitled, "Mosque and
Church: Their Contribution to Interreligious Harmony and Reconciliation."[18] Two papers by prominent Muslim participants merit special mention here, because of their pleading from a decidedly Muslim
point of view the acceptance and promotion of interreligious dialogue, especially with Christians. Syed Vahiduddin, former head of
the department of philosophy at Delhi University, pointed out the
Quranic basis for interreligious dialogue as advocated today: the
Islamic temper and ethos that transcend historical, institutional Islam

and in fact do not cease to challenge and call to self-questioning; "Quranic humanism" that follows directly from the way the Quran views human dignity, grounded in humankind's creation by and relation to the God of mercy. Vahiduddin stressed that in their common reference to transcendence, Muslims and Christians (and even those who fight for the cause of Allah without knowing that they are fighting for His cause) can and must, in the sense of Sura 3:52, pursue a common endeavor.

Professor Ziaul Hasan Faruqi, principal of Jamia Millia Islamia, New Delhi, made a strong plea in his paper for religious communities to open up to one another in dialogue and to thoroughly revise traditional attitudes and teachings. His message was that one must choose either to learn to live as a member of a world community composed of a number of different cultures, or not to live at all. We have to learn to live as partners, to develop a "mutual appreciation of each other's heritage based on the conviction of the equality of all as human beings in the eyes of God."[19] In simple words, we have to meet each other looking into each other's eyes and with open hearts.

To bring about this change in attitude and outlook, Z. H. Faruqi envisages action at both the intellectual and practical levels. Vis-à-vis the former, the first step should be to acquire a good and objective knowledge of various religious traditions. The second step should be to revise thoroughly our traditionally exclusivistic attitude. The original spirit of our respective religious traditions must be allowed to assert itself against the primacy of particular dogmas, rituals, and ceremonies. "Without a new theological approach to include all the world religions and the religious heritage of mankind and to find a respectable place for all religions in one's religious consciousness, the dream of inter-religious harmony will ever remain unrealized."

The third step must be an ever-deepening dialogue between adherents of the world religions. Dialogue is here seen as the effort "to establish a religious relationship with a person of another faith." In the context of world religions, it means to listen to each other's experience of the respective religion's traditions, and to share in a deeper union of mutual openness—even where irreducible differences of perception and expression remain.

A shared action, according to Faruqi, should be built on the common perception of what is, Quranically speaking, *ma'ruf*—that is, good, beautiful, just, and so forth. If the *ma'ruf* is one and the same for all mankind, then nothing should bar us from uniting and working together for a just social order, against all kinds of injustices, social, economic, and political, and from cooperating in doing things that make life good and beautiful.

This seminar stressed that certain initiatives have to be taken now. Both Christians and Muslims at the seminar felt that much needs to be done in the field of teaching, especially in institutions where community is formed, such as seminaries, *madrasas,* and institutes of Islamic and Christian studies. A number of Christian faculties of theology and philosophy schools as well as seminaries have started to institute basic courses on Islam and on Muslim life in India as part of their standard curriculum. Some participants, such as Professor Iqbal Ansari, director of the Institute of Islamic Studies of Aligarh University, expressed the conviction that their curriculum should allow teaching the Christian religion as Christians see it. Although the traditional syllabus of *madrasas* provides here and there for information and discussion of the elements of the Christian faith, it has always been within the framework and outlook of traditional Islamic thinking.

The need to collaborate on basic textbooks and anthologies on Christianity and Islam for use in Muslim and Christian religious higher educational institutions was also stressed. The Islamic Studies Association is now preparing a textbook on Islam, with special regard to Islam in India, for use in seminaries and possibly in secular institutions. Each chapter has been checked by a Muslim scholar of Islam. The exchange of scholars between Muslim and Christian institutions for religious instruction should also become common.

I will conclude with the latest Christian-Muslim initiative: In May 1985, twelve Muslim scholars and journalists from South Asia were invited to the Vatican Secretariat for Non-Christians in Rome to participate with Christian scholars in a two-day symposium on the theme of sanctity in Christianity and Islam. After the symposium, the group visited Assisi and Subiaco, two of the most venerable sites of the Franciscan and Benedictine traditions of spirituality. They also visited the catacombs and met with representatives of basic Christian communities in Rome. The initiative came from the Muslims who participated in the program. In his address to the group during a private audience, Pope John Paul II stressed the brotherhood and sisterhood of Muslims and Christians in the faith of Abraham, and pointed out the need for Muslims and Christians to discuss true holiness in obedience and worship to God.

The future of Christian-Muslim relations in India holds much promise if both Muslims and Christians heed the witness of "the countless numbers of good people around the world, Christians, Muslims, and others, who quietly lead lives of authentic obedience, praise, and thanksgiving to God and selfless service to their neighbor" and thus "offer humanity a genuine alternative, 'God's way,' to a world which otherwise would be destroyed in self-seeking, hatred and struggle."[20]

Notes

1. For an earlier, detailed treatment of the same topic cf. C. W. Troll, "Christian-Muslim Relations in India. A Critical Survey," *Islamochristiana* 5(1979):119–49.

2. The previous paragraphs are based on the perceptive analysis of the predicament of Islam in post-Independence India by W. C. Smith in *Islam in Modern History* (New York: The New American Library of World Literature, 1959), pp. 257–92.

3. *Notes on Islam* (Calcutta), June 1955, p. 49.

4. Ibid., May–June 1949, p. 60.

5. Ibid., November 1957, p. 113.

6. Ibid., June 1957, p. 55.

7. Ibid.

8. Ibid., September 1946, p. 1.

9. *All-India Seminar: The Church in India Today.* Bangalore 1969 (New Delhi: CBCI, 1969), pp. 342ff.

10. *Light and Life We Seek to Share. All-India Consultation on Evangelization.*

11. D. S. Amaloparvadass, ed., *Research Seminar on Non-Biblical Scriptures* (Bangalore: NBCLC, 1974), p. 620.

12. Neuner-Dupuis, *The Christian Faith* (Bangalore: T.P.I., 1973), 1032.

13. *Bulletin, Secretariatus,* 1975—X/2. no. 30, p. 257. Reprinted in *Journal of Dharma* 1 (1976): 267–83.

14. Ibid., pp. 255–56.

15. Ibid.

16. "Dialogue in India. A Challenge to Redeem Hope," in *Vidyajyoti, Journal of Theological Reflection* 49 (1975): 112.

17. *Islam and the Modern Age* 1 (May 1970): 7–8.

18. Cf. the report of the seminar by C. W. Troll in *Vidyajyoti,* 43 (1979): 16–24.

19. Quotations here refer to the cyclostyled papers of the seminar published in *Studies of Islam* (New Delhi), 1979.

20. *L'Osservatore Romano,* Venardi, 10 Maggio 1985, p. 4.

Muslims and Christians in the Philippines
A Study in Conflict and Efforts at Reconciliation

CESAR ADIB MAJUL

History has often demonstrated how, for a number of reasons, a dominant majority can come to resent the existence of a racial, ethnic, or religious minority. And when the minority possesses coveted resources, it is not difficult for the majority to rationalize its expropriative tendencies or actions. In turn, the minority, in order to survive, must search deep into its inner resources, reassert its identity, and in so doing increase its cohesion. When the identity is religious (even if the conflict has started as an economic one), the conflict often achieves a qualitative transformation with unanticipated ramifications. This is what has happened in the Philippines.

In the last two decades, the Philippines has witnessed communal conflicts between Muslims and Christians that have left a hundred thousand dead, displaced hundreds of thousands of Muslims from their ancestral lands, and witnessed the rise of a Muslim secessionist movement that cannot be simply wished away by the national government.[1] This movement has brought concern to the Muslim world, and affected not only the internal conditions of the country but its international relations as well. The communal conflict and resulting separatist movement are the cumulative results of an historical process spanning more than three centuries of the Spanish presence in the archipelago, more than three decades of direct American rule, and about forty years of government rule by natives who inherited the imperial mantle.

From the arrival of the Spaniards in 1565 to the latter part of the last century, the history of the relations between the Muslims and other inhabitants of the archipelago who became Christianized has been one of either chronic tension or actual war, instigated by the

This chapter was written just prior to the events that led to the overthrow of the Marcos regime in February 1986.

Spanish government for imperial, colonial, and religious ends. The events of the last two decades, although influenced by other emerging factors, cannot be fully understood without reference to how Spanish policies conditioned Muslim-Christian relations and how the United States government viewed such relations. This paper attempts to present briefly the historical causes of the conflict, how it has manifested itself in the last few years, and how recent efforts have been made by the government and by certain segments of the Philippine population (notably the religious one) to eliminate or at least reduce tension and conflict between the two communities.

As part of a slow but progressive expansion in the lands of the Malays in Southeast Asia, Islam secured its foothold in Sulu, in the Philippine south, by the end of the thirteenth century. But its northeast movement to other parts of the country was checked by the arrival of a Spanish colonial expedition in 1565. The Spaniards came with two clear missions: the Christianization of the inhabitants of the archipelago, and the expansion of the material domains of the Spanish monarch. By the end of the sixteenth century, except for the sultanate of Sulu and those of Maguindanao and Buayan on Mindanao island, practically the whole archipelago had been "pacified" by force of Spanish arms. By the first decade of the next century, the Christianization of the pacified inhabitants, their resettlement into quasi-urban population centers, and the establishment of a well-integrated Spanish colonial and ecclesiastical system was almost complete. The converted natives came to be called *indios,* while the unconquered Muslims were denoted as *moros*—the latter a reaffirmation in Castillian minds that they were coreligionists of the Muslims in Spain. The Spanish colonial government spared neither men nor resources to try to conquer the Moros and convert them to Catholicism. Points in Mindanao were outposts for imperial and religious aggression, and unsuccessful expeditions only served to further the Spanish resolve. After their successes in the Americas, they could not understand their failure in dealing with the relatively smaller population in Mindanao and Sulu. Even minor successes in causing disssension between the various sultans did not produce the desired results. The Spaniards did succeed in utilizing the converted natives to serve as spearmen, rowers, and carriers in their expeditions against the Muslims. In fact, the bulk of the expeditionary troops were natives who were explicitly instructed that the Muslims were the traditional enemies of their newly acquired faith. Thus were the Crusades transferred from a temperate clime to the tropics.

Due to a clear colonial policy and at a time in which the religious motive was predominent in society, these expeditions could not but have a religious color. Spanish friars invariably accompanied them, sometimes joining in the fighting and often being killed or captured. And friars found counterparts on the other side. Spanish chronicles vividly describe how "fanatic" Muslim *santones* were seen exhorting Muslim warriors to keep up the fight, and even joining the battle and getting killed.

Spanish friars saw to it that victorious battles were celebrated in Manila and smaller towns with masses and morality plays. These plays, called *moro-moro*, came to form a regular part of the repertoire of all town *fiestas* up to the eve of the Japanese occupation in 1941. They tended to ridicule Islam while portraying Muslims as evil and treacherous, if not downright ugly, creatures; Spanish soldiers, on the other hand, were seen as brave and gallant. The plays usually ended with a defeated Muslim sultan embracing Catholicism, or with his daughter embracing a handsome Christian warrior and accepting baptism. In the absence of an alternative medium of instruction and entertainment, it cannot be overemphasized how such plays conditioned generations of Filipinos to develop negative images of Muslims in general and of Moros in particular.[2] Members of the older generation vividly recall such plays, and one wonders how many of their present attitudes toward Islam and Muslims have been affected, consciously or otherwise, by plays that were the main source of entertainment before radios or movies became easily available.

The series of wars that pitted the Spaniards and their native allies against the Muslims spanned more than three centuries. They were called the Moro Wars by historians, and described as "piratical" acts by the Spaniards. They left deep scars still visible today in some Muslim lands, resulting in the destruction and depopulation of scores of Muslim villages and the capture or burning of thousands of sea craft, disrupting the time-honored commercial maritime activities of the Muslims. In the middle of the nineteenth century, all coconut and fruit trees on islands inhabited by Muslims were cut off or burned to render the islands uninhabitable. Hundreds of inhabitants were transported as far north as Luzon island to be forcibly converted to Catholicism. In the eighteenth century, before slavery was prohibited, hundreds of Muslim prisoners were branded and sold into slavery.

But Muslim retaliation was fearful, too. Muslim warriors often swooped down upon villages of converted *indios,* burned their homes and churches, and carried hundreds into captivity to be sold in the slave markets of the Dutch East Indies. (Other *indios* were retained as household slaves or workers in the farms and orchards.) Spanish records of the late eighteenth century reveal how the number of tributes from some Visayan villages had been reduced to almost nothing due to the depopulation caused by such raids. The *indios* were often defenseless, since the colonial government did not wish an armed population.

Dutch and British colonization of nearby Malay lands played a role in the gradual isolation of the Moros from their coreligionists, an isolation that forced them progessively to depend more and more on their own resources. While there was gradual reinforcement of such pre-Islamic institutions as the *datu*, or local chieftain, Islamic institutions were also strengthened. Moreover, in addition to prescribing the defense of family and land as religious duties, Islam was often used to rationalize unflinching loyalty to sultans and *datus*. In spite of linguistic and regional differences and occasional economic rivalries, Muslim groups often allied themselves for common defense, justifying such alliances on the basis of a common faith. Islam, indeed, provided the most important elements of identity, fostering a form of pre-nationalism.

But the isolation of the Muslims had its serious drawbacks. Principally, they were not exposed to some of the technological innovations then being introduced to the nearby colonies. For example, by the nineteenth century, the Spanish Filipino colony could boast a growing population, a government system of education and sanitation, a postal service, urban development, a degree of agricultural progress with a growing export economy, and so on—all of these developments absent in Muslim areas. Consequently, natural disasters and epidemics took a heavier toll of Muslim lives than in other areas of the archipelago.

In the first centuries of Spanish rule in the Philippines, the conquest and conversion of the Moros to Catholicism was a basic policy. Colonial and ecclesiastical officials viewed Islam as a false religion from which the Moros were to be delivered. However, in the closing decades of Spanish rule, due to republican or liberal ideas spreading in official Spanish circles as well as to some lessening of the religious motive in Spanish society, the newly declared policy was to transform the Moros into submissive subjects of the Spanish crown. Conversion ceased to have official sanction, although the Spanish clergy insisted that only if the Moros became Catholics would they be submissive subjects of Spain. While this represented a bid for official support for religious activities, the clergy had no compunction in revealing that evangelization could be used as a tool to serve the political ends of an imperial power. In any case, the last campaigns against the Muslims were supported by the Spanish clergy, which collected contributions from rich Chinese merchants as well as from schoolchildren for a cause that continued to be preached as religious.

The colonial government justified its ruthless campaigns not only by its avowed aim of doing away with the piratical and slaving activities of Muslims, but with the claim that it wanted to bring culture and civilization to the Muslims. The government pointed to the material progress of the Philippine colony as something the Moros could also eventually have, while protesting that it had no desire to convert the Moros. Yet a study of official documents reveals that the occupying powers continued to hope that, under proper administration, and after achieving the educational and economic level of the Christians, the Moros would choose to leave Islam. Meanwhile, to avoid criticism from liberal quarters, some Spanish priests asserted that in any case the Islam of the Moros was not the real Islam of traditional Muslim centers. Thus, to convert Moros to Catholicism was not really an attack against Islam, since the Moros were merely pagans disguised as Muslims. It is of interest to note that earlier missionaries claimed that Islam was forced upon the ancestors of the Moros by foreign Muslim merchants or adventurers, and was an intrusive religious institution; as such, there was of course nothing wrong in extirpating it in the Philippines.

It is difficult to be sure now to what extent the sultans and *datus* were impressed by the invitation to enter into what was portrayed as a superior culture. Obviously acceptance would cost them much of their traditional power and prerogatives. But what the Spaniards had failed to note was how deeply the Muslims and their chiefs cherished their religion and culture. Spanish superior naval power and weaponry and the enervating results of the long series of wars led many Muslim chiefs to make truces with the Spanish government, but not until official treaties stipulated that their religion was not to be interfered with. (Spanish officials saw these treaties as temporizing moves that would eventually integrate Muslim areas into the Spanish colony.)

In 1898, however, another power—the United States—wrested control of the Philippines. It is significant that one of the first things Spanish Jesuits submitted to American officials was a copy of a master plan for the evangelization, resettlement, and eventual assimilation of the Muslims into a colonial body politic—essentially the same plan previously submitted to the Spanish colonial authorities.³ American policy toward the Moros fell under the general mandate to develop, to civilize, to educate, to train in the science of self-government the Filipinos. In 1899, President William McKinley explained to a group of Protestant clergymen the reasons why he had decided to hold on to the Philippines. Disregarding the fact that more than eighty percent of the Filipinos had become Catholics under the benevolent tutelage of Spanish priests, McKinley opined that

> there was nothing left for us to do but to take them all, and to educate the Filipinos, and uplift and civilize and Christianize them, and, by God's grace, do the very best we could by them, as our fellow men for whom Christ also died.

Despite its president's pious claims, however, the United States never officially supported any move to convert the Philippine Muslims to Christianity.

The United States succeeded in another quarter where Spain had failed, however: the imposition of sovereignty over the Muslims. Superior weapons and special artillery decided the issue, and—at the cost of hundreds of dead Muslims—Muslim lands were finally incorporated into the new colony. Nevertheless, Islam was generally left untouched and Christian missionaries were neither supported or encouraged.⁴ (A few institutions contrary to American law, such as slavery, were proscribed.) Many American officials found Islam strange and believed that American tutelage would in the long run make Muslims abandon their beliefs and customary laws; in this, they failed to distinguish what was Islamic from what was pre-Islamic among the practices and institutions of the Moros. In any case, their basic assumption was that the superiority of American values would win eventual and grateful acceptance among the Moros. What they neglected to factor was that some of these values were of Christian origin, at least in the Muslims' eyes.

In their desire to raise the literacy level of the Moros, some American officers supporter a few Quranic schools. There was even one unusual officer who believed that it would be a good thing if the Moros knew more about Islam. His well-intentioned efforts to invite an Arab or Turkish teacher to the Philippines, however, met with grave suspicion from his superiors. American officials, engaged in the task of integrating Moros into the colonial body politic, could not have been happy to see foreign Muslims, such as Arab traders, come to the Philippine south, and the annual pilgrimage to Mecca did not elicit much sympathy.

It was probably such bias against or unfamiliarity with alternative religious systems that led Governor Leonard Wood to view with suspicion the work and recommendations of Dr. Najeeb Saleeby, the Arab-born author and educator who came to the Philippines as a surgeon with the American Expeditionary Forces and remained to serve in various civil offices having to do with the governance of the Moro provinces. Although a Christian, his knowledge of Arabic and Islamic history and institutions led Saleeby to develop a warm sympathy for the Moros and their *datus*. It is believed by some contemporary scholars that if Saleeby's recommendations had been accepted and implemented by American authorities, the present Philippine government would have less difficulty in solving the "Moro problem."[5]

One thing Americans were completely aware of was the ingrained hostility between Muslims and Christians due to historical factors. They knew that if both communities were left to themselves, bloody conflict might ensue. To remedy this, they brought in Christian officials to help raise the administrative sophistication of Muslims, introduce sanitation projects and improved agricultural techniques, and improve the public education system. A joint constabulary force of Muslims and Christians was created, and did some creditable work in enforcing law and order. The main idea behind these efforts was to make both communities cooperate for their mutual benefit, and perhaps to begin to feel that they belonged to the same polity.

But American officials looked at Mindanao as an island meant for agricultural exploitation by American businessmen as well as by settlers from other islands, and introduced Christian settlers into areas which Muslims considered their ancestral lands. The government declared large tracts of these ancestral lands public, and disposed of them accordingly. Soon, hundreds of settlers came on their own; many were poor, and were initially given seed and animals on loan by equally poor Muslim farmers. Some settlers were even "adopted" by Muslim families, and not a few of their children grew up as Muslims. The introduction of large numbers of settlers, however, later caused much hatred, suffering, and bloodshed in the Muslim lands.

The American promise of eventual independence for the Philippines alarmed Muslims, for the simple reason that Filipino national leaders meant to incorporate their lands into the projected republic. Muslims, especially their chiefs, did not look forward to being ruled by persons they dismissed as "Christian Filipinos." They asserted that they had entered into treaties with the United States, and not with the Christian Filipinos. *Datus* who had fought Americans in the past started to petition American officials both in the Philippines and in the United States that they be retained under American sovereignty in separate provinces until ready for their own independence, and for some time a few American officials considered this a viable possibility. A bill meant to satisfy Muslim aspirations was presented to the American congress, but the outcry of Filipino nationalistic leaders was great, charging American interests with sinister economic motives in Sulu and Mindanao. These leaders asserted that Muslims desired to be a part of the forthcoming independent polity, pointing out that Muslims and other Filipinos in the country had a common racial origin and that there would be no problem in the free practice of Islam for Muslims. But such assertions were made without consulting the Muslims or their leaders. In their declarations and manifestos, Muslims invariably expressed unhappiness at the prospect of rule by Christian Filipinos, who for centuries had waged war against them as hated allies of a colonial power intent on conquest and enforced conversion. Muslim religious leaders emphasized that never had Islam been more threatened, and most Muslims feared that the new national government in Manila would be a Christian Filipino government, not that much different from the old Christian Spanish version.

As a matter of history, the Muslims neither individually nor collectively participated in the Philippine revolutions of 1896 and 1898 against Spain. The attempts of Filipino revolutionary leaders to solicit Muslim support against Spain—and later against the United States—fell on deaf ears. A revolutionary movement aimed at transforming the *indio* into a Filipino had neither the sympathy nor the understanding of Muslims, who had no concept of transforming the *moro* into a Filipino. Thus, the nationalist movement during the American regime did not have the genuine participation of Muslims. For many years, even after independence in 1946, the terms *Filipino* and *Christian* were interchangable in the minds of the majority of Muslims, although at present such identification appears restricted to members of the oldest generation.

The inauguration of the Philippine Commonwealth in 1935 signified to Muslims that they would be ruled by Christian Filipinos. Unfortunately, in spite of the avowed mandate of the Americans, Muslims were not trained to participate meaningfully in an unfamiliar political process. In effect, they were simply handed over to Christian

Filipinos to be governed. The new president declared publicly that in the new system there would be no more sultans, *datus,* and other traditional leaders, and that the laws of the commonwealth would be applied to all with equal severity. This declaration alienated a significant number of Moro traditional leaders, who stood to lose much in the new system, since no efforts were made to have them participate in it. Moreover, Muslim religious leaders saw many elements in the civil code as contrary to Muslim law as well as to their customary law. The new educational system, for example, geared as it was to create a high sense of civic consciousness and national identity, also deemphasized regional and ethnic differences. Such aims, worthy as they may have been, served only to alarm Muslims, who saw the entire system as a means of eventually doing away with their cherished religion, culture, and traditions. Consequently, there was an initial shying away from the public schools, which prevented many young Muslims from becoming full participants in the mainstream of national life and from acquiring the skills necessary both to compete with Christians and to be of greater service to their communities. Confirming the worst Muslim fears were textbook stories featuring Muslim pirates, as well as illustrations of animals abhorred by Muslims as unclean. Additionally, many of the ethical principles used in prescribing family and social relations were of Western or Christian inspiration, and as such alien to Muslims.

During the Commonwealth period, very few Muslims occupied official positions. The top officials in Muslim provinces were Christians trained by Americans or imported from other provinces. What disturbed the Muslims was that the Christian Filipino officials seemed to regard them in almost the same way as had the Spanish and American authorities. Educated for the most part in Catholic schools, exposed to an American system of education, and having imbibed elements of Western culture and its modernizing influences, these officials considered themselves superior to the Muslims. It is likely, too, that many of them had been influenced by literature circulated against the Moros and exposure to *moro-moro* plays. They therefore viewed the Moros as wards to be educated by them in a superior culture.

The Church, too, looked to the Muslim lands as areas for proselytization and the saving of souls. Like its imperial predecessors, Filipino officialdom saw Mindanao as the "land of promise," an area that would increase the nation's agricultural wealth while providing homes for thousands of immigrants from densely populated provinces plagued by various agrarian troubles. During this Commonwealth period, a program was devised for an accelerated transport of settlers to Mindanao. It was not legally difficult to displace Muslims from lands which their ancestors had tilled for countless generations, since the concept of land titles was alien to Muslims and because the Commonwealth had already declared much such land to be public. Towns with Christian majorities and churches soon sprang up in areas where Muslims had long been in the majority, ruled by their own chiefs. They now became a minority—that is, to be sure, if they opted to remain in the area.[6] Countless Muslim families began life anew in less fertile regions, or in the interior of the island. The seeds of bloody land conflicts were being sown by the government, which neither knew how nor cared to read the danger signs. It was ironic indeed that the Muslims, who had managed to retain their lands in spite of vehement struggle with the Spanish government and its pressures to establish missions in their midst, would lose their lands under the peaceful aegis of a native government.

The Japanese invasion and occupation of Mindanao (1942–45) provided some Muslims the opportunity to regain their lands by frightening away the new occupants, who had no national government to protect them. Many Muslims became guerrillas, and often collaborated with Christian guerrillas against the foreign invaders. This was one aspect of political life in which they understood each other well.

After the war, a great deal of loose firearms and backpay money became available. Expectations concerning consumer goods rose, and a barter economy gave way to a money one. One aspect of the new sense of freedom was that hundreds of Muslims made the Mecca pilgrimage, or traded with and visited their coreligionists in Borneo and other nearby Indonesian islands. A few Indonesian teachers were invited to teach in the *madrasahs* or to become attached to mosques, and visits from foreign Muslims increased. Above all, there was an increased desire on the part of many Muslims, especially the young and the women, to know more about Islam.

When independence finally came in 1946, a few Muslim leaders—notably those who had won fame as guerrillas—got political positions, but most of the top offices in the Muslim provinces passed to Christians. And once again, in spite of Muslim protest, Christian settlers began to come to the Muslim provinces. This process was dramatically accelerated during the administration of President Magsaysay (1953–57) by a government program which settled ex-Communists, ex-soldiers, ex-prisoners, and others among the Muslims. Muslims were concerned, if not resentful, that these government-sponsored communities had better roads, better schools, better civic centers—and even irrigation projects. (The Muslims had no irrigation projects.) Land disputes became common, with occasional spilling of blood, and in the adjudication of these disputes it was obvious that the Christians had better access to the courts.

Muslims complained that there was no more land for them in Mindanao. They pointed to the high rate of unemployment in Sulu, which also had one of the lowest literacy rates in the country. There were also land conflicts between Muslims in Sulu, causing the dispossessed to form armed bands that roved the mountains. Moreover, the complaints were being voiced by a more conscious Muslim community, as Muslims were by this time attending both government and private schools, and hundreds of them had gone abroad to study at Al-Azhar in Cairo, on Egyptian government scholarships. They formed a pool from which a new *ulama*, with a heightened consciousness of Islam and the *umma*, emerged.

The complaints noted above and a general breakdown of law and order in some Muslim areas led the Philippine senate in 1956 to form a committee to inquire into the so-called Moro problem. It was led by Domocao Alonto, the lone Muslim senator, and its report pointed out that part of the problem was that the majority of Muslims did not consider themselves to be Filipinos. The report also revealed the chronic neglect of Muslims in the educational, economic, and political areas. Of its many recommendations, however, only one was implemented: the creation of a Commission of National Integration. This commission succeeded in sending thousands of Muslims to study in Manila, many of whom became professionals, and therefore better able to articulate the problems of their communities. Soon, there was a proliferation of Muslim student and professional organizations.

The Jabidah Massacre in March 1968, in which approximately thirty Muslim recruits in a secret government army project were summarily executed due to an alleged mutiny, galvanized Muslim fears that they would be forcibly dispersed as a religious community, and that Muslim lives were but little valued in Philippine society. The press gave large coverage to the army's role in the massacre, and other Muslim countries started raising questions. In May 1968, Datu Matalam of Cotabato announced the Muslim Independence Movement, aimed at an independent Islamic Republic of Sulu and Mindanao. Although it was probably no more than a desperate attempt to bring the plight of Muslims to national attention, the announcement further divided the Muslim and Christian communities even as it raised the expectations of the Muslims. Thousands of families transferred to safer places, with the result that mixed communities became rare. The number of refugees rose to alarming proportions,[7] and ominous rumors surfaced of Muslim youth being trained in guerrilla warfare in a neighboring country.

From the middle of 1970 through 1971, there was a systematic process to frighten Muslim families away from selected towns and areas in Cotabato and Lanao provinces, initiated and perpetuated by the so-called Christian Ilagas, a group composed mainly of Visayans specially trained for the purpose. Their method of selective killing of Muslims and mutilations of victims led thousands of Muslim families to flee their homes and farms. It can now be reasonably speculated that the Ilagas' mission was to see to it that no Muslims were left in selected areas to support Muslim candidates to political office; thus, only Christians would be left to vote for their choices among other Christians. (There is ample evidence that at least seven Christian candidates supported the Ilagas.) The Muslims counteracted with their own armed forces—the Blackshirts and Barracudas, who, by all accounts, were even tougher as well as more numerous. It was obvious to all observers, however, that the government constabulary forces sided with the Ilagas in any conflict with a Muslim group, and armed Christian settlers also cooperated with the Ilagas. When Ilagas attacked a Muslim village, it took a long time for government troops to arrive to protect civilians. Worse, Muslim groups fighting Ilagas often found government troops among the enemy. Muslim leaders could do little to rectify this situation, since many Christian candidates were former military officers who maintained contact with the armed forces. It was to be expected that in any conflict betwen Muslim and Christian armed groups, the military, composed mainly of Christian soldiers, would side with the Christians. It was a general principle in Christian quarters that the Muslims were the troublemakers.

The November 1971 elections demonstrated the success of the collusion between Christian politicians, the military, and the Ilagas, as political power in many areas formerly dominated by Muslims fell into the Christian camp. Pro forma investigations of reports of massacres of Muslims, in spite of general public knowledge of the identities of the military officers involved, were soon forgotten or set aside. Obviously, it would have been unwise for President Marcos to insist on investigations that would perforce justify Muslim charges of gross abuses on the part of the military; a plan for imposing martial law had been brewing in the president's mind for some time, and he would need military support to enforce such stringent measures. (Moreover, the Christian candidates who had won in the former Muslim strong- holds belonged to his political party.) An alleged Ilaga-Christian-army collusion led the Muslims to conclude that the coercive forces of the nation were being perverted to defend the interests of special seg- ments of society, and that Muslims were not getting justice in the country.

In September 1972, President Marcos declared martial law, in- cluding among his reasons the communal conflict in the south and the secessionist movement boiling there. The declaration, and subsequent government action to disarm Muslims, provoked clashes between the army and Muslims. The latter feared that, unarmed, they would be completely at the mercy of the Christians and the nation's military forces, which invariably sided with the Christians. This was the time and the setting in which the Moro National Liberation Front (MNLF) came into prominence.

The MNLF organizers were university graduates and young pro- fessionals who had trained abroad after the Jabidah Massacre. Their principal aim was the creation and maintenance of an armed force sufficient to protect Muslim communities from the Ilagas and other militant groups, but a larger aim was to serve as the instrument to raise Islamic consciousness and reform the socioeconomic conditions of the Muslims of the Philippines. The MNLF saw the Marcos govern- ment as not only insensitive to Muslim aspirations, but as an actual threat to their religion, culture, and institutions. Consequently, it declared that the only way to the freedom, happiness, cultural en- hancement, and communal progress of Muslims was through their political separation from the rest of the Philippines. Such an objective fit nicely with the Muslims' long history of struggle against Spanish and American colonialism by pointing out that the struggle con- tinued—this time against the existing Filipino colonialism. In clashes with the army, the MNLF often gave a good account of itself; it could put as many as 10,000 men in the field, men whose lineaments crossed linguistic and regional lines, while claiming the support or at least the sympathy of hundreds of thousands of Muslims.

The Muslim armed struggle under the leadership of the MNLF soon came to earn the sympathy of the Islamic Conference of Islamic Ministers (OIC), which since 1972 has passed a series of resolutions asking the Philippine government to aid the Muslims in returning to their lands and to restrain army aggression against them. Such international Muslim organizations as the *Rabitat* and the *Mutamar* have also made presentations to the government concerning acts of violence against its Muslim citizens. Various grand sheikhs of Al-Azhar have made similar protestations, and some Al-Azhar conferences have discussed the problems of Muslims in the Philippines. And even before the OIC took official note of such problems, various Muslim heads of state, notably Libya's Colonel Kaddafi, requested that President Marcos intervene to protect Muslim lives and properties.

This combination of Muslim international pressure, adverse publicity in the foreign press, and foreign sympathy and aid to the MNLF finally forced the Philippine government to give some attention to the Moro problem. It was forced to realize that, in spite of differences among the various Muslim states and rivalries among their leaders, the Muslims would close ranks in their resistence to and condemnation of the Marcos government. More important, the strength of the MNLF and the continuing conflict in the south were threatening the already weak fibers of the national community. On the premise that more economic benefits for Muslims and a measure of increased economic interdependence between them and Christians would lead to better relations, the government initiated a series of tentative steps that included the funding of certain rehabilitation projects, the offer of more banking facilities, encouragement for modest industrial projects, and an increased number of scholarships for Muslim youth. More positions in the national government were also given to Muslims.

Due to limited resources, however, the Marcos government's promises were not always fulfilled. The rehabilitation of destroyed mosques and *madrasahs*, for example, was effected mainly through a relief grant from the OIC and other Muslim organizations. Provinces with large Muslim majorities were merged into two separate regions and given certain token autonomous characteristics, to satisy provisions of the Tripoli Agreement of 1976 entered into by the MNLF and the Philippine government with OIC participation.

In an effort to convince Muslims that there was no official commitment to destroying Islam, presidential decrees were issued allowing Arabic as a medium of instruction in schools, certifying Muslim holy days as official holidays (for Muslims), and creating a Pilgrimage *(Haj)* Authority. Studies were made on how to upgrade the *madrasah* system so it could be formally recognized by the government. A prominent Muslim sultan who had fought Spain for almost fifty years was proclaimed a national hero, and a commemorative postage stamp was issued in his honor.

Of greater significance, however, was the president's approval of the Code of Muslim Personal Laws of the Philippines in 1977. Previously, the president, at the request of Muslim leaders, would periodically ask the Congress to pass a law recognizing Muslim marriages for an extended period of time. Such laws were temporary, based on the assumption that all Muslims would ultimately fall under a uniform civil law. The state was insensitive to Muslim Holy Law, especially as to matters of personal or family status. A great many Civil Code provisions were based on Christian or Western values, and as such never accepted by Muslims. Moreover, it was humiliating for Muslim dignitaries to have to make repeated special trips to the presidential palace to beg for extensions of a law grudgingly recognizing their marriages and, in the case of plural marriages or divorced parents, the legitimacy of their offspring. It is well known that the operation of the *Shari'a* best favors the existence of a Muslim community. Colonial powers have always recognized this, and in their attacks on Islam they often predicate citizenship on the abandonment of the *Shari'a*. In practice, however, Muslims have followed their traditional marriage laws, regardless of national laws.

The signing of the code in 1977 was the reward of many years of Muslim agitation and persistence. Years before martial law was established, the Muslim professional population had called for national recognition of Muslim law. This problem was brought to the Constitutional Convention in 1971 by delegate Michael Mastura, while former senator Mamintal Tamano strongly recommended the code before the highest officials of the land, including the president. Additionally, in December 1971, during an annual convention of Muslim lawyers, the problem of codification was brought before the delegates by this writer. Throughout this period, however, there was neither sympathy nor response from non-Muslim legal quarters. It was only after martial law was declared that the combination of frequent Army-MNLF clashes, international Muslim concern, and local Muslim agitation inclined President Marcos to finally consider the wisdom of promulgating a code. In 1973, he created a research staff to prepare an initial draft, and in 1974 appointed a presidential committee to come up with a more definite treatment. This committee, after consultation with Muslim religious leaders and lawyers, submitted its work to the president in August 1975, but it was not until February 1977 that he finally signed it into law.

After some years, a *Shariʿa* Institute was established, and various national seminars on the subject of Islamic law were held. Two years ago, special *Shariʿa* bar examinations were administered by the Philippine supreme court. Not till May 1985, however, did the president appoint ten of the successful examinees to serve as *Shariʿa* district court judges. The next month the appointees took their oaths of office, and soon after left for Cairo for further training.

The signing of the code in 1977 was flaunted by the government as proof to the Muslim world that it intended to go a long way to meet Muslim aspirations. However, the long delay in its implementation indicates not only its non-governmental origins but continued resistance in certain government quarters. Moreover, Christian Filipino lawyers are mainly influenced by Roman law and the Spanish Civil Code, which require the application of a uniform law for all citizens; the vast majority are ignorant of Islamic law. Lacking the necessary background in sociology or social studies, many do not appreciate the significance of a pluralistic society. The long history of the code and its tribulations sadly reflects that the *moro-moro* mentality still lingers within the corridors of Manila officialdom.

Nevertheless, government projects have brought a certain degree of peace and order in some Muslim areas and cooled revolutionary fervor among certain segments of the population, although there is a long way to go to achieve peace in such fever spots as Mindanao and Sulu. The autonomy provided by the Tripoli Agreement has not been fully realized, and the MNLF and other Muslim organizations within and outside the Philippines continues to blame the government.[8] Moreover, the bulk of Muslim refugees have been unable to return to their former homes, and—in spite of some significant withdrawal of units to Luzon—the army's continued presence in Muslim lands makes for a chronic tension that often erupts into bloody fighting. Soldiers are ambushed by Muslims avenging the death of loved ones, and army retaliation is swift and ferocious.[9] Soldiers tend to see all Muslims as enemies (for this is what they have often been taught) and fire indiscriminately, before asking questions. Many feel that they are hopelessly fighting an unseen enemy, are weary of the battle, and simply desire to return home. There have been cases of scions of prominent Muslim families being arrested by army authorities on the charge that they are MNLF sympathizers, and then released upon payment of ransom. Their parents then send them to the relative safety of Manila, thus depriving the community of the service of many bright young men.

Nor are army abuses confined to Muslims: if there is one thing Muslims and Christians can fully agree upon, it is that the Philippine army behaves in all respects like an army of occupation. Ironically, it is this abusive army that made possible the predominance of Christians in Muslim areas. Muslim leaders have recommended that the present troops be replaced by Muslim soldiers, but the government fears that any such massive withdrawal of present forces would invite the military arm of the MNLF to take over. The increasing presence of armed Communist bands in Mindanao, and alleged support for them from some Christian communities, may be another argument against army withdrawal.

Regardless of all that has been said and written about Muslim-Christian relations, however, a lot of water has passed under the bridge, and many previously held attitudes and prejudices have been somewhat moderated. At least one generation has been brought up in an educational system that fosters a national life, transcending narrow loyalties—a generation unexposed to the *moro-moro* plays, so to speak. To many of the present university population, religious differences are simply not very important, while increasingly, secular attitudes demand that history and social science textbooks do away with stereotyped portrayals of Muslims and other minorities and emphasize the Muslim role in the general struggle for freedom from colonialism as an integral part of Philippine history. The political atmosphere in the country now revolves more on issues of freedom, human rights, and economic upliftment, and Muslims are more commonly seen as victims than as villains. The thousands of Muslims in colleges and universities mix freely with their non-Muslim peers, and there have even been a few cases of intermarriage between Muslim and Christian students and professionals, with the male spouse usually the Muslim.

In the years immediately prior to the establishment of martial law, the Philippine press was quite free. It did not blanch at reporting the sordid details of military massacres of Muslims and the army's partiality to Christians, with the often sensationalized reports probably meant to embarrass the president or political party in power. Nevertheless, demanding more justice for Muslims and pointing out how communal conflicts endanger the national fabric, the press was a vital instrument in informing the general public about events and issues in the Muslim south.

An additional factor influencing Muslim-Christian relations is the number of skilled Filipino workers who go to other Muslim countries for contractual work—a figure that has reached 200,000 a year. Although generally isolated from the social life of the countries they work in, these workers come to realize that the Muslims "back home" are not an exotic minority but members of a vast religious community. Their image of Islam and of Muslims also changes after exposure to the impressive development projects in which they are involved. (A few such workers even convert to Islam for economic reasons, but the host countries make no effort to push the message of Islam.[10])

There have also been some preliminary Muslim-Christian dialogues, held on local and national levels by religious leaders, academics, professionals, and student leaders. On the national level, at least five such conclaves have been held, beginning in 1974. Most have taken place on the initiative of religiously inclined or civic-minded Christians in traditionally Muslim areas. The main purposes of the dialogues are for the participants to learn about each other's beliefs, examine points of contact, understand their problems as members of their respective religious communities, and devise ways to reduce communal conflicts and tensions, all in the hope that God, in His mysterious way, will bless such meetings and make them productive. The main source of inspiration for such dialogues is traceable to the Second Vatican Council's call for Catholics to enter into dialogue with Muslims. Various international conferences of Catholic bishops have subsequently discussed how "to reach out to Muslims," including the May 1980 synod of the Manila archdiocese. In spite of the initial Muslim suspicion concerning the aims of such dialogue, time has improved the quality of the issues raised as well as the quality of the ensuing discussions, and general goodwill seems to pervade the talks. (In the initial dialogues, some Muslims raised the question of whether the dialogues were veiled attempts to convert Muslims to Christianity, or to attempt to expose Islamic beliefs as inconsistent or untenable. In one such dialogue, a Muslim participant asked: "Can a Muslim committed to Islam live an Islamic life within the framework of a secular state dominated by Christians?")

Muslim participants have shown little inclination to know more about Christianity, but some at least have been eager to inform their Christian counterparts about Islamic beliefs—perhaps with the hope that if Christians know more about Islam they will be less prejudiced against Muslims. In any case, participants often say that they have come to know more of each other's beliefs and fears. The invariable conclusion of each dialogue is that, if all Muslims and Christians acted according to their religious dictates, there would be no conflict between them. Although there is merit in this pious conclusion, the immediate problem is the rectification of the refugee problem and destruction of properties. It is not easy to love a family of another faith who occupy one's former land, especially when the recovery of the property is made impossible by the martial presence of military men who are coreligionists of the occupiers.

Of interest and significance for the future are the yearly dialogues sponsored by the Dansalan Research Center (now called the Gowing Memorial Research Center), starting in 1981. Under Protestant sponsorship, the quality of the discussions are of a high order. Such topics as the pros and cons of intermarriage and the "revelation" that in some sectors of the Christian church the idea of conversion has not been entirely relinquished engage the participants. At the theological level, efforts are made to discover points of contact or similarities between Islam and Christianity. An occasional paper discussing such theological differences is submitted by Muslims.

Based on their own experiences with their followers, though, Muslim leaders have assumed that the Christian hierarchy exercises a strong moral influence on the faithful. In July 1971, at the height of the Ilaga depredations, Muslim leaders—political, religious, academic, professional—drew up a careful and lengthy manifesto exposing the problems in Muslim lands, and voicing their stand on the matter. Together with certain demands and appeals, the manifesto urged "the Catholic hierarchy and other Christian groups to exercise their moral and spiritual leadership to appeal to their co-religionists to respect Islam and the Muslims as the basis for peace and harmony."[11] No church official or Christian group made any response to the manifesto, leading the Muslim leadership to conclude that the Church was not adverse to the dispersion of the Muslim community, since this would inevitably favor the Christian element in Mindanao. The manifesto alarmed the government and Christians in Mindanao, as if they thought the Muslims were getting ready to declare a *jihad* against them.

Past meetings between Muslim leaders and the Church hierarchy have been difficult. One reason is the fragmented nature of Muslim leadership: it is not easy to find a single Muslim leader who can validly claim to speak for all Muslims. National decisions have often involved a consensus, which is difficult to secure since Muslims belong to different political parties, live in different regions, and are members of different ethnolinguistic groups. Even such a strictly religious group as an *ulama* organization is invariably regional. After the assassination of former senator Benigno Aquino in 1983, however,

Domocao Alonto Haji Ahmad, also a former senator as well as a prominent Muslim political and religious leader and founder of the Ansar ul Islam organization, visited Jaime Cardinal Sin, the archbishop of Manila, at the latter's official residence. They discussed the need for national reconciliation and how to bring more peace to the bloody south, and the cardinal expressed his sympathy for the sufferings of the Muslim refugees due to the civil strife. In a letter to Alonto thanking him for the visit, the cardinal pledged that he would, at the earliest opportunity, bring the problems of the Muslims to the attention of the political and military leaders of the country, including the president. Considering the cardinal's problems with the government due to radical elements in his flock, this gesture was quite charitable.

The current pope, John Paul II, is keen to have more harmonious relations including regular dialogue between the Muslim and Christian communities in the Philippines. As early as 1975, when the prefecture of Marawi—a city whose population is almost solidly Muslim—was being proposed, Pope Paul VI said that it ought to serve as a "reconciling presence among Muslims through dialogue of life and faith." The Manila synod of October 1979, in line with the spirit of the Second Vatican Council, spoke of the need to awaken among Christians a sincere concern for the problems of the Muslims, "both sociological and religious, particularly in the areas of social justice and family life," and to "overcome the communication gap existing between Christians and Muslims in the archdiocese."

Pope John Paul II's visit in February 1981 to Davao City (once a Muslim village, but now an almost wholly Christian city) included a message directed to the Muslims there. He addressed the Muslims as "brothers," and reminded them that they were the brothers of the Christian Filipinos, with whom they shared citizenship, regardless of cultural differences. Asking the Muslims to participate in building a harmonious future for their children and country, he encouraged the holding of dialogues. He reminded Muslims that it is only within the "framework of religion and its shared promises of faith that one can really speak of mutual respect, openness and collaboration between Christians and Muslims." In response, the Davao Muslims presented him with a letter which, after welcoming him, listed a series of complaints against the government, including military abuses. The letter also included an affirmation of the Muslim adherence to the *Shariᶜa*. In Davao, the pope was also able to meet with some Muslim officials who probably briefed him on government projects to aid Muslims.

The pope's visit was followed not long afterward by a pastoral letter from the bishop-vicar of Sulu and Tawi-Tawi (95 percent Muslim) exhorting "all Christians to respect the Muslims, their religion and culture." The letter explained that Islam, like Christianity, was monotheistic, and enumerated other theological similarities between the two faiths. It emphasized that "we will never dialogue in a friendly way unless we accept the Muslim as the sort of man he chooses to be." The letter ended with an appeal for Christians to free themselves from former prejudices while developing new attitudes towards Muslims. Along similar lines, Bishop Bienvendio Tudud of the Marawi prefecture published a few thoughtful articles on how to conduct Christian-Muslim dialogue. From the message of the pope to the recommendations of Bishop Tudtud, there has been no mention of conversion or of bringing Christ's message to Muslims.

Since the participants in the dialogue have been mainly religious leaders, professionals, and academics, some observers complain that they do not fully represent their respective religious communities. Such participants, however, due to their social position, are best able to influence their associates and institutions. Then, if they come to occupy positions of political or social power, their understanding and acquired tolerance may influence the setting of policies. A preview of the future was perhaps given when one participant claimed that, as a result of the dialogues, his missionary inclinations and those of some other clerics had vanished!

Such protestations to the effect that the age of conversion is gone or is going sit well with some Muslims in the Philippines. To other, more skeptical Muslims, however, such claims do not square well with what Datu Michael Mastura referred to as "the ominous implications" of a recent description of the Philippines, by Cardinal Sin, as being "the only Christian country in Asia," or of remarks of the papal nuncio, Monsignor Bruno Torpigliani, in which he defined the Philippines' role in "the evangelization of the region." For this reason, Cardinal Sin said, the Philippines should be sending not only religious but lay missionaries abroad. These missionaries, he pointed out, can be "professionals working and living abroad."[12] Datu Mastura made immediate reference to Christian missionary work in nearby Indonesia, where there is increasing resentment on the part of the Muslim majority toward such activity. Did the cardinal also mean "region" to include Muslim Malaysia, Chinese Singapore, or Communist Vietnam?

To some outside observers, Muslim fears of missionary activities in their midst appear to indicate a deeply ingrained psychological complex. A Christian dialogue participant once impatiently exclaimed to a Muslim participant: "If Muslims are so sure of their religion, why do they have to fear of missionaries converting them?" This question misses the point, however. In situations where there are thousands of uprooted Muslim families, where there are orphans, poverty, disease, and an absence of Muslim teachers, Muslims have reason indeed to fear Christian missionaries, who have resources and outside support as well as the protection of the authorities. Muslims, to be sure, do not fear conversion in Islamic educational centers or Sufi *taricats.*

On the intellectual and moral levels, one cannot but feel gratified and elated when the dialogues reaffirm the intrinsic value and dignity of the individual and his moral worth, recalling that there is an Almighty and Merciful God who guides the destinies of all people and that religious freedom is a cherished value in a democratic society. It may not be an exaggeration to claim that, on the individual level, these dialogues have produced mutual love and respect among people of different faiths. But on the institutional level, the highest form of understanding will not be reached until Christians are ready to accept the fact that Islam is also a revealed religion. This means that they must be willing to grant what Islam had always granted—that Revelation is found in both Islam and Christianity. Only then will statistically motivated conversions from all sides be thrust into the limbo of past dissensions.

In the communal conflicts in the 1960s and 70s, the military forces of the republic tended to side with and protect the Christian settlers, but the situation has changed somewhat. Army abuses are no longer confined to outrages against Muslims; there have been many instances of undisciplined or drunken soldiers breaking into the homes of peaceful Christians. Years ago, only the Muslims saw the army as an army of occupation, a host of Christian Filipinos succeeding the arms of Spain. Now, the Christians of Mindanao also see it as an army of occupation. For one thing, the writ of *habeas corpus* remains suspended in Muslim areas, in spite of having been restored in other provinces with the lifting of martial law in 1982—a situation that affects the legal status of the Christians living alongside Muslims in their areas. Moreover, many innocent Christians have been arrested or killed as suspected Communists. In fact, the so-called hamletization program aimed at regrouping citizens in manageable government-controlled settlements appears to be applied increasingly to Christian villages. A new variety of *Ilagas* (and identified as such) is appearing in Christian communities in the form of paramilitary units attached to the army. The Integrated Civilian Home Defense Force (ICHDF) in Zamboanga del Sur province is considered such a unit. Consequently, some Christian communities now find themselves in a situation similar to that faced by the Muslims vis-à-vis the Ilagas in the 1970s. Consequently, both Muslim and Christian communities in Mindanao now find it in their best interests to have the bulk of the army withdrawn from their homelands. Furthermore, both Cardinal Sin and Nur Misuari, the chairman of the MNLF, agree that the United States should cease military aid to the Philippines, for—in the cardinal's words—"it only goes to slaughter Filipinos."

Another problem facing both communities in Mindanao is the rising power and influence of the New People's Army (NPA) of the Communist Party, coupled with the increase of a radical element within some factions of the clergy. The army's hamletization of some Christian communities was justified on the premise of protecting them from the communists. Some critics expect that a combined MNLF-NPA force will give the Philippine government and army their biggest headache, but so far there does not appear to be any formal linkage or alliance between the two groups, although some contact is unavoidable since they operate in neighboring areas. It has been an element of government propaganda to charge that Nur Misuari is a communist with contacts with Filipino communist leaders, a charge obviously meant to deprive him of international Muslim sympathy and local Muslim support. A few ambitious Muslims have repeated this charge in an attempt to isolate Misuari from the MNLF, so that they may step in and control that organization. Before the foreign press and international Muslim organizations, however, Misuai has vehemently denied that he is a communist or has any formal link with the Communist Party. In any case, the presence of an increasingly better trained and more powerful communist armed group, with local support in western and southern Mindanao, will eventually require a response from the MNLF, as well as from those Muslims and Christians whose religious or ideological commitments lead them to view the rise of communism with alarm.

Much of the tension and armed conflict between Muslims and Christians is a testimony to the dominant majority's attitudes toward Muslims, exacerbated by government discrimination against or neglect of their cultural and religious aspirations. True, the government's inability to bring the Muslims up to a higher educational and technological level is due in part to the poor and "developing" character of the Philippines. Certainly, there are non-Muslim areas of the country with as much poverty and backwardness as Muslim areas, and government resources can only do so much. Unfortunately, this results in many government promises to the Muslims remaining purely verbal. The government is greatly to blame, too, for importing thousands of settlers from other islands to settle on Muslim lands, in order to solve the agrarian problems in the overpopulated provinces. In so doing, it made the Muslims, an historical people it was bound to respect and protect, pay a terrible price in terms of the loss of their ancestral lands. That the rights and interests of the Muslims were disregarded to satisfy the interests of another group can only be explained by the attitudes and ingrained prejudices of unenlightened government officials. Nevertheless, such injustices can be rectified in part with the return of most of the refugees to their former farms, with the government guaranteeing that no further such expropriations will take place. Without such remedial actions, deep resentment and conflict will continue to stalk the land.

Much can be accomplished toward peace if Muslims are helped to reach technological parity with other Philippine citizens, so that they can develop their own regions and reap the benefits thereof. At present, the few industrial improvements in Muslim lands are mostly for the benefit of Christian capitalists, managers, and employees. The exploitation of the natural resources of the remaining Muslim lands should not be left to the benefit of Manila capitalists who do not live in the land and who do not return anything to it. It is no wonder that Christian loggers are often ambushed in Lanao.

Increased opportunities for higher education, combined with the government's avowed aim to help upgrade the *madrasah* system, will go a long way to restore Muslim trust in government agencies. The appointment of a mufti in accordance with the code of 1977 may lead Muslims to forgive government footdragging on that matter. But it is of great importance that the declared autonomy of the two regions with Muslim majorities be genuine, and not merely a showpiece for international consumption. Indeed, such meaningful autonomy is a guarantee of the implementation of reforms.

In the sphere of the mind and spirit, continuing dialogues between Muslims and Christians can reduce those fears of Muslims that resulted from hundreds of years of turbulent history, and increase the number of Christians who accept Muslims as equal partners in a wider national community. For the problem of integrating the Muslims into the national community is not only a Moro problem; it is also a Christian problem. Too often, Christians identify membership in the national community in terms of their own values; thus, in an academic discussion I once heard a Christian exclaim, "The problem with the Moros is that they do not want to become like us!" What Christians ought to know and accept is that Muslims have a cherished faith, a set of moral values, and a system of laws they believe to be divinely inspired, and that to impose upon them an alternative set of values couched in secular terms not only does violence to them both as individuals and as a community, but risks bloodshed and sorrow. Muslims, for their part, must come to accept the fact that a honest partnership with Christians in the Philippines can bring beneficial results to all parties. In the long run, however, it will be the exemplification of Islamic virtues that will cause the Muslims to come to be viewed as worthy citizens and partners. And it is one of these virtues—that of bravery, and the willingness to fight and sacrifice for one's faith, rights, and dignity—that may yet serve to be the best guarantee for their survival as an *umma* in the Philippines.

References

Dansalan Quarterly. Published by the Gowing Memorial Research Center, Dansalan College Foundation, Inc., Marawi City, P.I. Useful for periodical reports on Muslim-Christian dialogues. Contains many important articles on Muslims in the Philippines.

George, T. J. S. *Revolt in Mindanao: The Rise of Islam in Philippine Politics*. Kuala Lumpur: Oxford University Press, 1980. Deals extensively with events leading to the rise of the MNLF.

Gowing, Peter G., and McAmis, Robert eds., *The Muslim Filipinos*. Manila: Solidaridad Publishing House, 1975. A good introduction to the history and institutions of the various Muslim ethnolinguistic groups.

Gowing, Peter G. *Mandate in Moroland: The American Government of Muslim Filipinos, 899–1920*. Quezon City: Philippine Center of Advanced Studies, University of the Philippines, 1977.

———. *Muslim Filipinos: Heritage and Horizon*. Quezon City: New Day Publishers, 1979. An excellent account of the history and institutions of Muslims of the Philippines as well as of their problems and aspirations.

Jacano, F. Landa, ed. *Filipino Muslims: Their Social Institutions and Cultural Achievements.* Quezon City: Asian Center, University of the Philippines, 1983. Contains sympathetic articles and an extensive bibiography.

Majul, Cesar A. *Muslims in the Philippines: Past, Present and Future Prospects.* Pamphlet. Manila: Converts to Islam Society of the Philippines, 1971.

————. *Muslims in the Philippines.* 2nd ed. Quezon City: University of the Philippines Press, 1973. Deals with the history of the Muslims in the Philippines from the earliest times to the eve of the American Occupation.

Mastura, Michael O. *Muslim Filipino Experience: A Collection of Essays.* Manila: Ministry of Muslim Affairs, 1984. Contains scholarly essays on Muslim experiences, problems, aspirations, and expectations in the Philippines.

Moro National Liberation Front, Central Committee, Office of the Chairman. "The Rise and Fall of Moro Statehood: Our Plight and Determination to Survive." 1974. Contains a rationale of the MNLF for secession.

Philippine Government, Ministry of Foreign Affairs. *From Secession to Autonomy: Self-Government in Southern Philippines.* Manila: 1980. Contains a copy of the Tripoli Agreement of 1976 and other documents.

————. Ministry of Muslim Affairs. *Code of Muslim Personal Laws of the Philippines.* Manila: 1983. Contains the official English version of the Code as well as an Arabic translation.

Notes

1. Out of a Philippine population of about 50 million, at least 4 million are Muslims. Ten ethnolinguistic groups are identified as Muslim, the largest of these being the Maguindanao, the Maranao, the Tausug, and the Samal. By comparison, about 85 percent of the total Philippine population is Catholic.

2. The first *moro-moro* plays were introduced by Jesuits in Manila in 1637 to celebrate a Spanish victory over the Maguinadanao sultan Qudarat, and became the models for future plays. After World War II, there were attempts by some Filipino romanticists to revive the plays as part of the Philippine literary heritage. Objections from some quarters that such a colonial heritage would only serve to revive animosities between religious communities finally prevailed.

3. This refers to the "Memoria del R.P. Pablo Pastells" (15 May 1892), included as an appendix in *Cartas de los PP. de la Compania de Jesus de la Mision de Filipinas, Cuaderno IX* (Manila, 1891).

4. In 1921 Frank Laubach, a noted Protestant missionary, wrote to Frank Carpenter, former governor of the Moro province, inviting him to head a venture that would spell the end of "the Muslim regime." The idea was to convert Moros to Christianity, and

then use them to convert other Muslims in Indonesia and even India. However, after a few years, Laubach began to question the morality of conversion. He eventually decided to concentrate on a literacy program that benefited hundreds.

5. To do justice to Leonard Wood (who once wrote to another American officer about his "uncontrollable antipathy" toward Saleeby), it must be mentioned that, after a few years, he came to appreciate the value of the good doctor.

6. For example, Cotabato province in 1939 was 55 percent Muslim and 45 percent Christian. In 1948, less than ten years later and in spite of the Japanese occupation, the Muslims represented thirty-five percent and the Christians sixty-five percent. In 1963, the government was administering colonies that included more than 25,000 Christian families and some 695,000 hectares of land. Since then, Cotabato province had been divided into four provinces to accommodate demographic changes.

7. In 1970, the number of Muslim and Christian refugees rose to 50,000. This number doubled the next year, and by 1973 the number (mostly Muslim) had passed the million mark. This was only in Mindanao. At present, just in Sabah, Malaysia, there are about 350,000 Muslim refugees from Sulu and Tawi-Tawi.

8. The MNLF, under the chairmanship of Nur Misuari, has consistently charged that the Philippine government has failed to honor its commitments to the Tripoli Agreement and that MNLF is therefore justified in reverting to its former secessionist stance. In his address to the plenary session of the fifteenth Islamic conference of foreign ministers held in Sana'a, Yemen Arab Republic, in December 1984, Misuari pleaded for OIC support for the creation of a Moro state independent of Filipino colonialism, and for eventual membership in the OIC. The OIC, however, while reiterating its support for the Bansamoro struggle for self-determination under MNLF leadership, believes that conformity to the Tripoli Agreement of 1976 can still serve as a basis for the peaceful solution to the problem of Muslims in the Philippines. But it officially noted and condemned what it believes is a refusal of Philippine government authorities to implement the agreement fully. At the fourth general meeting of the MNLF leadership, held on 5 March 1985, it was decided to make preparations for the formation of a provisional or interim government of a Bangsamoro Republic.

Even those Muslim groups who are not opting for secession agree that the government has failed to implement fully the Tripoli Agreement. In August 1985, the Moro Islamic Liberation Front (MILF), a splinter group of the MNLF under Hashim Salamat, asked all Muslim countries to impose economic sanctions on the Philippines for failing to keep its commitments to the Tripoli Agreement. Even Muslim leaders in the Philippines say openly that the present autonomy for regions 9 and 12 in the Philippine south is not a real one and does not adhere to the spirit of the Tripoli Agreement.

9. A recent case in point is an incident on Pata Island in February 1981 in which 124 Filipino soldiers were ambushed and killed, presumably by MNLF troops. Massive land, sea, and air operations, involving at least 15,000 government soldiers, were launched in retaliation. The civilian islanders suffered terribly, and out of an estimated 15,000 at least 2,000 were killed and 4,000 arrested. For some time, the survivors were not allowed to return to their homes and farms, and were in real danger of starvation. Muslims claim that the ambush was made because the soldiers had strafed homes of peaceful families, desecrated mosques, defiled Quran books, and abused Muslim women. All of these allegations were denied by the military, which blamed everything on Muslim treachery and untrustworthiness.

10. Often, prospective workers for Saudi Arabia would go to the Institute of Islamic Studies at the University of the Philippines, requesting that they convert to Islam and be issued certificates in the belief that this would enable them to get jobs more easily. They were informed that contractual work in Arab countries does not require any religious identification, and that, moreover, it was not a function of the institute to issue such certificates.

11. "Muslim Leaders' Consensus of Unity," *Manila Times,* 21 July 1971, p. 13.

12. "Islam in Asia: A Muslim Perspective," *Salsilah: A Journal of Philippine Ethnic Studies* 4 (1984): 5.

Index

THE VATICAN, ISLAM, AND THE MIDDLE EAST

was composed in 10-point Baskerville on a Mergenthaler Linotron 202 and leaded 2 points
by Coghill Book Typesetting Co.;
with display type in Tuck Roman Medium by Dix Type Inc;
and ornaments provided by Jōb Litho Services;
printed by sheet-fed offset on 50-pound, acid-free Glatfelter Antique Cream,
Smyth-sewn and bound over binder's boards in Joanna Arrestox B,
by Maple-Vail Book Manufacturing Group, Inc.;
with dust jackets printed in 2 colors
by New England Book Components, Inc.;
and published by

SYRACUSE UNIVERSITY PRESS
SYRACUSE, NEW YORK 13244-5160